Women's Experimental Cinema

ROBIN BLAETZ, *editor*

Women's Experimental Cinema

critical frameworks

Duke University Press   Durham & London   2007

© 2007 Duke University Press
All rights reserved
Printed in the United States of America
on acid-free paper ∞
Designed by C. H. Westmoreland
Typeset in Warnock Pro by Keystone
Typesetting, Inc.
Library of Congress Cataloging-in-
Publication Data appear on the last printed
page of this book.
Noël Carroll's article "Moving and Moving:
Minimalism to *Lives of Performers*"
originally appeared in *Millennium Film
Journal* 35–36 (2000). Reprinted with
permission.

Duke University Press gratefully
acknowledges the support of the American
Association of University Women, which
provided funds toward the production of
this book.

■

For Meredith and Gordon,

Augusta and Miranda,

and in memory of

Jay Leyda

Contents

◻

Acknowledgments

□

Although writers have provided individual thanks, certain names and institutions arise repeatedly and deserve special mention, including: Anthology Film Archives, Film-Makers' Cooperative, Canyon Cinema, *Millennium Film Journal*, P. Adams Sitney, Scott MacDonald, M. M. Serra, and Robert Haller. This project benefited from the generosity of the American Association of University Women in the form of a Summer Research Grant and from a number of Faculty Research Grants from Mount Holyoke College. I am grateful to all the writers who have been part of this project for their enthusiasm and commitment and for their substantial and passionate work. I want also to express my gratitude to my colleagues at Mount Holyoke College, particularly Elizabeth Young, Tom Wartenberg, Paul Staiti, Ajay Sinha, and Jenny Perlin, and to a number of others, including Cosmas Demetriou, Chris Holmlund, Kathleen McHugh, Adrienne McLean, James Meyer, Gordon Spencer-Blaetz, Ann Steuernagel, Patty White, Ken Wissoker, and two most helpful anonymous readers.

ROBIN BLAETZ

Introduction:

Women's Experimental Cinema

Critical Frameworks

◻

Experimental cinema has always been an art form in which women have excelled. As far back as 1942, when Maya Deren made the groundbreaking *Meshes of an Afternoon* with two people and a 16mm camera, countless women working in small-scale film and video have been creating a deep and wide-ranging body of film. Little of this work has entered into the many general histories that have been written about the cinema, but this is the fate of most avant-garde and experimental film (terms that I am using interchangeably here). Indeed, the dominance of narrative film-making and feature-length film has shaped criticism and scholarly work as much as it has production. While there are many experimental films that deserve increased attention, this anthology seeks to redress the absence of fifteen women artists through a series of critical essays that offer contextualized readings of their work.

In order to understand the reasons for recovering this work in particular, one must go back to the end of the 1960s and the beginning of the 1970s, when there was a window of opportunity for the assimilation of the rich field of women's experimental cinema into the wider arena of cinema studies. For this brief moment, scholars paid attention to both avant-garde film and the films that women were producing in ever-greater numbers in relation to feminism and increased opportunities for women in general. What happened during this period to obscure the presence of the women who had been working for the two previous decades and frustrate those artists seeking to further their careers in the years to follow? In order to get a sense of this historical moment and the causes of the lost opportunity, this introduction begins by focusing on several film festivals held during this period.

Certain male experimental filmmakers have received a narrow but steady stream of attention, with P. Adams Sitney's influential *Visionary Film: The American Avant-Garde* of 1974 firmly establishing a small group of artists in the history of the medium. Sitney's book, which was begun in 1969, was written during an extraordinarily rich time in the annals of the American avant-garde. The 1960s was a decade of growing interest in experimental film, particularly through the forum of the five International Experimental Film Competitions held in Belgium.[1] The festival was known for discovering new artists rather than furthering the careers of those who had established themselves by showing their work in previous years. However, the experimental film festival was no different than any other in that it remained a largely male preserve, which launched the careers of few women.[2] Although in the final competition in 1975 there were just twelve films out of seventy-four by women, no women on the initial jury, and one female judge out of five, women managed to win four of the ten prizes.[3] By the time the festival had run its course, many of the once struggling male avant-garde artists who had achieved a degree of fame in Belgium had found jobs teaching production in film studies programs in colleges and universities in the United States and no longer needed either the attention or the prize money.[4] Although a few women filmmakers had done well in the festivals, they received neither the critical consideration nor the jobs that accompanied it, and the field of avant-garde cinema was institutionalized as a thoroughly masculine one called the American avant-garde.

While scholarship about experimental film dealt largely with the newly evolved canon throughout the 1980s, Sitney had begun to reconsider his work. In fact he noted in each new version of *Visionary Film*, which reappeared in 1979 and 2002, that his lack of research in relation to the work of key women filmmakers had partially motivated the revised edition. For the second edition, he examined Deren and Marie Menken at greater length, and in the third, a longer list includes Yvonne Rainer, Su Friedrich, and Abigail Child. While this new attention was welcome, it was not able to make up for the initial elision. With some major exceptions, the women's work was more or less plugged in to a structure built around the notion of the romantic artist, and women's films seem to be peripheral to a tradition that had been defined as male.[5]

The chance to become known and supported as an experimental film-maker through university employment had diminished for women by the end of the 1960s. However, the early 1970s saw the birth of a remarkable number of film journals and festivals devoted to women's cinema inter-nationally. The first of the seven issues of the feminist journal *Women and Film* appeared in 1972, along with special issues on the topic in both *Film Library Quarterly* and *Take One*.[6] In June 1972, the First International Festival of Women's Films was held in New York City, followed two months later by "The Women's Event" at the Edinburgh International Film Festival. The next summer saw a festival of Women's Cinema at the National Theater in London and a Women and Film festival in Toronto. On one level, these festivals were quite similar; each one exhibited a transhistorical accumulation of feature, documentary, and experimental film by women, from the silent period to the present, sometimes divided into rather amorphous categories such as "Eroticism and Exploitation" or "Women: Myth and Reality" in the New York festival.[7] The intention is clear. The attendee is to be amazed and inspired by the plethora of women's work and the degree to which the films and their makers have been excluded from the field. The looseness of the programming was matched by the variety of discussions that were planned. In New York, for example, forums were held to consider the image of women in film, scriptwriting, women in television, programming and distribution, edit-ing, acting, directing, making documentaries, the question of a female film aesthetic, and the image of men in film.[8] The struggle to articulate whether women would be best served by analyzing the long history of misogynist imagery and women's attempts to work within the classical Hollywood system or by making images of themselves from scratch per-vaded this period of feminist film studies.

Yet even at this early date, critics of the festival such as filmmaker Joan Braderman observed that the haphazard collection of films presented what she called a misguided attempt to find a "female film sensibility."[9] The decontextualization of the films had the effect of making the films appear to be anomalous as works of art in a male tradition and skewing their reception toward "women's art" rather than simply art. The films chosen for the festivals were often feature films by the likes of Doro-thy Arzner, Mai Zetterling, or Agnes Varda, which had sometimes been briefly noted in film history books but rarely studied, and documentary films about women and women's history that had obvious appeal. Although there seems to have been quite a bit of experimental work shown in the New York festival, including a film or two by Deren, Menken, Gunvor Nelson and Dorothy Wiley, Chick Strand, and others, only one of the fifteen programs was labeled "Avant-Garde (Experimental) Films." B. Ruby Rich has written about these early women's film festivals in her memoir about her experiences with the feminist film movement in this period. She excuses what appears in retrospect to be arbitrariness as a research project and mission to rescue from oblivion the many unknown films otherwise absent from film history.[10] As might have been expected, the films shown and discussed during these festivals found their way into the college courses and books about women's film that were emerging at this time and began to form a canon. The minimal presence of experimental film at the festivals guaranteed that documentary films about contemporaneous issues (some of which were experimental in form) and films made by struggling foremothers would dominate the field of feminist film studies.

None of the films screened at any festival had as great an influence on film studies and on the fate of women's experimental cinema as the discussions held at "The Women's Event" at the Edinburgh Festival of 1972. At these seminars, some open only to women, scholars such as Claire Johnston and Laura Mulvey began to introduce the psychoanalytically based film theory that would change the direction of the entire field of film studies.[11] Questions proposed in the festival handout laid the path for years to come. For example, in relation to documentaries about women, the organizers asked whether the films had offered a critique of their place in society or merely reflected dominant ideology. Even more to the point, they raised a series of questions: Are there "specifically feminine values which emerge from the work of women directors? Must women directors totally reject masculine values and invent something entirely different? Or, conversely, what function does the feminine critique of ideology have?"[12] In the end, this final query carried the most weight. The conclusion that films were influential and harmful to women to the degree that they were structured through invisible editing to satisfy male desire for visual and literal dominance shifted the attention of feminist scholars from women's films to films about women. Cinematically experimental investigation of female subjectivity such as that found in Deren's *At Land* of 1945 began to seem far less compelling than understanding the effect on millions of women of Hollywood's melodramas of the same period, such as *Mildred Pierce* (Michael Curtiz, 1945). Few scholars noted that in describing the far-from-innocent workings of this style of filmmaking that is so familiar that it appears not to exist at all, both Mulvey and Johnston call for a countercinema to take its place.[13]

It is with this countercinema that *Women's Experimental Cinema: Critical Frameworks* is concerned. The essays commissioned for this volume are meant to revive attention to a number of films that have fallen through the cracks of both the history of the American avant-garde and feminist scholarship. Quite a few of the filmmakers covered are no longer working, some of them have died, and all deserve the consideration of the discipline of film studies in order to be understood, appreciated, taught, and preserved. The writers of the essays in this volume have sought to present the work of these filmmakers as broadly as possible. To use and expand the light metaphor used by André Bazin and other film theorists, in which the theater is a chandelier in comparison to the random aim of the usher's flashlight that is cinema, I would hope that this anthology would function like a lighthouse.[14] These essays are both radiant in themselves as they guide scholars toward this submerged work but they also offer a warning of the dangers of failing to pay attention to the fate of this fragile medium. The ultimate goal of this book is to insert the work of these less known filmmakers into film history, widely conceived to include, for example, the American avant-garde, minimalism, or ethnography, and also to enrich the definition of feminism in the cinema.

The anthology has a particular interest in filling a lacuna in the history of experimental film. As the situation now stands, a student using some of the textbooks in the field might come away thinking that the filmmaker Carolee Schneemann was exclusively an actress and a muse. These essays intend to suggest the full complexity of Schneemann's art and that of the other filmmakers discussed. In addition to expanding the canon of avant-garde cinema and feminist film, this collection also reveals intriguing similarities between various women filmmakers who rarely knew each other but who worked in the evolving historical circumstances that slowly changed women's social roles in the second half of the twentieth century. While the editor and the individual writers wish the book to encourage its readers to explore beyond its boundaries, this introduction suggests a number of characteristics common to some of these filmmakers, which differentiate their work from the more familiar films of the artists who work within the context of feminist theory. These artists who have received considerable attention, particularly Laura Mulvey, Sally

Potter, Chantal Akerman, and Yvonne Rainer, make films that are directly related to the scholarly work that deconstructed the patriarchal structures of the cinema in order to understand its seductive appeal. Except for a chapter on Rainer's first film, *Lives of Performers* (1972) and reference to her *Privilege* (1991) in the conclusion, this book contains no new scholarship about these filmmakers. This introduction seeks to highlight some of the most obvious of the characteristics common to those filmmakers working outside of feminist theory to provide a point of entry into the films.

Since the late 1980s, however, ever more writers, including Scott MacDonald, William C. Wees, and Wheeler Winston Dixon, have been considering women's cinema in the broader field of avant-garde film history. In addition, feminist theorists such as E. Ann Kaplan, Annette Kuhn, and Judith Mayne have paid attention to certain women artists since the 1970s. More inclusive approaches to the field, which embrace a broader variety of films, have been written by Lucy Fischer, Lauren Rabinovitz, B. Ruby Rich, and Alexandra Juhasz. In addition to addressing the work of some of the filmmakers considered in this anthology, these writers use analysis, personal reflection, and/or interviews to contextualize the work in relation to Hollywood film, the social and political context of the 1960s and 1970s, and feminist filmmaking as a broadly defined movement. Recently, the material about certain women filmmakers has begun to thicken, with entire books and even several volumes devoted to the likes of Rainer, Deren, and Joyce Wieland. As more and more scholars and publishers tackle the challenges of researching women experimental filmmakers, the odds increase that the films will still be here for the generations to come.

The one question that is bound to arise in perusing the table of contents of this book is, why these filmmakers and not others? Regrettably, there are no chapters on Sara Kathryn Arledge, Freude Bartlett, Julie Dash, Storm de Hirsch, Tracey Moffatt, Anne Severson, and many more.[15] An anthology can contain only a certain number of essays, of course, but in these cases there were simply no scholars currently willing or able to write about these artists. In other cases, such as that of Yoko Ono and certainly Deren, the reconsideration of their life's work has already begun.[16] For the most part, however, the filmmakers included in this anthology are those who have achieved recognition, if not from the field at large then at least from the small group of scholars involved with experimental cinema.

Introduction to the Filmmakers and the Essays

Many of the connections between the filmmakers considered in this anthology are simply the result of the era in which they started working. Most of the artists discussed are primarily filmmakers, although several also work in video. Because of the dominance of the North American avant-garde between the 1950s and 1970s in the art world and in colleges and universities, many women were exposed to experimental cinema and began to make it themselves. Thus, most of the filmmakers are American, and all either worked in the United States or are involved in contemporary political or aesthetic concerns familiar to U.S. scholars. Joyce Wieland, for example, was Canadian, but she worked side by side with her husband, Michael Snow, one of the key members of the North American avant-garde. Although there are many international women filmmakers, past and present, whose work deserves recognition, this anthology's national focus seeks to rectify the commonly held notion that the American avant-garde was exclusively male. The filmmakers to be discussed include Marie Menken, Joyce Wieland, Gunvor Nelson, Yvonne Rainer, Carolee Schneemann, Barbara Rubin, Amy Greenfield, Barbara Hammer, Chick Strand, Marjorie Keller, Leslie Thornton, Abigail Child, Peggy Ahwesh, Su Friedrich, Cheryl Dunye, and several others who are discussed briefly in the book's conclusion.

It is not the aim of this book to write an overarching history or construct a movement that would include or explain each filmmaker who is studied. In fact, what is most exciting about much of the analysis of the films in this book is the degree to which the work often cannot be inserted in a coherent way into any preexisting history of avant-garde film. The films, many of which appear to be incoherent and difficult to read in their intentional or unintentional challenge to classical Hollywood cinema, share only the quality of speaking, albeit in many voices, of a sense of something missing. In my own essay, "Amnesis Time: The Films of Marjorie Keller," I have called this element the "lost object" to express a notion common in much of the work presented in the book.[17] The title of one of Leslie Thornton's films, *Adynata*, a word meaning the expression of the impossibility of expression, is yet another and perhaps the most appropriate term to describe much of the cinematic work examined in this volume.

One of the more striking aspects of the essays is the degree to which they revise the current impression of the filmmaker in question. To a large extent, women filmmakers in general are most often discussed when their films can be seen as lyrical meditations, vaguely in the tradition of Jonas Mekas or Stan Brakhage but less constructed.[18] There is evidently something that seems appropriate about a woman making poetic film, or what David James calls the "film diary" as opposed to the "diary film." Whereas the film diary is the unsophisticated record of the filmmaker's world, the diary film mediates the raw, unplanned material shot in daily life with editing, other kinds of material, and sound.[19] Yet the broad stroke with which the adjective *lyrical* is applied to women's film becomes symptomatic of either a refusal actually to examine the work or discomfort with the films themselves. A case in point is found in the work of Marie Menken, the first filmmaker examined. Menken's gestural camerawork, heavy editing, and manipulation of the surface of the film influenced Brakhage and Mekas, but her work is not necessarily primarily lyrical, as it is almost always described. As Melissa Ragona discusses in her essay "Swing and Sway: Marie Menken's Filmic Events," Menken was not interested in her subjective responses to her perception of her domestic world but rather simply recorded footage of what she saw around her to use as fragmentary elements in the creation of films that may or may not have been substantively connected to her life. Likewise, a film such as Joyce Wieland's *Handtinting*, featuring girls in motion, may appear to be merely expressive but is formally rigorous with its looping, flipping, and abrupt editing used to comment on alienation and entrapment. As Paul Arthur suggests in "Different/Same/Both/Neither: The Polycentric Cinema of Joyce Wieland," Wieland is no poetess of the cinema, nor does she simply quote the films of those working in the lyrical tradition. Instead, Wieland engages in a critical dialogue with the avant-garde itself. Other filmmakers whose work has been mistakenly thought of as closer to the film diary than the more complex diary film include Keller, Schneemann, and Friedrich. This work is neither simply introspectively connected with women's consciousness raising nor is it derivative of the films of male counterparts. Although many of the filmmakers cite the influence of Brakhage, Mekas, Gregory Markopoulos, and Bruce Baille in the lyrical vein, and Bruce Conner, Hollis Frampton, and Snow regarding found footage and structural cinema, the women's work sometimes deconstructs or repudiates, occasionally quotes, but often has nothing to do with its counterpart in the traditionally defined American avant-garde.

The tendency to categorize and dismiss women's filmmaking as simple diary, particularly in its early years, has had the unfortunate consequence of rending the pervasive irony and humor of much of this work invisible.

Menken again provides a clear example; her playful, formally complex animation films of the early 1960s, such as *Hurry! Hurry!*, with its racing sperm, are little known, most likely because they contradict the sense of her as a film poet. Another case in point is the work of Gunvor Nelson. In her essay "Excavating Visual Fields, Layering Auditory Frames: Signature, Translation, Resonance and Gunvor Nelson's Films," Chris Holmlund does not let the reader forget Nelson's *Schmeergunz*, an aggressively funny film made in 1966 that contrasts mass media images of female beauty with drain cleaning and vomiting in reverse. Similar examples could be provided for most of the filmmakers, whose perceptive intelligence when facing the world, and particularly women's place in it, necessarily manifests a sense of humor. As filmmakers such as Friedrich, Ahwesh, and Dunye have gained greater visibility, it has become ever more apparent that wit and irony are not foreign elements in women's experimental cinema but perhaps the most omnipresent characteristic of all.

While current women artists working in cinema unabashedly refer to themselves as filmmakers, previous generations often not only called and continue to call themselves artists, *tout court*, but also persist in working in their original media. Wieland is the only person to have worked in textiles, but she is joined as a painter, printmaker, and installation artist by Menken, Nelson, Thornton, Schneemann, and others to a lesser degree. The title of M. M. Serra and Kathryn Ramey's essay, "Eye/Body: The Cinematic Paintings of Carolee Schneemann," stresses the degree to which the cinema is not always the privileged mode of creation but rather a tool in a larger, often kinesthetic project. However, as Paul Arthur significantly indicates in his work on Wieland, the very heterogeneity that makes these artists so interesting has been partially to blame for their lack of visibility in an art world that tends to categorize artists by medium. Those artists who came from dance, on the contrary, seem to have been better able to integrate their practices and gain recognition as filmmakers, perhaps because the dance film has a history broad enough to include them. Noël Carroll's "Moving and Moving: From Minimalism to *Lives of Performers*" and Robert A. Haller's "Amy Greenfield: Film, Dynamic Movement, and Transformation" trace Yvonne Rainer's and Greenfield's use of the cinema as a choreographic partner, albeit in very different ways.

Diversity in the backgrounds brought to the cinema, ranging from the arts noted above to the institution building carried out by both Chick Strand, who was also an ethnographer, and Marjorie Keller, who was a film scholar, is matched by the variety of political positions taken by the filmmakers. While some of the earliest women covered may have been less likely to have been part of the feminist movement, simply because of when they were born, there are others, such as Nelson, Rainer, and Thornton, who distinctly stated at a certain point that their art was not feminist. Of the others, there is a broad range of political activity, ranging from direct involvement in the women's movement and larger social justice issues to theoretical work in the burgeoning field of film studies. The most visible of women filmmakers over the past several decades have been lesbian, most likely because their work has been investigated and publicized in anthologies and conferences specifically concerned with issues of identity and representation and the broader field of queer studies.[20] Chuck Kleinhans's "Barbara Hammer: Lyrics and History" examines the filmmaker whose wide-ranging work and vigorous self-promotion have made her one of the best known of not only lesbian filmmakers but all women filmmakers. Although almost half of the women studied in this volume identify themselves as lesbian, the writers have not restricted their studies to this aspect of the work alone but have looked at the films in their widest possible context.

Whether or not various filmmakers identify themselves or their work as feminist, almost all share the feminist-inspired tendency to employ nonhierarchical, collaborative production practices. To a striking degree, these artists coauthored films, worked with a company of actors and technicians who sometimes even alternated roles, and engaged in a dialogue about their art in the larger context of women's cinema. Film history sometimes has interpreted these practices as indicating a lack of competence or confidence rather than as pioneering new modes of social relations. Associated with this approach to production were the sustaining efforts by Strand and Keller, particularly, on behalf of the distribution, exhibition, and critical reception of the avant-garde through work with, most notably, Canyon Cinema in San Francisco and Film-Makers' Cooperative in New York, respectively.

The films themselves are enormously experimental and diverse in form and method. One of the more audacious formats in all of avant-garde cinema is that used by Barbara Rubin in *Christmas on Earth* of 1963. As Ara Osterweil notes in " 'Absently Enchanted': The Apocryphal, Ecstatic Cinema of Barbara Rubin," the seventeen-year-old Rubin used two 16mm projectors at once but projected the films onto a single screen so that the images of sexual activity were appropriately layered, one permeating the other. The creative use of technology is further reflected in the wide variety of formats employed. While the early filmmakers were limited to Super 8 and sometimes 16mm film, Ahwesh currently chooses to use Super 8 and many more periodically return to 16mm in this digital age. On the other hand, as Kathleen McHugh notes in "The Experimental 'Dunyementary': A Cinematic Signature Effect" and Janet Cutler observes in "Su Friedrich: Breaking the Rules," both Dunye and Friedrich use or aspire to work in 35mm film to reach the broadest possible audience. Most of the artists make single films, although several are working in more complex forms such as installation. Mary Ann Doane writes of open-ended film projects in her essay, "In the Ruins of the Image: The Work of Leslie Thornton," and Maureen Turim considers serial films in "Sounds, Intervals, and Startling Images in the Films of Abigail Child."

The work of all of these filmmakers tends toward documentary rather than fiction, necessarily expanding the definition of documentary through the choice of subjects and formal experimentation. While the films of Rainer, Friedrich, and Dunye are also concerned with narrative, almost all of the filmmakers find their raw material in their own worlds and lives. As suggested, the use of domestic space and autobiography has been somewhat to blame for the misapprehension of much of the work considered in this book due to its association with the unconstructed home movie or film diary. But as Paul Arthur reminds us, the kitchen table that appears repeatedly in Wieland's work is just as emblematic and rich as the iconic cabin in Colorado that appears so often in Brakhage's films or Andy Warhol's Factory (and the same could be said for Nelson's family homes or Schneemann's cats). Like Menken and Keller in particular, Wieland films her familiar life at home because it is there and because it provides exemplary material with which to create political film. The assumption that these films romantically document "feminine" matters involving the home, love relationships, children, or birth could hardly be further from the truth.

The most perilous but popular focus in these films is the female body itself, and its use has been the prime cause of the split between women filmmakers and feminist theorists that this book implicitly addresses. Many of the filmmakers have blurred the line between performer and observer in their work as a means of investigating the thorny issues surrounding the representation of the female body. The modes of approach are myriad, ranging from almost total elimination of the body to complete exposure—and sometimes combining the two. In all of the films, from Wieland's fragmentation and magnification of body parts to Keller's refusal to show more than a small section of the body, and then never the part that the camerawork would lead one to expect, the filmmaker's presence is strong. The interrogation of the body's status as a cultural and linguistic sign, rather than a natural object, is pervasive and constant. Alternately, from Nelson's capturing of the body performing the most mundane acts, such as inserting a tampon or vomiting, to Rainer's flat, quotidian movements of bodies dressed in street clothes in *Lives of Performers* of 1972, the filmmakers challenge the traditional means and rationales for objectifying the female body.

The most contentious and risky variation is the full exposure of the naked female form, which has alternately been perceived as a celebration of the autonomous and liberated body or a frankly embarrassing example of naive essentialism. While Child and Ahwesh integrate exposure with fragmentation through formal means, stressing repetitive gesture and everyday movement in the former and the dissolution of the image-bearing emulsion itself in the latter, others go for full disclosure. Schneemann and Rubin are the most notorious in this regard, and their 1963 films *Fuses* and *Christmas on Earth* were unavailable for viewing for many years as a result. Rubin's film explores every possible combination of male and female bodies in a style that reveals all but also fragments, masks, and distances in a continual metamorphosis in which the camera is an active partner. Due to its relatively straightforward celebration of heterosexual sex between two beautiful and identifiable people, *Fuses* has been the lightning rod. Schneemann intended literally to envision her bodily perception of her world in all its layers of complexity and to reject the nudity of patriarchal discourse that objectifies the body in favor of the nakedness of the subject. Theorists, however, derided the film for its naïveté in believing that its intention to show the unclothed female body in a nonsexist way could be read by the film's viewers. Greenfield's films, in which the naked body is featured as well, have been equally problematic for theorists, despite the filmmaker's claim that the absence of clothing rejects the fetishization of conventional eroticism and allows the powerful body in action to dominate. Perhaps because of their outsider status and the unfamiliarity of the images, lesbian filmmakers have been freer to depict the naked body, and several artists, including Hammer and Friedrich, have dealt with both the aging and diseased body in addition.

In order to create images that challenge conventional representation of the female body and the limitations of classical Hollywood structures in general, all of the filmmakers experiment with the medium. One of the greatest misconceptions about this experimentation is that its often startling and vexing variations from the linear and orderly norm signify incompetence. On the contrary, the technique that signifies amateurism and disorder is quite intentional and often formally complex; the loosely shot footage is invariably heavily edited. Menken's loose, gestural camerawork—copied by the majority of the filmmakers who followed her—is emblematic in its extremity. Not only did Menken hold the camera as she walked but she allowed her cigarette smoke to drift into the shot and took little care to clean her lens. The shakiness, the movement in and out of focus, the inclusion of the flash frames at the end of the film roll, and general home-movie look of the shots call attention to the filmmaker and prevent the illusion of transparency and clarity so valued by both Hollywood and the structural filmmakers of the late 1960s. As Maria Pramaggiore discusses in "Chick Strand's Experimental Ethnography," at least one filmmaker went so far as to dance with her camera in hand to stress the subjectivity of her gaze and her relationship with her subject. While the gestural camera dominates, Rainer, Thornton, Friedrich, and Dunye privilege static, frontal camera placement. Regardless of the various techniques used for achieving distance through camera positioning, the filmmakers are united in their intensive use of associative or disjunctive rather than linear editing.

The temporal span of this book reveals many interesting formal and thematic developments and transformations over the decades, but few as intriguing as the progression from the dirty aesthetic of Menken's work to the pop culture–centered one of Ahwesh and Dunye. As William C. Wees explores in "Peggy's Playhouse: Contesting the Modernist Paradigm," Ahwesh takes as her field not only the medium itself, but also its entire history of representation. Her ironic, impertinent, free-flowing, and seemingly carelessly made films challenge authority on every level, from the notion of the well-made film to the importance of the stable subject. Dunye joins Ahwesh in this confrontation, finding her cinematic self, as McHugh puts it, in situation comedies of 1970s television. This confluence in which Dunye's postmodern, media-created surfaces return us to what Ragona calls Menken's comprehension of the world as "extra-terrestrial ephemera" is one of the book's more interesting revelations. While Rainer's work would appear to be far from that of Menken, Ahwesh, or Dunye, her simultaneous investigation of her domestic world, her filmic narrating of the stories taken from this realm, and her self-reflexive meditation on the ways in which Hollywood has influenced her telling participate in a similar investigation of interiors versus exteriors.

The evocation of surfaces, whether natural or media-created, suggests perhaps the single most prevalent formal device among all the filmmakers: a layering of images. Both a literal means of construction and a powerful metaphor, the technique has its origins in weaving and working with fabric, the kinds of gendered labor in which Wieland originally worked as a textile artist and in which women have traditionally found themselves as editors. Holmlund responds to this quality in Nelson's work by shaping her essay around the metaphor of archeology. She sees the films as centered on the revelation of what is beneath both the material and the metaphysical worlds as revealed first through decay and time and then through the work of the camera. Strand's and Keller's films are equally focused and formed through superimposition on both the visual and aural tracks, while Schneemann's original copy of *Fuses* was made up of so many layers of celluloid and paint that it was almost impossible to print. This search for what lies beneath surface appearance and convention is also carried out, in Friedrich in particular, through the literal scratching away of the film's emulsion.

Concurrent with the visual layering is the interweaving of the sound track. In the vast majority of films, disjunction reigns between image and sound and within the audio track. As both Child and Keller make quite clear in their writing, the complex sound tracks are not casual collages of sound but are scored in relation to specific images. Others, such as Nelson and Strand, work more loosely in the creation of tapestries of sound made up of conversation, music, ambient noise, and silence. On the other end of the spectrum, Rainer and Thornton work with speech and printed text, sometimes in combination with more diffuse sound, in order to investigate language itself. While Rainer foregrounds narrative and the effect of the voice through recitation rather than performance, Thornton's particularly rich sound tracks manifest and explore what Doane calls the "archive of endlessly mutable, significant sound."

The notion of the archive is present not only in the audio track but also in the visual one in the form of found footage. The previously shot film or video images, advertising imagery, or, in the case of Ahwesh's *She-Puppet* (2001), a video game are juxtaposed with original footage and sound to refer to and comment upon the larger cultural context, particularly the mass media. Strand's practice of using found footage to forge a dialogue in her overtly ethnographic project is duplicated less deliberately in the work of other filmmakers. Child, one of the most well-known of all found footage filmmakers, joins Thornton and Rainer, to a lesser extent, in using imagery from silent cinema to explore the history of the cinematic representation of women. However, Child also uses found imagery in abstract ways, creating rhythmic mosaics in which people become ma-chinelike, in a tradition that hearkens back to the earliest cinema of attractions.[21] As one might expect, the excess of fragmentation, layering, and interweaving of sounds and images from the filmmaker's experience and film history give rise to a degree of surrealism. Keller notes in her scholarly work on Jean Cocteau and Joseph Cornell that the cinema itself, with its reality effect, allows the improbable to enter the real world to a degree unparalleled in any other art form. With notable frequency, many of the films evoke and comment upon the sometimes humorous and often surreal disassociations between patriarchal culture and women's lives within it.

If there is any thematic link connecting the work of these fifteen film-makers, it would be that of looking beneath and uncovering. What is revealed below the literal and metaphorical layers in the films takes many forms but in almost every case involves emotion. Some filmmakers quite deliberately have sought to unveil the passions. Strand turned to film-making from ethnography out of frustration with her male colleagues, whose self-imposed distance from their subjects created what she felt to be inaccurate impressions and even false data. Film, when used creatively rather than as a recording device, had the potential to reveal something authentic about the encounter with the subject. In a different manner but a similar spirit, Rainer left dance for film in order not to simply express emotion corporeally, which she had rejected as ideologically misguided in dance, but to both represent and analyze emotion. Where her work in dance revealed the "essential conditions of dance," as Carroll suggests, her work in film allowed her to investigate what might be called the essential conditions of life.

At least two filmmakers worked even more specifically to uncover the complex feeling and sentiment behind the veneers of both life and the well-made film. Schneemann and Keller made films in reaction to Brak-hage's films about sex and birth. They worked in different ways to get be-neath the beautiful and striking surfaces for which Brakhage was known to reveal the sense of relentless becoming and overwhelming intensity that more closely approximate for women the experience of the physi-cality of love and family life. This search for a means to represent emotion was pervasive in the work of filmmakers who started working before the 1980s. At times the exploration involved a specific context or event, but often the field was more amorphous, as in Nelson's moody, resonant films, which arouse the desire to explore beneath the surface without necessarily revealing what is found. On the other hand, the work of more contemporary filmmakers such as Friedrich, Ahwesh, and Dunye seems less constricted by what is to them a distant avant-garde film history that valued the repression of emotion both in structural film and even in ostensibly more expressive modes.

What then finally can be made of the layers, the fragments, and the archeological metaphors that resonate in and through these films? What do the filmmakers find? For some, particularly Rainer, Hammer, and Friedrich, something substantial is recovered through accumulation and juxtaposition, resulting in analysis and critique. The past and the means through which it has been constructed are revealed to be questioned, understood, and either accepted contingently or rejected. For others the process is less clear-cut. In the work of Nelson, Schneemann, Strand, and Greenfield, the archeological process suggests images of what lies beyond words and even beyond consciousness in ways that are impossible to articulate but are surely of interest for their ability to disturb. In this same vein but with a more precise vision, Keller suggests that nothing remains of experience that has not entered into language. Her films are full of empty spaces, both materially in the form of blank leader and in the world she records, but they also show where this irrecoverable past, now a lacuna, interrupts the logic of cohesive narratives and history itself. Keller's paradoxical reliance on the evidentiary status of photography and cinema recurs in the work of Thornton and Child. All three are interested in what has not been spoken and remains unspeakable, but which lies embedded in the patriarchal discourses that overtly block further investigation. Like many of the filmmakers, they look in the least promising places and often locate through cinema, not truth, but something that rings true. Finally, for the most contemporary of the filmmakers, particularly Ahwesh and Dunye, there is no pressure to attempt to reveal anything (although, of course, they do). McHugh notes Dunye's rejection of the very notion of her own invisibility, which the filmmaker sees as a negative quality used in power relations. The younger filmmakers accept the surface of the culture in which they live, parodying and inventing with self-reflexive glee, secure in the knowledge that the era in which those few men in charge of the isolated avant-garde film journals and festivals had the power to determine visibility or lack thereof is past.

In introducing this volume of essays, I have mentioned all of the authors and the titles of their work at least once to the degree that they particularly exemplify a specific trait common to all or some of the group, and certainly not in accordance with their greater or lesser importance. Each of the sixteen essays that follow, fifteen of which were written for this anthology[22] and the last of which introduces several filmmakers not discussed in individual chapters, adheres to a similar trajectory. Each scholar concentrates on his or her own area of expertise, and the approaches and styles of the essays vary in enlightening ways. But every writer provides specific social, political, or artistic contexts for understanding the filmmaker and her work, along with exemplary critical readings of a representative sample of the films, in an overall length deemed appropriate to the particular methodology used. The essays are organized somewhat chronologically to suggest their historical development in relation to experimental film in general and their connections to other artistic and scholarly spheres, social movements, and political activity.

By way of conclusion, and encouragement, the anthology ends with an essay by Scott MacDonald on the pedagogical challenges of teaching women's experimental cinema. MacDonald's description of the practical problems he has faced is sobering but helpful. His own selection of exemplary films for classroom use extends the breadth of this book, reinforcing the conviction held by all of the writers that the group of filmmakers discussed here could easily be tripled. This anthology, we hope, is simply one phase of a larger project that will be continued and extended by readers and students who are inspired to conduct further archival research, engage in comparative scholarship, and teach the films that make up the loosely defined canon of women's experimental cinema. In concrete terms, the material uncovered here ought to appear in databases that can facilitate an ongoing project. Likewise, this book, with its not-so-ulterior mission of preserving the films of experimental women filmmakers, would fulfill its highest function if it inspired film festivals requiring high-quality prints of the work. Finally, although the field of film studies must fight for the future of 8mm and 16mm projection, it must also seek funding to create digital versions of the material, which are essential for classroom use and, in some cases, for the purpose of preservation. As the Women Film Pioneers project, which deals with women in silent film history, has discovered, every year that passes makes the recovery of lost films and tenuously preserved information more difficult, more frustrating, and less successful.[23] I speak for all of the writers in this anthology in expressing my belief that the history of cinema will be greatly impoverished if it loses the legacy of these filmmakers and their work.

Notes

1 Organized by Jacques Ledoux, the first Belgian festival, the Festival International du Film Expérimental and Poétique, was held in the summer of 1949, the second, the Experimental Film Competition, was held in Brussels in the spring of 1958, and the rest of the events were titled International Experimental Film Competition and held in Knokke, with the third held from December 25, 1963, to January 2, 1964, the fourth during the same dates in 1967–68, and the fifth and final one during the same period in 1974–75.

2 The records of the festival at the Cinémathèque Royale de Belgique indicate that women's work was a minimal presence in the festival, with 5 percent or less representation from North America overall, and even these women were most often present as part of a male/female couple.

3 Keller, "Report from Knokke-Exprmentl 5,"28–33. Keller notes particularly the number of purportedly feminist films in the festival that were essentially sexist male fantasies, and she makes an equally strong case against women's films that she sees as banal psychodramas. She also remarks on the festival's unfortunate exclusion of 8mm and Super 8 films, both of which were less expensive to shoot and more easily available to women filmmakers.

4 Michelson and Sitney, "A Conversation on Knokke and the Independent Filmmaker."

5 Patricia Mellencamp notes in *Indiscretions: Avant-Garde, Video, and Feminism*, that many approaches to the avant-garde, particularly Sitney's *Visionary Film*, serve primarily as investigations of the romantic artist—who is by definition male—in which women can only be muses, critics, lovers, or mothers (19). I note, however, that Sitney's latest work in progress encompasses the films of Marie Menken, Abigail Child, and Su Friedrich, among others.

6 *Women and Film* 1, nos. 1–6, and 2, no. 7 (1972–75); *Film Library Quarterly* 5, no. 1 (1971–72); and *Take One* 3, no. 2 (1972).

7 For a list of all the films shown, see D. Kaplan, "Part 3: Selected Short Subjects/First International Women's Film Festival," 37–39.

8 Martineau, "Women's Film Daily," 36.

9 Braderman, "First Festival of Women's Films," 87.

10 Rich, *Chick Flicks*, 29–39.

11 See Johnston, "Women's Cinema as Counter Cinema" and Mulvey, "Visual Pleasure and Narrative Cinema."

12 Martineau, "Women's Film Daily," 37.

13 As early as 1973, the editors of *Women and Film* 1, nos. 3–4 (1973): 5, made the following plea: "For this issue of *Women and Film*, we received countless articles on the commercial product and disproportionately few writings on independent films made by women even though these films represent in quantity, form and content, the most significant contribution of these last 12 months of cinema history. . . . [Feminists] spend 90% of their energy giving

attention to men's works thereby ironically validating them and confirming their right to monopolize all spheres." The editors then call for improved distribution and exhibition of women's films, the establishment of archives, particularly for fragile 8mm film, and, crucially, for the theorizing of feminist cinema. Little did they know that the growth of theory would further erode scholarly work on women's cinema, except for those films that overtly worked in opposition to classical Hollywood film. By 1974, in the next to last issue of *Women and Film*, Julia Lesage wrote in a footnote to her essay, "Feminist Film Criticism: Theory and Practice," that little had been written about experimental film because "these films are not as accessible for rental as narrative films, nor have we considered what role these films play in a feminist cinema." She then makes a plea for "the greater support of experimental filmmaking by women" (18).

14   Bazin, *What Is Cinema?*, 107.

15   While Patricia Mellencamp's fascinating work in progress on Moffatt was not suitable for this project, it will undoubtedly appear in another format soon.

16   See Munroe and Hendricks, *Yes Yoko Ono*, and Nichols, *Maya Deren and the American Avant-Garde*, in particular.

17   I note that I am not referring to the lost object of psychoanalytic theory. I do not read the films and their diverse representation of formal and thematic gaps and holes with the prescriptive theoretical assumption that the absence of the mother is the motivating force of desire and thus language. Instead I see in this work something more amorphous that is, if not outside of the discourse of patriarchy, clearly a threat to its dominion.

18   Both Mekas and Brakhage worked almost exclusively in their domestic spaces, filming family, friends, homes, and the natural world around them. See Sitney, *Visionary Film*, for further information about both directors.

19   James, "Film Diary/Diary Film," 147. I note that James's own articulation of the movement between the two approaches is complex and not particularly based on gender.

20   See the Women Make Movies web site for an extensive list of film festivals devoted to lesbian or gay and lesbian film (www.wwm.com/resources).

21   See Gunning, "The Cinema of Attractions."

22   Carroll's essay about Rainer's well-known *Lives of Performers* both is shorter than most of the other essays and has been published previously in *Millennium Film Journal*. It is included because it has received little exposure and it offers a suggestive contextualization of Rainer's work in regard to minimalism and to structural film, the dominant avant-garde practice in the late 1960s and early 1970s.

23   The Women Film Pioneers project, located at Duke University under the direction of Jane Gaines, seeks to make public information about the women who worked in all capacities in the earliest years of the film industry. See www.duke.edu/web/film/pioneers.

MELISSA RAGONA

Swing and Sway

Marie Menken's Filmic Events

□

Marie Menken (1910–70) is one of the least recognized experimental filmmakers of her generation. Menken's influence on filmmakers like Willard Maas (her husband and collaborator), Stan Brakhage, Jonas Mekas, Norman McLaren, Kenneth Anger, Maya Deren, and Andy Warhol is vast and varied. Brakhage has written the most lucidly and candidly about Menken's life. Indeed, he claims that Menken was one of the most important influences on his "lid-swinging" or "ways of seeing" through the camera eye.[1] In step with Parker Tyler, who claims that Menken was "one of the very first to endow the handheld camera with an elementary sort of dance pulse" or a signature "swing and sway,"[2] Brakhage argues that the fluidity of Menken's camera was revolutionary for filmmakers during the 1950s and 1960s who still felt they had to "imitate the Hollywood dolly shot, without dollies."[3] The smooth pan that implied the invisibility of the camera, a seamlessness without human error, was a norm that Menken challenged with her "free, swinging, swooping handheld pans."

Menken's use of film as a new perceptual medium—especially one that could be manipulated as an object—suggested several paths down which one could travel aesthetically. As Brakhage implied, her work inspired him to think about the relationship of paint to film and eventually painting on film, a process he began to explore in the early 1960s. He describes

Menken's approach to the film strip, in a similar way to his own during this period: "When she came to film, then she looked at it first of all as a 'thread' of many shades and colors to be woven or 'spun out' into related patterns. She would hold the strips of film in her hand very much as she would strands of beads to be put into a collage painting. She would hang the film strips on clothespins and, after much meditation and often without running them through a viewer at all, would cut them together."[4] As Sitney describes, "a quarter of Brakhage's oeuvre was made without using a camera," but unlike Menken, Brakhage moved toward an abstract expressionist penchant for medium-specific painterliness, individuality, and the uniqueness of the painterly mark in film. In contrast, Menken's later work led her more and more toward viewing film as an event-based medium. Closer to Fluxus performance aesthetics and Pop Art's quick play with the readymade, Menken's animations played skillfully with both the objecthood of film (making the viewer aware of film frame, projection surface, shot arrangement, and montage sequence) as well as film's performativity—its ability to animate the inanimate, to reveal critical relationships between media: film frame and painterly canvas, audio and image, language and figure.[5]

Born in 1910 in New York to Lithuanian immigrant parents, Menken began painting in her early twenties. In the mid-1930s, she received a residence-grant from Yaddo, an art colony in upstate New York, where she met the poet and filmmaker Willard Maas, whom she married in 1937.[6] Cecil Starr writes that she "worked as [Hilla] Rebay's secretary" for the Gallery of Non-Objective Painting (later known as the Guggenheim Museum) in order to support her work as a painter during this period.[7] In her position as Rebay's assistant, Menken attended many film screenings or "Concerts of Non-Objectivity," organized by Rebay which included films by Hans Richter, Viking Eggeling, Oskar Fischinger, and Norman McLaren. From the mid-1940s until the time of her death in 1970, Menken worked as a night-time manager of the Foreign News Department at Time-Life in New York.[8] Outside a few, very brief reviews of her shows at the Tibor de Nagy and Betty Parsons galleries in New York, not much is known about Menken's early painting, but by the 1950s she had begun experimenting with other media, including sand, collage, assemblage, and installation.[9] Film seemed to provide the logical step that would bring her work into more kinetic arrangements and allow her to explore the Duchampian chance operations that she was already engaged in with painting.

In the inaugural show of the Tibor de Nagy Gallery in 1950, Menken

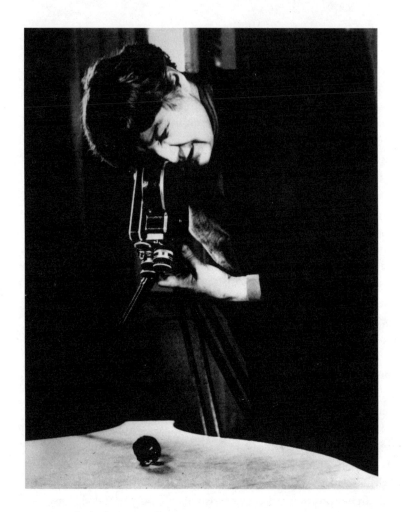

Marie Menken at work. Courtesy of Anthology Film Archives.

was surrounded by a new second school of New York painters: Franz Kline, Larry Rivers, Elaine de Kooning, Grace Hartigan, Harry Jackson, Alfred Leslie, Robert Goodnough, and Helen Frankenthaler.[10] While this second school defied the orthodox abstract expressionism of the color field painters like Mark Rothko, Barnett Newman, Clyfford Still, and Adolph Gottlieb, they still remained devoted to the material of paint—a medium that Menken found limited, and which she began to explore and extend through film. Her engagement in the worlds of Fluxus (through her friendship with Robert Watts) and Pop Art (amplified by her involvement in Warhol's film projects) further inspired her rejection of abstract expressionist concerns with the specificity of paint and canvas.[11]

Menken used film as a way of rethinking painting and sculptural problems, in particular the transition from abstract expressionism to Pop and conceptual projects. The latter can be most clearly read in her ironic title, *Pop Goes the Easel* (1964),[12] or in her explicit works on painting like *Mood Mondrian* (1963) or *Drips in Strips* (1963). Most commonly, Menken's talents have been read through her poet husband Maas's work, focusing on her contribution to the film poem or film sentence. This is underlined by Jonas Mekas's description of her work in his 1962 *Film Journal*: "The structure of Menken's filmic sentences, her movements, and her rhythms are those of poetry."[13] In the scant critical literature on Menken produced primarily by Brakhage, Sitney, and Mekas (more recently by David James and Scott MacDonald), Menken is lauded as one of the great film diarists, as a film poet, and as one of the important inventors of the lyrical tradition in film.[14] In this essay, I hope to reveal how these critics and filmmakers, in their efforts to celebrate her within the purview of their own achievements (Brakhage and Mekas are central players here), reduce the specificity and complexity of her work. While Menken was interested in the materiality of cinematic language, her strategies are more deeply concerned with ungrounding the easel-based practices of drawing and sculpture through film. Film not only freed her from canvas and brush but allowed her to critique the verticality and stasis of 1940s painting and object-based practices. Her handheld camera produced a frenetic vertigo on sculptural, architectural, natural, and domestic objects, while her play with animation stretched the borders of film frame and event. Cinematic writing with light (as seen in *Moonplay, Lights, Greek Epiphany*, and *Night Writing*, all combined in *Notebook*) replaced painterly values; perception, not paint, became medium.

The Notebook: Quick Sketches and Events

Menken's work addresses a moment in painting and art making similar to the modernist turn taken by Gertrude Stein in the early twentieth century. Stein, privy to the worlds of Pablo Picasso, Georges Braque, and Camille Pissarro, was interested in the shape and duration of the fragment; consequently her writing was more of a response to painting than literature. As Brakhage has noted, the influence Menken had on his work was in step with the inspiration Stein had asserted upon him, "continually draw[ing] [him] toward the material of [his] daily living rather than 'literature.' "[15] The notion of a "notebook," journal, or diary has played a central role in framing Menken's filmic work critically.[16] As indicated above, she is often referred to as a film poet, one of the first to use the film journal as a form. One of my contentions, however, is that the history of the film diary, which is placed squarely at the center of Menken's invention, uses only a very specific definition to propagate this genealogy.

David James gives an exhaustive treatise on the differences between the film diary and the diary film. In brief, he argues that the film diary delivers immediacy, raw daily life; it privileges a single textual sense, that of the subjective position of the filmmaker. In contrast, the diary film is mediated: "it subjects the original images to sounds and disjunct visual material."[17] The impossibility of a pure version of the former (unmediated, the problem of the ever-slipping present, the presence of the unstaged filmmaker) has been a main critique of this genre.[18] But James gives Mekas credit for approaching the contradictions of the film diary with panache: "Mekas was the first fully to articulate this combination of imperatives—the need to respond immediately with the camera to and in the present, and the need to subjectivize that recording—as the essential conditions of the film diary, and the first fully to turn them to advantage, and eventually to invest filmic attention to daily life with religious significance."[19]

Menken, on the other hand, is inscribed by James as an extension of feminist diary writing of the 1970s, "where introspection and self-awareness were understood as individual participation in a collective historical recovery."[20] After Menken, he cites work by Chantal Akerman, Storm de Hirsch, Su Friedrich, Marjorie Keller, Yvonne Rainer, Amalie Rothschild, Carolee Schneemann, and Claudia Weill as a continuation of this tradition. In contrast, male experimental filmmakers, such as Andrew Noren, George Pinkus, and Mekas, began utilizing the film diary approach only after 1960s avant-garde filmmaking models lost steam (he seems to be referring to structuralist film). In short, Menken's invention of the film diary is valued as something unique because it strongly influenced Mekas and Brakhage. Moreover, it is read as an existential, anti-structural move, a more enlightened form than the subjective works offered by "people of color, women, and gays."[21] In contrast, Mekas's and Brakhage's form of the film diary are presented as having more structural rigor, as well as being informed by the open, more personal, feminist-inspired essay.

Menken's *Notebook*, I would like to argue, is closer to quick sketching than journal writing—and it does not reflect the kind of subjective auto-biography and existential angst that works like *Walden* (Mekas, 1964–69) or *Anticipation of the Night* (Brakhage, 1958) represent. Menken's collection here—"Raindrops," "Greek Epiphany," "Moonplay," "Copy Cat," "Paper Cuts," "Lights," "Night Writing," "The Egg," and "Etcetcetc."—is a playful sketchbook of manipulated nature, animated objects, and moving cutouts. From the beginning of this series, Menken was not engaged in exercising the internal world of the film diary, its registering of the un-adulterated, subjective view of the filmmaker. Instead, she created a kind of frenetic artifice out of natural events. For example, in "Raindrops," she pushes nature's clock prematurely: "As she waits behind the camera for a drop of rain on the tip of a leaf to gather sufficient mass to fall, we sense her impatience and even anxiety lest the film will run out on her; so an unseen hand taps the branch, forcing the drops to fall."[22] "Raindrops" characterizes, in a sense, the kind of manipulation that Menken regularly engaged in with her work; she was not interested, as Mekas was, in registering her "state of feeling (and all the memories)" as she filmed a particular object, action, or scene. As Sitney has so cogently argued in *Visionary Film*, Menken "tampered" with her handheld work. She was not interested in the "straightforward observational film" but rather wanted to incorporate her own sordid hand, even if it registered her cigarette smoke as it wafted into a particular shooting session.[23]

In *Notebook*'s "Greek Epiphany," "Moonplay," "Lights," and "Night Writing," Menken treats natural and artificial light with equal valence. Menken's experimentation with light as a medium was informed both by her own fascination of transposing other media (painting, light, sculpture) into filmic contours, and also by the proliferation of art works that took "light" as both subject and modus operandi. Artists like Julio Le Parc, Dan Flavin, Chryssa, Larry Bell, Robert Irwin, and James Terrell (just to name a few) were interested in light, perception, movement, and illusion as a central part of their art practices during the mid-1960s, continuing

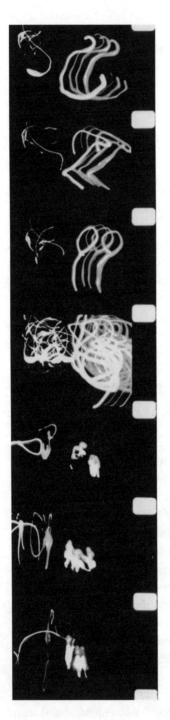

From Marie Menken's *Lights*, 1966.
Courtesy of Anthology Film Archives.

into the 1970s and, in some cases, up into the present. Menken's fascination with neon lighting, as presented in "Night Writing," as well as in her 3-D works at the Tibor de Nagy Gallery in December 1950, is echoed in the work of Dan Flavin, in which light has the ability to transform an environment. But where Flavin and Bell were interested in having their audiences confront light as a sculptural object (as in Flavin's exposed fluorescent fixtures or Bell's light boxes), Menken was closer to Irwin in her efforts to reveal the hypnotic effect of light divorced from any object. In "Night Writing," we are confronted by "such quick movement" that the red and green neon lights seem to be "brilliant calligraphy on the screen."[24] In "Greek Epiphany," candlelight—at first discernible, analog light—becomes abstracted into color, marking an anonymous pattern, rather than an orthodox religious, representational ceremony. A similar transformation takes place in "Lights" when a Christmas tree is inverted and its lights take over the screen in 3-D forms. Moreover, an analogy is made between the tree lights and the lights in an adjacent building, removing any narrative context from the sense of the decorative. Likewise, in "Moonplay," the moon as it moves with lightning speed across the sky seems to appear more like a flashlight or strobe, flattening any sense of depth of field on the screen. There are two versions of "Moonplay"; one was made for *Notebook*, and the other, made a bit later, develops the themes Menken had begun in her first short sketch. The latter is set to music by Teiji Ito so that the moon moves—through stop-motion animation—frenetically, wildly with the quick-changing score. As Sitney has noted, the night photography of Menken's "Moonplay," its fast panning, fusing of foreground and background, as well as its elimination of depth are borrowed by Brakhage for *Anticipation of the Night*. "A short mixture of what Marie Menken called both 'Moonplay' and 'Night Writing,' here [in Brakhage's *Anticipation of the Night*] intercut, prepares the transition to an amusement park, where older children take rides in the night . . . the lights of the park behind them have next to no depth on the screen."[25]

The flatness of the screen is even more prominent in Menken's animation pieces in *Notebook*: "Copycat," "Paper Cuts," "The Egg," and "Etcetcetc." Inspiring to Norman McLaren and a host of younger, contemporary animators, including Lewis Klahr, Janie Geiser, Emily Breer, and Martha Colburn, Menken's animation work nonetheless has been ignored or mentioned briefly in critical discussions of her work.[26] This is most likely because this work, which is playful, irreverent, and abject, does not fit the prevailing model of her as a lyrical film poet and keen observer of everyday life. "Copycat," a brief study in diagonals, is in some ways more successful than the longer *Mood Mondrian* (1963). Rather than having her camera race over the structure of a painting, as she does in *Mood Mondrian*, Menken allows the structure of diagonals—their play against one another—to constitute the movement of the film. Reminiscent, sans sound, of McLaren's *Lines Horizontal* and *Lines Vertical* (1961–62), Menken's "Copycat" reveals the formalist energy of abstraction, commenting once again on the tabula rasa of the film screen and pointing back at its artificial borders to the edges of its proscenium square. She also pokes fun at the alleged symmetry of the modernist diagonal. When repeated, diagonals copy each other endlessly, outwitting each other with new juxtapositions, threatening to misalign themselves in asymmetrical patterns, but always moving in similar directions and finding order next to each other.

Likewise, in "Paper Cuts," Menken manipulates blue, red, and pink forms through space so that they play off and against each other. Solidified into relationships because of their color, the pinks team up against the blues, the blues against the reds, and so forth. Sand animation is put to use in a way reminiscent of her earlier work in sand painting. For example, two pink forms shove off of a silvery background (a kind of sandy glitter), signaling a brigade of pink forms that march, in full force, across the screen. They proceed to infect (a favorite Menken animation ploy) a collection of what appear to be green leaflike forms. The latter become leaves of an orange, but are then quickly deconstructed as abstract forms, which fly off the screen at the end of the film.

Prefiguring the Brothers Quay's films such as *Street of Crocodiles* (1986), Menken's "The Egg" is a neogothic study of a skeleton that magically acquires an egg, which comes swinging into the picture and settles into a lower cavity of the skeleton. Then, some kind of red, gelatinous glitter seeps into the picture frame, invades the skeletal body, and frees the egg from its position.[27] This sense of an entropic world where objects infect or invade objects is a recurring theme in Menken's animation. Her sense of humor, however, often steps in and converts a potentially dark scene into slapstick. In "Etcetcetc." Menken is depicted hopping up and down with two dogs on a rooftop (their seeming motion created by stop animation). Intercuts to a busy highway or scenes whipping by from inside a moving train are interspersed with return shots of a woman and two dogs jumping, endlessly, up and down. At one point, the viewer is given the point of view of one of the dogs from the roof looking down and observing the moving traffic of the city. The film's absurdity is equaled only by *Hurry! Hurry!* and *Go Go Go*, two films that are often cited as serious masterpieces (in particular, by Brakhage). These films all exhibit the same kind of humor as her graphic animations through ironic repetitions: in the former, of racing sperm, in the latter, of frenetic urban people.

Menken's *Notebook* was not an attempt to present an unmediated, purely autobiographical or photographic diary of the present. Seeing and recording, the subject I and the camera eye were not collapsed into one another. As Maureen Turim has made clear, the definition of the lyrical film, with its "I'm behind the camera, so this is my view" approach, coincides with the precepts of the autobiographical, journal-like film.[28] For Menken, what the camera could see was as important as what she saw in her mind's eye; reality and artifice were fused in Menken's films, which offered up often uncanny, otherworldly depictions of the mundane. Menken was aware of the impossibility of this kind of filmmaking outside the frame of a utopian project. Thus the problem that Mekas and Brakhage faced in their efforts to present raw, immediate experience, namely, the "intrusion of present consciousness over footage from the past," did not plague Menken. She used the time lags implicit in pop culture and stop-motion photography as ironic signposts that pointed more toward a tabloid consciousness (like Warhol's) rather than to the interior space of diary film. Unlike Mekas and Brakhage, well-meaning, self-proclaimed chroniclers of the "truth" of their times, Menken was naughty, irreverent, and willing to sacrifice the authenticity of an image for a fabricated version which offered up a surface that might reveal more fully the underside, the flipside of the cultural record. Mekas and Brakhage were fascinated by Menken, not because she represented some kind of authentic film poetess, as they often proclaimed, but because she registered what were, for them "heavy" moments in nature and urban life in flippant, jubilant ways. As Mekas has written,

There are moments in *Arabesque* and in *Notebook* that are among the most inspired sentences in filmic poetry. Does Menken transpose reality? Or condense it? Or does she, simply, go direct to the essence of it? Isn't poetry more realistic than realism? The realist sees only the front of a building, the outlines, a street, a tree. Menken sees in them the motion of time and eye. She sees the motions of heart in a tree. She sees through them and beyond them. She retains a visual memory of all that she sees.

She re-creates moments of observation, of meditation, reflection, wonderment. A rain that she sees, a tender rain, becomes the memory of all rains she ever saw; a garden that she sees becomes a memory of all gardens, all color, all perfume, all mid-summer and sun.[29]

Menken's ability to catch the "everyday," a garden, a walk, a city street, is lauded as good, avant-garde practice. She exercises a careful, sensitive eye, a rhythmic handheld camera, and an aesthetics of low production values (a pawned camera and natural lighting and settings). She is a master observer, capturing the lyrical worlds of gardens (*Glimpse of the Garden*), the rococo of Moorish architecture (*Arabesque for Kenneth Anger*), or the abstraction of cracked sidewalks (*Sidewalks*). But Menken also had a keen sense of the art world—the sculptures of Isamu Noguchi, the paintings of Piet Mondrian, the pop objects of Andy Warhol, and the Fluxus-inspired sculptural toys and games of Robert Watts. As often noted, Menken played an alcoholic mother next to Gerard Malanga in *Chelsea Girls* and was a frequent visitor at Warhol's Factory (Warhol also visited her and Willard Maas in their Brooklyn apartment). In five of her twenty films currently in circulation, she traces the move made in the American art world from European modernism to abstract expressionism to Pop Art and Fluxus and comments in sardonic and clever ways on the limitations and potentiality of each movement through the medium of film.

Menken's Camera Eye on Sculpture and Painting

Most critics have concentrated on Menken's *Visual Variations on Noguchi* (1945), lauding it as one of her finest achievements in terms of shot rhythm (her kinetic camera work at play), image-sound relations, and light values (its rich fields of black and white). As Brakhage, one of her most avid fans, declares: "Marie Menken's 'Open Sesame' to me was that *Visual Variations on Noguchi* was the first film I had ever seen which completely not only admitted but capitalized on the fact that the camera was handheld."[30] Sitney cites *Visual Variations on Noguchi* as one of the key influences on Brakhage's early lyrical turn. While several critics laud the frenetic movement Menken was able to capture in this first film, she is reinscribed by Mekas back into the more static image of a film poet: "She transposes reality into poetry. It is through poetry that Menken reveals to us the subtle aspects of reality, the mysteries of the world and the mysteries of her own soul."[31] For Sitney, camera movement stands center stage for the lyrical film: "In the lyrical form there is no longer a hero; instead, the screen is filled with movement, and that movement, both of the camera and the editing, reverberates with the idea of a person looking."[32] Although Sitney does not situate Menken in traditions of Romantic poetry as Mekas does, his complex interpretation of the lyrical (as acute, critical observation achieved through the simultaneous acts of seeing, filming, and editing) collapses in the context of Romantic criticism about Menken during the 1970s and 1980s. In contrast to most film criticism during this period, Parker Tyler puts his finger on the pulse of Menken's original technique, naming the "nervous, somewhat eccentric, rhythmic play" which she injects into seemingly static images.[33] Indeed, he points to the tension she often (but not always) creates both "to and from the photographed field," as well as "back and forth before it."[34] He cites her achievement in terms of creating an "extra" or "third" dimension on the flat film screen. In other words, her work exhibits an awareness of film as playing a central role in the expanded field of both sculpture and painting. Building on the work of Robert Rauschenberg, Menken is able to expose the intimacy between 2-D and 3-D forms—exploiting their asymmetry in order to create new spatial relationships.

For instance, *Visual Variations on Noguchi* is a playful celebration of Noguchi's work. Menken opens with a whispering voice-over. We are taken deftly down into the sculpture by a camera that careens along the edges of Noguchi's sculpture, making it fleshlike, bringing us closer and closer to the sculpture's texture, its body object. Cavernous voices signal depth and the presence of water, as if we are slowly being submerged. Then, as quickly as we have descended, an upward vertiginous camera movement heaves our vision to the top of the sculpture, which is luminescent and seemingly spinning. Then, Menken's signature "swing and sway" causes us to lose orientation as vertical and horizontal axes vanish. White, abstract forms (photographic fragments of the sculpture) seem to soar through space, reminding us of her ability to animate the most static of objects—to confront us, through film, with the plasticity of sculpture and, in turn, with the sculptural aspects of film.

Menken told Brakhage that *Noguchi* was an attempt to capture "the flying spirit of movement within these solid objects."[35] It was a landmark piece for independent cinema, freeing up many other independent filmmakers from the commercial aesthetic of what she called the "Hollywood dolly shot."[36] But even more profoundly, this piece marks the beginning of Menken's long relationship with plastic and painterly works; she went on to use Mondrian's *Broadway Boogie Woogie*, Warhol's *Brillo Boxes* and *Silkscreen Portrait Series*, and Robert Watts's *Eggs*. Menken's work demands a more complex reading, one that the frame of film poetry or the lyrical movie cannot deliver. Her bravado included a profound knowledge of contemporary art and an interest in bringing about radical changes in the perspectives available to both art and film worlds. Her first show at Tibor de Nagy Gallery in December 1950 was described by Joe Le Sueur, editor and author (of a memoir on Frank O'Hara) as an affront to the admirers of haute abstract expressionism:

> "Come after six to the opening," she urged me, "because that's when the fun begins." She went on to explain that it would be nightfall by then, so that her phosphorescent paintings—some were attached to the ceiling, as I recall—would glow in the dark when John Myers turned off the lights. Well, she was right; it was a lot of fun. For one thing, there were untoward goings-on in the dark and much giggling. Eventually, two policemen arrived to break up the party. Excited by the prospect of a gallery that would be devoted to what she called "fun in art," Marie was full of big plans that night for the gallery's future, plans, as it turned out, that came to naught when John and Tibor promptly began exhibiting the likes of Rivers, Frankenthaler, and Freilicher.[37]

Noguchi had already been made when Menken made her splashy debut in the New York art world. Film, for her, would soon overtake painting and directly inspire her rethinking of canvas, light, and object-audience positions. Her installation-like work for the Tibor de Nagy show illustrates an assemblage aesthetic that predates Robert Rauschenberg's *Combines* of the mid-1950s. Its projection from the ceiling—across and toward horizontal works on the wall—interrupts the viewer's traditional line of gallery vision. It also threatens, from above, the visitor's line of travel across the gallery floor. This emphasis on an object's performative potential was already evident in *Noguchi*, with Menken's camera movement activating the potential movement of a sculpture's plastic lines. The sound-image relations in *Noguchi* further emphasize what transformed into the event structure of objects in later Fluxus-inspired work. There is a playful, ironic relationship to sound as well; a goofy, low, grumbling voice leads us into the nether areas of the sculpture (as mentioned above, we have a sense that we are being submerged both sonically and optically). Then, a broken neo-noir narrative punctuates the sudden twists and turns around the sculpture. The glissando of piano parallels the glissando of camera. An operatic voice underscores the effect of a sudden zoom.

Menken theorized film's relationship to painting in *Dwightiana* (1957), *Mood Mondrian* (1963), and *Drips in Strips* (1963). *Mood Mondrian* comes closest to repeating the strategies she uses in *Noguchi*; it attempts to follow the rhythms Mondrian sets up, racing along verticals, then cutting unexpectedly to horizontals. And though the five-and-a-half minute film is silent, Menken is experimenting with "visual sound" or "eye music," which Brakhage would later extend and name "visual music." Menken describes *Mood Mondrian* as "a film of a painting of a sound" or "visual boogie rhythm." The latter most accurately captures Mondrian's own assessment of what he was attempting to do in this work: "The painting might be interpreted as a representation of music, and that it is not—my work is free from music."[38] Instead of "composition," Mondrian was interested in working with "rhythm" and "opposition" from about 1937, which was the beginning of his transatlantic painting series in which *Broadway Boogie Woogie* plays a prominent role. Menken was drawn to his work in the way she was drawn to Noguchi's, because of its acoustic, kinesthetic, and rhythmic explorations within the realm of the visual.

A similar tactic is used in her earlier *Dwightiana* (1957), except that in addition to sound-motivated rhythmic patterns, Menken uses animation to "move" the image in unexpected, novel ways. She begins this piece with paint dripping down over blue and black title designs—these drips will appear quite literally, again, in *Drips in Strips* (1963). But here paint's heavy gravity is juxtaposed against animation's ephemeral agility. First, Menken syncs each drip with a percussive stroke on a talking drum from accompanist Teiji Ito. This opening tableau is followed by the animation of a kaleidoscope of brightly colored objects moving over one of Dwight Ripley's Miro-like paintings which exude a kind of magic realist aesthetic (griffin-like figures move in a surreal garden). Here, as she does in her other painting-related films, Menken comments on the use of foreground and background, screen and frame, as well as 3-D versus 2-D space. Ripley's paintings work both as flat planes, exposed as painterly surfaces, and as open fields in which animated objects enter or scurry across in agitated, jazzlike patterns. Menken uses sand animation to further decenter the picture plane of each painting, rearranging focal points through a system of "cover up" and "reveal." Then, objects—necklace strands, bits of jewelry—take command and seem to be consuming their sand background as they move across the screen. Studies of stasis versus movement, aggregate versus solo constellations dominate the film, accentuated by Teiji's insistent music.

In *Drips in Strips* (1963), Menken delivers a Jackson Pollock–like slapstick; the viewer can see the shadow of her hand as she splatters paint onto the filmed canvas. She delivers a version of action painting, with the kineticism increased by the agility of the moving camera. The film opens with black drips, then hot pink paint just dribbling down a canvas. The camera swings from side to side, top to bottom, reverses. Close-ups of hot pink, presented in slow motion, are surprised by sudden injections of white and black drips, recalling the opening shot. We watch the process of painting through the lens of the camera, each frame documenting the density of the paint, until the final frame is completely saturated with strips of drips.

Contrary to most critical assessments, this film illustrates not Menken's desire to paint through film, but rather her sardonic comment on the process of painting itself. Menken described *Drips in Strips* as "spattered paint responding to gravity, forming its own patterns and combinations of color."[39] *Drips in Strips* has more of a relationship to the event-inspired scores of Fluxus than to the drip canvases of abstract expressionist painters. Its equation *drip* = *strip* comments more on Menken's own replacement of painting with film, as well as on her interest in the structural possibilities of art making, a decided focus on process over content and event over object production. Brakhage claims to have learned this lesson from Menken, who claimed, "I was prepared to accept the far greater reality, to the film artist, of the strip of film as opposed to the images it makes (under certain conditions of extreme mechanization) on the screen."[40]

Menken's *Notebook* is a testament to her agility with filmic event structures. Her turn from abstract expressionist references to a focus on an aesthetic of surfaces—transparency, translucence, sheen, shine, and reflection—informed both the work of Andy Warhol, but even more profoundly, the work of Fluxus artist Robert Watts (each of whom she made the object of a film). As Menken herself said, "these are too tiny or too obvious for comment"; the raindrops, paper cuts, moon plays, night writings, and egg games are objects from the natural world examined as if they were extraterrestrial ephemera, emitting light, color, and humor. In her *Notebook* films, a ludic volley plays itself out between the luminous edges of nature (raindrops, the moon) and the frenetic perimeters of urban culture (Christmas lights, neon signage). The mistaken focus on Menken's lyrical beauty made by Brakhage, Mekas, and MacDonald has been well propagated, simply by a lack of information about Menken, that her identity as a film poet of great sensitivity (especially partial to filming gardens) has overshadowed the sardonic, witty, playful Fluxus side of both her animations, as well as her attempt to address the emerging moment of an aesthetics of surface during a time when artists were still occupied with material substance, structure, and procedural form.[41] Even when Brakhage tried to typecast her as a "cinematic poet" arguing that she "made a translation of poetic possibilities into the language of cinema," he also pointed out that she reminded him that "there is enough English poetry to read in a lifetime, why bother with attempts at translations from other languages?"[42]

Embedded in Menken's work is an explicit critique of the lyricism of abstract expressionism, as well as any direct equations made between poetry and film. Only in her collaboration with her husband Willard Maas, in *Geography of the Body* (1943) or *Image in the Snow* (1950), does she come close to articulating a Romantic poetics of film. Her work with lights reveals a fascination with surface and emulsion rather than the sheer poetic force of any particular subject. Like Warhol, Menken was interested in the status of objects and their objecthood. In fact, in much of Menken's work, objects and subjects are given equal weight, imbued with a structural equivalence through the material force of film.

Pop Goes the Easel: Menken Films Warhol

In her film *Andy Warhol* (1965), which she considers a "document" rather than one of her more adventurous constructions, Menken plays with the fine line that can be found running across all her work between irony and an almost neorealist grit. This tension can be felt even in her own description of her Andy Warhol film: "A long day in the life of Pop artist Andy Warhol shortened into minutes: a document." Her implied reference to Warhol's "labor"—a long day for Andy—is repeated in the structure of the film, centered on Warhol's work activities at the Factory, and points to the durational quality of his time-based artworks. Especially in her documentation of the construction of his Brillo boxes—with Gerard Malanga, his underpaid line worker, in assistance, viewers are made privy to the symbiotic tie Warhol established between artistic production and commodity aesthetics. As has been well discussed, Warhol's work ethic was Herculean; his own recreation of surplus value was generated by his ability to bridge the gap between culture's mourning of the loss of "real" textures of the preindustrial past and the "real" labor that was considered "lost" and outmoded by the new market of plastics, synthetics, and multiples. Menken teases out this relationship by opening the film with her characteristic interest in reflective surfaces: mirrors, chandeliers, windows. The opening shot is an image of Malanga's reflection in a mirror as he works to package 120 wooden Brillo Box simulacra made for the Stable Gallery in New York (in 1964, a year before Menken's film of the same was released in 1965). She moves then from Warhol climbing a ladder to Malanga and Warhol stretching out paper, with the grid of manufactured boxes in the background. This "mirror of production" is played out as glittering surface and both reflects faux industrial labor and reveals the "work" in the work of art. Other handheld revelations include the seeming excess of wealth that hangs over the squalor of the art workers' bathroom, where a gaudy chandelier hangs over a slightly dirty toilet. The latter image mirrors Menken's own gritty street camera aesthetic: dirt in the lens, unclean edits, and drunken camera movements.

As Sitney has argued, Menken also had a propensity to "incorporate the extraneous reflection of herself and her camera, even her cigarette smoke, into an animated fragment, [making] the very nervous instability of the hand-held camera a part of the rhythmic structure of several films."[43] In making *Andy Warhol*, she also is making a "copy" of her own aesthetic personality—one that had an affinity with Warhol's work ethic (as her sixty-hour weeks at Time-Life testify)—as well as his vacated but ever present voyeuristic gaze on everyone and everything around him. In one of the most interesting moments in the film, Menken turns Warhol into the mechanical, serial self he always claimed to be ("I am a machine"). Menken, at once brutally and playfully, mechanizes him in front of his serial work of Jackie O, ending the sequence with Warhol encountering his own mirrored reflection.

The aggressive serial repetition that Menken achieves through pixilation (or single framing) marks a shift in her work from 1963 to 1965 that makes it difficult to place her in the realm of traditional collage aesthetics, as Brakhage attempted to do: "What Marie essentially 'mothered' into film was cinematic collage."[44] Menken relied less on paratactical strategies, as the modernist collagists had, and more on a reflective asymmetry—mirroring Warhol, within her filmic portrait of him, back onto himself. Warhol's reflection, to which Menken circles back, also references his reflection in *Empire* (1964) in the window of the Time-Life Building. Menken's presence in Warhol's life was not really as a Warhol Superstar (which only really happened after her appearance as Malanga's mother in *Chelsea Girls*) but rather as one of the powerful people (known as "the Body") to whom Warhol was attracted. As has been documented in the scant literature on Menken, she and Willard Maas threw some of the most important star-studded parties (hosting Edward Albee, Marilyn Monroe, Arthur Miller, Truman Capote, et al.) long before Warhol's Factory attracted a "scene." The wonderful, sometimes disparaging myth which is continually retold is that Albee fashioned his renowned play *Who's Afraid of Virginia Woolf?* after Menken and Maas's tumultuous relationship. Many of the art luminaries mentioned here, including Brakhage, Menken, and Maas, often acted in each other's work or served as inspiration for idiosyncratic characters and plots, prefiguring Warhol's notion of a Factory Superstar.

Menken's interest in Warhol was connected to their common project of an increasing excision of "personality" (or, in the other direction, a hyperinflation as seen in the superstars) from film and painting. Viewers became consumers, celebrating, to borrow from Benjamin Buchloh, "their proper status of having been erased as subjects."[45]

By 1967, Menken had become interested in the work of Fluxus artist Robert Watts and made a short animation piece, *Watts with EGGS*, in which she animates his chrome-casted *Box of Eggs*. The film opens with lights reflected in the eggs (of course), then, through single framing, pixilates a man's hand arranging eggs in different patterns. The hands (those of John Hawkins) fill the box back up with eggs.[46] Next, the eggs do the same routine, but more magically, more serenely, without the assistance of the hands. Menken also introduces a string and a feather duster into animated action, so that the eggs, one by one, seem to be coming directly out of the duster (objects infect objects). By the end, the eggs are magically back in their box. Like Warhol, Watts drew attention to the status of art as a mere commodity. His *Box of Eggs* (1967), like his earlier *Chrome Fruits and Vegetables* (1964) cast from the actual objects, were meant to be displayed in their appropriate crates, complete with marked prices, as if they were as dispensable and replaceable as the produce in a grocery shop. A related work by Watts is *Whitman's Assorted Chocolates* (1963–64). By presenting the art object as a facsimile of something real rendered useless, Watts expressed with clarity one of the fundamental propositions of Pop that Buchloh also says Warhol had articulated, namely the juncture between shared experience and its expression in the form of a generally recognizable sign.[47] The event structure of Watts's work paralleled Menken's effort to create an event-based film. Watts was interested, as Menken had been in her earlier work as a painter, in how the performative and participatory could be activated. Another important level of aesthetic inquiry that Watts's own projects inspired in Menken was her own fascination with objects as items of fetish.

Like Watts's work, Menken's films are filled with objects that have light-reflective surfaces; Menken was fascinated with the translucency and transparency of industrial plastics and other synthetics. Her object-rich films point to the perceptual volley she employs between a deflected gaze—away from objects and toward their gleam, their surface, and a hyperengaged viewing of substitute objects. In this way, Menken reposi-tions cinematic subjectivity, especially during this period as it is posed in terms of a lyrical, poetic camera eye, within the experience of objects rather than that of subjects. She locates the event structure of film not in the participatory aesthetics of John Cage, Robert Rauschenberg, and Allan Kaprow but, like Warhol, in the "real rituals of participation within which mass culture contains and controls its audiences."[48]

Finally, if we can read Menken beyond the framework of the personal diary film or a Romantic poetics of film, which is how she has been thus far inscribed in experimental film history and theory, then we will be able to discover a filmmaker who was engaged in more formal questions about the relations of surface (of screen, of objects), of frame (microlevel of movement), and of montage (interval and rhythm). She toyed with the lyrical aesthetics of film that surrounded her: she added humor, sullied it with quick, dirty moves, and challenged its authenticity by questioning the borders between the real and the contrived, document and perfor-mance. Animation, especially, allowed Menken to twist the conventions of both painting and filmmaking; she moved adroitly between the media of paint and light, canvas and screen. She had a keen awareness of the relationship between still and moving images. Like the filmmaker Robert Breer, who also began his career as a painter, Menken was interested "in the locus of the tension between the static and the moving."[49] Without including Menken, Sitney traces the interests of experimental animators like Breer, Len Lye, and Harry Smith back to the historical avant-garde's innovations in graphic cinema, namely the work of Viking Eggeling, Hans Richter, Fernand Leger, and Marcel Duchamp. Borrowing from Clement Greenberg's analysis of the use of language or type in Cubist painting, Sitney argues that an "absolute frontality" which lies outside "the repre-sentational context of the picture" was used by graphic cinema, as well as more contemporary work like Breer's.[50] The emphasis on surface (used by Lye, Breer, and Smith) is traced, by Sitney, back to the collage aes-thetics of Braque and Picasso; they affected flatness by simulating the separation of surface as produced by print and stencil techniques. While Breer and his contemporaries are situated in relation to the early graphic cinema artists, Menken is placed by Sitney within the aesthetic paradigm of 1950s abstract expressionism. MacDonald corroborates Sitney's claim:

"Menken's freewheeling camera moves her imagery in the direction of abstraction—evoking the gestural dripping or brushwork of Pollock and de Kooning."[51] This reading, however, is too reductive—especially in light of the fact that she shared Breer, Lye, and Smith's motion graphic sensibility and had an intimate relationship to the work of Warhol.

Menken's filmic sensibility is less gestural and more deeply imbedded in the Pop and conceptual projects in which she was immersed. The worlds of Robert Watts, Andy Warhol, and Kenneth Anger intersected with hers in profound and surprising ways. Her films, like Warhol's canvases, depict not images or pictures, but rather, to borrow from George Brecht, an event. Menken's animated films need to be read with and against her live-action work in order to reveal her brief but poignant studies in perception and cinematic reception. In her lifelong project to find a space between the abject and the lyrical, the object and its surface, Menken left a rich legacy for contemporary filmmakers like Jennifer Montgomery, Peggy Ahwesh (apparent in the entropic *Color of Love* and *Scary Movie*), and animators like Martha Colburn, Jacob Ciocci, and Cory Arcangel, whose obsessions with the grit and gleam of found objects and vacated subjects flit across the screen caught in animated fits of anguish, despair, and glitter.[52]

Filmography

Currently in Distribution

Please note: the lengths, titles, and exact dates of Menken's films are difficult to figure definitively. The lists below have been largely culled from the *Film-Makers' Cooperative Catalogue, no. 7* as well as from personal discussions with P. Adams Sitney.

> *Visual Variations on Noguchi*, 1945 (4 min.): sd., b&w; 16mm
> *Hurry! Hurry!*, 1957 (3 min.): sd., col.; 16mm
> *Glimpse of the Garden*, 1957 (5 min.): sd., col.; 16mm
> *Dwightiana*, 1957 (3 ½ min.): sd., col.; 16mm
> *Faucets*, 1960 (5 min.): si., b&w.; 16mm
> *Eye Music in Red Major*, 1961 (5 ½ min.): si., col.; 16mm
> *Arabesque for Kenneth Anger*, 1961 (4 min.): sd., col.; 16mm
> *Bagatelle for Willard Maas*, 1961 (5 min.): sd., col.; 16mm
> *Moonplay*, 1962 (5 min.): sd., b&w; 16mm
> *Mood Mondrian*, 1963 (5 ½ min.): si., col.; 16mm
> *Drips in Strips*, 1963 (2 ½ min.): si., col.; 16mm

Notebook, 1963 (10 min.): si., b&w and col.; 16mm
  (*Notebook* includes nine sections: "Raindrops," "Greek Epiphany,"
  "Moonplay," "Copy Cat," "Paper Cuts," "Lights," "Night Writing," "The
  Egg," and "Etcetcetc.")
Go Go Go, 1962–64 (11 ½ min.): si., col.; 16mm
Wrestling, 1964 (8 min.): si., b&w; 16mm
Andy Warhol, 1965 (22 min.): col.; 16mm
Lights, 1966 (6 ½ min.): si., b&w.; 16mm
Sidewalks, 1966 (6 ½ min.): si., b&w.; 16mm
Excursion, 1968 (5 ½ min.): sd., col.; 16mm
Watts with Eggs, 1967 (2 ½ min.): si., col.; 16mm

Films Menken worked on by Willard Maas
Geography of the Body, 1943 (7 min.): sd., b&w; 16mm
Image in the Snow, 1950s (29 min.): sd., b&w; 16mm
Narcissus, 1956 (59 min.): sd., b&w; 16mm[53]

Films Menken worked on by Maya Deren
At Land, 1944
Very Eye of Night, 1958[54]

Currently Undistributed

Several of these films are undergoing preservation at Anthology Film Archives.
The film titles have sometimes changed several times and some have been
given provisionary titles by Anthology for the purposes of identification. Below
is the information available at the time of this publication.

Pop Goes the Easel, 1964
The Gravediggers from Guadix, 1958 (50 min.; incomplete)
Zenscapes, 1969 (3–5 min.): si., col.; 16mm
Women in Touch, 1960s
Here and There with My Octoscope (unfinished, first shown at the Charles
  Theater in New York, 1961): si., but intended to add sd.; 16mm

Notes

1   Brakhage's epistemological approach to the camera's ability to see is described in "Metaphors on Vision": "Yet I suggest that there is a pursuit of
knowledge foreign to language and founded upon visual communication, demanding a development of the optical mind, and dependent upon perception
in the original and deepest sense of the word" (12).

2 Tyler, *Underground Film*, 158.

3 Brakhage, "Marie Menken," 38.

4 Ibid., 41.

5 In the brief space of this article, it is not possible to explore the larger trajectories I suggest here, especially Menken's interest in the relationships between sound and image and language and figure. Menken's exposure to the work of John Cage, James Tenney, Merce Cunningham, and Isamu Noguchi encouraged her to think inventively about the performativity of language and sound. We begin to see this tested in *Visual Variations on Noguchi*, a film she made while she was immersed in her work for Cunningham—through Noguchi's commission—as well as in her silent, rhythmic *Mood Mondrian*. As I argue throughout this essay, Menken was interested in the shared performative valence between subjects and objects (as well as silence and sound). The Gryphon Group, which she cofounded with Willard Maas in the mid-1950s and whose members included Ben Moore, Charles Boultenhouse, Gregory Markopoulos, and Charles Henri Ford, mirrored the interdisciplinary work of Fluxus in their use of "distinguished artists in other fields," including composers Ben Weber, Alan Havhaness, John Cage, James Tenney, John Gruen, and Lucille Dlugoszewski (who also composed scores for many of the Gryphon films). Notions of chance and indeterminacy, as well as Cage's redefinition of silence as the "absence of intended sounds," pulse throughout Menken's work. See "About the Gryphon Film Group" (1950s) in Menken's archival file at the Filmmakers' Cooperative in New York. I also think Tom Beard's curating of the films of the Gryphon Group, "All Words Are Flesh," *Ocularis*, January 30, 2005, and his accompanying program notes point to Gryphon filmmakers' interest in the materiality of language through the body. E-mail correspondence, January 2006.

6 Brakhage, "Marie Menken," 34. Sitney shared a short curriculum vitae of Marie Menken's with me, which lists her as "Special Technician, Civilian, US Army Signal Corps, Photographic Center, Astoria," creating special effects for training and Army documentary films (building miniatures and dioramas) from 1941 to 1945. It also cites her as having worked for *Fortune Magazine* in the 1950s but gives no job details.

7 Starr, "Hilla Rebay and the Guggenheim Nexus," 7.

8 Tony Conrad described Menken's complete and total rule over the news department at Time-Life. Even toward the end, when she would come to work completely drunk, she was able to retain control because she simply knew her job better than anyone else. Basically, without her, they were lost. Personal conversation, February 2004.

9 Several short reviews (mostly one sentence) exist of Menken's shows. In 1949, at the Betty Parsons Gallery, she had a two-person show with Ad Reinhardt. In 1951, Parsons gave her a one-woman show. See *Art Digest*, November 1, 1949, for a review of her first show; see *Art Digest*, February 15, 1951, for a

review of her solo show at Parsons. See *Art News*, April 1951, for a mention of her show at the Tibor de Nagy Gallery in New York.

10   The Tibor de Nagy Gallery, founded by Tibor de Nagy and John Meyers in the winter of 1950, was at first formed as a challenge to the Peggy Guggenheim Collection (which represented the so-called first school of American painters). Encouraged by Jackson Pollock, Lee Krasner, and Clement Greenberg, de Nagy wanted to create a gallery that would fill the void left by Guggenheim's move to Europe in 1947. But de Nagy was primarily a financier, and he eventually hired the British polymath, Dwight Ripley, whom he described as "a genius, a painter, poet, a linguist, a botanist, a collector, a pianist, an alcoholic, a millionaire." Ripley was also one of Maas's male lovers, as well as a good friend of Menken's (as attested to by the use of his garden in *Glimpses* as well as her homage to him, *Dwightiana*). See Wilkin, *Tibor de Nagy Gallery*.

11   Menken appears in the following Warhol films: *Screentests* (1964–66), *The Life of Juanita Castro* (1965), *Bitch* (1965), *Girls in Prison* (1965), and *The Chelsea Girls* (1966).

12   This title has multiple reference points. Del Lord's *Pop Goes the Easel* (1935) stars the Three Stooges. *Pop Goes the Easel* was also the title of a television program in 1962, filmed by Ken Russell on Pop Art, and in 1963 was used as an exhibition title for one of the first Pop Art retrospectives in Houston, Texas. This undistributed film, along with several other titles, has been unearthed by Anthology Film Archives, but at the time of this publication the films were not available for viewing. Martina Kudlacek, an Austrian filmmaker who directed *In the Mirror of Maya Deren* (2001), is working on a documentary film on Marie Menken, as well as a book-length project.

13   Mekas, "Praise to Marie Menken," 47.

14   Sitney's discussion of the lyrical tradition in film is too complex and far-reaching to discuss here. Often, the lyrical is mistakenly reduced, as Sitney has charged, to "a quality rather than a mode; that is as if it were the opposite of 'dry,' 'stark,' or 'harsh'" (e-mail correspondence, June 14, 2005). Sitney's use of *lyrical* involves the rethinking of modernism as an extension of the radical breaks lyrical literature made in the late eighteenth and early nineteenth centuries. Especially key to his understanding of the lyrical is its focus on the production of space through the movement of the body (personal discussion at the Getty Museum in Los Angeles, 2005). Sitney has included a much larger discussion of the work of Menken in his forthcoming book on serial films, in which he addresses primarily Menken's kinetic camera movement—and her affirmation of the "actual flatness and whiteness of the screen."

15   Brakhage, "On Marie Menken," 91.

16   James, "Film Diary/Diary Film"; MacDonald, *The Garden in the Machine*.

17   James, "Film Diary/Diary Film," 165.

18   See Turim, "Reminiscences, Subjectivities, and Truths," 193–212.

19   James, "Film Diary/Diary Film," 154.

20   Ibid., 150.

21   Ibid., 151.

22   Sitney, *Visionary Film*, 160.

23   Ibid, 160–61.

24   Ibid., 161.

25   Ibid., 164.

26   Martha Colburn's gritty cutout work, as displayed in *There's a Pervert in our Pool!* (1998) and *Spiders in Love: An Arachnogasmic Musical* (1999) is especially relevant in thinking about how Menken's legacy has been extended.

27   It should be noted here that, according to Brakhage, Menken had had a "still-birth child" early on in her relationship with Maas, which was a traumatic experience for her. This macabre depiction of an egg—entering, then exiting a body—could possibly have been inspired by this early loss. The autobiographical, if it enters her films at all, is not, of course, the center of her work. Her animations, including "The Egg," were structural fantasias.

28   Turim, "Reminiscences, Subjectivities, and Truths," 195.

29   Mekas, "Praise to Marie Menken," 47.

30   Brakhage, "On Marie Menken," 91.

31   Mekas, "Praise to Marie Menken," 47.

32   Sitney, *Visionary Film*, 160.

33   Tyler, *Underground Film*, 160.

34   Ibid., 158.

35   Brakhage, "Marie Menken," 38.

36   Ibid.

37   Wilkin, *Tibor de Nagy Gallery*.

38   Cooper and Spronk, *Mondrian: The Transatlantic Paintings*, 35.

39   Menken's statement about *Drips in Strips* appears in the *Film-Makers' Cooperative Catalogue, no. 7*, 370.

40   Brakhage, *Scrapbook*, 91.

41   Buchloh, "Robert Watts," 544. I am indebted to Buchloh's analyses of Andy Warhol's and Robert Watts's work in terms of event structures. His critical approach to Warhol and Watts deeply informs my approach to Menken and her work.

42   Brakhage, "Marie Menken," 42.

43   Sitney, *Visionary Film*, 161.

44   Brakhage, "Marie Menken," 41.

45   Buchloh, "Andy Warhol's One-Dimensional Art," 514.

46   John Hawkins was a filmmaker who collaborated on the films of both Menken and Maas.

47   Buchloh, "Andy Warhol's One-Dimensional Art," 499.

48   Ibid., 485.

49   Sitney, *Visionary Film*, 272.

50   Ibid.

51   MacDonald, *The Garden in the Machine*, 58.

52   Jacob Ciocci (a.k.a. Paper Rad) and Cory Arcangel (a.k.a. Beige) are artists whose work, in part, includes video and computer animation or "found animation" culled from the Internet and the detritus of digital signals and analogue machines. For example, Ciocci's most recent video installation, *Super Highway* (2005), uses found animation material across a variety of Internet sources, and Cory Arcangel's *Super Mario Clouds* (2005) is based on the *Super Mario* game for Nintendo's NES game console.

53   Sitney writes, "Menken collaborated with Maas and George Barker on *Geography*, and she is the female nude in it. She acted in *Image in the Snow*. For *Narcissus*, she carved a model of the row of Roman imperial heads (for a trick shot or two)" (e-mail, January 20, 2006).

54   Menken animated the chess sequence for Maya Deren's *At Land* (1944), and she plotted the moving constellations for Deren's *Very Eye of Night* (1958). These references are noted in Marie Menken's curriculum vitae (see note 5).

PAUL ARTHUR

Different / Same / Both / Neither

The Polycentric Cinema of Joyce Wieland

◻

Handtinting (1967–68)—a five-minute silent study of young girls danc-ing, swimming, and observing one another by Joyce Wieland (1931–98)—has a quality that is reminiscent of cognitive dilemmas in some of her other films but that has few counterparts in avant-garde cinema of the sixties. The playful tone of *Handtinting* matches the energies of its human subjects, suggesting a lyrical romp in the tradition of perhaps Shirley Clarke or Marie Menken, while its narrow focus and set of recur-ring formal gestures point to an underlying conceptual rigor more in tune with the work of Wieland's occasional collaborator and close friend Hollis Frampton. We quickly recognize that a handful of rather banal images, all taken in the same institutional setting, is being repeated according to an insistently rhythmic pattern, with the girls' bodily movements abruptly cut short before completion. It is apparent as well that certain shots are looped and laterally flipped, confounding an already tenuous relationship to straightforward recording. A faint correspondence surfaces between looking and performing. Brief segments of clear leader separate what are intuited as possible cycles or ordered variations. Finally, selected passages are tinted in several different colors and there are occasional bursts of tiny perforations on the image surface, further distancing our involve-ment in the profilmic scene.

For viewers even partially familiar with key avant-garde idioms and

From Joyce
Wieland's
Handtinting,
1967–68. Courtesy
of Canadian
Filmmakers'
Distribution Center
and Joyce Wieland.

their accompanying critical debates, *Handtinting* offers a surprising range of almost equally plausible insights concerning Wieland's method of construction, the film's relevant aesthetic frameworks, and its appropriate sphere of discursive meaning. Speculation that Wieland derived a logical system for the sequencing of shots—a burgeoning compositional strategy that P. Adams Sitney would in 1969 dub "Structural Film"[1]—is ballasted by a contrary feeling that rhythmic elements are quirky and unstable, more visually expressive than coolly rational. In other words, by connecting the film's syntax to its pictorial content, one could describe the looping of shots as symbolic of entrapment or the jolting cadences as claustrophobic, indicative of psychological alienation or dislocation experienced by the awkward African American and white teenage subjects (such a reading is enhanced by knowledge that Wieland's footage consists of outtakes from a sponsored documentary on Job Corps training for which she served as camerawoman). Unlike so-called minimalist films surfacing in the late 1960s, *Handtinting*'s representational specificity strikes us as far from arbitrary, a mere backdrop against which heightened cognizance of film's materiality becomes the "real" content—as was frequently claimed of structuralist exemplars.[2] Neither the subtly erotic mobilization of female bodies nor the documentary undertow of depicted events fits neatly with the demands of a strictly modernist agenda, yet they are clearly insufficient as markers for even poetic fringes of nonfiction realism.

An ancillary tension arises between the manual application of fabric dyes and needle perforations—techniques adapted from Wieland's well-defined art world vocabulary of wall hangings and textile constructions—and the blunt facticity of photographed events. To the extent that denaturing of the photographic image through manipulation of the film-strip was associated with anti-illusionist strategies—as in films made during the same period by Stan Brakhage and Carolee Schneemann, among others[3]—Wieland's disruptions carry an additional charge by inscribing an explicitly feminine craft tradition, thus simultaneously undercutting and embellishing the activities of the frolicking young workers. Work, indeed gendered artisanal labor, becomes a potent subtext here and elsewhere, equally deflecting the lyrical avant-garde's nature-oriented surface metaphors and minimalism's single-minded emphasis on materiality. This creates a sort of categorical hesitation, an inability on the part of the spectator to immediately or unproblematically fix a preferred "angle" of signification. The effect mirrors on a global level ambiguities over the status of individual shots in *Handtinting*—and also in *Sailboat* (1967–68), *Catfood* (1968), and *Reason Over Passion* (1967–69)—in which discernment of exact repetition, variation, similarity, or optical distortion is deliberately scrambled.

The juggling of seemingly antithetical formal options is not unique to Wieland, yet, as *Handtinting* makes clear, her borrowing of established cinematic codes is underwritten neither by parodic nor by ironic motives: the offhand shots of the girls, for instance, are never placed in visual quotation marks. Instead her abiding strength, evidenced in quite different projects, is to foster deft exchanges between indexical and figurative image qualities just as, in a similar spirit of confrontation, she yokes narrative cues to aleatory structures, parries looming sentimentality with political anger, counters allegory with pictorial literalism, and uses historical reference to slice through experimental cinema's romantic obsession with the phenomenological present. To be sure, the invocation of history is for Wieland, as it is for the American avant-garde in general, predominantly a matter of film history and art history. Yet in this regard, also, she manages to carve out an exception through her intensifying engagement with Canadian cultural themes and questions of national identity. It is as if difficulties of "identification"—extending from the technical provenance of a given shot to the arena of generic affiliation to narrative mechanisms of character subjectivity (germane to her semicommercial narrative, *The Far Shore* [1975])—provides a master trope from which Wieland's vision of cinema proceeds.[4]

Public Images

It is not enough simply to argue that Wieland challenged or bridged boundary distinctions among independent film factions of her time. That rebellious scene was awash with as many iconoclasts—how does one assign stylistic fealty to Jack Smith, or Harry Smith?—as champions of nascent aesthetic ideologies, of which Wieland's then-husband Michael Snow, a key figure in the inauguration of structural film, is a prime example. Wieland herself was said to occupy a position somewhere between the front lines of formal innovation and outright disregard for the (admittedly obscure) clamor of 1960s avant-garde polemics. Unlike Frampton and Brakhage, or even Snow, Wieland did not produce theoretically inflected writings in support of her creative impulses, and in fact she lamented the influx of film theory into noncommercial practice. The trajectory of her rather brief career can be mapped across a bundle of alternative, historically vibrant stylistic options that remain always fluid and plural. My assertion of a polycentric—as opposed to a unicentric or decentered—aesthetic sensibility is certainly congruent with her methods as a gallery artist and, if nothing else, it helps vitiate critical perspectives that celebrate increasing formal complexity or the progressive working out of a series of medium-specific "problems" or conundrums.[5] The inability to settle on a unitary rubric through which to explain the development of, and relationship among, her films can be considered simultaneously as a virtue and a curse.

It is, then, not farfetched to declare that an interpretive "crisis" in naming, convened around her work, is as emblematic of the avant-garde's typical strain of cultural resistance as it is integral to the meaning of Wieland's overall project. To be sure, some of her most perspicacious commentators insist on roping her into a discrete ideological framework. Sitney and Regina Cornwell, for instance, attempt to claim Wieland for the modernist camp. A cadre of woman writers led by Kay Armatage, Kass Banning, and Lauren Rabinowitz, following in the wake of initial critical assessments, discover in the films a wellspring of feminist ideas that in essence repudiate the masculinist ethos of high modernism. More recently, R. Bruce Elder and Bart Testa make the case for Wieland as a "pioneer of postmodernism."[6] It is difficult to think of another canonical filmmaker for whom the same critical impasse pertains. A number of supporters—including Sitney, Cornwell, Banning, and Michael Zryd, in a metacritical essay, "'There Are Many Joyces': The Critical Reception of the Films of Joyce Wieland"—readily acknowledge multiplicity or "elusiveness" as a primary feature of the oeuvre yet need to recuperate Wieland's aesthetic profligacy as either dictated by external circumstance or as an index of the movement or sensibility being touted; only Zryd implies that the classificatory slippage in her films can function as a coherent stance in its own right. Moreover, some writers have maintained that Wieland's dual careers in film and art, and her heterogeneity within these separate domains, actually proved detrimental to her career, and to adequate appreciation of her accomplishments. Jay Scott writes: "It has been difficult for Wieland because she is a woman, and it has been difficult for critics because she has been *too* womanly . . . too recklessly fecund."[7] Hence a strange brand of special pleading, to the point of victimology, surrounds Wieland's public image.

A review of the literature reveals persistent allegations that either her gender, her Canadian textual orientation, her involvement in the art world, or a combination of factors, foreclosed proper recognition within the experimental film pantheon. While it is undeniable that the work of women filmmakers was occasionally ignored or dismissed by critics and institutions, especially during the 1960s, the idea that Wieland's reputation was hobbled by unspoken or inadvertent bias is nonsense. Wieland herself grew disenchanted with the rising competitiveness of the New York avant-garde milieu—in contrast to an early delight in what she perceived as an impoverished but casual spirit of collaboration and cooperation—and came to resent her exclusion from the "art of cinema" roster selected by Anthology Film Archives in 1970, a leading factor in her move back to Toronto.[8] Nonetheless, by almost any common yardstick for avant-garde "success," Wieland had a stellar career. In its prime, from 1964 to 1973, she produced fourteen films with a total running time of roughly three and a half hours. The better part of the next three years was spent laboring on the hybrid feature *The Far Shore*, whose critical and popular failure precipitated her withdrawal from moviemaking. Several years before her death, Wieland managed to complete two projects begun much earlier, only one of which, *A and B in Ontario* (1967–84; cocredited to Hollis Frampton), recasts concerns central in her core films.

Compared to the most celebrated filmmakers of her generation, Wieland's output was relatively small, yet, unlike other female avant-gardists whose work reached maturity during the same period, her films were the focus of considerable public attention.[9] A cursory, unscientific survey of one-person appearances and inclusion in important museum programs and catalogues in both North America and Europe suggests that Wieland's films were widely seen, to some extent riding the coattails of critical interest in minimalist styles and, in all likelihood, serving as a token

Joyce Wieland.
Courtesy of
Anthology
Film Archives.

woman at a historical juncture that witnessed increasing pressures across a spectrum of cultural production for the representation of women.[10] In addition, Wieland is one of the few female filmmakers discussed in early histories of the American movement.[11] Arguably, her growing prestige as a Canadian gallery artist created unique crossover opportunities in which to analyze and promote her films, as is evident by the amount of coverage she received in art magazines and in the culture pages—especially in Canadian newspapers.

As counterintuitive as it might sound, in the context of late-1960s ideas about the vicissitudes of creative work and the political struggles with which those ideas are typically imbricated, Wieland's gender, her formidable art world presence, and her Canadian roots were probably distinct advantages, rather than disadvantages, in pursuit of the meager rewards available to experimental film artists.[12] This of course begs the question of what constitutes success in this marginal precinct and what, if anything, such success might mean in the reckoning of Wieland's body of films. While a fuller discussion of institutional patterns and operations is outside the scope of this essay, it is nonetheless important to keep in mind specific social openings, as well as obstacles, that were characteristic of avant-garde cinema during its moment of greatest public exposure and most acute internal divisions.[13]

The Political as Personal

Attempts to hammer Wieland's work into a critical mold receptive to the tenets of modernism, or Canadian nationalism, or whatever, frequently overlook the degree to which her films were a product of their time, attentive to and reciprocally amplifying key themes and utopian social aspirations associated with the 1960s counterculture. Her films are connected to that period's wider turbulence not in the hackneyed rubric of "peace, love, and expanded consciousness" but in Wieland's tripartite commitment to use film—or more accurately, cinema—as a vehicle with which to skewer entrenched values, to abrogate conventional limits separating discrete mediums or artistic spheres, and to model a set of desired social relations through the exigencies of film production. As David James contends, a radical edge of 1960s cinema was its rejection of medium-specific modernist paradigms by assaulting "boundaries between genres, between media, between art and non-art, and between art and life, and often in a way that called into question the fetishism of the commodity art object." James goes on to suggest that because film, a touchstone for the collision of art and commerce, served as a meeting ground for various creative disciplines, it became a privileged arena for engendering new modes of opposition.[14]

Despite occasional resentment at what she viewed as a lack of recognition, Wieland was dedicated to an ethos of collaboration, to confronting male-centered myths of creative autonomy by foregrounding film's reliance on collective labor. Indeed, more than half of the twenty films listed in her filmography feature some form of outside cooperation, ranging from the large-scale interactions required for the production of *The Far Shore*, to the composition of musical tracks and help with purely technical services, to the sharing of directorial credit on six projects. Admittedly, a subset of films is patently solipsistic in their self-reflexive focus, yet there is also an unmistakably dialogical principle informing much of her best work. For example, even the industrial titles made for the austere studies *1933* and *Sailboat* (both 1967–68) command a presence that differs significantly from standard film titles; their duration and visual disjunction from the images they ostensibly caption direct attention to the source of their nonartisanal manufacture, hence to an "interpersonal" confluence of authorship.[15] In a more complex register, the performative and interdetermining mise-en-scène of Wieland's portrait of a Quebecois political activist, *Pierre Vallieres* (1972), simultaneously overturns idealist assumptions of documentary transparency

From Joyce Wieland's *Sailboat*, 1967–68. Courtesy of Canadian Filmmakers' Distribution Center and Joyce Wieland.

while granting her subject considerable latitude in dictating a mode of verbal address.

Among a host of revisionist tendencies in art world practices of the 1960s was a belated acceptance of what had previously been pigeonholed as crafts, in particular ceramics and textile weaving. Wieland was an early proponent of the integration of so-called elite and populist visual forms, although the skilled female participation on her elaborate gallery pieces remained, for the most part, anonymous.[16] In film, however, Wieland's collaborations are both more upfront and even-handed. By far her most extreme statement of cinema as a process of interlocution, the unjustly neglected *A and B in Ontario* evolves as an improvised dance for two camera operators starring Wieland and Frampton. They play a recorded game of peek-a-boo across a series of pictorially cogent locations, beginning with a domestic interior redolent of Wieland's earlier work, proceeding through the sort of urban byways that appear in Frampton's films and winding up at the seaside, a setting crucial to both filmmakers. The effect is similar to an unhierarchal version of Dziga Vertov's *The Man with a Movie Camera*, in which perceived coordinates of seer and seen, figure and ground, the spontaneous and the tightly choreographed, are in constant flux.[17] *A and B* starts off by poking fun at the construction of point-of-view couplets but soon transforms itself into a kind of epistemological double portrait.

Planted at opposite ends of *A and B*, the cozy apartment and pan-

oramic landscape represent the alpha and omega of Wieland's icono-
graphic universe. It is possible that the two most famous, generative, and
multivalent spaces in 1960s cinema are Warhol's Factory and Brakhage's
cabin in the Colorado mountains. For each locale, the physical bearing
and quality of light, its human inhabitants and visitors, plus the surrounding environment, mediate at every turn the kinds of films fabricated there.
In retrospect, both are modern incarnations of the classical artist's studio,
a motif that at least since nineteenth-century French painter Gustave
Courbet has been freighted with mercurial negotiations between work
and leisure, social demands and private reflection. Add to those two
emblematic spaces a third, Wieland's urban domicile or, more precisely,
her kitchen. As she puts it, "The kitchen table has been at the core of my
art since I was a child," describing the thrust of her early aesthetic as
"trying to make a point about housewife art and wife art and woman's
art."[18] The table, a cardinal site for the intermingling of work, consumption, and conversation, figures in *Water Sark*, *Catfood* (1968), and *Rat Life
and Diet in North America* (1968). Slightly extending the visual ensemble,
Dripping Water (with Michael Snow, 1969) focuses on a kitchen sink,
while *Patriotism* (1964) takes place in bed. In every case, a common
household—that is, "womanly"—chore is referenced and summarily
transformed: setting the table; feeding the cat; taking care of pet gerbils;
dealing with a leaky faucet; rousing (arousing?) a sleepy guest. These
seemingly mundane tasks become the premise for formal investigations
or, alternatively, political satire. Her aesthetic elevation of the quotidian,
however, never quite banishes an underlying ambivalence, constructing
domestic life as at once imaginatively liberating and entrapping.

Few commentators have failed to note the historically loaded intersection of domestic and social regimes in Wieland's films.[19] Recalling the
now-degraded slogan that emerged during the onset of feminist protest
at the end of the 1960s, "the personal is political," critics have tended to
frame her explorations of domestic space as symptomatic of broader
struggles to reclaim from an oppressive history of unpaid, undervalued
labor the traces of an authentically female identity. The salutary rereading of objects and activities conferred as "female"—as in the kitchen as
atelier—constitutes a significant axis in Wieland's "home movies," but it
is hardly the entire story. *Rat Life*, a caustically funny "beast fable" in
the spirit of Beatrix Potter,[20] uses props, intertitles, and found images to
spin a tale about draft dodgers, antiwar resistance, and the dream of a
Canada immune from U.S. domination. Despite invective aimed at imperialism and extralegal suppression of dissent, Wieland's gerbil-inmates

retain disquieting affinities with the plight of housewives: "They were haunted little characters . . . little victims no matter how nicely they were treated."[21] In her work in general, whatever pleasure is extracted from the trappings of domestic life is often accompanied by yearnings for escape, epitomized by nondomestic street noise in the sound tracks to *Catfood* and *Dripping Water*.

Assertions of common cause between women's groups and national movements of self-determination were endemic to the period, and this rhetorical confluence surfaces again in *Pierre Vallieres* and *Solidarity* (1973). The former is remarkable in its elegant structure and thrilling blend of politics and cinematic reflexivity. For nearly thirty minutes, a gigantic close-up of Pierre Vallieres's mustachioed mouth—similar to the legendary "Rosebud" image in *Citizen Kane*—fills the screen. A fiery orator, Vallieres speaks in French in relaxed, conversational tones. English subtitles provide a loose translation of his analyses of economic exploitation of Quebec's French-speaking population and possible avenues of redress. Vallieres's words are heard even over blank passages of leader when the camera is being reloaded—also heard are extraneous sounds of the film crew in action—and at some point a slight gap in the synchronization of voice and image becomes noticeable. In a coda, after the interview is finished, Wieland pans across a nondescript interior to a large window, holding on a snowy rural vista until the film roll flares out.

A topic of particular concern to Vallieres is the pivotal position of women in the Quebecois revolt, their demands for "liberation" intimately bound up with the vanguard politics of working-class resistance. His argument is at once supplemented and deflected by Wieland's formal ensemble. Needless to say, it is a bit disorienting to audit a speech whose sole visual reference is the speaker's mouth. A blatant sensuality radiates from this image, a function of scale, color, and the strangely isolated undulations of Vallieres's orifice, and it is impossible to miss its vaginal resonance. Mouths are prominent motifs in 1960s art. Wieland had sketched and made early paintings of lips, as well as fanciful genitalia,[22] and *Water Sark* has shots of the filmmaker's mouth distorted through a magnifying glass. An entire subclass of Warhol films revolve around oral gratification of various types, and lips are emphasized in Warhol's paintings as well as in Pop canvases by Tom Wesselman and others.

In *Pierre Vallieres*, the central image sustains a virtually oracular series of paradoxes: simultaneously masculine and feminine, confined and emancipated; the throne of language and an autonomous hub of visual interest; an organ emitting culturally specific discourse that is heard by non-French viewers as purely abstract sound. For good measure, subtitles further split and complicate our apprehension of verbal content, since it is impossible to attend equally to all three "mediums": sound, printed speech, and pulsating image. Finally, in an era of heightened truth claims by cinema verité advocates and practitioners, *Pierre Vallieres* demolishes naive documentary assumptions of a natural seamlessness between image and sound, undercutting in the process the notion of intimate, transparent representations of singular personalities—the celebrity portraits on which 1960s verité built its reputation. Here formal tensions point to potentially discordant social messages, a refusal to reduce the interests at stake to simple slogans. The film's ostensible unity conspires to foreground divisive conflicts for which language—in its broadest sense—serves as symbolic marker.

Wieland in effect turns Vallieres's mouth into a landscape, every tooth and scraggly mustache hair a topographic feature or species of exotic flora. Landscape proper, the provisional solution to domesticity's burden of female enclosure, is a preeminent theme in Canadian painting and independent film.[23] Wieland was certainly attuned to her culture's landscape traditions, paying double-edged homage to the role of pastoral settings in shaping the terms of national identity through an array of humorous paintings and fabric constructions.[24] In film, landscape takes center stage in the long, once again deceptively straightforward *Reason Over Passion*, which her technical collaborator Hollis Frampton somewhat cryptically declared "the Canadian film that will sum up the sixties."[25] It is probably her most celebrated work, and much has been written about its formal rigor, its ambiguous treatment of charismatic leader Pierre Trudeau—in an optically manipulated portrait that interrupts an otherwise continuous East-West sea-to-sea journey from Cape Breton to Vancouver—and Wieland's shrewd handling of nationalist symbology, including flag design, insignia, musical anthem, and iconic locales.[26]

Not only were basic techniques and materials (rerecorded or optically denatured original footage, appropriated music and speech, printed texts) part of a roster that was recycled from film to film and transposed across the breadth of Wieland's artistic output, but the title itself (a phrase taken from a speech by Prime Minister Trudeau) had been applied to a painting and an assemblage. What is different from her small-scale, condensed perspective in previous films is the advent of a survey or inventory as structuring device. In fact, *Reason* is hinged on a double survey: a series of moving snapshots, following the change of seasons into

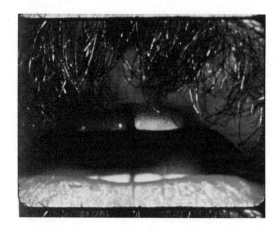

From Joyce Wieland's
Pierre Vallieres, 1972.
Courtesy of Canadian
Filmmakers' Distribu-
tion Center and Joyce
Wieland.

From Joyce Wieland's *Reason over Passion*, 1967–69.
Courtesy of Canadian Filmmakers' Distribution
Center and Joyce Wieland.

winter, taken more or less progressively across the length of the continent; and a set of 537 computer-generated permutations of Trudeau's title phrase running as cadenced subtitles. Despite a host of internal discrepancies and digressions, critics were quick to slot *Reason* into the structural camp; indeed, Barrie Hale contended, "It is to the filmic formality of the traveling shot what *Wavelength* is to the zoom."[27]

While understandable, such a characterization is far from complete. As she does elsewhere, Wieland recalibrates a familiar documentary genre, the travelogue, which was a staple in the filmic legacy of John Grierson's National Film Board of Canada, an institution whose anodyne boosterism was in many respects anathema to 1960s experimentalists. To be sure, the cross-country journey has an apposite, countercultural, context: that of many spiritual-aesthetic quests realized by the likes of Bob Dylan, Allen Ginsberg, Ken Kesey, and in a filmic register, by David Rimmer, Bruce Baillie and, most famously, by avant-garde fellow traveler Dennis Hopper in *Easy Rider*.[28] That this was almost exclusively masculinist artistic territory makes Wieland's intervention all the more exciting.

Her treatment of Trudeau in the portrait, or "love poem," lodged in the film's middle panel—analogous to the central panel of the Canadian flag —triggers yet another key issue from the period's cultural baggage, the contradictory need for, and deep suspicion of, enlightened national leadership. Young, hip, and intellectually adroit, Trudeau inspired guarded fealty from a spectrum of Canadian political factions, including feminists and environmentalists. *Reason* both caresses and deconstructs original footage of Trudeau, nestling his slow-motion movements in one of Wieland's signature soft oval frames. On the other hand, her crude rephotography creates the impression of jerking him around like a puppeteer, freezing then temporarily releasing his body in a manner that pushes an erotic embrace in the direction of sadism.[29] It is not just in this section that frictions between "reason" and "passion," as aesthetic options as well as existential axioms, come into play. The dissolution of the title into nonsense words throws language, and the rational operations it subtends, into the sensory cauldron of rhythmic images. And although the recording of landscape shots is not especially expressive—as it would be for someone like Brakhage—it is rife with enough small quirks and deflating lapses to subdue any impression of harsh, systematic logic. In this way Wieland calls into question, if she does not outright reverse, the dictum announced by the title. Could there be a more apt generational shibboleth than privileging emotional realities, passion, over stodgy reasonableness?

"Untutored" Vision Impaired

Water is incontestably a totemic element in Wieland's films; it permeates her image catalog, seeps into film titles, and burbles along on various sound tracks. It is wielded as the antithesis of the mechanical, generates symbolic associations with the feminine, and even conspires to foreground cinema's apparatus, especially the flow of filmstrip through projector. In *Dripping Water*, for example, the sink can be read as a container or frame past which the steady descent of droplets reminds us of the intermittent yet continuous state of film projection. For the last scenic image in *Reason Over Passion*, Wieland logically offers a western seascape; instead of a live shot, however, she uses the face of a tacky postcard. Incessant camera movement in the body of the film invests this still image with a rather canny sign of closure, but the shot has another, heretofore unnoticed, valence: it rhymes with, and slyly trumps, the still photograph of waves at the conclusion of Snow's *Wavelength*. That there could be an ongoing intertextual dialogue in the work of married avant-gardists is hardly shocking—recall that Wieland makes a brief appearance in *Wavelength*, and that several Snow films take place in domestic lofts or enlist common household objects—but what that prospect suggests about the inevitability of representation and allusion in Wieland's work is historically striking, and quite prescient.

In 1963, Brakhage issued his enormously influential credo, *Metaphors on Vision*, that begins with the oft-cited challenge: "Imagine an eye unruled by man-made laws of perspective, an eye unprejudiced by compositional logic, an eye which does not have to respond to the name of everything but which must know each object encountered in life through an adventure in perception."[30] His call for an "untutored eye" was at the heart of an aesthetic that mobilized cinematic resources—focus, light exposure, superimposition, camera movement—toward the creation of a purely "autonomous" image, a photographic moment capable of deflecting or subverting a viewer's ability to automatically absorb what appears on screen into a litany of familiar (nominal) attributes. Watching film shot using this method might require considerable effort to identify a brown, underlit, wiggling shape as the family dog. Structural filmmakers later rejected Brakhage's poetic idioms, especially his reliance on editing to foster metaphoric connections, while retaining a similar belief in self-contained, low-level signifiers whose quotient of social reference is, as it were, at once minimal and superseded by reflexive engagement with cinema's physical properties, such as flatness, the illusion of motion, and so on.[31]

Despite her critical and interpersonal entanglements in the structural film initiative, Wieland characteristically fashioned an idiosyncratic position that could simultaneously borrow from, critique, and transcend stylistic prerogatives identified with each camp. Further, one of the thorniest paradoxes in Wieland's entire oeuvre is the dynamic between originality and allusion. Her early paintings are marked by a combination of abstract expressionist and Pop Art influences, including Warhol, Jasper Johns, Robert Rauschenberg, Claes Oldenburg, and Willem de Kooning.[32] Traces of contemporary art, along with muted allusions to Dutch still life and French Romanticism, as well as bows to indigenous artistic cadres like the Group of Seven resurface in films such as *Sailboat*—with its Warholian commercial veneer—and *Water Sark*, in which shots of the filmmaker's grotesquely magnified mouth recall the focus of de Kooning's famous "Woman" paintings.[33] In addition, a number of films implicitly invoke or carry veiled references to cinematic styles or canonical works. Not surprisingly, the bulk of intertextual cues are directed at avant-garde, rather than Hollywood narrative, sources—unlike quotations in, say, Kenneth Anger's *Scorpio Rising* (1964) or Baillie's *Mass for the Dakota Sioux* (1963–64).[34]

Admittedly, quotation and allusion are not totally absent from reigning avant-garde idioms of the sixties; indeed, Bruce Conner's collage approach had a powerful impact on many filmmakers, including Pat O'Neill and Scott Bartlett. Yet what Wieland does revolves less around quotation than what I want to call "critical dialogue," an approach that anticipates the flood of postmodern appropriation in succeeding decades. Although she employed found materials in various gallery pieces, her sole exercise in filmic collage, *Barbara's Blindness* (with Betty Ferguson, 1965), bears an oddly adversarial quality. Indebted equally to Conner and the great Canadian collagist Arthur Lipsett, the film builds off a cheesy morality tale about a young girl's sensory impairment and its imaginative compensations, produced most likely for classroom or public service venues. *Blindness* uses match cuts to enjamb extraneous images that convert the subject's outing in a garden into a series of looming disasters involving elephants, mummies, and mushroom clouds—apocalyptic reverberations of which are shared by Conner and Lipsett. The theme of childhood sensory experience is of course a primary, even primal, concern in Brakhage's films of the period, and Wieland's breezy treatment of

From Joyce
Wieland's *Water
Sark*, 1964–65.
Courtesy of Cana-
dian Filmmakers'
Distribution Center
and Joyce Wieland.

perceptual innocence is filtered by a distinctly female perspective, as if expressions of visionary experience are a priori mediated by gender.

Blindness also contains several instances of amusingly obtuse inter-titles—"Two years later"; "Once upon a time"—nearly identical to those in Salvador Dalí and Luis Buñuel's *Un chien andalou* (1928) or Fernan Leger's *Ballet mécanique* (1924). Wieland's increasingly complex han-dling of printed language, culminating in *Rat Life and Diet* and *Pierre Vallieres*, can be said to intersect a diverse group of filmic sources: French avant-garde classics of the 1920s; Snow's obsession with punning; Framp-ton's career-long interrogation of the theoretical properties of language versus image; the informational inscriptions used by National Film Board documentaries and—a probable target of *Rat Life*—the Disney nature films that swept the continent in the late 1950s.[35] Once again, Wieland's interest in disjunctive yet illuminating pairings of language and image presage an onslaught of this motif by later avant-gardists such as Peggy Ahwesh and Leslie Thornton.[36] Sometimes the inferred intertext has the aura of an inside joke; for instance, the closing shot of snowy woods in *Vallieres* looks suspiciously like the shot that concludes Frampton's *Zorns Lemma* (1970).[37] At other times, the reference is more diffuse, as in the possible linkage between *1933* (1967–68), the historical date and the street scene it captions, and the documentary tradition of the City Sym-phony, Walter Ruttman's *Berlin* (1927) or Jay Leyda's *A Bronx Morning* (1931)—in this case, Wieland constructs not a poetic symphony but a brief, repetitive musical riff.

To take a final instance of Wieland's polycentric approach to allusion, and in lieu of a summary statement of her manifest originality, consider the rich skein of reference unleashed by *Water Sark*. This work has been taken as prima facie evidence of the filmmaker's feminist convictions,[38] but as usual it enfolds a broad compass of possible meanings. Briefly, *Water Sark* is a stridently self-referential "kitchen table" film in which a variety of immediate objects is examined almost palpably by the camera, often through huge close-ups, in an increasingly complex play of mirror reflections, refractions through liquids and glass surfaces, and virtual superimpositions. At first the scrutinized shapes are primarily vessels (a teapot, bowl, drinking glasses, a translucent paper globe) and plants; after a few minutes, Wieland herself, her face and body—costumed, as well as naked—becomes the central image. Manipulating camera, mirror, and at times a magnifying lens, Wieland playfully exhibits her lips, breasts, and belly from unusual angles, creating visual rhymes with earlier objects based on similarities in shape, color, and movement. The frame is frequently split into confusingly adjacent—bordering on cubist—perspectives. At one level, then, *Water Sark* is a performative self-portrait in which the body is a field of potential reference that controls, as it creates analogies with, its surrounding domestic milieu.

The elevation of prosaic objects through rhythmic articulation and isolation within the frame is a dominant strategy in *Ballet mécanique*, a film that juxtaposes the visual regimes of kitchen and factory. *Water Sark* can be unpacked as a response to not only Leger's film but also Vertov's *The Man with a Movie Camera*, insofar as it constitutes an inquiry into the epistemology of observer and subject, how what is seen by the camera is mediated by the physical position and determinate motives of the filmmaker. Hence it is a film about the nature, and the limits, of subjectivity in cinema. As such *Water Sark* proposes a mischievous, if also heartfelt, response to another celebrated avant-garde lyric dealing with (male) subjectivity and women's bodies, Brakhage's *Window Water Baby Moving* (1959).[39] Where Brakhage uses rapid montage to make comparisons between his wife Jane's breasts or pregnant belly, seen half-submerged in a bathtub, and celestial bodies, Wieland eschews grandiose metaphors for a lilting mélange of corporeal identity, filmmaking identity, and domestic self. Typically, the film registers not as angry repudiation but as quizzical, often humorous, rejoinder. For an artist who disdained the idea of cinema cut to the specifications of aesthetic theory, and whose resistance to historical inequalities never veered toward didactic peroration, *Water Sark* demonstrates an acuity and capaciousness of critical insight that has seldom penetrated the alternatively insular and bitterly parodic discourse of the American avant-garde.

Filmography

Tea in the Garden (with Warren Collins), ca. 1956 (4 min.): sd., b&w; 16mm
A Salt in the Park (with Warren Collins and Michael Snow), ca. 1958
    (5 min.): sd., b&w; 16mm
Larry's Recent Behavior, 1963 (18 min.): sd., col.; 8mm
Patriotism, 1964 (4 min.): sd., col.; 8mm
Patriotism, Part II, 1964 (3 min.): si., col.; 8mm
Water Sark (sound track: Carla Bley, Mike Mantler, Ray Jessel), 1964–65
    (14 min.): sd., col.; 8mm
Barbara's Blindness (with Betty Ferguson), 1965 (17 min.): sd., col.; 16mm
Peggy's Blue Skylight (music: Paul Bley), 1964–66 (11 min.): sd., b&w; 8mm
Handtinting, 1967–68 (4 min.): sd., col.; 16mm
1933, 1967–68 (4 min.): sd., col.; 16mm
Sailboat, 1967–68 (3 min.): sd., col.; 16mm
Catfood, 1968 (13 min.): sd., col.; 16mm
Reason Over Passion/La Raison avant la passion, 1967–69 (82 min.): sd.,
    col.; 16mm
Rat Life and Diet in North America, 1968 (14 min.): sd., col.; 16mm
Dripping Water (with Michael Snow), 1969 (10 min.): sd., b&w; 16mm
Pierres Vallieres (sound: Judy Steed), 1972 (30 min.): sd., col.; 16mm
Solidarity, 1973 (11 min.): sd., col.; 16mm
The Far Shore, 1975 (105 min.): sd., col.; 35mm
    Producers: Joyce Wieland and Judy Steed; screenplay: Bryan Barney, from
    an original story by Wieland; cinematography: Richard Leiterman;
    editing: George Appleby, Brian French; music: Douglas Pringle; cast:
    Frank Moore, Lawrence Benedict, Celine Lomez, Sean McCann,
    Charlotte Blunt, Susan Petrie.
A and B in Toronto (sound editing: Michelle Moses; editing: Susan Rynard,
    Wieland; with Hollis Frampton), 1967–84 (17 min.): sd., b&w; 16mm
Birds at Sunrise (optical and technical: David Bennel; sound editing:
    Michele Moses; editing: Susan Rynard, Wieland), 1972–86 (10 min.): sd.,
    col.; 16mm

Notes

1 Sitney, *Visionary Film*, 347–73.

2 I have never entirely accepted the idea of the empty signifier in structural film. I argue against the evacuation of the image in, for instance, my essay on urban topographies, "The Redemption of the City," in *A Line of Sight*, 42–59.

3 What I have in mind here is Brakhage's use of paint as visual correlative

of, especially, bodily fluids and plant matter. For a related reading of Schneemann's Brakhage-influenced *Fuses* (1964–67), see James, *Allegories of Cinema*, 317–21.

4 Hollis Frampton, in a 1971 recorded conversation with Wieland, takes a similar view: "The continuous retrieve of all your concerns seems . . . to be a series of things that happen out of 'context,' then because it is so insistent, to demand some kind of re-evaluation of what we think 'context' is in film" ("I Don't Even Know about the Second Stanza," 163).

5 The relevant critical doctrine here is of course that of Greenbergian modernism, but a late-romantic variation of that schema is evident in Sitney's *Visionary Film*.

6 Nearly all the substantive critiques of Wieland's films have been collected in Kathryn Elder's anthology, which is truly remarkable in its scholarly dedication. An invaluable feature of the book is Elder's summary, "Joyce Wieland: A Bibliographic Guide to the Film Literature," which references newspaper and magazine items and even incidental critical remarks in essays devoted primarily to other filmmakers (213–51).

7 Scott, "Full Circle," 22. Elder makes a similar point in her foreword to *The Films of Joyce Wieland* (5).

8 K. Elder, "Bibliographic Guide," *The Films of Joyce Wieland*, 243; see also Banning, "The Mummification of Mommy," 34.

9 Elder's bibliography lists 330 entries between 1963 and 1999. Of these, approximately one-third consist of newspaper reviews and obituaries; the rest range from essays in scholarly journals to reviews in prestigious magazines such as *Artforum* and *Artscanada*. Carolee Schneemann, who was active in New York in the late 1960s and received considerable notice for her scandalous performances and gallery work, has had very little written about her films. Gunvor Nelson, who began making films in 1965 and completed nine films through 1975, and who, like Wieland, was married to a well-known filmmaker, Robert Nelson, had a stake in gallery art, and collaborated with other women on various projects, was until recently able to garner no more than a handful of write-ups; see *Gunvor Nelson and the Avant-Garde*, ed. John Sundholm. Even the work of Yvonne Rainer, undoubtedly the best-known and most influential feminist filmmaker of the last thirty years, generated fewer public notices; the bibliography contained in the self-edited monograph *The Films of Yvonne Rainer*, features just over one hundred entries. I want to make it clear I do not believe that the sheer number of written notices translates automatically or without qualification into magnitude of public acclaim. My point is simply that the idea of Wieland's career as underappreciated is, to my mind, unfounded.

10 This assessment is drawn in part from Elder's "Bibliographic Guide," and in part from examining film rental records of the Film-Makers' Cooperative in New York City. To a far greater extent than the avant-garde idioms that preceded and followed it, structural film was an almost exclusively male initiative

(the only other woman who comes to mind is Vickie Z. Peterson). For two examples of Wieland's participation in groundbreaking museum shows, see the catalogues *Form and Structure in Recent Film*, edited by Dennis Wheeler, and *New Forms in Film*, edited by Annette Michelson.

11 See, for example, Curtis, *Experimental Cinema*, 188–89. Although Sitney was an early supporter, featuring Wieland's work in the initial iteration of his structural film essay, she is barely mentioned in *Visionary Film*. On the other hand, Jonas Mekas consistently publicized her shows in his *Village Voice* columns, and she figures prominently in Mekas's published collection *Movie Journal*.

12 At the risk of (further?) betraying a condescending, New York–centric view of Canadian culture, its relatively compact and localized circuits of art production afforded, at least for a time, greater access to regular press coverage and the veneer of a less fractious network of administrative support.

13 Unfortunately, the field of institutional history in avant-garde studies is largely *terra incognito*. Zryd, an energetic proponent of this approach, offers a useful overview of conditions in Canada, albeit focusing on a slightly later period: "A Report on Canadian Experimental Film Institutions, 1980–2000." Lauren Rabinovitz makes a salient contribution in *Points of Resistance*. A number of chapters in my book *A Line of Sight* adopt critical or empirical perspectives on institutional dynamics.

14 James, *Allegories of Cinema*, 98. Regrettably, James's magisterial account of the 1960s makes only passing reference to Wieland's oeuvre.

15 As a young woman, Wieland worked as a graphic designer for an animation company on industrial film assignments. Her first personal films, made in collaboration with coworkers including Snow, are described as parodies of commercial idioms (see Elder, *The Films of Joyce Wieland*, 2–3). The influence of advertising design is evident in later work such as *Sailboat*. By the same token, her working-class background and affinity for shared manual labor operates as an intriguing, if unacknowledged, subtext in a number of films. Her initial fascination with the New York avant-garde scene was in part predicated on her feelings of economic solidarity: "There was a whole cinema language that people were inventing—without money" (quoted in Elder, 3).

16 See McPherson, "Wieland," 11–20; also Scott, "Full Circle," 21–24.

17 It is worth pointing out that in documentary practice women have historically flourished as editors, a prominent example of which is Elizaveta Svilova's role in the films of Dziga Vertov.

18 Frampton, "I Don't Even Know about the Second Stanza," 172.

19 Banning, "The Mummification of Mommy," 33; Rabinowitz, "The Development of Feminist Strategies in the Experimental Films of Joyce Wieland," 109; also Magidson and Wright, "True Patriot Love," 85.

20 Rabinowitz, "The Development of Feminist Strategies in the Experimental Films of Joyce Wieland," 107.

21 Armatage, "Kay Armatage Interviews Joyce Wieland," 156.

22 Scott, "Full Circle," 25.

23 Bart Testa offers a useful overview of the cultural obsession with landscape, relating its larger implications to a diverse group of avant-garde films, in *Spirit in the Landscape.*

24 Banning, "The Mummification of Mommy," 30–32.

25 Frampton, "I Don't Even Know about the Second Stanza," 179.

26 Banning, "The Mummification of Mommy," 32; Rabinowitz, "The Development of Feminist Strategies in the Experimental Films of Joyce Wieland," 111–13; Lellis, "*La Raison avant la passion*," 57–63.

27 Elder, *The Films of Joyce Wieland*, 224.

28 I address the literary precedents and wider cultural implications of this typically 1960s ritual trek in "*Quixote* and Its Contexts," 32–55.

29 Lellis helpfully observes that over the course of the film "Wieland give[s] us a sample of just about every possible level of abstraction for the notion of Canada," including of course Trudeau himself ("*La Raison avant la passion*," 59). Wieland's own statement reaffirms this line of argument: "I decided to unite the leader to the land and cement it with his words . . . not so much cement as spread them across a continent" (quoted in McPherson, "Wieland," 19).

30 Brakhage, *Metaphors on Vision*, n.p.

31 That the structural group was aware of, and perversely engaged with, the debate about image "purity" is evident in this comment by Snow on Wieland's *1933* (1967–68): "You will find out, if you didn't already know, how naming tints pure vision," *Film-Makers' Cooperative Catalogue, no. 7*, 490.

32 Scott, "Full Circle," 25.

33 In a delicious comment on *Pierre Vallieres*, Wieland explains: "I am interested in lips as subject matter. . . . Through the mouth you can meditate on the qualities of voice, the French language, Revolution, French Revolution, Gericault's colour, etc." (quoted in Elder, *The Films of Joyce Wieland*, 222).

34 The exception to her general disengagement from idioms of dominant cinema is *The Far Shore*, which several historians have linked to D. W. Griffith and to Sirkian melodrama (see Scott, "Full Circle," 26; Rabinowitz, "*The Far Shore*," 119–26).

35 Although I can locate no comments by Wieland, or her critics, citing the malign influence of the Disney series, as an early animal rights and environmental activist it would have been fitting for Wieland to transform Hollywood's familiar rodent allegories into a utopian political tract.

36 For a fuller discussion of this trend, see Arthur, *A Line of Sight*, 166–73.

37 It is possible that Frampton returned the favor in *Poetic Justice* (1972), with the otherwise enigmatic appearance of a rubber glove, an object that figures prominently in *Water Sark*.

38 Armatage, "The Feminine Body," 135–46.

39 Armatage describes the formal emphasis on shape, texture, and color in *Water Sark* as a version of the "Brakhagian moment of ecstatic vision in which all the senses concatenate together" (ibid., 138). I can't argue with this characterization but feel that there is more at stake in Wieland's recasting of Brakhage's idealized relation to his domestic space.

CHRIS HOLMLUND

Excavating Visual Fields,

Layering Auditory Frames

Signature, Translation, Resonance,

and Gunvor Nelson's Films

☐

Of Signature and Translation

Swedish artist Gunvor Nelson (b. 1931) is well established within avant-garde circles. Arguably she is best known for her work in the Bay Area in the mid-1960s and early 1970s. From 1970 to 1992 she taught at the San Francisco Art Institute; in 1993 she moved back to Sweden. Over the years, her work has frequently been shown at European and North American festivals, there have been several one-woman shows in her honor, and she has received many grants and awards.[1] With twenty films, five videos, and one video installation[2] to her credit as of 2006, one might well say, with Steve Anker, that her "films compose one of the great bodies of independent work in the history of the medium."[3]

In the male-dominated contexts of 1960s avant-garde film, however, friends and acquaintances like Bruce Baillie, Bruce Conner, and Stan Brakhage were among those foremost in the West Coast "eye."[4] It was perhaps inevitable, therefore, that Nelson and collaborator Dorothy Wiley should initially be received as feminist filmmakers, especially since their first collage film, *Schmeerguntz* (1965), wittily contrasts 1940s–1960s mass media constructs of what femininity "should" be (via clips and collages taken from the Miss America pageant, television fitness shows, and magazine advertisements) with Wiley's daily routines while pregnant with a second child (we see her, for example, cleaning gunk from a sink, and struggling to put on a garter belt, stockings, and boots).

Yet the film does not focus exclusively on women, though both Nelson and Wiley's experiences as young mothers helped shape it. (Nelson appears fleetingly with her young daughter Oona near the end.) Nelson herself has always eschewed the label "feminist,"[5] maintaining that in the case of *Schmeerguntz* she was simply working with what she had at hand.[6] Indeed, as will be clear, her work is "impossible to categorize either in gender or geographical terms."[7] The films, all shot on 16mm, are strikingly different, but certain themes, attitudes, and approaches modulate across them and carry over, if in altered fashion, to the videos as well.

As a way into contemplation of her 1980s and 1990s work in particular, I weave my comments here around the concepts of signature (evoked in part through my subtitle) and translation (indicated solely as movement within and between media boundaries). Though I occasionally invoke some of the early films (in particular *Schmeerguntz* and *My Name Is Oona* [1969]), I focus on the films made between 1984 and 1991 for three principal reasons: (1) they are less well known in the United States; (2) they illuminate aspects of the earlier films; and (3) they provide salient bridges to the contemporary video pieces. In what follows, I concentrate on four of the five "field studies" (*Frame Line* [1984], *Light Years*, *Light Years Expanding* [both 1987], and *Natural Features* [1990]). I also look at Nelson's two investigations of Kristinehamn (*Kristina's Harbor* [1993] and *Old Digs* [1993]), and at her silent short, *Time Being* (1991). In passing I mention the two nonlinear "features" (*Red Shift* [1984] and *Before Need Redressed* [1994]), and the fifth field study, *Field Study #2* (1988).

In Nelson's case, I argue, signature and translation acquire specific tonalities. Her films are intensely personal and at the same time abstract; many are surrealist; several include family members and Nelson herself; many incorporate animation and painting. All are carefully, if often barely perceptibly, structured around contrasts of color, rhythm, light, line, form, and texture. That six of the twenty-four works that Nelson has authored are actually coauthored is thus not a problem to establishing signature in the sense either of authorship or of characteristic elements.[8] Nelson's measured shaping of sounds and placement of silence provide, moreover, a third sense of signature, one reminiscent of "time signature" and "key signature" in music.

Equally important are Nelson's multiple engagements with translation. Among the several definitions listed in *Webster's New Collegiate Dictionary*, I find suggestive are: (as noun) "1a: a rendering from one language into another" and "1b: a change to a different substance, form, or appearance: conversion"; (as verb) "1a: to bear, remove, or change from one place, state, form or appearance to another," "2a: to turn into one's own or another language," "2b: to transfer or turn from one set of symbols into another," and "3: to enrapture."

The better to bring out Nelson's shapings of signature and translation, I present my observations in three movements. In the first, "The Art of Commuting/The Commuting of Art," I examine translations among forms, materials, and media and investigate the ways Nelson references travel, both between the United States and Sweden and also around Sweden. The discussion of space—and necessarily, also, of memory—at the close of this section is intended as span to the second, "Silencing Sounds/Sounding Silences." Here I touch on Nelson's unmooring of language and probing of "signature" in the more musical sense, via her stress on aural textures, rhythms, and voicing. In the third movement, "The Need for Multiple Meanings," I engage further with language, addressing Nelson's surrealist play with words, generic expectations, and film conventions, and also return to her emphases on the material components of film and video texts via titles, title cards, and concern with screening conditions.

In a coda, I argue that because such diverse modalities of signature and translation flow through Nelson's work, a third term, *resonance*, is needed, beyond signature and translation. In all her films—and now in her videos, too—emotion and mood predominate, fueling, prompting, soliciting *our* necessarily diverse reflections, ruminations, and interactions. There are no, can be no, fixed conclusions about the "puzzling pieces" that Nelson proffers.[9] As indicative of her recent transformations, I close with a glance toward her videos, briefly discussing *Snowdrift (a.k.a. Snowstorm)* (2001).[10]

The Art of Commuting/The Commuting of Art

From her first film to her latest video, *Trace Elements* (2003),[11] Gunvor Nelson has experimented with translations among forms, materials, and media. Trained as a painter and lithographer, first in Sweden and then at Mills College,[12] she never received any formal film training.[13] Consistently, she has been interested in "fields"—both in the sense of what the camera "sees" and the artist recombines, and in the sense of what an archaeologist looks for. Frames and layers are prominently displayed

From Gunvor Nelson's *Frameline*, 1984. Courtesy of
Gunvor Nelson.

in her animated work; strikingly, there are few focus shifts. In the five
"field studies" (that is, *Frame Line, Light Years, Light Years Expanding,
Field Study #2*, and *Natural Features*),[14] Nelson juxtaposes, morphs, and
examines photographed, painted, sketched, and real elements within a
single frame and frame to frame, using animation stands and optical
printers. To take just one example: straight lines metamorphose into
featherlike strokes at the end of *Frame Line*, a twenty-two-minute black-
and-white collage film. Somewhat similarly though later, *Kristina's Harbor* meditates on the resemblances between cubes, rectangles, triangles,
pyramids, and prisms.

In many films, Nelson paints over, drips liquids onto, or cuts out
substances. *Natural Features* is probably the most open-ended in this
regard. No predictable patterns are to be found, and although the emphasis is clearly on faces, these are rarely "natural," but better described
as works in progress or happenings. Examples abound: what seems a
face emerges from quickly sketched lines; a photographed face is seen
through a pane of glass, and then partially disappears under paint drops
or brush strokes. Sometimes faces are shown upside down; sometimes
only parts of heads are seen. Nelson's own face is briefly and dimly
glimpsed on a few occasions, seen through water or in a mirror. Often her
finger or hand manipulate objects chosen without apparent rhyme or
reason: there are a pear in gold foil, a dead bird, toy cars, a top, bits of film,
puzzle pieces, newspaper clippings, tubes of paint, and so on.

Repeatedly, Nelson ponders "natural" transformations. Sometimes these involve changes from one state to another, as when in *Before Need* and *Before Need Redressed* a hot iron is placed atop a block of ice, which begins to melt. Often she observes the modulations brought about through aging or decay. In *Red Shift*, a fifty-minute film she has described in the Canyon Cinema catalogue as "a film in black and white about relationships, generations, and time," three generations of mothers and daughters (played by family members) interact; their conversations take place within two basic time frames, one past, one present. Another woman's voice is interspersed with theirs: she reads offscreen from Calamity Jane's letters to the daughter she never knew and only briefly saw. At one point we see Nelson's eighty-year-old mother, Carin Grundel, with difficulty dress;[15] later, in close-up, a hand (Nelson's) reaches out and gently touches her mother's wrinkled face; she breaks into a joyous smile. And "natural" transformations appear in the collage "journeys" around Sweden and through time that form the heart of *Light Years* and *Light Years Expanding* as well, as when apples in various states of decay appear within landscapes. (Rotting apples also figure in *Frame Line*.) In *Kristina's Harbor* and *Old Digs*, Nelson finds garbage floating down the river, and many dead birds. "Ideas grew out of the footage as I was working on it," she wrote. "The town was rebuilding and digging up the old.... I remember I wanted a journey up the river, back into many meanings, memories, and dreams. And more."[16] Her last film with Wiley, *Before Need Redressed*, excises many of the lengthy dialogues of *Before Need* (1979)[17] but retains what Anker calls the "oblique narrative raising questions on aging, the breakdown of the body, the inability to learn, and the shadowy world of memory."[18]

Translations provoked by travel and/or instigated by memory underpin most of the recent films. Nelson herself downplays their "Swedishness,"[19] yet Swedish critics and audiences unfailingly notice how often Swedish markers appear. Astrid Söderbergh Widding comments in *Svenska Dagbladet* that Nelson's Swedish dialogue in *Red Shift* is "surprisingly stilted," then continues: "It's tempting to think that Nelson's long time living and working in the U.S. gave her a special relationship both to her home region in Värmland and to her family in Sweden. She seems to look at all of this from a distance, at the same time with great respect and devotion. It's striking how often she returns home in her films—only, it would seem, to discover that home had in part become *unheimlich*, foreign."[20]

Many of Nelson's 1980s and 1990s films were, of course, shot in Sweden, with Stockholm's Filmverkstan a prime source of technical help.[21]

From Gunvor
Nelson's *Red Shift*,
1984. Courtesy of
Gunvor Nelson.

What is most important, however, is that Nelson transmutes Sweden in her work. For although things Swedish often trigger connections to memory and to family, always these are filtered through film or via video: in Nelson's case, meditation on media typically accompanies and conveys other content. For me, Sweden thus functions in these works as a kind of *källa*, a word which translates variously as "spring," "source," and "well" (and thereby happily also signals the many references to and images of water and fluids in most of the films, including several, such as *Fog Pumas* [1967], *Moon's Pool* [1973], and *One and the Same* [1972], that were shot in the United States). Because the transfiguration of "Swedish" traces is so core to the post-1980s pieces, the fact that Nelson continues at times to be labeled a "West Coast" filmmaker represents an acute failure by Anglophone critics to perceive how "transnational objects . . . challenge translation."[22] Among U.S. critics, only Nelson's longtime colleague Steve Anker, in effect, underlines the importance of these cross-cultural translations, writing of *Trollstenen* that "the distances of geography and time encouraged her to adopt a critical and analytical position when contemplating memories or artifacts from the past, as well as in considering how best to generate accompanying contemporary material. This led to a second focus, on the nature of images as tissues of memory—the materiality and illusory power of images themselves—and how they can be manipulated as objects and given further resonance within a larger photographic work."[23]

Primarily shot and edited in Sweden, *Frame Line* is exemplary in this regard. For Henrik Örrje, the film is "a personal depiction of Stockholm and impressions after many years away";[24] Filmverkstan's catalogue terms it "an abstract sketch of Stockholm seen with Swedish-American eyes like glimpses . . . to be at home and foreign at the same time."[25] Throughout, bits of Stockholm are offered as fragments of memory; near the end, a few bars of the Swedish national anthem are played on a flute.[26] The image track proffers pieces of a puzzle, images of people walking in the streets, many postcards on which Nelson paints or writes, views of Stockholm taken from a boat, sketches of shapes, lines, and twirling boxes. Periodically, there are shots of Nelson's face, hair, or hands; there is also much, much more.[27]

Both *Light Years* and *Light Years Expanding* extend the scope of Nelson's commutations, moving from Stockholm now to tour southern and central Sweden.[28] Though some shots are repeated across the two films, each has its "own" footage and its own distinct rhythm: *Light Years Expanding* moves more rapidly. The sound tracks also differ. Neither film contains much synchronized sound, yet in *Light Years*, briefly, dogs can be heard barking as they are seen on screen; in *Light Years Expanding*, English, presumably emanating from a car radio, is fleetingly audible. Because he himself is Swedish, Anders Pettersson is able to specify that in these two road trips, Nelson moves from Skåne to Blekinge to Dalarna to Klarälven, but the film operates without geographical logic.[29] "Realist" chronology is also absent: sometimes it is summer, sometimes there is a bit of snow. If anything, ur-Swedish signs proliferate: time and again "Falu" red[30] houses and barns, churches, woods, rivers, and fields flash past. Some images are shot in color, others in black and white; some are taken from car windows; others include Nelson's layered animations.

Yet if the emphases on translation and commutation are stronger in the later films, Nelson's 1969 *My Name Is Oona* already explored memory, imagination, travel, and translation. Here Nelson's seven-year-old daughter Oona appears on horseback and costumed in a cape, blonde hair flying as she rides as if she were a John Bauer fairy tale princess; in closing, perhaps intermingling her own childhood fantasies with her daughter's, Nelson softly sings snatches of a Swedish folk song. No translation is offered.

Silencing Sounds/Sounding Silences

Nelson's untranslated song offers quiet closure to a film organized around two types of recordings. The first is of her young daughter repeating, mantralike, "My Name Is Oona," in many looped versions. The second (recorded by Steve Reich) is formed by Oona's recitation of the days of the week. Volume and tempo accelerate and decelerate; solo utterances are interwoven with choral ones. Words become differently meaningful, even mystical, as what is melodic and rhythmic about language moves forward. Haunting images—of Oona on her horse in the woods and the fields, wrestling with a friend, smiling in close-up—are rendered in a variety of ways. In the beginning, trees are seen in positive and negative images. Other scenes are rephotographed in close-up so that the grain is visible; a few are slowed down.[31] Always, they move "with" the sound track.

But attention to the "silence" of sounds and the "sound" of silences shades all of Nelson's work. In *Schmeerguntz*, Nelson and Wiley devoted much care to editing the sound track. There the rapid images find their equivalents in the staccato splicing of songs and snippets of recorded conversation and voice-over narration; there are no fade-ins or -outs. The visual/audio combinations are often ironic: a polka accompanies a photographic collage of priests dancing in circles in the snow; a male voice says, "And he kissed her again," as vomit pours (in reverse motion) back into a woman's mouth; "I Could Have Danced All Night" accompanies shots of a toilet being cleaned.

In her later work, Nelson shies away from such relatively straightforward associations, opting instead for more musical signatures.[32] She refuses to include her two-hour-long family meditation, *Trollstenen*, in retrospectives, in part because it incorporates translated interviews; in part because she finds the film too long. Yet in every film, although in some more than in others, key and meter, placement and pitch, rhythm and dynamics, variation and theme, color what we see. As in Bach fugues, sound tracks form other "lines," other "voices," that attend to and peel off from the images. In many films, there are bursts of synthesized music, bars played on actual instruments, screeches, shouts, bits of song, whistles, bells. *Natural Features*, for example, incorporates the sound of a car radio searching for stations, scraps of music, the singing of the film title, and stretches of silence; on the visual plane, cut-outs, photos, mirrors, toys, puzzle pieces, ink, and paint flash past in waves of color and shards of shapes. Nelson is intrigued by the impact pacing has, commenting, "If you would use two strong sounds after each other, the second sound would diminish or drown the first one. . . . A sound reverberates in your brain long after it has subsided if no other sound has followed. . . . It is being repeated in you. . . . I like the idea of being able to prolong a sound in this manner."[33]

In *Kristina's Harbor* and especially in *Old Digs*, sounds break away from images while silences interrupt and pace sounds. Shot at the same time, on a return to Sweden in 1990, Nelson typically distinguishes the

From Gunvor
Nelson's *My Name
Is Oona*, 1969.
Courtesy of Gunvor
Nelson.

From Gunvor Nelson's *Old Digs*,
1993. Courtesy of Gunvor Nelson.

two via their image tracks. *Kristina's Harbor*, she says, represents what she found above water around her hometown, Kristinehamn; *Old Digs* what she found below and associated with the "unconscious." Many of the visuals in the latter are reflections of trees, buildings, and people in water. Yet the sound tracks are equally distinctive. In *Kristina's Harbor* snatches of voices speak in Värmländsk dialects and talk about what it is like to live in Kristinehamn; sometimes they mention why they have chosen to stay there. Occasionally (although not often) their commentary is translated into English. A few titles are also given in English: almost immediately "I am so in love with my little town" appears; soon after, a young man says the same thing, in Swedish. In *Old Digs*, in contrast, though images of literal excavation again appear, Nelson's archaeological explorations have moved deeper. Words recede into a background buzz of indecipherable murmuring and mumbling. Other aural elements, such as clock tones and a rainstorm, come and go, bereft of readily identifiable visual anchors.[34]

Nelson's interest in voicing extends to a respect for silence qua silence, as well. Made when her mother was ninety years old (she died not long after), the eight-minute, black-and-white *Time Being* audaciously refuses sound and thereby becomes, I feel, Nelson's most powerful film. There are three principal sections, each punctuated by gestural camera work. A prelude offers two photos of Nelson's mother. In one, she stands upright and energetic on skis in long shot; in the other, she smiles at the camera/ photographer in close-up. Briefly, one of the photos "shakes." In stark contrast, the first and longest section contains *no* camera movement or editing. Instead we see Carin Grundel in close-up, lying prone on a nursing home or hospital bed, face partially averted from the camera, her mouth sunken, struggling to breathe. Though her eyes flicker open from time to time, she seems not to realize that anyone else is in the room. Suddenly, an interlude: the camera pans wildly around the room, there are a few edits, and then all fades to black. The second section, again a fixed long take but now a medium shot, shows Carin lying immobile in the same position. After another brief interlude, the camera moves back farther still, gazing steadily in fixed long shot at Carin's body in bed, revealing tree branches outside the window, flowers on the sill, an empty bed to one side. For a moment, the sun comes out, then goes away; the light changes to near white, for Nelson "creating a widening of space, a holy moment."[35] Finally, the camera pans slowly to the floor, showing as the last image the sandaled feet of Nelson herself.

By film's end, silence has become unbelievably expressive, underscoring time, suggesting being. Aware of the impact that these alternations between fixed and frenzied movements, duration, and silence have, Nelson makes no stills from it available.[36] As she says:

> When you see a film without sound, you're forced to confront your own thoughts and your own fears. Without sound one can hear one's own voice more clearly and from that find distance and room to look for the personal meaning the film may have. . . . The question of balance, lack of balance, is something that's very important to me. . . . If everything has the same value, nothing is underlined or emphasized. I am very careful about trying to find the right scale of color and emphasis.[37]

Nelson's balancings and unbalancings of sound and silence, movement and image, clearly move space and time into dimensions other than those inhabited by mainstream feature-length film. Deleuze's insights in *Le Temps-Image* also apply to Nelson's projects of layering and excavation:

> When the acoustic is no longer an extension of the visual, the acoustic and the visual become two distinct layers of a "stratigraphic" space. . . . the visual image never reproduces what the voice utters, and the sound track never describes what the image shows. However, even if the two domains are incommensurable, they are not without relation. There is in fact a complementarity between sound and image based on their strategic dissociation. . . . The relation between sound and image requires a rotation of visible surfaces or an excavation of pictured landscapes.[38]

The Need for Multiple Meanings

Nelson's burying and unearthing of meanings, messages, forms, and relations is profoundly marked by surrealism. Like the surrealists, Nelson is fond of dreamlike and punning visuals: most obviously so in *Fog Pumas*, *Before Need*, and *Before Need Redressed*. Speaking to students I taught at the University of Stockholm, she said she tried in the latter two films to capture "the beauty of our strange obsessions." (The title, *Before Need*, alludes to a sign in a chapel that advertises cubicles for funeral urns.) Like the surrealists, too, Nelson delights in nonsensical, if allusive, intertitles. In *Natural Features* several, all in block letter type, are interspersed among the images. Some, for example: "RECENT EXCAVATIONS," "PLEASE EXCAVATE," "SUNKEN TERRAIN," "EXCAVATION IN PROGRESS"—implicate spatial strata; two, "IN PLAIN VIEW" and (the last) "POSSIBLE SOURCE OF

ERROR," suggest, then question, knowledge. The earlier *Frame Line* also plays with intertitles, among them "gedigna visioner" (reluctantly leaving behind),[39] "all remote, random," "and in harmony," "sightseeing," "greetings from," and "lingering notes." For me, these hint at a foreigner's/exile's sensitivity to shifting meanings and varying contexts, at the difficulty of speaking in a language not one's own, at the difficulty of speaking in a language one has been away from. One might similarly regard the strange sayings of "Lout Sue Sez" that pepper the image tracks of *Before Need* and *Before Need Redressed* or the cryptic proverbs scattered throughout *Red Shift* (e.g., "the praise is not pudding," "the earth is frozen for lazy swine," "naked as a frog," "kind children wait till they get nothing").

The joy Nelson takes in torquing film conventions and challenging genre expectations is obvious everywhere. In *Light Years* and *Light Years Expanding*, for example, she reworks painting traditions of landscapes and still lifes: decaying apples placed over a photograph of snowy forests or within a landscape, on top of fence posts. In *Natural Features* she flouts the traditional ways film credits are shown: the title is first spoken, then, a bit later, sung, later still, painted. Further bending convention, intertitles reading "by Gunvor Nelson" and "Thank you" appear halfway through the film, that is, slightly later than (but still well before) the other credits appear. Only the acknowledgments of financial and technical assistance appear, as usual, at film's end, although these are sung, not written. As Nelson told my class in Stockholm, she always tries "to look at things from a slightly different angle, so a thing doesn't refer only to itself."

To this end, many of Nelson's films foreground the camera's presence; all explore editing. Significantly, from *Schmeerguntz* on, close-ups prove revelatory, if also elusive, permitting everyday objects to manifest hidden meaning. In *Light Years*, a finger pokes at a tiny green worm; in *Red Shift*, a hand wipes steam from a mirror, cleans a hairbrush, sorts jewelry in a drawer; in *Old Digs* dead birds and a beetle loom large. Beginning with *Schmeerguntz*, she comments, "I discovered how beautiful things *look* through the camera. . . . A melon or dirty dishes, seen with a lens in close-up, were translated into something else. . . . The camera became like binoculars; you zero in on a small area and isolate it, and it becomes more precious *because* it's selected."[40]

Never has Nelson forgotten the rapture of visual translations, obtained through a camera, modified through animation and painting, and organized in editing. The titles she chooses signal her sensitivity to and

From Gunvor Nelson's *Light Years*, 1987. Courtesy of Gunvor Nelson.

appreciation of her materials: *FRAME LINE, RED Shift, LIGHT Years, LIGHT Years Expanding, FIELD Study #2, Natural FEATURES, TIME Being, Tree-LINE/Träd-GRÄNS, Snowdrift (a.k.a. SNOW Storm)*, and *TRACE ELEMENTS* (save for the word *SNOWDRIFT*, the capitals represent my emphasis). Many convey openness and nonfixity thanks to words like *shift*, *drift*, and *expanding*.[41] Clearly, this insistence on forms and processes stems from her background as a painter. No wonder, then, that she prefers to be called an "artist"; she dislikes the label "director": for her, painting and film are intimately linked. As Anker puts it, Nelson "has managed to transform her passion for the feel of pigments applied on flat surfaces to the paradoxically non-physical interplay of shadow and light. Her films are sensual immersions into sound and image, where every flicker contributes, through its rhythm and texture, to the content of the composition."[42]

No doubt because she is so fascinated by field and form, Nelson is extraordinarily precise about how her work should be presented and preserved. At the premiere of *Frame Line* at Canyon Cinema, she covered the emergency exit signs with black cloth to ensure darkness. When she showed *Old Digs* to my students, she insisted on turning the volume *down*, cautioning them that they were not meant to try to understand the snippets of voices that punctuate the film save, perhaps, to register "old age" via tremors or pitch. She sends detailed instructions with the PAL video copies of *Tree-Line* and *Snowdrift (a.k.a. Snowstorm)* she provides to projectionists, trying to get their attention. In the case of *Tree-Line*, some words are underlined, others are written in red (here rendered as italics): "The *sound* should be set as *loud* as possible *at the first titles*. In the *picture the black should be black.* The video is almost B/W except for some blue." With *Snowdrift (a.k.a. Snowstorm)*, the indications are given in capital letters, and underlined: *"PLEASE* SHOW WITH SLIGHTLY MORE CONTRAST THAN NORMAL." It took literally years to restore *Light Years*. (It took nine trail prints, Nelson wrote me, to give the film the correct color and density; luckily Pacific Film Archive covered the costs). The *Frame Line* original negative was quite damaged; dirt was ingrained in the surface so that it could not be cleaned. "Prints from *Frame Line* have a lot of white spots, like snow. This shows up a lot because the film is so dark," Nelson wrote me, sadly. "It is not the restoring lab's fault. I am very unhappy that no 'clean' prints can be made . . . It was very costly to get this far and now I do not have the money to tackle *Red Shift*."[43] This is lamentable, for with *Red Shift*, "the original negative splices are coming apart and no new prints can be made. A real problem with the old films, and it takes a lot of time and effort to time them again in a new lab. MY old labs are closing."[44] Nelson wants her work to be experienced at its best, in good prints, under the best possible screening conditions. Nonetheless she recognizes that even the most exacting assembly, the most painstaking presentation, does not and cannot control reception. Nor would she wish to do so, for she is eager to convey and share her sense that multiple meanings are not just desirable but necessary.

Beyond Signature and Translation, Toward Resonance

Personally, I am touched by the ways that Nelson's works often think "through the body," emphasizing tactile relations and/or relationships between women. At the same time, I deeply respect and sincerely value her and Chick Strand's, and others' desire *not* to be referred to as "women artists," but rather to be considered "artists," *tout court*. Times have changed, but Dorothy Wiley's delight that people occasionally wondered whether *Schmeerguntz* was made by a man or a woman[45] remains pertinent: the art surely matters more than the maker. Despite my frequent invocation of Nelson's background and what she has said to me and to others, moreover, I do not want to weight unduly biography or authorial voice. As Janet Staiger cautions, we must beware the "fallacy of assuming filmmakers' statements about their work are obvious (and do not require the same sort of textual attention as texts such as their films). After all, they are part of the author's techniques of the self."[46] Though I have tried to provide a sense of the range of critical reception, clearly I find some comments more helpful than others; a few, as I have indicated, are incorrect.

I have focused in this essay on the 1980s and 1990s films in hopes that, increasingly, others will share my enthusiasm for them. Yet I know that I am not alone in valuing Nelson's more recent work. While it is true that, as Anker writes, Nelson has "lost the popular interest her earlier films had achieved," it is also true that "her work is being increasingly applauded by avant-garde establishment critics Fred Camper, Robert Haller and Jonas Mekas."[47] Other avant-garde filmmakers, too, prize her contributions, among them Brakhage, who underscored in 1994 how much he liked her work. He had seen a good deal of it but singled out the 1988 *Field Study #2* in particular, finding it had "affinities" with his own work. As he put it, *Field Study #2* was analogously "about remembrance, which includes hypnagogic vision or moving visual thinking to counterbalance the dangers of nostalgia or sentimentality."[48]

There are, of course, salient differences between Brakhage's and Nelson's *oeuvres*. Unlike Brakhage, Nelson has never sought to project "a single, authoritative perspective or understanding of the world."[49] In her work, in contrast, explorations of new perspectives, investigations of new media, are of the essence. Listening to and watching her films and videos, I find myself opening to what cannot be expressed through language; I wonder about what may exist beyond consciousness; I pay enhanced attention to sounds and silences, rhythm and movement. But how, as a critic, to convey adequately to others through words my sensory impressions and fleeting reflections? I imagine I feel somewhat as Nelson herself does. In most interviews she says something like the following: "As soon as I've said something I instantly realize everything I haven't managed to express. And what I've said acquires too great an importance. I feel sad at being able to express so little of everything I feel, think, and know about film creating/making."[50]

Yet especially with avant-garde work, there cannot simply be interpretation, let alone decipherment. I am reminded of Roland Barthes's insistence that "every text is eternally written *here and now*. The active relationship between creator, work, and viewer . . . yields 'multiple writings' that resist foreclosed interpretation."[51] At issue with Nelson's films must also be *resonance*, not just signature or translation. Viewer "vibrations" will necessarily vary, and whether, how, these works are grouped will sound additional, differing tones and highlight other, shifting lusters.

Meanwhile Nelson's musings on media and memory continue, now with and through video. When I met her in 1997, she was immersed in the challenge this new world presented, both exhausted and invigorated by the opportunities it offered. Characteristically, she looked forward to the greater independence and control that shooting and editing on video would afford her; characteristically, too, the videos she has completed since then pay great attention to her materials.

With video, however, both the characteristics of the medium and quality of the equipment she owns further encourage minimalism. Her second video, *Snowdrift (a.k.a. Snowstorm)*, is exemplary in this regard.[52] It begins and ends with snowflakes flying against (another) Falu-red log wall. From the start, behind the gestural camerawork, diagonal lines encounter horizontals. First subtly, then overtly, we are made aware of the framing of the image by what Widding calls the "curtain of snow."[53] As the video progresses and the snow continues to fall, the snowflakes are animated and abstracted, becoming blobs, lines, and dashes. At times these renderings are reminiscent of video "snow," yet they vary in tempo, alter direction, and even revolve as colors pulsate out and in, punctuated by moments of black and white. In a middle section, an oval plaque of a moose (another quintessentially Swedish marker) can be glimpsed.[54] Nearer the end, lines metamorphose into rectangular planes, then turn back again to lines; always "real" images interrupt or mingle with animated ones. Busier than usual, the sound track is marked by its own augmentations and diminutions: blowing snow becomes white noise; dissonant synthesized sounds, syllables sung by a choir, clangs (from a bell?) alternate with silence. As the work ends, "by Gunvor Grundel Nelson" appears through the snow in white outlined by black, then the image fades to white and finally goes dark, leaving behind memories of visual and audial variations that echo on, "like a sound that only reminds us of a word."[55]

The more I experience, savor, and reflect on Nelson's films, and now her videos, the more grateful I become for her ceaseless searching.[56] As she explains, each work begins with a strategy or an attitude in mind, then proceeds as an investigation of what it should be. She finds happiness in the surprise, the revelation, and enjoys both the freedom of filming and the strictness of editing.[57] *I* like that Nelson makes a point of

From Gunvor Nelson's *Snowdrift*, 2001. Courtesy of
Gunvor Nelson.

listening to her material,[58] that she is sensitive to nuance and context, that
she plays with visual and musical dynamics, that she considers both
iconic and plastic dimensions, excavating visual fields and layering auditory frames.

Filmography

Schmeerguntz, 1965 (15 min.): sd., b&w; 16mm
Fog Pumas, 1967 (25 min.): sd., col.; 16mm
Kirsa Nicholina, 1969 (16 min.): sd., col.; 16mm
My Name Is Oona, 1969 (10 min.): sd., b&w; 16mm
Five Artists: BillBobBillBillBob (with Dorothy Wiley), 1971 (70 min.): sd.,
    col.; 16mm
One and the Same (with Freude Solomon-Bartlett), 1972 (4 min.): sd., col.;
    16mm
Take Off (with Magda), 1972 (10 min.): sd., b&w; 16mm
Moon's Pool, 1973 (15 min.): sd., col.; 16mm
Trollstene, 1973–76 (120 min.): sd., col.; 16mm
Before Need (with Dorothy Wiley), 1979 (75 min.): sd., col.; 16mm
Frame Line, 1984 (22 min.): sd., b&w; 16mm
Red Shift, 1984 (50 min.): sd., b&w; 16mm

Light Years, 1987 (28 min.): sd., col.; 16mm
Light Years Expanding, 1987 (25 min.): sd., col.; 16mm
Field Study #2, 1988 (8 min.): sd., col.; 16mm
Natural Features, 1990 (30 min.): sd., col.; 16mm
Time Being, 1991 (8 min.): si., b&w; 16mm
Old Digs, 1993 (20 min.): sd., col.; 16mm
Kristina's Harbor, 1993 (50 min.): sd., col.; 16mm
Before Need Redressed (with Dorothy Wiley), 1995 (42 min.): sd., col.; 16mm
Tree-Line/Trädgräns, 1998 (8 min.): sd., col.; video
Bevismaterial: 52 Veckor (*Collected Evidence: 52 Weeks*), 1998 (4 x 30 min.): installation
Snowdrift (a.k.a. Snowstorm), 2001 (9 min.): sd., col.; video
Trace Elements, 2003 (9 min.): sd., col.; video
True to Life, 2006 (38 min.): video
New Evidence, 2006 (22 min.): video

Notes

Warmest thanks to Gunvor Grundel Nelson for her suggestions and feedback. Thanks also to Steve Anker and Paul Arthur for stimulating discussions about Nelson's work, and to John Sundholm, Astrid Soderbergh Widding, and Anders Pettersson for engaging conversations and for sharing their own essays, in English and Swedish, on Nelson. I am privileged to have been a part of a conference held in Nelson's honor in August 2002 in Karlstad; the opportunities to rescreen several of the films, hear speakers, and participate in question/answer sessions there were invaluable. Lastly, thanks to Scott MacDonald, who first suggested that I contact Gunvor on one of my many trips to Sweden.

1   Other teaching posts included a year at San Francisco State University from 1969 to 1970 and a semester in 1987 at the School of the Art Institute of Chicago. Nelson acquired dual U.S.-Swedish citizenship only in 2002. For additional biographical details, see note 13 and Sundholm, "Biography," 110–11. Nelson's awards include a Guggenheim, two NEA grants, and a Rockefeller Foundation grant. For a more complete, but partial, listing of other grants, awards, and shows, see Pettersson, *Gunvor Nelson*, D-uppsats, Bilaga, 4. Additional bibliographic information can be found in Holmlund, "Gunvor Nelson," 131, and Pettersson, *Gunvor Nelson*, 82–85.

2   The installation, *Collected Evidence: 52 Weeks*, is comprised of four thirty-minute videos, slides, photographs, images lit from behind, computer graphics, and more.

3   Anker, "The Films of Gunvor Nelson," 9. Anker's essay, published in Sundholm, *Gunvor Nelson: Still Moving*, is partially available online. See www.filmint.nu/netonly/eng/excerptnelson.html.

4   Earlier films that Nelson has mentioned having been important to her at the time include Dalí and Buñuel's *Un chien andalou* (1929), Jean Cocteau's *Beauty and the Beast* (1946), and Maya Deren's *Meshes of the Afternoon* (1943).

5   For readings of Nelson's early films as feminist and feminine, see DiMatteo, "Gunvor Nelson"; Fischer, *Shot/Counter Shot*; Gill, "The Films of Gunvor Nelson"; D. Nelson, "Imagery of the Archetypal Feminine"; and Richardson, "An Interview with Gunvor Nelson and Dorothy Wiley."

6   Comment made after the screening of *Schmeerguntz* at the 2002 conference, "Gunvor Nelson: Still Moving i ljud och bild," held in Karlstad. In their joint 1971 interview with Brenda Richardson, Wiley was more open to the promotion of women's art as art *by* women, although she has not sought to position herself as a "woman artist" either. See Richardson, "An Interview with Gunvor Nelson and Dorothy Wiley," 37. Wiley's single-authored films, all available from Canyon Cinema, include *Zane Forbidden* (1972), *The Weenie Worm* (1972), *Letters* (1972), *Cabbage* (1972), *Miss Jesus Fries on Grill* (1973), and *The Birth of Seth Andrew Kinmount* (1977).

7   Anker, "Gunvor Nelson," 118.

8   The five early cosigned films include *Schmeerguntz, Fog Pumas, Five Artists: BillBobBillBillBob, One and the Same*, and *Before Need*. Except for *One and the Same*, which was made with Freude (Bartlett), all were made with Dorothy Wiley. (The later *Before Need Redressed* was, too.) One might consider a sixth early film to be coauthored as well: *Take Off* star and producer Magda claimed coauthorship, to Nelson's dismay.

9   Pettersson, "Interview," 154.

10   Others write this title differently, as *Snowdrift/Snowstorm*, as *Snowstorm*, even as *SNOWDRIFT/SNOWSTORM*. I am using the title Nelson proposed and prefers (personal correspondence, January 10, 2005).

11   For discussions of *Trace Elements*, see Pettersson, "Interview," 160–61 and Sundholm, "Gunvor Nelson and the Aesthetics of Sensual Materiality."

12   At Mills, she studied with abstract painter Richard Diebenkorn. She also studied art at Humboldt State University and the San Francisco Art Institute (then called the California School of Fine Arts).

13   For a time Nelson worked as an editor at a television station, but she and Wiley received only thirty minutes of instruction in how to use a camera (from Robert Nelson) before they started filming *Schmeerguntz*.

14   Nelson regards all of her animation films as "field studies," she says, because "the area that the animation camera lens sees is called a 'field.' *Take Off* (1972) was partly re-filmed with an animation camera, so it was supposed to be the first" (Pettersson, "Interview," 156). With respect to *Take Off*, however, critics usually stress feminist elements, with B. Rich describing it in the *Canyon Cinema Catalogue* as "a forceful political statement on the image of women and the true meaning of stripping" (254). Although the piece begins and ends with animation, the "body" of the work focuses on an aging stripper (Ellion

Ness) as she takes off her clothes, facing front; the camera at times "dances" with her. Then her legs, ears, breasts, arms, nose, and head come off. Last her torso hurtles off into space. Nelson manipulates the images she has filmed in several ways, adding superimpositions, shifting speeds, and fragmenting Ness's body.

15 Since the shots do not appear in a logical temporal order (first Carin puts her stockings on, then she begins to put her stockings on), both the dailiness and the struggle of the task are implicated.

16 Pettersson, *Gunvor Nelson*, 68.

17 Nelson and Wiley cut much of what people say.

18 Anker, "Gunvor Nelson and the American Avant-Garde Film," 119.

19 See, for example, Helmersson, "Filma är som att måla."

20 Widding, "Ett kabinett," 9, my translation.

21 In contrast, of the earlier films only *My Name Is Oona* and *Trollstenen* enlist Swedish images or sounds.

22 Marks, *The Skin of the Film*, 79.

23 Anker, "The Films of Gunvor Nelson," 18. Asked in 1971 whether there "is anything in your character that's specifically Swedish," Nelson replied, "Dreams. And a general feeling of order, a classical type of form which is ingrained." See Richardson, "An Interview with Gunvor Nelson and Dorothy Wiley," 38.

24 Pettersson, *Gunvor Nelson*, 86.

25 Filmverkstan catalogue, 25, my translation. In a description written for Canyon Cinema, Nelson herself describes the film as "an eerie flow between the ugly and the beautiful; about returning, about roots, and also about reshaping." See *Canyon Cinema Film Video Catalogue*, 7.

26 Nelson hints at the national anthem at other points in the film as well. She emphasizes that she "tried to do something really unusual with the national anthem so that even Swedes might not see it at first." See Pettersson, "Interview," 155.

27 Described by the American Museum of the Moving Image as a fragment of a trilogy of the homeland, Nelson nonetheless maintained, "that's not what I focused on." See Pettersson, *Gunvor Nelson*, 85, my translation.

28 Since she had so much footage, Nelson atypically worked on both films at the same time. Usually she completes one film or video before moving on to the next.

29 Nelson herself says that she visited an aunt in Lund, a sister in Blekinge, and friends in Stockholm and around Kristinehamn. See Pettersson, *Gunvor Nelson*, 85. There are also, she tells me, some winter shots from further north, in Dalarna (e-mail, January 19, 2005).

30 The color originated in the city of Falun, in Dalarna, hence the name. During the first two decades of the twentieth century, many Swedish homes were painted this particular tone of red: for the national romantic style then in

vogue, the color was emblematic of tradition. To provide contrast, shutters, door frames and window frames were usually painted white. The colors are still popular today.

31 Early blurbs obtained from Canyon Cinema include a quote from Amos Vogel's *Village Voice* review and Karyn Kay's program notes. Vogel says that the film, which screened at the second Whitney Museum avant-garde series in 1971, "captures in haunting, intensely lyrical images, fragments of the coming to consciousness of a child girl." He finds Nelson "the revelation of the program . . . [a] true poetess [*sic*] of the visual cinema." See *Canyon Cinema Film Video Catalogue*, 2–3. Kay writes, "Oona is transformed into an eerie, almost dream-like figure. The everyday, the personal, takes on dramatic proportions. The child is no longer simply a child, but she is representative of feminine myths of beauty and strength." For more about *My Name Is Oona*, see Anker, "Gunvor Nelson and the American Avant-Garde Film," 115–16; MacDonald, "Gunvor Nelson," 188–89; and Pettersson, "Interview," 143–44.

32 Nelson is even more attentive to sound in the videos, Sundholm argues, because visuals are less precise with video. See "Gunvor Nelson and the Aesthetics of Materiality."

33 Pettersson, "Interview," 158.

34 Widding describes the film as "a tightly-knit meditation about a place, both well known and foreign, both carried in memory and changed beyond recognition" ("Ett kabinett," 9, my translation).

35 Personal correspondence, January 10, 2005.

36 See Sundholm, "Gunvor Nelson and the Aesthetics of Sensual Materiality."

37 Pettersson, *Gunvor Nelson*, 67, my translation.

38 Rodowick, *Gilles Deleuze's Time Machine*, 145, 149. Rodowick/Deleuze are speaking of Duras's and Straub-Huillet's experimental fiction films and Claude Lanzmann's documentary *Shoah* (1985). Compare Steve Anker's assessment: "each gathered image [I'd add and underline, "each collected sound"] was a fragmentary, recovered object which was uniquely and visually expressive unto itself, and which lent itself to being sutured into tapestries of complex emotional resonance and multiple meanings" ("Gunvor Nelson and the American Avant-Garde Film," 119).

39 *Gedigna* means both "solid" and "native."

40 MacDonald, "Gunvor Nelson," 186.

41 The title of the first book in Swedish devoted to her work, *Still Moving i ljud och bild*, was Nelson's suggestion. See Andersson, "Technology and Poetry," 74. Once again, Nelson's word play combines Swedish (which translates to "in sound and image") with English; it also evokes time ("still moving"), travel ("moving"), and, of course, core aspects of film and video, that is, stills and movement.

42 Anker, "The Films of Gunvor Nelson," 9.

43 Letter, January 10, 2005.

44 E-mail, December 9, 2003.

45 See Richardson, "An Interview with Gunvor Nelson and Dorothy Wiley," 37, for Wiley's comments about a screening held at Reed College.

46 Staiger, "Authorship Approaches," 52.

47 Anker, "Gunvor Nelson and the American Avant-Garde Film," 122.

48 Ganguly, "Stan Brakhage," 148.

49 Anker, "Gunvor Nelson and American Avant-Garde Film," 123.

50 Pettersson, "Interview," 162. Compare, for example, "when I utter something, I immediately feel all the things I've *not* said, and what I *have* said inevitably takes on too much importance" (MacDonald, "Gunvor Nelson," 183–84).

51 Barthes, "The Death of the Author," 145.

52 For other discussions of *Tree-Line* and *Snowdrift (a.k.a. Snowstorm)*, see Andersson's insightful analysis in "Technology and Poetry," Sundholm's brief treatment in "Gunvor Nelson and the Aesthetics of Sensual Materiality," and Widding's excellent "The Material World Transformed."

53 Widding, "The Material World Transformed," 132.

54 Nelson told me that the moose was her neighbor's and was placed in a window across from her apartment at the time. Here again, then, is an example of how she taps and transforms the everyday, incorporates the personal, and transports the national in/through her art.

55 Andersson, "Technology and Poetry," 98.

56 Nelson's confession to Pettersson is telling: "I have tried not to repeat myself. . . . I am afraid of becoming 'too skillful.' . . . You risk losing that which is unique and that which you have not done before" ("Interview," 148).

57 Response at the 2002 Karlstad conference.

58 As she says, "surprising solutions can be had with the most 'deficient' of material if you let it speak to you: if you learn what really is in the film" (Pettersson, *Gunvor Nelson*, 80, citing a five-page handout compiled for the editing classes Nelson taught, 1983–85, at the San Francisco Art Institute).

NOËL CARROLL

Moving and Moving

From Minimalism to *Lives of Performers*

□

In retrospect, *Lives of Performers* strikes one as an allegory of its time—of Yvonne Rainer's (and the avant-garde film world's) movement from minimalism to something else. The film begins with rehearsal footage of the dance *Walk, She Said*, which gives every appearance of being a minimalist exercise devoted to the exploration of movement as such.[1] Though a rehearsal (and, therefore, by definition, something that looks toward the future), this dance, oddly enough, points back to the past—to minimalism, with its commitment to a modernist aesthetic of austerity. In a narrow sense, the dance rehearsal points backward to Rainer's own distinguished career as a choreographer—a career that she was, with *Lives of Performers*, preparing to exchange for a career in filmmaking. From another, wider, angle, one can also gloss the rehearsal material from *Walk, She Said* as a synecdoche for the aesthetic milieu of the time, where not only the dance world but the worlds of fine arts and film were all dominated by minimalism, the film world variant of which was structural film.

Sandwiched in between the shoots of the rehearsal is the "real" content of the film. Sally Banes has called *Lives of Performers* a backstage musical—that is, we get a view of the fictional lives of the performers, ostensibly in between their rehearsals of the minimalist *Walk, She Said*. Thus, what is excluded by minimalist mandate from *Walk, She Said*— emotion and narrative—becomes the focus of the film we see. What is backstage comes on stage, while what should be on stage, by minimalist standards, is actually backstage, since it is only a rehearsal.[2]

Walk, She Said is an eminently minimalist-sounding title. *Walk* signals the commitment to ordinary movement on the part of minimalist choreographers, especially those associated with Judson Church and now called "postmodern." *Walk*, of course, could aptly describe a work like Steve Paxton's *Satisfyin' Lover*, where forty-two performers pace across the stage at their everyday cadence. Minimalist works like this were committed to discovering the essential conditions of dance as well as the minimal conditions of dance perception.[3]

Similarly, in the entire phrase—"Walk, she said"—the verb *walk* appears in the imperative mood, revealing the essential nature of choreography as a matter of instruction, of the type that Rainer herself exemplifies in the rehearsal footage in *Lives*. In this way, the expression "Walk, she said" is nothing short of a score for the most stripped-down, essential piece of minimalist choreography imaginable. Thus, the rehearsal footage in *Lives* represents art at its most abstract and pared down, setting up a contrast to what sits between its appearances—the seemingly messy, complicated lives of the performers, no longer depicted in their universal aspect as mere walkers—mere bodies in movement, neatly and sharply deployed in space—but fictional lovers with shifting psychological states, occupying an unstable inner space.[4]

If *Walk, She Said* stands as a specimen for the type of choreography that obsessed ambitious artists of the early 1970s, it also corresponds to the aesthetic inclinations of the filmmakers who dominated that moment in American avant-garde cinema called "structural film," represented most illustriously by Michael Snow, Hollis Frampton, and Ernie Gehr. Structural filmmakers—like the minimalist postmodern choreographers —attempted to pare down whatever seemed extraneous in their work in order to discover the nature of film. They sought to shrink their repertoire of devices to just those that would foreground the essential elements of the medium. If a film like *Wavelength*—a zoom shot, sometimes interrupted, of a loft—contained anecdotal or narrative material, it was there only in order to be parodied and, ultimately, to be bypassed in favor of the real star of the show: cinema as personified by the play of pure cinematic devices, such as the zoom shot, itself predicated upon engaging the audience in a rarefied act of apperception regarding the conditions of the cinematic experience.[5]

Moreover, if a structural film contained language, it was there not so much for what it said, but as another specimen for minimalist interrogation, dissection, and analysis. Just as the minimalist choreographer attempted to peel dance down to its core, so structuralist filmmakers used austere design to explore what made film film, narrative narrative, and language language. Thus the placement of *Walk, She Said* at the opening of *Lives* symbolizes the kind of aesthetic venture, the kind of film that Rainer "should" have been making, given the taste of the time, thereby setting up a studied contrast to the film to come—not only literally the film to come in the next seventy minutes or so, but the film to come in the larger sense of the kind of avant-garde film that would eventually displace structural filmmaking from the center of attention to a position nearer the periphery.

If, as the Russian formalists argued, art history is an affair of shifting dominants, then the movement from *Walk, She Said* to the lives of performers in this film prophesies a shift from the dominance of structural film, with its commitment to minimalist aesthetics, to a reengagement with life—the *Lives of Performers*—which, perforce, involves a return to narrative and emotion, subjects excluded from the minimalist program in favor of pure artistic, formal, and perceptual research.

Nevertheless, though *Lives of Performers* returns to the very human and impure topic of the passions—returning to well-known scenarios of courtship, fear of rejection, jealousy, betrayal, insensitivity, anger, reconciliation, and ambivalence—the film does not take up these issues oblivious to the ambitions of modernism.[6] For while aspiring to tell stories about the loves of performers, Rainer also, at the same time, wants to comment analytically on the nature of narrative—or, at least, certain aspects thereof—in this film.

One way to appreciate this is to recall how generic the narratives in the film are—or, rather, how they are made to appear generic. For example, there is, for the viewer, the recurring question of who the narrative is about, due to the frequent, uncertain, underdetermined juxtaposition of word and image. Is the text about this person or that person; this couple or that couple? Because of the ambiguity of the spoken and written references in the film, these questions force themselves on the viewer again and again. Moreover, the ambiguity of the spoken and written references in the film—vis-à-vis the ongoing narrative—serves to generalize the scenario: to suggest that this is the story of many people or that stories themselves are (very often) generic. That is, we lay them on the experiences of many different people—on many different characters—monotonously.[7]

In this way, generic narratives might be thought of as clichés, and, of course, we have been alerted to the importance of cliché to Rainer's

Valda Setterfield in Yvonne Rainer's *Lives of Performers*, 1972.
Courtesy of Anthology Film Archives.

conception of *Lives* by the opening quotation from Leo Bersani: "Cliché is, in a sense, the purest art of intelligibility; it tempts us with the possibility of enclosing life within beautifully inalterable formulas, of obscuring the arbitrary nature of imagination with an appearance of necessity." Through Bersani's quotation, that is, Rainer heralds her sense of the nature, function, and appeal of the generic narratives she is about to explore.[8]

Here it is also interesting to consider the use of the psychoanalyst Carl Jung in *Lives*. In a number of her films, Rainer employs what might be thought of as psychoanalytic reference points. In *Journeys from Berlin*, Jacques Lacan plays this role; in *MURDER and murder*, Joan Rivière. In *Lives*, the psychoanalytic reference point is Jung, whom Rainer mentions four times and quotes approvingly in the film, notably in the section in which still photographs of *Grand Union Dreams* are shown. But what is the relevance of Jung to *Lives*? I think it is this: Jung believed in the psychic existence of archetypal or stereotypical characters and narratives, templates according to which we make sense of life.

For Jung, epic narratives of the gods, such as those alluded to in the photographic montage of *Grand Union Dreams* in the early portion of *Lives*, are archetypal narratives of this sort. Thus, Rainer might be interpreted as using this Jungian narrative to register the point that many (most?) narratives, such as those to follow, have a stereotypical cast. That is, the voice-over narration of events in the personal lives of the performers, when juxtaposed against the mythic material from *Grand Union Dreams*, suggests that these personal tales are instances of mythic narratives.[9]

Though deployed to limn the experience of individuals, these myths are nevertheless generic. Thus, by sounding this refrain, Rainer remains enough of a committed modernist so that if she is going to tell stories, her modernist conscience also requires her to tell us something about the nature of such stories.

Perhaps the clearest example of generic narration in *Lives* is the trio among Shirley Soffer, John Erdman, and Valda Setterfield. Executed in a medium shot with the dancers facing the camera, it is accompanied by offscreen commentary, read by Setterfield, which begins: "You might describe it that way. It's also a story about a man who loves a woman and can't leave her when he falls in love with another woman." As Setterfield recounts the various affective permutations circulating this virtually archetypal love triangle, the three dancers reorient themselves toward and away from one another—sometimes lying down, sometimes hugging, sometimes somersaulting, but mostly just changing facings. Each change of facing is unavoidably read as a shift in affection, given the commentary.

Ironically, without the voice-over commentary, this dance would appear as a quintessential minimal dance, a piece of moving geometry, bereft of emotional qualities. But the accompanying narrative overlays a charge of passion. As the man turns away from one woman to the other, in the context of the voice-over, it is natural to interpret this as signaling an alienation of affection. However, the voice-over narrative makes it difficult to correlate precisely the women in the dance with the women in the text.

They are called No. 1 and No. 2, and if this is not abstract enough, it is hard to keep track of which one is which relative to the story. The spectator, especially on an initial viewing, cannot be sure that she has consistently mapped the spoken narrative onto the visuals. Which one of the dancers is No. 1 and which one is No. 2 is tauntingly ambiguous for the normal viewer.[10] Yet this, I submit, is not a mistake on Rainer's part, but a way to manipulate the viewer's experience of the dance in order to motivate the theme that this perennial tale of the love triangle is a generic narrative, one that might fit the plight of either of the women, and, by extension, others. It is, of course, a story that we have all told about ourselves or others—more than once—in our own lives.

One part of Rainer's reflexive investigation in *Lives*, then, emphasizes, as I have already indicated, the generic aspect of narratives. Another phenomenon that Rainer takes up for examination is the paradoxical effect of narrative, and perhaps particularly visual narrative, to possess an aura of finality—the "appearance of necessity," as Bersani says—despite the fact that narratives are made up of a contingent ensemble of events and reversible choices. Thus, in *Lives of Performers*, characters are often played by different actors,[11] and scenes are putatively rehearsed and played in alternative ways, though each instantiation of the written text appears absolutely authoritative visually. At one point, for instance, Setterfield seems to think aloud about how she should play a scene—one involving an entrance into a room already occupied by John Erdman and Shirley Soffer.[12] Then, what follows is nothing less than an elaborate inventory (including as many as ten variations) of how she might enter (or even not at all enter) the room.

This is an exercise in the subjunctive mood, an exploration of alternative, possible narrative worlds, pointedly reminding us that, though the modal status of narratives—perhaps particularly visual ones—feels like some kind of necessity, it is really, with respect to fictional constructs, nothing more than a matter of possibilities carefully staged and advanced from a repertoire of contingent choices.

Throughout *Lives*, we see emerging in Rainer's film work a preoccupation with theory, which will become one of her signatures as a cineaste. But even in its earliest appearance, we note that she is not a doctrinaire theorist, but rather one who tries to motivate and to make available to audiences theoretical insights through their experience of the film. The insights she has to offer about the nature of narrative in *Lives of Performers* are not dictated at the audience as they might have been in so many New Talkies; rather, they emerge from one's experience of the film.[13] For instance, Rainer's insight into the generic nature of narratives, despite the appearance of particularity that dominates individual narratives, emerges from the simultaneous ambiguity and tempting applicability of the narratives with which the viewer is confronted while trying to match the spoken text with the visuals. This, in conjunction with the allusions to Jung, should encourage the informed viewer, maieutically, to an appreciation of the putatively archetypal dimension of narrative structure.

Similarly, the play of necessity and possibility—of the indicative and the subjunctive—in the deep structure of the film is something that Rainer makes available to the audience through demonstration rather than protestation, committed as she has been not just to advancing theoretical points, but to making theorists—that is, to engendering the participation of audiences willing to reflect thoughtfully on the stories, images, and their reciprocal configuration as they encounter them in *Lives*. If Rainer succeeds in disclosing the apparent necessity of narratives as, in part, a function of their generic structures, she also deconstructs that appearance by underscoring that such narratives are really composed from a network of contingent possibilities, alternative artistic choices of the sort she exhibits.

With Rainer's concern with narrative comes an interest in the emotions, since the emotions are the most common engine for the production of action in our fondest stories of human affairs. That is, the emotions are the springs that make action happen, which, in turn, becomes the stuff of stories.

As is well known, Rainer has said that she moved from dance to film in order to pursue her interests in the emotions. But though this is a cliché of Yvonniana, Sally Banes has asked the good question of why Rainer had to embrace film in order to approach the emotions, since the dance of her immediate predecessors—the moderns, including, most notably Martha

Graham—made the emotions their privileged domain.[14] But as Banes points out, that sort of approach to the emotions—the modern-dance approach—was not available to Rainer, and not simply because of her avowed minimalism.

The modern-dance approach involved exhibiting, expressing, or projecting emotion—making it visible on the surface of the body in a way often predicated upon arousing emotions in the audience. Modern dancers sought to provoke emotion as they showed it forth bodily. Emotion from one body was designed to infect other bodies, igniting feeling in spectators.

Yet this approach was antithetical to Rainer's concern with emotion, which, paralleling her interests in narrative, focused on reflecting on the nature and structure of the emotions—on their stereotypical or archetypal scenarios—rather than on being caught up in their rhythms, swamped by affect and, in the worst case, wallowing in it. This is why, I hypothesize, Rainer moved from choreography to film, since film allowed her the opportunity to reflect on the emotions dispassionately. Whereas existing dance vocabularies tended to absorb audiences rather than to afford a space for reflection—indeed, since the presence of any emotional body in dance is apt to infect the audience affectively—Rainer moved from dance to film in order to secure a space for reflection, to distance the audience from emotive engulfment, setting emotion at a remove where spectators could observe the emotional states of characters as if under a microscope.[15]

It may sound strange to speak of film as a means for "anaesthetizing" emotions for the purpose of observation. So many genre films—from action and suspense films to horror and melodrama—are about activating emotions, not about scrutinizing them. But what Rainer saw as a filmic possibility was the option of dissecting emotional states, of dissolving them into their parts in a way that not only undercut their potential infectiousness but dismantled them for one to view their parts dispassionately and contemplatively.

What Rainer realized was the possibility of separating the parts of an emotion—of prying apart the inside and the outside—and redistributing said parts across the various visual and linguistic channels of cinematic articulation—intertitles, voice-over, and visual enactment, both photographic and cinematic. We often speak of channeling our emotions. In *Lives*, Rainer rechannels and redistributes the emotions of her characters across several informational tracks, separating the behavioral and the propositional dimensions of emotions so that one can reflect on

From Yvonne Rainer's *Lives of Performers*, 1972. Courtesy of Yvonne Rainer.

each dimension coolly, without being caught up in the holistic emotional undertow.[16]

The characters are often literally frozen, or, at least, frequently deadpan, as we hear or read of their inner turmoil. Their demeanor is not only a sort of realistic acknowledgment of the suppression of affect among modern middle-class professionals, but also a device to keep the audience on the outside looking in—rather like anatomists of affect.

Just as Brechtian acting techniques, including the third person deliveries of lines, alienate the actors from their characters, so the disembodied verbal affect distantiates the viewer, so that one can chart the repetitions, stereotypes, and generic structures in the emotional lives of the characters, including romantic syndromes of approach and avoidance, patterns of reconciliation, envy, betrayal, and anger.[17] Moreover, additional distantiating devices, including the low-key acting style, the ever-so-discreet frontal medium shots, and the foreswearing of emotionally aggressive close-ups,[18] decouple affect from gesture, thereby short-circuiting the likelihood of the bodily emotional infectiousness that is the hallmark of much modern dance and most popular film.

Nevertheless, if most of the film brackets or deemphasizes the bodily expression of emotion, concentrating on the mental or propositional content of the emotive states portrayed, the bodily realm is not forgotten. The film reinstates it, so to speak, in the coda, an enactment of a series of stills from the published scenario of G. W. Pabst's *Pandora's Box*, which sequence is nothing so much as a catalog of a range of stereotypical bodily manifestations of emotional states. By means of this protracted montage of photographic recreations (each pose is held for twenty seconds before it is relaxed), Rainer is able to set forth for reflection readily recognizable, recurring forms of emotive appearances, thereby continuing her meditation on the generic structure of the emotions at the same time that the film reunites emotive thinking with its natural habitat in the body.

Most of this coda is silent, and the stillness of the sequence—in terms of both movement and sound—along with the narrative decontextualization of the images invites the viewer to scrutinize these highly legible, in some cases conventionalized, expressions of emotion almost diagnostically. That is, appropriately defamiliarized, these poses become opportunities to contemplate the generic face of emotion.

At the same time, the relevance of this coda to the rest of the film is reflective, reminding us of the emotive upheaval that underlies the putative lives and loves of the performers who have engaged us for most of the film so far. At one point, a snatch of the Rolling Stones song "No Expectations" intervenes, about which B. Ruby Rich comments: "In a stagy replica of the 1928 melodrama, the four characters get to exhibit extremes of emotion never displayed in the preceding footage. Lest the viewer, however, thereby assume that the emotions themselves were not in evidence (albeit devoid of a matching acting style), Rainer slyly matches the last three minutes of the 'stills' to the Rolling Stones song . . . of yet another affair of the heart gone wrong."[19]

However, even if in the "Lulu" section Rainer finally grants the emotions some measure of bodily visibility (and audibility), both the "heat" of the acting style and the music are buffered by the configuration of cinematic strategies, so that the audience, instead of being affectively inflamed, stays at a meditative distance, clinically taking note of the generic emotive forms of fright, abandon, passion, amusement, and derangement. Thus, it is as if in the coda, Rainer returns to the home territory of modern dance—to the topic of the embodiment of emotion—but with a difference. For by presenting the intense expression of emotion, as abstracted from a silent expressionist film, in the medium of effectively still images, she has arrested their contagious powers, calling forth contemplation rather than empathy, kinetic or otherwise. Thus, in turning to film, Rainer discovered a way to acknowledge and address the life of the emotions, without being overwhelmed by it.

Filmography

Lives of Performers, 1972 (90 min.): sd., b&w; 16mm
Film about a Woman Who . . . , 1974 (105 min.): sd., b&w; 16mm
Kristina Talking Pictures, 1976 (90 min.): sd., col.; 16mm
Journeys from Berlin/1971, 1979 (125 min.): sd., col.; 16mm
The Man Who Envied Women, 1985 (125 min.): sd., col.; 16mm
Privilege, 1990 (103 min.): sd., col., b&w; 16mm
MURDER and murder, 1996 (113 min.): sd., col.; 16mm

Notes

The author expresses his gratitude to Yvonne Rainer and Sally Banes for their comments on an earlier version of this article. A version of this article was presented at a talk at the conference on the work of Yvonne Rainer, sponsored by the Humanities Institute of New York University, April 1999.

1   *Walk, She Said* was performed at the Whitney Museum on April 12, 1972, as part of a larger piece by Rainer titled *Performance.* Several other sections of *Lives of Performers* were also recycled from this material, including the "Lulu" coda.

2   Sally Banes, "Dance, Emotion, Film: The Case of Yvonne Rainer," talk at the symposium on the work of Yvonne Rainer sponsored by the Humanities Institute of New York University, April 1999.

3   Annette Michelson refers to this tendency as "autoanalytical" in her pioneering article "Yvonne Rainer, Part I," 58.

4   In her famous "NO manifesto," when Rainer said "no to moving and being moved," this referred, as Banes has shown, to being moved affectively and to moving the audience emotionally. Thus in *Lives*, Rainer is taking up the issue of emotion in dance that had been generally exiled during her more minimalist moments. See Banes, *Dancing Women*, 223.

5   In personal correspondence, Rainer has objected to my analogy between Snow's zoom shot and the Judson use of ordinary movement, like walking. She points out that whereas the zoom might be a unique feature of motion picture images, walking is not a unique feature of dance. We all walk even when we are not dancing. This disanalogy is well observed. It leads me to think that when we speak of minimalist essentialism, we need to keep in mind that there are at least two types. One type seeks after the basic features of an art form, which are unique to it. The other looks to fundamental features—building blocks, if you will, of the art form—whether or not they are unique to it. Snow's essentialism with respect to the zoom shot is an example of uniqueness essentialism; the Judson use of walking is more a matter of building-block essentialism—it strips

the choreography down to its most minimal or basic elements, but not in a way that marks it off as distinguishable from ordinary walking. It is a matter of getting down to essences, but not categorically distinct essences.

6   It may seem strange that I keep calling Rainer's project in the late 1960s and early 1970s "modernist," since she is associated with postmodern dance. However, postmodern dance was not postmodernist. It was a revolt against the modern dance and, in that sense, postmodern, but it essayed that revolt in the name of a reflexive interrogation of movement as such. Thus, though postmodern, it was also modernist in its ambitions, as was minimalism, despite Michael Fried's deprecations. Postmodern dance was minimalist dance and, for that reason, not postmodernist, as that concept was to evolve in the late seventies as a foil to minimalism. Admittedly these labels can be confusing, especially if one tries to use them as they were used in the relevant historical context. For further terminological clarification, see Banes, *Terpsichore in Sneakers*, xiv–xv.

7   As Peggy Phelan points out, *Lives* is concerned with "the most ubiquitous narrative of all, the love story" ("Yvonne Rainer," 13).

8   In her essay "A Likely Story," Rainer asks, "Can the presentation of sexual conflict or the presentation of love and jealousy be revitalized through a studied placement or dislocation of cliches borrowed from soap opera or melodrama?" Since *Lives* is subtitled "a melodrama," it is hard to resist reading this as a rhetorical question stating her intentions with respect to that film.

9   Phelan notes: "Rainer's attraction to emotional narrative also led her to conceive of her own life as a sort of 'mythic' source" ("Yvonne Rainer," 11).

10   In personal correspondence, Rainer has pointed out to me that the ambiguity of the enactment of this triangle is heightened in what immediately follows it. After the dance, there is a close-up of Shirley Soffer asking, "Which woman is the director most sympathetic to?" Then, also in a close-up, Valda Setterfield replies: "I think No. 1, maybe simply because she appears first." But this does not clarify anything, since neither woman appeared first in the image; the indeterminacy about which one is which therefore doggedly remains, perhaps even more uncomfortably than before. See Rainer, *Lives of Performers* (script), 67–68.

11   On the soundtrack, for example, Rainer says: "Did I mention that I'm going to be taking some of John's parts?"

12   Rainer, *Lives of Performers* (script), 72–73.

13   Though I have elsewhere argued that avant-garde artworks, including films, can rarely produce theories in any full-blooded sense of the terms, I nevertheless do refer to Rainer's interests in *Lives* as theoretical. I do so not only because filmmakers, as a matter of historical fact, often think of themselves as involved in theorizing, but also because I do not deny that filmmakers can illustrate (as opposed to proving) theoretical insights. In this way, they may be thought of as tutoring audiences—frequently, as in Rainer's case, maie-

utically. And though tutoring theory is very different than making theory, there is no compelling reason to refuse the label "theoretical" to the former—so long as we are aware of what we are doing. Moreover, it is in this sense that I would call *Lives* theoretical. For further discussion of this issue, see Carroll, "Avant-Garde Film and Film Theory" and "Avant-Garde Art and the Problem of Theory." Judith Mayne makes the interesting point that Rainer's filmmaking can also be considered theoretical in the sense that it constantly undermines or, at least questions, reigning film world theories dialectically. This is especially true, I think, of *Journeys from Berlin/1971* and *The Man Who Envied Women*, but less pertinent, I believe to *Lives*. See Mayne, "Theory Speak(s)." For a similar conception of *Journeys from Berlin/1971*, see Noël Carroll, "Interview with a Woman Who."

14   Banes, "Dance, Emotion, Film."

15   It is true that Rainer explored emotional material in live pieces such as *Grand Union Dreams, Performance*, and later the staged version of *Story about a Woman Who* . . . . But, I speculate, even treating emotional material on stage in her own distancing idiom, was not, from her point of view, as effective as rendering it on film. For as long as the human body remains present to the spectator, the potential for emotional response is highly likely. Film, on the other hand, can be used in such a way that the medium itself becomes an alienation technique in its own right (by decorporealizing, disembodying, and, thereby distancing the human presence of the performers from the audience).

16   For an account of the different components of emotional states, see Noël Carroll, *The Philosophy of Horror*, chap. 1.

17   Rainer makes clear her interest in the generic structures of the emotions in a letter to Nan Piene following a screening of *Lives of Performers*. She writes: "The more I get into it the more I see how such things as rage, terror, desire, conflict, et al., are not unique to my experience the way my body and its functioning are" (*Work, 1961–1973*, 238).

18   There are, of course, close-ups in *Lives*. But two things need to be said about them. Where there are close-ups of people's faces, they are not emotionally arresting, because, with the exception of the "Lulu coda," the performers' faces are generally impassive and, in addition, sometimes almost still. This makes it very hard to read their emotional significance. Thus, though close-ups of faces, they are not emotionally infectious ones. One of the only deviations from this norm that I remember occurs when Valda, slyly smiling in a medium close-up, turns away from Fernando after their discussion about her solo.

As well as close-ups of faces, the film also contains a wealth of close-ups of "detached," sometimes decontextualized, body parts—feet, midsections, and the like. Frequently this occurs while emotionally significant material is being read on the soundtrack. But these close-ups tend to decouple the affect of the words from the images. By fragmenting the human body in this way, Rainer depersonalizes it, rendering it anonymous and denuding it of its expressive powers.

When we see shots of the legs or shoulders of characters, these do not visually narrate the situation in a way that stimulates an affective response, even if such a response might be appropriate, given the accompanying text. Though these shots in some sense illustrate the story, not only do they fail to engage the viewer emotionally, they even block such reactions, disposing us toward calmly heeding the flatly delivered propositional content of the emotional states, rather than being revved up by their bodily manifestation.

19   Rich, "Yvonne Rainer," 6.

M. M. SERRA AND KATHRYN RAMEY

Eye/Body

The Cinematic Paintings of Carolee Schneemann

□

I'm still a painter and I will always be in essence a painter. . . . Painting doesn't have to mean that you're holding a brush in your hand. It might or it might not. It might be a camera. It might be a microphone. It might be your own body that when you go inside the frame and when you adjust your focus you see that the materiality of what you're working with might include yourself in a force field.—Carolee Schneemann

Pioneer artist Carolee Schneemann (b. 1939) works in a variety of media, including painting, kinetic theater, moving images, and installations. She was a founder of the Judson Dance Theater Group, a participant in early "happenings" in New York City, and as a filmmaker, the creator of *Fuses* (1964–67), *Viet-Flakes* (1964–66), *Plumb Line* (1968–72) and *Kitch's Last Meal* (1973–75). Before she completed her first film, Schneemann had incorporated 16mm film into her kinetic theater performances in an effort both to challenge the viewer's expectations of representation and to push the boundaries of the audience's perception of time, space, and movement. Throughout the mid- to late 1960s and the 1970s, a synergy existed between her painting constructions, kinetic theater, and projected films. In the intervening years, Schneemann has produced multimedia installations, performances, videos, and sculptural objects, and has continued to be an influential force within contemporary art. She has also been a prolific writer regarding her own work and working process.

To understand the significance of Schneemann's film work, this essay will explore her emergence as an artist through painting, sculpture, and kinetic theater and determine how film and video became an inevitable and necessary extension of these forms. Because of her extensive theoretical and critical insight into her artistic practice, this essay will use Schneemann's concept of the "eye/body"—the seeing, active artist agent—to interrogate the films and performances and to reflect her importance both as an avant-garde filmmaker and as a pioneering multimedia artist and author.

Schneemann works to disrupt aesthetic and cultural limitations between painting and its extended materials and to question acceptable gendered conventions. Painting is where she began her formal concentration on landscapes and drawing from life; even as a small child she was interested in representing time formulations in space. For instance, Schneemann remembers drawing sequential images of feet descending a staircase in an attempt to imagine what happens in the suspended motion between the steps.[1] Her early interest in kinetics, the visual representation of the temporality of motion, coupled with her youthful exposure to the corporeality of the human form through her father's at-home medical practice, shaped the foundations for some of Schneemann's most important contributions to artistic and filmic practice. As the art historian Kristine Stiles notes, Schneemann portrays those things observed by the eye through the eye/body, creating a physical counterpart for that which is actual, drawing "the observer's attention to the connection *between* actual things and conceptual representations *through* the material of the body."[2]

The term *eye/body* comes from one of Schneemann's photographic series, *Eye Body: 36 Transformative Actions for Camera* (1963), in which she integrated her naked body with snakes, fur, fragmented mirrors, and other objects in ritualized actions within her "painting constructions," in her fur district loft.[3] Schneemann turned a traditionally "passive, aestheticized" object in art—the female form—into an active artist as agent of her own making, breaking artist/subject and audience/object expectations. This use of her body signaled a change in her working process. Schneemann had moved from a cramped working space in Illinois to a large loft space in New York City, which liberated her to create dimensional painting constructions. Schneemann's participation in Claus Oldenburg's *Store Days* and other happenings in the early 1960s had also expanded for her "painterly arenas" in which the participants functioned as embodied material in action. Schneemann states: "I decided to be combined with my work as an additional 'material'—real, physical: to let my body be a further dimension of the tactile, plastic character of the constructions."

With *Eye Body* Schneemann incorporated her physical body into the form of her work for the first time, permeating the boundaries between artist and work, interior and exterior, and merging the inner eye of the artist/subject, the seeing eye of the artist/agent, and the eye of the viewer. As Rebecca Schneider points out, *Eye Body* suggests "embodied vision, a bodily eye—sighted eyes—artist's eyes—not only in the seer, but in the body of the seen."[4] Although "body art," or the inclusion of the self or self-image, has become iconic in contemporary art, in the 1960s, Schneemann encountered intense critical objection to the inclusion of her body in her work. Nevertheless, Schneemann's positioning of herself within the piece as medium and as an active seeing agent, as well as her insistence on emphasizing the body as a collage material, contributed to her groundbreaking work in kinetic theater.

Kinetic Theater: Performances and Happenings, 1964–1977

Schneemann credits her insight into gender politics with her "discovery," while still a student in 1959, of Simone de Beauvoir's *The Second Sex*. Living at the time in Vermont with musician James Tenney, she was isolated in her desire to influence the boundaries of gender roles among artists. However, once in New York, she recollects a "coming together of young dancers; almost all women: Yvonne Rainer, Deborah Hay, Trisha Brown, Elaine Summers, Lucinda Childs, Ruth Emerson, Judith Dunn. . . . We knew that no one was going to take over the meaning of the body and new forms of motion except us. It was protofeminist."[5] As the 1960s progressed, Schneemann initiated "Environment for Sound & Motion," kinetic theater presented at the Living Theater, choreographed for Rainer, Arlene Rothlein, Malcolm Goldstein, Andre Cadet, and others. Schneemann reflects about this time: "It is increasingly difficult to realize how presumptuous we were and the pressures of tradition. The roles of women were still rigidly fixed or fixated. An exceptional woman performer, beautiful and skilled, was acceptable. But a band of self-determined young women poised to challenge and change the only field in which a woman could singularly excel—that was a source of excitement, outrage, and shock."[6] Members of this group went on to become the Judson Dance Theater, with whom Schneemann began to make some of her most memorable and influential kinetic theater works.[7]

Meat Joy (1964), one of Schneemann's earliest and well-documented kinetic theater performances, was created by invitation from Jean-Jacques Lebel for the Festival of Free Expression held in May 1964 in Paris. In a letter to Lebel, Schneemann wrote that she worked with the Judson Dancers "for love of their non-dance movements and their aggressive, expansive interest in changing the very physical traditions which have given their bodies extraordinary scope and strength."[8] Schneemann drew her inspiration for *Meat Joy* from "dreams sensations images" recorded in journals as far back as 1960, conjuring a rapport with Antonin Artaud and the visceral quality of French butcher shops.[9]

In his manifestos, Artaud argues against the traditional training of actors, suggesting instead that they be trained "like dancers, athletes, mimes and singers." He wanted theater to revert to undiluted spectacle, and in *The Theater and Its Double* he states that "this quality of pure theater, this physics of the absolute gesture which is itself idea . . . this gives us a new idea of what properly belongs to the realm of forms and of manifested matter.' "[10] Schneemann responded to Artaud with *Meat Joy*. In *Meat Joy*, there are loosely identified couples and a serving maid in a starched apron who functions as a stage manager, entering among the performers with trays of props, including sausages, raw fish, chicken, plastic, and paint. Performers call out to the maid for cues, for shifts in the actions, often depending on her for their movement sequences. All of the cast members excepting the maid arrive in street clothing and other costumes, which they eventually strip off to reveal feather bikinis or, in the central woman's case, portrayed by Schneemann, a bikini of tiger fur. While *Meat Joy* was choreographed in terms of visual movements (diagonal, vertical, clustered, or broken apart) or sequenced in terms of the timing of certain events, it was essential to Schneemann that the participants, having rehearsed contact improvisation for several weeks, responded spontaneously to each other and to the introduction of objects around them as well as the score, the lights, and the audience. The score of *Meat Joy* contains prerecorded narration from texts formative to Schneemann's development of the work and vocalizations of her attempts to learn French. The sound track layers extracts of pop songs ("Blue Suede Shoes," "Tutti Frutti," "That's the Way Boys Are," and "I Like Bread and Butter"), interspersed with audio recordings of the calls of fish vendors made from Schneemann's hotel window on the rue de Seine.

Michael Benedikt asserts that Schneemann's use of the human form in *Meat Joy* is a profound extension of the principles of abstract expressionist gestural paintings. He writes: "Its basic idea is also one of Abstract Expressionism's: That, in the contest of a sufficiently active and gestural painting style, virtually any subject can serve to fill an essential abstract gesture or painting stroke with the necessary element of content. Schneemann's contribution to both a later phase of Abstract Expressionism and the Happening was to fulfill these gestures with an element that has seldom been treated as anything *but* abstract in both painting and theatre: the human form."[11] In *Meat Joy* the human form extends the dimensions of painting into active time, and the body is both the surface of the painting and the brush, the subject and the content, the artist and the art.

Schneemann's use of her naked form as both subject and author also confronts the established power dynamics ensconced within the artistic tradition of the time. Asked why she used her naked or nearly naked form in her performances and films, Schneemann replied, "In some sense I made a gift of my body to other women."[12] Schneemann's use of the explicit body could evoke violent responses from some male audience members in the mid-1960s. In her book *More Than Meat Joy*, Schneemann writes: "I was astounded when in the midst of *Meat Joy* [in Paris] a man came out of the audience and began to strangle me. Steeped in the writings of Wilhelm Reich I understood what had affected him but not how to break his hold on my neck!"[13]

As Schneemann suggests, Wilhelm Reich theorized that sexual repression could lead to explosive aggressive behavior. Further, in his treatise *The Mass Psychology of Fascism*, Reich asserts that institutionalized repression of natural sex impulses could lead to mass brutality, the destruction of nature, and even war. The idea that sexual repression could activate violent and aggressive behavior in individuals and society is a theme that has carried through much of Schneemann's work. In the video *Vesper's Stampede to My Holy Mouth* (1992) and the multichannel video projection *Devour* (2003–4), Schneemann juxtaposes fractured images of erotic pleasure with documentary fragments of bombings, shootings, and explosions.[14]

In the mid-1970s, despite the cultural and artistic impact of happenings, kinetic theater, and other "embodied" art work, Schneemann recognized that many of her contemporaries continued to perceive aesthetic representations in painting, plaster, or performances as "real" and thus reproduce the same repressive social moralities that exist in the day-to-day world. Schneemann states that her motives for using naked or nearly naked human forms in her performances were "to break into the taboos against the vitality of the naked body in movement, to eroticize my guilt-ridden culture, and further to confound this culture's sexual rigidities— that the life of the body is more *variously* expressive than a sex-negative society can admit."[15] Schneemann used the explicit body to expose cultural taboos. By being female, naked, and an artist she laid bare the relationship between the passive female form and artistic creativity as traditionally being one of passive object and active artist. Extending her concept of "eye/body," she became the active agent artist, using her naked body as medium while retaining creative control.

Although she had gained significant critical acclaim for her painting and performance work by the early 1960s, as always, Schneemann was not to be contained by medium or artistic practice. She began incorporating photography and film into her performances in the mid-1960s and was moved to create several stand-alone films. In her groundbreaking film work Schneemann further confronted her viewers' expectations regarding the creative act and the usually eroticized and objectified female body. The following section is a chronological examination of her evolving film and video work, which incorporates both the social and personal historical context in which the work was produced, as well as close readings of the films themselves.

The Celluloid Body: Schneemann's Film Work

Schneemann's development as a filmmaker began in the late 1950s in New York, where she met her future partner and collaborator, the musician James Tenney, while she was on leave from Bard College and attending the New School for Social Research and Columbia University. At this time, Schneemann met Stan Brakhage, Tenney's high school friend who was traveling east from Colorado. Schneemann describes an early meeting: "We were so broke, we shared one bowl of spaghetti on 42nd Street. We were each from provincial little towns far from the dynamics of NYC, where growing up our gifts had been regarded as a kind of unmanageable damage. Finding each other was miraculous. We fantasized that Stan was the future of film and poetry, I was the future of activated painting transformed as time, and Jim was the future of music conceived as spatial dynamics."[16] Although Brakhage was an important influence on Schneemann's acquisition of film as a part of her artistic arsenal, she states that film "somehow became inevitable," as photography had permeated the visual materials of artists throughout the early 1960s. She began using film as central to her performances and installations during this time.

Schneemann acknowledges the importance of her relationships with Brakhage and Tenney and insists on the artistic and social significance of their shared, aesthetic explorations. Schneemann recollects that Brakhage looked at her work with interest and engaged in conversations about aesthetic theory during the time when he was making psychodramas such as *Desistfilm* (1954) and *Reflections on Black* (1955). She states that she "was trying to convince him then that black and white and the surrealist tradition (in film) was a dead end." She suggested, "that he look at form, that he look at painting and that there were de Kooning and Pollock waiting in terms of dimensionality and the shift out of Cezanne's fracture of the plane." Within this close friendship, Schneemann, as Tenney's partner, was also expected to perform traditional female duties such as shopping, cooking, cleaning, and not dominating the conversation.

Since Schneemann did not own a camera, she often borrowed equipment from her male friends. She remembers that their attitude was ambivalent: "Yes, I want to help you . . . but don't bleed on my camera . . . Don't mess up the machinery." *Fuses* was inspired by Brakhage's *Window Water Baby Moving*, the 1963 film in which Stan filmed his wife, Jane, giving birth to their first child. Despite the courageous and gorgeous physicality of the film, Schneemann was distressed that Jane, who often held the camera, was never given credit as a cocreator. As Schneemann states, Jane Brakhage "was the muse and he [Stan] had always the visionary, structural authority over the work." In *Fuses*, she wanted to explore "the loving fuck preceding birth." In an interview with Scott MacDonald, she noted that *Fuses* was also "in part an answer to Brakhage's *Loving*," a 16mm color film that features Schneemann and Tenney. Ostensibly Brakhage made the film because of his enthrallment with their dynamic sexual and sensual relationship. But in Schneemann's words, "*Loving* failed to capture our central eroticism and [with *Fuses*] I wanted to set that right."[17] In *Loving*, Brakhage was the observer-voyeur, but in filming herself with Tenney, Schneemann returns to the "eye/body," which includes the eyes of the artist-as-subject, the eyes of the artist as filmmaker, and the gaze of the viewer.

Fuses (1964–1967)

Fuses was shot on a borrowed 30-second wind-up 16mm Bolex with short ends of film from other filmmakers' commercial jobs.[18] As Schneemann

From Carolee
Schneemann's
Fuses, 1964–67.
Courtesy of Carolee
Schneemann.

painted, etched, stamped, and dyed the surface of the heavily collaged film, it became a physically thick, textured film object. The difficulties that this film has faced since its creation, due to its explicit sexual content, began in postproduction. For example, when Schneemann mailed each 100-foot roll to the laboratory in Pittsburgh to be developed, she had to attach a letter from a psychiatrist stating "the enclosed material represents an archetypal study of the cross," because the FBI randomly searched film labs for pornographic material during this period. The difficulties only increased when the printer almost refused to print the film because of its physical density.

Filmed and edited from 1965 to 1967, *Fuses* is silent, its title suggesting both its combustible nature and also the form of the film. *Fuses* merges layers of imagery over painting, superimposing images of Schneemann and Tenney making love within changing seasons and in their domestic surround. Schneemann has written of the rationale behind the film's form:

> Paint is the power of extending what you see or feel, of intensifying the physicality of perception. I wanted the bodies to be turning into tactile sensations of flickers. For the viewer to be lost in the frame—to move the body in and out of its own frame, to move the eye in and out of the body so even as viewers could see everything desired, the perceptions would be in a state of dissolution, optically resembling some aspect of the erotic streaming in the bodies—which cannot be a literal translation. It is a painterly, tactile translation edited as a music of frames.[19]

Fuses explores Schneemann's erotic relationship with Tenney and their domestic space over a period of several years. The film was inspired by the shameless appreciations of their cat Kitch, who would watch their sensual activities and was a constant companion. Schneemann hung the hand-wound camera from a lamp or placed it on a chair or bed, and often the film frame and focus shift as the bodies, more preoccupied with their lovemaking than being filmed objects, merge and blur in and out of focus and frame. Schneemann welcomed the fluidity between the camera, the human and feline subjects, and the domestic space and incorporated the fortuitous randomness of the captured images within the formal structure of the film. In addition, in her exacting editing process Schneemann worked with archetypal female symbols inherent in the imagery, such as the open windows, the ocean, a hillside bush at dusk, cows, her cat, the close-focused vulva, and masculine symbols, such as the silo, Christmas trees, decorative balls, and the penis, both flaccid and erect. *Fuses* is remarkable for its intentional and formal editing of the spontaneously filmed images. First-time viewers often overlook the intricacy and delicacy of the film's formal structure because they are overwhelmed by the film's explicit content with its variety of (hetero)sexual practices, including fellatio, cunnilingus, and a range of positions of intercourse and expressions of orgasm. With this film in particular, multiple viewings are required to gain an appreciation for Schneemann's remarkable filmic/painterly construction.

Fuses is first and foremost an organic whole; even the titles are painted, scratched, and performative. The titles are in white printed over a variety of different colored backgrounds, superimposed over each other, with punch holes, scratches, and paint sometimes obliterating them altogether. Repeated in various fonts, they include a credit for James Tenney, as well as for Kitch the cat. The title sequence is followed by a splice mark and a vertical brush of black ink against a warm orange-red, unfocused image. The first sequence is a dense weaving of very close-up, warm-toned images of a nipple, a pulsing vagina, Kitch, and pubic hair, which cuts to blue-toned shots of Schneemann running on the beach in different directions, both toward and away from the camera. These images are intercut with vivid green trees shot through an open window, with a floral curtain blowing in the breeze, and cuts to interior shots of a silhouette of Kitch and then to images of Schneemann and Tenney coupling, with warm-toned flesh emerging from and receding into the darkness. Even in these first few minutes it is possible to see the complexity and intricacy of Schneemann's editing structure—what she describes as mathematical counts for each gesture duration—that alternate between warm- and cool-toned images, the exterior, natural space and the interior domestic space, the cat, the window, the ocean, the exterior of the home, and a huge variety of fragmentary images of erotic engagement.

Throughout the film, Schneemann captures Kitch gazing at the couple and out the window. Kitch is at once herself as well as representative of the gaze, the eyes of the filmmaker/editor, and the presence of the viewer/spectator. Kitch embodies not just the seeing eye, but also the internal eye of the artist paying homage to Schneemann and Tenney's loving relationship as they pass through the seasons in their domestic space. The first quick frame of fellatio is superimposed and inverted over a silhouette of trees and Kitch sitting in a window. This sequence is followed by frames of the cat on the window sill, intercut with sequences of the penis in the mouth, with the surface of the film speckled with paint. A densely painted superimposition of varying positions and body parts follows both in extreme close-up and in medium shots, some of which are well-lit and focused while others drift from focused to blurry.

The density of its construction, the fragmentary images of the naked body, and the egalitarian treatment of the lovemaking mark *Fuses* as significantly different from other representations of sexual acts, most notably, pornography. Pornography both then and now most often conforms to a strict narrative code with sustained full-body shots of the sex act culminating in one or more men ejaculating.[20] By showing multiple ejaculations and female orgasms layered, painted, scratched, and stamped, Schneemann frustrates any attempt by the viewer to read this film for conventional pornographic pleasure. What became a dilemma for many viewers often became apparent when she screened the work in progress for feedback from her fellow artists and filmmakers. There were some critical, defensive responses such as: "This is narcissistic exhibitionism. . . . When does he really get off? . . . Aren't you just showing off your body?" It was clear that in *Fuses*, Schneemann broke some powerful cultural taboos. As she later reflected in a 1993 videotape, *Imaging Her Erotics*, made with Maria Beatty:

WE WHO ARE
ADDRESSING THE TABOOS
BECOME THE TABOO.
THE SUPPRESSORS
ARE CONFUSED.
THEY CANNOT
DISTINGUISH IMAGES
FROM THE IMAGE
MAKERS.

By foregrounding herself as artist and image, Schneemann confounds cultural expectations about the sexualized female nude. One of the primary functions of a taboo in culture is to instantiate power relations. In *Fuses* Schneemann is an active agent of her own sexuality *and* the artist/visionary who creates and presents her own image. She not only broke cultural taboos about the representation of male and female sexuality but also challenged the tradition of the female nude in Western art as muse and passive object by being the active creative force behind the image. Schneemann, through her formulation of the eye/body, is the participatory eye of the subject returning the gaze of her lover, of the viewers, and of herself as artist/editor/creator.

One of the first public screenings of *Fuses* was at Cannes, in a sidebar called "Radical Films of 1969." Schneemann recalls standing in the back of the theater with Susan Sontag. At the end of the screening of *Fuses*, there was a great agitation in the front of the theater with men jumping up and down, howling, and slashing the seats with razors and knives. The police had to be called. Sontag surmised that male audience members responded so vociferously because the film did not fulfill their pornographic expectations with its visual fractures and its egalitarian representation of genitals and of orgasm. As in *Meat Joy*, *Fuses* activated visceral responses.

Viet-Flakes (1965)

Schneemann not only broke boundaries by integrating the naked body into her performances and films, she also used her aesthetic production to critique the social/political milieu in which she lived. Her 1967 kinetic theater performance *Snows* was in response to the United States military involvement in Vietnam. Although Vietnam became known as the first televised war, in the mid-1960s there were very few images of atrocities against Vietnamese civilians covered by the United States press. Schneemann gathered images and information from European and radical papers, which she then photographed and filmed to become projections in *Snows*.

The performance was technically innovative, using three 16mm projectors, five films, three audiotapes, a light machine, and a color organ, as well as stage and floor lights. Schneemann's technical description of the piece includes the following:

> *Snows* was realized with the assistance of technicians from Bell Telephone Laboratories, soon to become known as EAT—Experiments as Art and Technology. All of the electrical systems were controlled by the audience,

without their knowledge. A third of the seats were wired with contact microphones feeding into an SCR switching system to which all other motors were connected. Schneemann's cue sequence incorporated all the possible variations in their electrical equipment, which could be altered by the unconscious motions of the audience as they responded to the films, sound and performance activations.[21]

In other words, during the performance, the audience, unaware of their contribution, controlled the electronics, the slide projectors, and film projectors so that they could speed up or slow down the images depending on how they were responding to the graphic horror.

In a recent lecture at the Kitchen in New York, Schneemann was questioned about whether the use of this imagery in art making is an aestheticization of war. Making reference to the recent war in Iraq, she said, "we don't even see these pictures of graphic violence anymore. There is a removal from our culture of the effects of our technological power."[22] She discussed how most American media representatives during the war in Iraq have operated through the grace of the military and participated in their own censorship, noting as well that the U.S. military bombed the Baghdad hotel where the European press was staying, as well as the main Iraqi television station. As though predicting our society's increasing isolation and denial of culpability, at the end of *Snows*, the performers were wrapped in tin foil, covered in flour, blindfolded, and sent out to walk planks placed over the audience's seats.

In his book about the 1960s, *Allegories of Cinema*, David James acknowledges Schneemann's film *Viet-Flakes* as one of the earliest Vietnam War protest films. Schneemann began shooting footage for *Viet-Flakes* while producing *Snows*. Although *Viet-Flakes* is important for its staggering images, the inventiveness of its process is significant as well. She began shooting the stills with a film camera that she had borrowed from experimental filmmaker Ken Jacobs, but she soon realized that the camera did not have a close-up lens. Unable to wait to get another camera, she rushed to the store to purchase several magnifying lenses, which she taped to the camera lens. By moving the layered lenses as she was filming, Schneemann created a form of live animation. She describes that she "could present a degree of abstraction so that the photograph of the falling bombs looked like a Rembrandt drawing—out of focus—and then bring the literal referent into its disturbing focus: a thatched house in flames. So the discrepancy seemed appropriate to go from an aestheticized detail into its concrete monstrousness." The sound track, made in

From Carolee
Schneemann's
Viet-Flakes, 1965.
Courtesy of Carolee
Schneemann.

collaboration with Tenney, layered brief edits of fragments of 1960s popular music, Vietnamese chants, Bach, and orgasmic keening heard as a train shunted.

To a contemporary audience, many of the images of Vietnam from *Viet-Flakes* may seem disturbingly familiar: half-naked children running in front of tanks, figures on fire, and people being executed. The newspaper clippings are rephotographed, almost lovingly caressed by the camera, moving from an abstract pointillism into shocking focus. It is this process, coupled with the sound track of monks chanting, the wailing, and Bach fragments, that gives the impression of moving vertiginously back and forth from the quotidian to the ecstatic to the monstrous, as if in an effort to make sacred images of civilians and soldiers whose lives have been brutalized. In *Viet-Flakes*, Schneemann performs a filmic alchemy, ritualistically turning static paper and ink into streaming celluloid. As part of a broad-based response to the Republican National Convention in New York City in August of 2004, Chrissie Iles, curator at the Whitney Museum, along with the artist Sam Durant, programmed a collection of short films called *War! Protest in America, 1965–2004*. The inclusion of *Viet-Flakes*, singled out for its power by Roberta Smith of the *New York Times*, testifies to the enduring legacy and relevance of the film and the power of the artist to bear witness.

Plumb Line (1971)

In 1968, Schneemann was distraught over the endless involvement of the United States in Vietnam and left for Europe, where she began editing the second part of her autobiographical trilogy, *Plumb Line*. While *Fuses*, the first installment in this trilogy, had been an ecstatic exploration of her relationship with Tenney, *Plumb Line* explores the darker side of an obsessive love affair. Schneemann describes the film as "an exorcism of a relationship that went bad."[23] *Plumb Line* was shot in Super 8 and then step-printed at the London Filmmakers' Co-operative on an optical printer that Schneemann convinced a patron to donate. As with *Fuses*, *Plumb Line* is an intricate construction that can be analyzed in terms of five or six semidiscrete sections. The collaged sound track assembled by Schneemann often functions contrapuntally with the images and is of a complexity that Scott MacDonald argues is at least the equal of Peter Kubelka's *Unsere Afrikareise*. Whereas *Fuses* is concerned with exploring the physicality and domesticity of heterosexual love, *Plumb Line* investigates sexual politics and hypermasculinity. Schneemann states, "The plumb line stands for a phallic measure, a phallic exploration and determination of space."[24]

Schneemann's romantic partner in this film is a carpenter/artist. The film opens with a bronze plumb (a weight, often of lead, suspended on a line and used especially to determine a vertical direction or distance) in front of a projected image of the man's face, which seems to measure the "true" of the man or the romance with him. The film image seems to skip in the projector gate as the screen begins to burn behind the man's head. The image cuts to one of Schneemann looking out a window. A four-frame image of unsplit 8mm with the left side overexposed is then shown, and Schneemann writes the title *Plumb Line* in reddish brown, bloodlike paint on the screen on which the film is projected. As her hand sweeps over the title dripping with water, she writes her name and the date (1968). A red flare flashes as this title sequence ends. Throughout the film Schneemann emphasizes the use of the vertical, particularly through the repeated use of the split four-frame images, to reinforce a measure of "phallic space" and obsessive desires. However, by choosing a plumb line as a metaphor for the relationship, she is utilizing a tool of his trade, visually appropriating it for her own. Although this film explores the destructive potential of eros, ultimately it provides catharsis as Schneemann reconfigures the relationship through the mechanics of the lens and the split frames of optical printing.

The first section after the opening is a kaleidoscopic vision of interiors. Schneemann starts to reveal her relationship with a handsome, virile man. The sequence begins with textured paper tape at the head of the film roll, giving the impression that Schneemann is leaving in the rough edges, the artifacts or skin of the film itself. Early on there is a red vertical frame line that mirrors the plumb at the beginning and then four images/

From Carolee Schneemann's *Plumb Line*, 1968–71. Courtesy of Carolee Schneemann.

frames, as regular 8mm film is split and doubled within each 16mm frame. The right side mirrors the left in shots of interior space. This sequence is followed by double exposures: a close-up of a hand holding a teacup over a long shot of two windows from inside a room, with a man in silhouette in the distance in front of a window, and a close-up of the man's feet over a long shot of him sweeping the floor with a long-handled broom. The close-up changes to a bookshelf that is out of focus and then the man alone as the camera zooms in and out. The serenity of these interior shots functions as a prelude to the impending dissolution of the relationship. This first section ends in darkness and a hallway and what looks like a naked reflection in a mirror in a dark room. At first it appears to be a man, and then perhaps Schneemann herself. The figure moves closer to the camera just as the film becomes red, ending with a flare.

Four sections follow. The first occurs in Venice, with a seemingly autonomous Schneemann examining exterior space, the people in it, and their relationship to the space, light, and beings that surround them. The second section features several shots of a solitary cat poised within the busy and crowded Piazza San Marco. In section 3, the camera scrutinizes the man, showing him driving, kissing Schneemann, and running naked in the ocean. It reveals a close-up of his genitalia, as well as scenes in

London and an increasing sense of tension between the two people. In section 4, the relationship dissolves as sound is suddenly introduced, providing aural evidence of Schneemann's psychic fracture, as transcribed from the film.

> "I can't stand the sun . . . they've been giving me a lot of pills . . . some of the pills they put me to sleep . . . for 4 or 5 hours . . . they took me to eat and when I came back . . . they put all these little bits . . . of things on my plate . . . that look like hideous sculptures . . . and had nothing at all to do with food . . . I found out I lost six pounds overnight . . . one of them was a brown folded over piece of . . . dough and inside of one was four pieces of asparagus . . . and inside another was a piece of . . . sausage . . . with something on it . . . brown . . . combining it with the pancake . . . It might have been cheese . . . and inside another was something that I couldn't recognize . . . like a mushroom that had rotted . . . or a piece of a heart that had been left in the sun . . . and had become speckled . . . and they said "please eat some of it . . . it will make you strong."
>
> [The woman moans, sounds of a cat crying, and sirens.]

Schneemann states that "this quoted text from *Plumb Line* was made by me flipping on a tape recorder as I wandered through my studio in a state of emotional collapse triggered by the endless Vietnam atrocities and the dissolution of my long relationship with Tenney." This emotional outpouring is as confrontational as Schneemann's physical nakedness in her earlier work. Schneemann takes viewers through the very eye of her sorrow and asks them to engage with her pain. This section provides a catharsis that allows Schneemann in section 5 to edit a ritualistic reworking of the earlier footage. Schneemann reclaims her sanity as a woman and as a filmmaker. By burning, step-printing, multiplying, and fragmenting, Schneemann exorcises psychic chaos and transforms it into a work of art. As the second film in her autobiographical trilogy, *Plumb Line*, in contrast to the lyrical eroticism and sexual equity of *Fuses*, explores the emotional pain of unequal power relations. By submitting the film documentation of this experience to the physical manipulation of her optical printing and postproduction process, Schneemann transforms her intimately emotional and personal experiences.

Kitch's Last Meal (1973–1978)

Schneemann returned to New York from England with filmmaker Anthony McCall as the Vietnam War drew to a close and began work on

From Carolee
Schneemann's
Kitch's Last Meal,
1973–78. Courtesy
of Carolee
Schneemann.

Kitch's Last Meal, a double screen, Super 8 film with sound on cassette (with screenings ranging in length from two to five hours). The final film in Schneemann's autobiographical trilogy, *Kitch's Last Meal* is based ostensibly on her cat, Kitch, her constant and most valued traveling companion for over nineteen years. Kitch is featured looking on while she and Tenney are making love in *Fuses.* Schneemann says that with *Kitch's Last Meal* she wanted to make a film about the intimacy of daily life, but when she looked at her early reels she thought they were too diaristic and programmatic. So she decided to make the film a double-screen projection, with two images projected simultaneously. The editing of this film then became extremely complex as she worked between two reels, never seeing them simultaneously, to create a dynamic tension between their images and structure.

The sound in *Kitch's Last Meal* is striking for its insistence on the normalcy of the day-to-day life of a cat living and dying in an artist's home. Schneemann records the ordinary sounds of the domestic and creative space, the conversations between her and her lover (McCall), the refrigerator door closing, a dish dropping into the sink, and the sound of the train moving along the tracks behind her farmhouse. Over this aural tapestry, she can also be heard reading her own writing about the position of woman in the white, male-dominated Western art world. A text that was later featured in her performance *Interior Scroll 2* describes how her work is received by the experimental film community and responds to the critique of her work by structuralist filmmakers (reproduced here on the facing page).

Kitch's Last Meal has received little critical attention for two reasons, the first of which is that it has remained on Super 8 with sound on cassette as a double-screen projection, which makes it difficult to show. The second reason for its obscurity, perhaps more pernicious, is a legacy that Schneemann has fought throughout her life. It is a film about things that were despised and disregarded by the filmmakers and critics who were her peers in the 1970s. It is about the fragility of life, the tenderness of intimacy, and the sorrow of loss. As such, it fell outside of and protested against the aesthetic and conceptual categories of the cannon of experimental film at that time.

In 1977 Schneemann was invited by Stan Brakhage to introduce a program of erotic films by women at the Telluride Film Festival, in which her films *Fuses* and *Plumb Line* were featured. After her arrival in Colorado, she discovered that the program was titled "The Erotic Woman" and the festival brochure cover depicted a naked male flasher opening his raincoat to reveal no genitals, but a text written on his chest "Fourth Telluride Film Festival." She was outraged that various films by women should be presented as standing for "the erotic woman" or defining what is erotic for all women. She staged an "action" as her introduction where she read the text from *Kitch's Last Meal* from a scroll that she pulled from her vagina as she stood painted with Telluride mud atop a small Victorian stage.[25]

This performance was a recreation of her 1975 *Interior Scroll*, which was enacted at the *Women Here and Now* conference in East Hampton, and in which the scroll text was a passage from her book *Cézanne, She Was a Great Painter*. Whereas the first event was within the context of painting exhibits and performances, her Telluride action was an outraged protest at the ways in which explicit films made by women continued to be pigeonholed and reduced to "erotic films" to be consumed by men. It is important to note that the "structuralist filmmaker" referred to in the

[Text from Schneemann's performance *Interior Scroll 2*]

I met a happy man
a structuralist filmmaker
—but don't call me that
it's something else I do—
you are charming
but don't ask us
to look at your films
we cannot
there are certain films
we cannot look at
the personal clutter
the persistence of feelings
the hand-touch sensibility
the diaristic indulgence
the painterly mess
the dense gestalt
the primitive techniques
(I don't take the advice of men
who only talk to themselves)
even if you are older than I
you are a monster I spawned
you have slithered out
of the excesses and vitality of
the sixties . . .

he said you can do as I do
take one clear process
follow its strictest
implications intellectually
establish a system of
permutations establish
their visual set . . .
I said my film is concerned
with DIET AND
DIGESTION
very well he said then
why the train?
the train is DEATH as there
is
die in diet and di in
digestion
then you are back to metaphors
and meanings
my work has no meaning
beyond
the logic of its systems
I have done away with
emotion intuition
inspiration—
those aggrandized habits
which set artists apart from
ordinary people—those
unclear tendencies which
are inflicted upon viewers
. . .

it's true I said when I watch
your films my mind wanders
freely. . . . .
during the half hour of pulsing dots I
compose letters
dream of my lover
write a grocery list
rummage in the trunk
for a missing sweater
plan the drainage of pipes for
the root cellar. . . . .
it is pleasant not to be
manipulated
he protested
you are unable to appreciate
the system the grid
the numerical rational
procedures—
the Pythagorean cues—
I saw my failings were worthy of
dismissal I'd be buried
alive my works lost . . .
he said we can be friends
equally though we are not artists
equally I said we cannot
be friends equally and we
cannot be artists equally
he told me he had lived with
a "sculptress" I asked does
that make me a "film-makeress"?
"Oh no," he said, "We think of you
as a dancer."

monologue is not McCall, Schneemann's partner from 1971 through 1976, as many people assumed, but a veiled reference to critic and film scholar Annette Michelson, who, according to Schneemann, could not look at her films. As Schneemann said in an interview with Scott MacDonald in 1988, "It's a double invention and transmutation: it's not to a man but to a woman [disguised in a male pronoun]. The projected quotes are from her students."[26] In other words, as David Levi Strauss queries when discussing the continued absence of women artists like Schneemann in the canon of art history: "Is the suppression, exclusion, and neglect of women artists with radical social imaginations somehow built into the notion of 'art history' " and by extension film history and criticism?"[27] If historians and critics cannot look at the work and cannot explain it to their students, it will continue to remain outside film and art history.

The 1980s to the Present: Videos, Installations, Writing

Kitch's Last Meal is the last celluloid film Schneemann made. It also signaled in many ways her move away from the experimental and avant-garde film community as a venue for her work and a move toward more extensive writing projects and site-specific installation and performance work. In the 1970s and 1980s, Schneemann contributed some of the most important multimedia performances of the time. She continued to foreground the body of the artist as medium and further developed her elaborate lexicon of feminist symbols and histories. At the same time, she began using video to create work for or about her various performances and installations.

In 1992, in collaboration with Victoria Vesna, Schneemann created the video *Vesper's Stampede to My Holy Mouth*, examining the historical parallels between the torture and maiming of cats and women through witchcraft trials, genital mutilation, and the destruction of goddess religion. Schneemann's love and respect for cats, stemming perhaps from one of her first memories of a cat staring into her cradle, continued to inspire her work. In the early 1980s, she created a furor with her photo collage *Infinity Kisses*, which featured 140 self-shot prints of Schneemann being kissed by her cat, Cluny. Cluny died in 1988, but Schneemann claims that he was reborn in Vesper, with whom she had a similarly ardent physical relationship.[28] In *Vesper's Stampede to My*

Holy Mouth, Schneemann discusses the then-current war in Lebanon and the destruction of historic goddess sites. She connects the gratuitous violence being done to the Lebanese and Palestinian people and the annihilation of the archeological sites in the region—which are a source of human history and sacral worship—with the misogyny of centuries of censorship of women's voices, the abuse of their bodies, and the androcentrism that allows the abuse and enslavement of men, women, children, and animals.

In the 1990s Schneemann produced several installations that continued to explore the body, some from the perspective of its dissolution. In *Mortal Coils* (1995), she responds to the deaths of seventeen of her friends in the previous three years. While the installation is a tribute to these dead friends it is also a response to Schneemann's perception that our culture has lost the significant rituals that helped to deal with death. Expressions of grief are seen as irrational, and there is no place for the very physical manifestations of loss to find release. In *Mortal Coils* Schneemann creates a projection system of transparent images moving across space through a system of four slide projectors on dissolve units with motorized mirrors. This kinetic installation includes seventeen motorized manila ropes suspended and revolving from ceiling units and walls covered with enlarged "In Memoriam" text. *Mortal Coils* creates a space that is at once a place to surrender to memory and a space in which one's grief can be confirmed. In *Plague Column* (1995) she explores issues of health and illness through images of mutating microscopic cells within a cluster of video monitors, surrounded by walls that are covered in photographic prints of enlarged colorized cells.

During a 2003 lecture at the Kitchen, a woman in the audience asked Schneemann about the difference between her use of her body in the 1960s and in her current work. She responded that in the cultural climate of the 1960s, "the body was in flux, transposition, every issue had to engage the body. But currently the body no longer belongs to the adventures, the risks that my imagery entered." Schneemann avers that the body in art since the 1970s has been commodified, and she compares it to the occupation of New York City by big business, saying, "the body in 'Performance Art' has become centered in cultural ambitions, novelistic narratives, self-display, confessionals."[29] It is not that Schneemann has stopped using her body "as a source of knowledge" or inspiration or medium, but that popular culture has commodified the ways in which the body can be used to transgress boundaries that surround and constrain

Carolee Schneemann. Courtesy of Anthology Film Archives.
Photo: Joan Barker.

art making and social practice. In her most recent work, *Devour* (2003–4), Schneemann returns to double-screen projection, albeit in video, juxtaposing images of "political disaster, domestic intimacy and ambiguous menace" as gestures "both human and mechanical."[30] Now in 2005, with the explicit torture images of Abu Ghraib, the pleasured nude body is further constrained by trauma and shame.

As Schneemann has changed the ways in which she uses her body in her art, the meanings she makes from and through it have evolved. Her life-long endeavor has been to reinscribe the human on the body and to insist that her artistic vision come through her physical experience. Carolee Schneemann persistently enacts the "eye/body," the seeing, active artist agent and continues to make work that challenges convention and expands our understanding of what painting, performance, and film are or can be.

Filmography

Meat Joy, 1964/1991 (6 min.): sd., col.; video (edited by Bob Giorgio and
  Carolee Schneemann from original film footage of 1964 NYC
  performance, filmed by Pierre Dominique Gaisseau, re-edited for video in
  1991)
Viet-Flakes, 1965 (11 min.): sd., col.; 16mm
Fuses, 1964–67 (22 min.): sd., col.; 16mm
Plumb Line, 1968–71 (18 min.): sd., col.; 16mm
Kitch's Last Meal, 1973–78 (variable units 20 min.—4 hrs.): sd., col.; Super
  8, sound on audio cassette
Up to and Including Her Limits, 1974–77 (60 min.): sd., b&w; video
Interior Scroll (withheld from circulation by the videographer Dorothy
  Beskind), 1975 (40 min.): sd., b&w; video
Up to and Including Her Limits, (1973–76) 1984 (25 min.): sd., col.; video
Vesper's Stampede to My Holy Mouth, 1992 (15 min.): sd., col.; video
Imaging Her Erotics (video interview by Maria Beatty in collaboration with
  Carolee Schneemann), 1993 (5 min.): sd., col.; video
Interior Scroll—The Cave, 1993–95 (12 min.): sd., col.; video
Known/Unknown—Plague Column 1996 (videoloop): sd., col.; video
Vespers Pool, 1999 (8 min.): sd., col.; video
Devour, 2003–2004 (8 min.): sd., col.; DVD

Notes

1 Unless otherwise noted, all quotations in reference to Schneemann's personal or aesthetic history are drawn from a personal interview with the authors
in 2003.

2 Stiles, "The Painter as an Instrument of Real Time," 9, emphasis in original.

3 Schneemann, *Imaging Her Erotics,* 56.

4 Schneider, *The Explicit Body in Performance,* 35.

5 Juhasz, *Women of Vision,* 87.

6 Correspondence with Schneemann, August 23, 2005.

7 Schneemann, *More Than Meat Joy,* 32.

8 Ibid., 62.

9 Benedikt, *Theatre Experiment,* 357.

10 Artaud, "The Theater and Its Double," 222.

11 Benedikt, *Theater Experiment,* 355.

12 Schneemann, *More Than Meat Joy,* 194.

13 Ibid. See Reich, *The Mass Psychology of Fascism.*

14   Correspondence with Schneemann, August 23, 2005.

15   Schneemann, *More Than Meat Joy,* 194.

16   Correspondence with Schneemann, August 23, 2005, to elaborate the memory first described in 2003 interview.

17   MacDonald, *A Critical Cinema,* 142.

18   Because Schneemann screened her projects at festivals and other venues and then continued to work on them, her films are often listed with a variety of production dates or a span of years. In accordance with the artist's wishes, we have listed the films as they are dated on the filmmaker's biography on her web site, www.caroleeschneemann.com/bio.html.

19   Haug, "Interview with Kate Haug," 43.

20   For further research on a feminist interpretation of pornography as a film genre, see Williams, *Hard Core.*

21   Correspondence with Schneemann, August 23, 2005.

22   Schneemann, "Disruptive Consciousness," video.

23   MacDonald, "An Interview with Carolee Schneemann," 10.

24   MacDonald, "Carolee Schneemann's Autobiographical Trilogy," 29, 31.

25   Schneemann, *Imaging Her Erotics,* 154–55.

26   MacDonald, *A Critical Cinema,* 143.

27   Levi Strauss, "Love Rides Aristotle through the Audience," 320.

28   Schneemann, *Imaging Her Erotics,* 264.

29   Schneemann, "Disruptive Consciousness," video.

30   Schneemann, "Press Release for *Devour.*"

ARA OSTERWEIL

"Absently Enchanted"

The Apocryphal, Ecstatic Cinema of Barbara Rubin

◻

We're in the months of love; I'm seventeen years old. The time of hopes and dreams, as they say—and here I am, getting started—a child touched by the finger of the Muse—excuse me if that's trite—to express my fine beliefs, my yearnings, my feelings, all those things poets know—myself, I call them spring things.—Arthur Rimbaud to Théodore de Banville, Charleville, May 1870

Unlike most female experimental filmmakers discussed in this anthology, Barbara Rubin (1946–80) was neither a skilled practitioner nor a prolific director. While Rubin was frequently seen wielding a camera at some of the most outrageous media events and happenings of the sixties, there was often no film in her camera.[1] On the occasions when her camera was fully loaded, much of the noncanonical footage that has been attributed to Rubin appears strikingly amateurish.[2] More a woman with a movie camera than a committed documentarian, Rubin nevertheless transformed the role of the camera from its most obvious function as a recording apparatus to a literal agit-prop with which to provoke her audiences. Challenging the presumed distinction between performer and observer, as well as the privileging of the products of filmmaking above the process of manipulating a camera as a corporeal extension, Rubin revised what it meant to be an experimental filmmaker in the 1960s.

Although Rubin conceived of many ambitious film projects, she only

Barbara Rubin in Andy Warhol's *Screentest*, 1965. Courtesy of the Andy Warhol Museum.

completed two films.[3] *Christmas on Earth*, made by the seventeen-year-old novice in 1963 with a 16mm Bolex borrowed from Jonas Mekas, is one of the most sexually explicit, beautifully hallucinatory films to emerge from the 1960s. *Emunah* (codirected by Pamela Mayo, 1972), which Rubin completed after her conversion to Hasidism, juxtaposes footage of Allen Ginsberg with Hebrew text and photographs of concentration camps.[4] Conceptually, *Emunah* implies reconciliation between Rubin's two seemingly incompatible worlds—the New York Underground art scene and the Hasidism toward which she later turned. Unfortunately, *Emunah* lacks the inspiration of her earlier work and fails to deliver more than a nebulous glimpse of the appeal Judaism held for Rubin.[5] Rather than illuminating the mysterious link between the corporeal materialism of *Christmas on Earth* and the spirituality of Rubin's religious quest, *Emunah* projects the filmmaker's sentimental longing onto the figure of Ginsberg, who is seen reading kaddish at the Royal Albert Hall in London and lingering at the gravestone of William Blake.

Had Barbara Rubin never picked up a camera, or appeared in front of one, her contributions to the art, music, and literary countercultures of the time would have still been considerable. Although her pose on the back cover of Dylan's album *Bringing It All Back Home*, where she is seen massaging Dylan's curls, suggests a certain passivity, Rubin was anything but an onlooker.[6] On the contrary, Rubin's multiple roles as an organizer, agitator, and innovator in the artistic and musical milieus of her time had profound and lasting effects on the cultural developments that have increasingly become associated with the 1960s. Initially through her friendships with Jonas Mekas and Ginsberg, and then through her own determination, Rubin infiltrated the Underground scene, serving as a catalyst

Barbara Rubin in Jonas Mekas's
Walden, 1964–69. Courtesy of
Anthology Film
Archives.

for the interaction between individuals whom she regarded as the best
minds of her generation. Although Andy Warhol's biographer Victor
Bockris characterizes Rubin as a "squirrel extraordinaire,"[7] she was, in
fact, much more than a local emissary, although she frequently delivered
musical celebrities like Donovan, Dylan, and the Byrds to Warhol's Factory. Jonas Mekas's poignant film *Scenes from the Life of Andy Warhol*
(1982) briefly captures Rubin's collaborative spirit in action. Following
footage of Rubin conversing at a café table with Ginsberg, Peter Orlovsky,
and other Beats while the pyrotechnics of the Exploding Plastic Inevitable flicker in the background, an intertitle asserts, "We were all there
because of Barbara."[8]

In this essay, I investigate the trope of the masquerade as it relates to the
astonishing sexual representations in *Christmas on Earth* as well as to Bar-

bara Rubin's life and career beyond the film. By situating Rubin's work in the milieu of the early avant-garde film community of the 1960s, the changing legal and artistic landscape of sexual representation, and Rubin's own tumultuous biography, this essay aims to articulate the historical conditions that made Rubin's filmmaking career both possible and theoretically problematic. Through a brief comparison of Rubin's "sexperimental" cinema with films by the other female experimental filmmakers Carolee Schneemann and Yoko Ono, this essay establishes the ways in which *Christmas on Earth* simultaneously intersects with and departs from the work of Rubin's female contemporaries. Although this analysis inevitably privileges *Christmas on Earth* over Rubin's other, mostly uncompleted film projects, it also takes into account Rubin's more "apocryphal" work, including her activities as an Underground film organizer. Finally, by demystifying the circumstances of Rubin's biography, this essay interrogates the presumed rupture separating Rubin's early ventures as a filmmaker and her eventual renunciation of experimental cinema.

While Rubin's obscurity can be partially attributed to the unusual circumstances of her biography, the overwhelming absence of critical attention reveals the extent to which Rubin's only known finished film challenges dominant preconceptions about the limits of sexual representation in this period. While the sexually transgressive work of contemporaneous avant-garde filmmakers such as Warhol, Jack Smith, and Kenneth Anger has been salvaged in the post-Stonewall era of queer identity politics, Rubin's work remains decidedly unclassifiable. More sexually explicit than either *Flaming Creatures* (Jack Smith, 1963) or *Scorpio Rising* (Kenneth Anger, 1963), both of which were charged with obscenity, *Christmas on Earth* neither suffered nor benefited from the notoriety associated with these films.[9] Furthermore, despite Rubin's status as a female experimental filmmaker, *Christmas on Earth* is not a characteristically "feminist" film, although its orgiastic beauty focuses on the myriad erotic possibilities of the body. Like many female experimental filmmakers of her generation, Rubin never identified herself as a feminist. Like the term *queer*, which has been belatedly affixed to the homoerotic films of Warhol, Smith, and Anger, the notion of a consciously feminist avant-garde did not hold currency until the late 1970s (and was still not always welcomed by female filmmakers) and would thus be anachronistic to apply here. Nevertheless, the quixotic trajectory of Rubin's career reveals both artistic and personal struggles that were doubtlessly influenced by the fact of Rubin's gender in a male-dominated social and cultural milieu.

Like many of the artistic legends from the 1960s, Rubin died young, at age 35, leaving a myriad of counterfactual questions for subsequent generations to ponder. Constantly reinventing herself, Rubin was less the proverbial chameleon, which alters its hue in order to assimilate to its environment, than a caterpillar in a constant state of flux and becoming.[10] Like many of the artists of her generation—including both Dylan and Ginsberg, whose own (temporary) returns to Judaism were reputedly inspired by Rubin's growing interest in religion—Rubin underwent a quest for spiritual meaning that involved dramatic revelations and recantations. However, unlike many of these artists who underwent publicly acknowledged religious phases, Rubin remained committed to Judaism. From the time of her discovery of Hasidism in the late 1960s, to her death in 1980, Rubin never returned to the ethos of drug experimentation and free love that she previously epitomized. After Rubin severed nearly all of her ties to the New York avant-garde community and moved to a religious community in France in the early 1970s, the threads that tied her so closely to the cultural developments of the 1960s tapered off and eventually disappeared.

In hindsight, Rubin's endless mutability seems nothing less than the quintessence of the 1960s. Donning a turban over her shaved head, draped in flowing rags, and aglitter with bangles, Rubin looked hippie before it was acceptable, or even recognizable to do so. Although her persona hinged upon the appearance of spontaneity, Rubin had an uncanny way of stumbling onto the defining scenes of her generation. Undoubtedly, many of Rubin's debuts were more than accidental (she was known to consciously seek out celebrity); others seem more serendipitous. According to Rosebud Pettet, who hitchhiked around the country with Rubin in the early 1960s, the two teenaged girls "just happened" to arrive in Berkeley in 1964 at the height of the free speech movement. While Berkeley students rallied en masse to Mario Savio's rhetoric, Rubin recognized an opportunity to exercise her own personal freedom. In the midst of one of the most incendiary student rebellions in history, Rubin bought a razor at the local drugstore, chopped off all of her hair in the middle of Sproul Plaza, and threw the strands of it into the crowd in a gesture of defiance. Despite the appearance of being absolutely kindred with the counterculture zeitgeist, Rubin was simultaneously ahead of and behind her time. Although she pioneered multimedia, multiple-projection extravaganzas decades before this became the norm in installation art, her nostalgia and longing for the immigrant Yiddish culture of her ancestors drew her deeper and deeper into the religious traditions of the past.

A middle-class Jewish girl from Queens, Rubin came to the Underground film community in New York as a teenager. Unlike the average teenager, however, Rubin had just been released from a juvenile correction facility for her vast experimentation with drugs that had begun, paradoxically, after swallowing a handful of the diet pills with which she had been instructed to manage her weight.[11] Through her uncle, William Rubin, who then managed the Gramercy Arts Theater where many avant-garde film screenings were held, Barbara was introduced to Jonas Mekas, by far the most important advocate of Underground cinema as well as the founder of the Film-Makers' Cooperative and, later, the Anthology Film Archives. At the request of her uncle, who was attempting to find a creative outlet for some of Barbara's more irreverent behavior, Mekas hired Barbara to assist at the Coop. In 1963, Rubin borrowed Mekas's 16mm Bolex camera and over the course of three days filmed *Christmas on Earth*, the "most sexually explicit film to startle the preporn avant-garde."[12] Originally called Cocks and Cunts before being retitled after a phrase from Arthur Rimbaud's epic poem "A Season in Hell," *Christmas on Earth* consisted of two black-and-white thirty-minute reels, which Rubin customarily projected simultaneously, one inside the other. With the placement of various color filters on the projector lens, and the addition of an ad-hoc sound track culled from any available radio, the already densely layered *Christmas on Earth* became a multimedia performance evocative of multiple meanings and mutating effects.[13] The rich, resplendent textures of *Christmas on Earth* approximate the blinking, magical lights of the holiday to which the film's title refers. Nevertheless, the affinities between the traditional family celebration and Rubin's quite libidinous version of the fantasy plenitude of Christmas end with the kaleidoscopic display of colored lights.

According to playwright Richard Foreman, who, along with his then-wife Amy Taubin, was an intimate friend and early supporter of Rubin, *Christmas on Earth* was originally shown unedited. Originally featuring long, "poignant" takes of lovemaking between painted and costumed Underground stars Gerard Malanga and Naomi Levine as they fornicated in nearly every position imaginable, *Christmas on Earth* was continually reedited for each performance. Foreman maintains that it was Rubin's exposure to the rapid montage of Gregory Markopoulos's films that inspired her to slice the original into dynamic fragments that, from his perspective, enhanced the kaleidoscopic effect of the film while diminishing its emotional affect. Although critics praised the reedited film for its virtuoso, seemingly deliberate juxtapositions, Rosebud maintains that Rubin, bare-breasted and high on amphetamines, actually randomly parsed the film, dumped the fragments into a wastebasket, and mindlessly reconstructed it. Indeed, Rubin's euphoric description of her method of production seems to verify Rosebud's account:

A week out of nine months of mental hospital indoctrination and I meet Jonas and he gives me a camera and film love and trust and I shoot up down around back over under and shoot over and over speedily slow back and front end, the subject chosen by the creeping souls of the moment cocks and cunts, love supreme can believe to fantasy I then spent 3 months chopping the hours and hours of film up into a basket and then toss and toss flip and toss and one by one absently enchanted destined to put it together and separate onto two different reels and then project one reel half the size inside the other reel and then show it and someone tells me what a good editing job I did.[14]

In *Christmas on Earth*, at least five nude bodies are seen engaged in a variety of different sexual acts, including heterosexual genital penetration, homosexual anal sex, fellatio, cunnilingus, and masturbation. When watching the reels individually, one observes significant differences between reels A and B that are obscured when the film is seen through Rubin's preferred method of double projection. Reel A, for instance, privileges corporeal fragments much more than reel B, which is dominated by images of complete bodies. Commencing with a shot of a nonerect penis as it bobs up and down, reel A delivers a startling sequence of extreme close-ups, including the face of a woman screaming in ecstasy, fingers spreading open the lips of a vagina, an anus puckering open and shut, and a penis as it grows tumescent. Through Rubin's use of superimposition, penises suggestively overlap with faces, fingers appear to probe a mouth that simultaneously locks lips with labia, and tongues seem inserted in anuses. True to Rubin's original title *Cocks and Cunts*, reel A presents a seemingly endless array of genitals. Vaginas and anuses are repeatedly spread open, as if inviting the camera (and the observer) to penetrate these tempting apertures.

Orifices, however, are not the only organs that shift shape in *Christmas on Earth*'s frenzied game of hide and seek. Presaging the outrageous work of film and video artist Vito Acconci, who daringly recorded himself with his penis hidden between his thighs in a series aptly titled *Conversions* (1971), *Christmas on Earth* subjects the male genitals to a sequence of dramatic transformations. In addition to including shots of swelling and diminishing erections, *Christmas on Earth* also includes images in

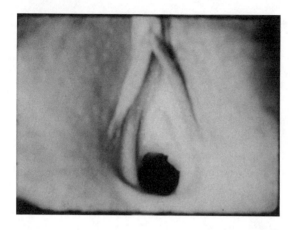

From Barbara
Rubin's *Christmas
on Earth*, 1963.
Frame enlargement.

which the penis retreats from visibility. At a certain point in the film, a
man pulls his testicles over his cock, hiding it beneath the bulge of his
scrotum, before allowing it to pop out a few seconds later. As with the
myriad images of spread orifices, this gesture suggests an insatiable swallowing, the body attempting to consume itself.

At the end of the first reel, the camera pulls back to belatedly deliver an
establishing shot. Extricated from the tangle of body parts, the camera
focuses on a group shot of the performers, who wear lavish amounts of
exotic body paint. The main female protagonist is painted almost entirely
black, except for white regions covering her breasts and stomach, which
transform her torso into a spectral mask. The four members of her male
harem, who sit surrounding her on the floor, are painted white. Not only
does Rubin's use of body-paint situate sexual adventure in the ritual
practices of the primitive other, but it also makes it quite difficult to
distinguish between the participants, let alone decipher which body part
belongs to whom.

Rather than inviting the spectator to identify with any one of these
performers, as in a classical narrative film, *Christmas on Earth* privileges
the viewer's identification with the apparatus itself. At one point in the
first reel, the camera rhythmically zooms in and out as the lips of a vagina
are pulled open and shut. Many critics have articulated the ways in which
Rubin's use of double projection simulates the act of sexual penetration.[15]
What has not been noted is the way in which the thrusting motion of the
camera acts as a surrogate for the viewer by facilitating the desired penetration of the onscreen images.[16] In this intensifying "frenzy of the visible," Rubin's characteristically wild camera movements enable not only
the ecstatic scrutiny of bodies splayed open, but the nearly tactile inter-

action between the observer and the observed as well. Like a lover so enthralled that she cannot decide where to cast her eyes first, Rubin's camera pans and swerves, enters and retreats. As the first reel ends in a blur of flickering white blotches, the participants wave at the camera, breaking the established Hollywood taboo against directly addressing either the apparatus or the implied audience. Like Shakespeare's Puck, the sexual "shadows" in *Christmas on Earth* humbly bid their audience farewell, acknowledging the artifice of their performance and the dream-like splendor of their visions.

The epilogue of the first reel is the subject of the second reel. Panning over the supine figure of the lacquered woman, Rubin's camera, like Willard Maas's in *Geography of the Body* (1947), explores the body as unfamiliar geographical terrain, at the same time that it insists upon sexual congress as a rapturous game of role-playing. Through the de-familiarizing effects of the paint, bodies become inscrutable juxtapositions of hill and valley, positive and negative space. Peering out from an inky expanse of torso, breasts develop eyes, and the sensuous rolls of the stomach grin like a Cheshire cat. Although reel B includes close-up images of body parts, it is significantly more oriented toward whole bodies and the performance of recognizable albeit taboo sexual acts. Whereas reel A creates the impression of interpenetrating body parts largely through the technique of superimposition, reel B offers diverse tableaux of nonsimulated sex. Through double projection and super-imposition, it appears that many more than five bodies are visible. As Sally Banes has observed, these techniques produce "a seemingly endless array of breasts and penises, vulvas and exploring fingers—enough to belong to a crowd."[17]

Like Eadweard Muybridge's late-nineteenth-century photographs of human locomotion, Rubin's celebration of corporeal splendor exposes the metamorphoses of bodies as they engage in various actions. Whereas Muybridge necessarily excluded the body's involuntary reactions to sexual stimulation from his nearly exhaustive compendium of corporeal motion, Rubin explores both the voluntary and involuntary gestures of bodies engaged in a spectrum of sexual acts. At times, the performers in *Christmas* ostentatiously pose for the camera, as when the woman squeezes the folds of her stomach into a smile, or when one of the men spreads the cheeks of his ass open as he lies with his legs spread above his head. At other times, however, the bodies in *Christmas on Earth* depart from deliberate or theatrical gestures, permitting the audience to glimpse unstaged, involuntary confessions of corporeal pleasure. In what may be the first "money shot" in experimental cinema, ejaculate rushes from a man's trembling penis following a rather frenzied display of masturbation and anal sex between two male partners.

Rather than privileging this moment of corporeal truth over the manifold displays of unverifiable sexual pleasure in the film, however, Rubin treats male sexual climax as only one of the myriad possibilities of bodily ecstasy. Instead of culminating the erotic explorations in *Christmas on Earth* with this shot, Rubin insists upon the continuity rather than the cessation of sexual pleasure implied by orgasm, by immediately cutting to images of undiminished sexual plenitude. Although shots of male orgasm would not dominate the representation of sexual pleasure until the explosion of hard-core pornography in 1972,[18] as a hard-core film *avant la lettre, Christmas on Earth* presciently resists the kind of teleological impulse that would circumscribe later forms of visual pornography.

In her essay "Film Body: An Implantation of Perversions," Linda Williams persuasively argues that Muybridge's studies of human motion fetishize the female body through the addition of superfluous props that insist upon the constructed status of femininity. By comparing Muybridge's photographs of women with his photographs of men, Williams observes that while male nudity is treated as a natural or self-evident component of the scientific study of the body, Muybridge's representation of female nudity is oversaturated with narrative meaning. Whereas male bodies are generally displayed without adornment, and are seen engaged in banal activities like walking, catching, and throwing, women are often posed in intimate rituals of dressing and undressing, caressing and flirting. Frequently draped in diaphanous veils and accompanied by unnecessary props, Muybridge's women engage in a primitive form of striptease that both presupposes and implants the perceived artifice of the female gender.[19]

Like Muybridge, Rubin relies heavily on veils and other types of costumes that simultaneously mask and reveal the human figure. However, rather than merely disguising the female body through excessive ornamentation, Rubin also represents masculinity as a thoroughly constructed artifice. Instead of objectifying the female body while preserving the agency of the male subject, Rubin disperses masquerade's duplicity over both genders. Transformed into erotic objects through the geometrical designs inscribed on their bodies and the masks and other ornaments that they wear, here the male performers occupy what is typically considered the "feminine" position by rendering their bodies serviceable for penetration. Although critic Amy Taubin has observed that the

From Barbara
Rubin's *Christmas on
Earth*, 1963. Frame
enlargement.

"dilemma" of *Christmas on Earth* "is maternity and its place in a definition of female sexuality,"[20] it seems that the film as compellingly presents
the related desire of the male to open himself and his body as woman. In
spite of the copious images of male genitalia, the structuring desire of the
film is the ontology of the orifice, the urge to be spread, penetrated, and
occupied. In *Christmas on Earth*, the dichotomies between male and
female, subject and object, and "top" and "bottom" cease to obtain as the
relationship between anatomical difference and prescribed sexual roles
collapses in an orgy of fluid exchanges.

As Banes has argued, Rubin's creation of "a fantastical, Orientalist
sexual space" enables the white woman, "recast as a woman of color," to
be "sexually available in a way that white women are not supposed to
be."[21] Freed from the sexual guilt that historically accompanies white
womanhood, here women partake in the giving and receiving of a host of
sexual favors without suffering the attendant social consequences of perceived promiscuity. Similarly, the men in Rubin's film pursue an expanded notion of sexual sovereignty. Painted to resemble vaguely primitive creatures, the men alternate between performing heterosexual and
homosexual acts, implying that this kind of unregulated bisexuality is a

natural feature of human desire that has been repressed by Western society. Taking advantage of the widespread cultural double standard that persistently accepts provocative images of "native" sexuality while prohibiting images of Western or Caucasian nudity, *Christmas on Earth* proffers the perceived "innocence" of the native sexual encounter as one of many roles that can be taken up in the erotic adventure.

Much as in Jack Smith's *Flaming Creatures*, the outrageously "costumed" players in *Christmas on Earth* are free to express conventionally taboo sexual desires through the use of both the racial and sexual masquerade. Prefiguring Warhol's *Couch* (1964), which exhibits a range of both homosexual and heterosexual encounters on the eponymous piece of Factory furniture, *Christmas on Earth* depicts the sex act as an infinitely variable encounter whose pleasures cannot be circumscribed by the "norm" of heterosexual copulation.[22] Yet unlike *Couch*, whose constant exchange of sexual partners suggests the extension of the capitalist marketplace into the private sphere, Rubin's intimation of a precapitalist ritualistic domain of pleasure hearkens back toward an imagined sexual utopia, unpolluted by the political economy of the present. Like Carolee Schneemann's *Fuses* (1964–67) and Stan Brakhage's *Cat's Cradle* (1959), *Christmas on Earth* is a film documenting human sexuality that includes footage of a cat. While this may seem like a superficial or facetious similarity, the different approaches to feline representation in these works reveals significantly divergent sensibilities on the part of their respective directors. Whereas both Schneemann's and Brakhage's homages to lovemaking include the cat presumably as a signifier of the mode of coupled domesticity from which sexual intimacy emerges, *Christmas on Earth* humorously juxtaposes a pair of cats engaged in sexual intercourse alongside images of people fucking. Rather than referring to the domestic sphere that often includes a beloved house pet as accessory, *Christmas on Earth* situates its explorations of human sexuality on a continuum of corporeal fornication that includes the expression of animal lust.

As David James and Sally Banes have argued, the projection technique of *Christmas on Earth*, in which one reel forms a smaller square within the other, results in an interpenetration that is analogous to the sex act itself. In his book *Allegories of Cinema*, David James has noted both Rubin's struggle as a female filmmaker in a cinematic vanguard largely dominated by men, and the way in which this struggle is allegorized formally through the "labial" interpenetration of Rubin's double projection: "Figuring female bi-labialism both in its representation of the vagina and in the intercourse of one screen with other, it [*Christmas on Earth*] suggests allegorical readings of image production and re-production. It polemically asserts the double-ness, the plurality, moving towards the polymorphous-ness, of the female against the fetishizing of the male that is figured, filmically, in the phallomorphism of single projection and, socially, in the circle of filmmakers associated with the New York Cooperative at that time."[23]

James's observations about the ways in which the literal and symbolic "double-ness" of Rubin's images constituted a potent challenge to the male-centered avant-garde film community are persuasive. Confronted by films in which male directors attempted to figure female sexual pleasure through phallocentric conventions and the illusion of mutual authorship, avant-garde filmmakers like Rubin, Schneemann, and Yoko Ono decided to make their own cinematic documents of the body. However, while it is useful to situate the corporeal films of these three female directors in relation to each other in order to distinguish an important alternative to experimental sex films authored by male directors, there are also important distinctions that merit recognition. Schneemann decided to make *Fuses* as a result of her dissatisfaction with Brakhage's representation of her lovemaking with her partner James Tenney in his films *Loving* (1957) and *Cat's Cradle* (1959). However, as the aesthetic of *Fuses* reveals, Schneemann's debt to Brakhage is substantial. Although she obtains directorial control of the representation of her own body, Schneemann does not manage to emancipate her film from Brakhage's cinematic signatures. Through the copious amounts of superimposition, repetition, upside-down shots, as well as her dyeing, stamping, and scratching on the film itself, *Fuses* pays significant homage to the very father it is anxious to displace. Stylistically, *Fuses* and *Christmas on Earth* bear considerable resemblance to each other, in their shared use of the superimposed, multilayered image, as well as their rapid juxtaposition of corporeal fragments with images of whole bodies engaged in sexual intercourse. Unlike *Fuses*, however, Rubin's brilliant innovation of double-screen projection in *Christmas on Earth* manages to incorporate experimental cinema's primary trope of the ruptured image while simultaneously critiquing the patriarchal inflections of the single frame.

In its materialist celebration of the body and body parts, *Christmas on Earth* also corresponds to the early motion-study films of Ono, including *No. 1 Eyeblink* (1966) and *No. 4 (Bottoms)* (also known as *Fluxfilm #16*, 1966). By focusing on the up-close movements of particular body parts in these films, Ono defamiliarizes the viewer's relation to the geography of the human physique at the same time that she challenges the observer's assumptions about the relation between anatomy and gender. Looking closely at the buttocks presented in *No. 4 (Bottoms)*, or the slow-motion blink of Ono's own eye in *Eyeblink*, body parts and corporeal motions once familiar begin to take on an abstract life of their own, as do the many magnified orifices in *Christmas on Earth*.[24] Fittingly, critic Kristine Stiles has compared Ono's expansion of the erogenous zone to French feminist Luce Irigaray's description of woman's pluralistic eroticism. Woman, Irigaray argues, "has sexual zones just about everywhere."[25] For Irigaray and other feminist theorists, Freud's phallocentric notion of sexuality ignores the multiple sites of corporeal pleasure constitutive of female sexuality. Like Rubin, Ono did not regard sexual plurality and multiplicity as the sole property and privilege of the female body. On the contrary, Ono extended the notion of plurality to include masculinity as well as femininity. By including male bodies as the subject of her cinematic inquiries into human motion, Ono simultaneously rejected "the traditional isolation of the female body as a subject of separate erotic observation, surveillance, and control."[26]

Despite the undeniable difficulty of being a female filmmaker in a male-dominated experimental film community, the critical tendency to employ essentialist or anatomical notions of femininity—including bilabialism, plurality, and doubleness—in relation to experimental films by women is problematic. Rather than privileging the bilabial properties of female anatomy over the supposed oneness of the male anatomy, *Christmas on Earth* deessentializes the anatomical body of both sexes by depicting the flesh in a constant process of metamorphosis. While the goal of this essay is not to submerge Rubin's inspired spontaneity in dense theoretical constructs, Mary Ann Doane's notion of the masquerade, in which femininity is theorized as a mask that can be donned and removed, seems a more appropriate frame through which to approach *Christmas on Earth*.[27]

Far from attesting to the naturalness or authenticity of native sexual culture or the feminine body, the various masquerades in *Christmas on Earth* suggest the ways in which sex and gender always already involve role-playing and the notion of being-as-performance. Like Schneemann, Rubin objectifies the female body in addition to fetishizing the racial or ethnic other. Several times during the nearly thirty-minute film, the woman's body "becomes configured as an abstraction of a face—her breasts become eyes, her pubis a mouth."[28] Whereas the woman's actual face is transformed into a mask by the decorative paint, her sexual organs are presented as a substitute for the defining features of her visage. Like René

Magritte's painting *The Rape* (*Le Viol*, 1934), Rubin's reconfiguration of the female body as face reduces woman to a notion of pure carnality at the same time that it analogizes the female genitals to an all-consuming, insatiable orifice. However, unlike the misogynist trope of the *vagina dentata*, which conflates the mouth and the female genitals as a response to the male's fear of castration by the woman,[29] Rubin's visual conjunction of these two cavities suggests the polymorphous, nondiscriminating pleasures of what is known in psychoanalysis as oral eroticism.[30] In an onanistic gesture akin to Freud's interpretation of the masturbatory practice of thumb-sucking, the woman also presumably finds sexual satisfaction from her own body, as a rather feminine hand is seen stroking the lips of the vagina.[31]

Unlike Magritte's painting, whose title implies the violence associated with the objectification of the female body, *Christmas on Earth* celebrates this objectification as a strategy that enables women to pursue a variety of sexual pleasures. Since, as Banes observes, the female "body itself has oxymoronically become a mask," it can deflect the penetrating gaze of the spectator even as the camera "unmasks" the body's most private parts.[32] In Rubin's film, sexuality is never associated with violence or violation, even as bodies are exchanged between multiple partners. By celebrating the joys of sex and the wonders of the female body as a highly iconic, oversaturated visual object willingly submissive to the prodding, penetrating and thrusting extremities belonging to other (mostly male) participants, Rubin precociously challenged the kind of emerging feminism that would trade organized activism for individual pleasure.

According to Rosebud, Rubin was fully aware of the effects that her film would have upon the audiences of the day. For an eighteen-year-old girl, untutored in the arts of cinematography and editing, to make a film more explicit than any of the Underground films by established (male) experimental directors of her generation, quickly created a sensation. However, unlike Jack Smith, whose notorious *Flaming Creatures* propelled him to the center of numerous legal battles and earned him a reputation for obscenity, Rubin's sexual precociousness quickly transformed her into a beneficent, otherworldly innocent in the eyes of her public. In his review of the film published in *Film Culture* in the summer of 1965, Mekas waxed elegantly about the cinematic candor with which Rubin approached the sex act:

> *Christmas on Earth*: A woman; a man; the black of the pubic hair; the cunt's moon mountains and canyons. As the film goes, image after image,

the most private territories of the body are laid open for us. The first shock changes into silence then is transposed into amazement. We have seldom seen such down-to-body beauty, so real as only beauty (man) can be: terrible beauty that man, that woman is, are, that Love is.

Do they have no more shame? This eighteen-year-old girl, she must have no shame, to look at and show the body so nakedly. Only angels have no shame. But we do not believe in angels; we do not believe in Paradise any more, nor in Christmas; we have been Out for too long. "Orpheus has been too long in Hell."—Brakhage.

A syllogism: Barbara Rubin has no shame; angels have no shame; Barbara Rubin is an angel.

Yes, Barbara Rubin has no shame because she has been kissed by the angel of Love.[33]

While Mekas continued to be the most devout guardian and champion of Rubin's oeuvre, the deliberate naïveté of these original reflections has unwittingly diminished the import of Rubin's film. Rather than explicating the insistently corporeal mode of address that makes *Christmas on Earth* such a significant departure from other Underground films of the period, Mekas's ethereal syllogism disavows the sheer physicality of Rubin's exploration of bodies. Although Underground film historian Parker Tyler himself was prone to characterizing Underground films as infantile, primitive, and gimmicky, he astutely critiques Mekas for disavowing the "stark erotic subject matter of the film" through a patently "deliberate effort to replace black magic with white" and "to saturate adult sexuality with a 'childlike' innocence."[34] Although Rubin promotes the stereotypes of both primitive sexual excess and the unselfconscious "innocence" of native culture, she does so strategically, with an intense degree of self-reflexivity. By appropriating these stereotypes, Rubin negotiates an alternative space in which to perform a critique of hegemonic notions of gender, identity, and sexuality.

With the exhibition of *Christmas on Earth*, Barbara Rubin quickly became one of the central figures of the emerging artistic vanguard. On New Year's Eve 1963–64, Rubin, along with Mekas and P. Adams Sitney, led the charge to show *Flaming Creatures* illegally at the Third International Experimental Film Exposition in Knokke-le-Zoute, Belgium. After smuggling her film into the projection booth in the canister of Stan Brakhage's *Dog Star Man*, Rubin and her associates tied up the secretly compliant projectionist, locked themselves in the room, seized control of the switchboard, cut the lights, and began to show to film. Even after the authorities arrived and attempted to halt the screening, Rubin remained undeterred. As a riot erupted, Rubin shouted encouragement to the audience while hurling curses at the police. Unrestrained by the probability that she could be prosecuted for showing the film (exhibitors in New York had already endured imprisonment and formidable legal battles on account of showing Smith's film), Rubin attempted to project the film on the face of the Belgian Minister of Culture.[35]

Avant-garde film historian Sitney recalls Rubin's zeal as she traveled from Belgium to Cannes, Paris, Munich, and Italy. While Sitney longed to find an established audience and suitable exhibition venues for avant-garde cinema, Rubin was more committed to "showing films in the street and starting a revolution." Although they were both dedicated to gaining exposure for experimental cinema, Rubin was driven by the impulse to expand the meaning of cinema beyond the confines of the screening room and thus to eradicate artistic "censorship" in even its most benign manifestations. As she followed Sitney around Europe, Rubin frequently canceled screenings that he had labored to organize, preferring to project films on crowded streets and empty sky.

While many of her colleagues at the time remember Rubin as a nurturing, spiritual being, others, like Sitney and Ken Jacobs, recall Rubin's public impieties as brazen profligacy. These critics fail to take into account the ways in which Rubin's shock tactics employed the cinema as an instrument to challenge the bourgeois parameters of social etiquette as well as to expand the role of the media in the counterculture revolution. Conjuring the outrageous tactics of the Dadaists, Rubin used her camera to provoke and disturb, frequently transforming highbrow publicity events into carnivalesque debacles in which social hierarchies were inverted and ridiculed. As one of the primary organizers of the *Andy Warhol Up-Tight* series, Rubin both appalled and delighted audiences that had gathered for a glimpse of the New York Underground at various colleges and speaking venues. On January 13, 1966, Warhol was invited to be the evening's entertainment at the New York Society for Clinical Psychiatry's forty-third annual dinner, held at Delmonico's Hotel.[36] Bursting into the room with a camera, as the Velvet Underground acoustically tortured the guests and Gerard Malanga and Edie Sedgwick performed the "whip dance" in the background, Rubin taunted the attending psychiatrists. Casting blinding lights in their faces, Rubin hurled derogatory questions at the esteemed members of the medical profession, including: "What does her vagina feel like? Is his penis big enough? Do you eat her out?"[37] As the horrified guests began to leave, Rubin continued her interrogation: "Why are you getting embarrassed? You're a psychiatrist; you're not supposed to get embarrassed." The following day, the *New York Times* reported on the event; their chosen headline, "Shock Treatment for Psychiatrists," reveals the extent to which Rubin's guerrilla tactics had inverted the sanctioned relationship between patient and doctor, expert and amateur.

By the late 1960s, Rubin's anarchistic spirit began to wane as she became more interested in observant Judaism. In 1968, Rubin moved to upstate New York to live with Allen Ginsberg and Peter Orlovsky on Ginsberg's farm in Cherry Valley. According to Gordon Ball and Rosebud, Rubin engineered the relocation of Ginsberg, with whom she had lived sporadically in New York, in order to live out her idyllic fantasy of bearing his children and growing old with him in the country. Although Rubin's desire for a pastoral romance with Ginsberg seems incompatible with the poet's avowed homosexuality, their unusual relationship did not in fact exclude erotic encounters. According to Ball, who lived with them on the farm, Ginsberg had "made love to Barbara on the dark green carpeted floor of the Coop/Jonas's apartment" after seeing her film.[38] True to the model of fluid sexuality Rubin had represented in *Christmas on Earth*, in which sexual preference was less a permanent identity than a position that could be temporarily occupied and then exchanged, Rubin's relationship with Ginsberg defied the rules of codified sexual behavior. Judging from Rubin's deep and passionate kiss with actress/filmmaker Naomi Levine, recorded in a yet unpreserved sequence of Warhol's *Kiss* (1963),[39] Ginsberg was not the only one who experimented with partners of both genders.

Although Rubin had always been interested in spirituality (Foreman remembers Rubin poring over the books in his library, seeking quotations for an anticipated "Anthology of Light"), it was during this period that she became involved in the rites and rituals of organized religion. Ball attributes Rubin's seemingly contradictory embrace of Hasidism to her deep disappointment upon learning that Ginsberg did not share her fantasy of domestic bliss. Other friends, however, account for Rubin's conversion through narratives of continuity rather than rupture, situating Rubin's transformation on a continuum with her ongoing attraction to different modes of expanded consciousness that included the liberal use of mind-altering drugs and the hallucinatory perceptions afforded by multimedia happenings. Nevertheless, by the time Rubin returned to New York City, she had changed her name to Bracha, the Hebrew equivalent of Barbara, and had begun to keep kosher, light Sabbath candles, and don a religious head covering.

At this point in Rubin's biography, details become vague and perspectives collide. According to Brett Aronowitz,[40] Rubin's immersion in Hasidism amounted to brainwashing by a cult; Rubin was gradually stripped of the traces of her irreverent personality by the dogmatic and retrogressive gender practices of religious fundamentalism. On the other hand, both Wendy Clarke and Rosebud insist that Rubin remained a renegade in spite of her adoption of stringent religious traditions.[41] Rosebud, who lived with Rubin on the Lower East Side during the time of Rubin's increasing religious zeal, insists that Rubin interpreted religious strictures to her own end, often in defiance of acceptable conventions of piety. For example, Rosebud maintains that Rubin insisted on wearing a turban even though she was not married and thus not required to according to the tenets of orthodoxy. Clarke contends that it was Rubin's interest in Kabbalah—which was not considered an acceptable area for women's study—that inspired her embrace of Hasidism rather than any attraction to the rules and regulations of religious fundamentalism.

From this perspective, Rubin's entry into the gender-divided world of Hasidism may be no more startling than her participation in the male-dominated experimental film community of the early 1960s; in both situations, Rubin survived by rewriting the rules according to her needs, flying in the face of convention when necessary. Furthermore, Clarke describes the Hasidic enclave in Brighton Beach to which Rubin belonged as a bohemian commune, full of like-minded artists, rather than a traditional orthodox community. In this light, Ball's claim that Rubin's first husband, rabbinical student Mordecai Levy, was not a born Jew but an enlightened convert, suggests that Rubin's "caterpillar changes" did not stop at the temple threshold but continued to influence her associations with other kindred changelings. Although Rubin's marriage to Levy ended after little more than a year, the bizarre image of their wedding ceremony further illuminates the extent of Rubin's dual citizenship. According to Rosebud, "young girls stood on rickety chairs to peer over the mechitza at Bob Dylan and Allen Ginsberg dancing on the men's side."[42]

Despite the desire to find another, more utopian way of accounting for her religious conversion, certain facts of Rubin's biography make it nearly impossible to maintain that Rubin remained entirely of double consciousness. In a note addressed to Leslie Trumbull, then director of the Film-Makers' Cooperative, Rubin, calling herself Brache,[43] ordered the destruction of the only print of *Christmas on Earth*, a request that has thankfully not been fulfilled.[44] After divorcing Levy, Rubin married a French painter named Pierre Besancon; shortly afterward, they moved to France and settled in a Hasidic community. After giving birth to a half dozen children in as many years (although she is rumored to have been warned by doctors not to have any more children due to her excessive weight gain and slight frame), Rubin died of a postnatal infection in 1980, two weeks after the birth of her youngest son, Aaron. According to the "Preliminary Report of the Death of an American Citizen Abroad," posted two years later by an American Vice Counsel in Lyon, Rubin was buried in the Jewish Cemetery in Ceffois-le-Bas, Haut Ruin, France.[45] Long before her death, Rubin had severed all ties to the New York art world and experimental film community.

While Rubin's conversion to Hasidism has frequently been cast as a postlapsarian repentance of the sexual excesses of her youth, the strategies employed in *Christmas on Earth* actually provide a key with which to deconstruct Rubin's seemingly radical surrender of the pleasures of the material world. In an interview with Rubin conducted by Mekas for the *Village Voice* in 1972, "Bracha" rather candidly discusses the paradoxes of orthodox Judaism, which she had already been practicing for several years. Despite her acknowledgment of many "male chauvinist pigs in Torah," Rubin praised the divergent, often surprising gender roles advocated by Hasidism:

> Torah holds that the man and the woman is like a microcosm of the universe. And Torah says, the woman isn't the one of softness—it's the man. It says, a woman is hard, she's filled with judgment. In Torah, the male is the external force, and the woman is the internal force. External meaning that the man's function in the universe is not going out and getting a job, and doing all that; in Torah, the woman does light. The woman takes care of the literal, physical world, and the man takes care of the spiritual. But without the interchange between the man and the woman, the spiritual world goes crazy, it flies away. Like men tend to fly away. And the female world, which is literal, tends to be harsh, and it gets so harsh that it's like nature, starts to destroy. So there always must be that interchange, you see, between the two.[46]

Given this interpretative spin, it is less shocking that Rubin should choose to pursue something as "extreme" as Hasidism after making the shamelessly corporeal, sexually dazzling *Christmas on Earth*. True to the ethos of fluid gender identifications that Rubin presented, as well as the insistently materialist tone of her approach to the body, Rubin's postconversion commentary reveals the extent to which she managed to incorporate her trademark of fierce femininity into organized religion. Taking into account Rubin's penchant for the exploration of ritual and performativity, it may be misleading to assume that Rubin's last role as pious Hasidic hausfrau was any more essential than the other masquerades—as Underground organizer, sexual outlaw, and irreverent filmmaker—that Rubin assumed in her ongoing emergence from the skin of the self's cocoon.

Had Barbara Rubin disappeared from the Underground community immediately after completing her first film, *Christmas on Earth* would remain one of the most compelling testaments to the spirit of experimental cinema of the 1960s and the counterculture, as well as a work of unparalleled formal and aesthetic consequence. While many critics have dismissed Rubin's later work in regards to her precocious debut, it is only through an examination of Rubin's entire, apocryphal career that the uniqueness of her vision, and the attending difficulty of her struggles as artist, woman, and filmmaker, begin to come into focus. In an environment in which it was nearly impossible for an untrained, underage woman to break into a world of established male auteurs, Rubin took flight, soared to unexpected heights, and offered unqualified glimpses of beauty along the way. In the process, Barbara Rubin answered the question that had been posed to her, generations before, by Rimbaud in "The Impossible," *A Season in Hell*: "When are we going to take off, past the shores and the mountains, to greet the new task, the new wisdom, the defeat of tyrants and devils, the end of superstition—to worship—the first to do so!—Christmas on this earth!"[47]

Filmography

Christmas on Earth, 1963 (29 min.): si., b&w; 16mm
Emunah (with Pamela Mayo), 1972–73 (18 min.): si., col., b&w; 16mm

Notes

1 In his journal entry for June 23, 1966, Jonas Mekas writes, "I have seen Barbara Rubin going through entire evenings of shooting with an empty camera" ("On the Tactile Interactions in Cinema," 248).

2 Callie Angell, assistant curator at the Whitney Museum of Art and director of the Andy Warhol Film Project, has distinguished the footage Rubin shot for the *Andy Warhol Up-Tight* series from Danny Williams's on the basis of Rubin's barely legible imagery. However, compared with the intimate clarity of Rubin's camera in *Christmas on Earth*, her wild, spinning camera movements and habitual underexposure seem to indicate the deliberate refusal to acknowledge the established rules of filmmaking rather than the simple lack of proficiency.

3 *Christmas on Earth Continued* (1965), coauthored by Rubin's friend Rosebud Pettet, was conceived as a billion-dollar fantasy epic that required the construction of a massive fairy kingdom in Ireland and the casting of virtually every significant enfant terrible from the music, literary, cinema, and art worlds, including Jean Genet, Lenny Bruce, the Beatles, Bob Dylan, Marianne Faithful, the Supremes, and Marlon Brando.

4 Belasco, "A Note from the Underground," 50.

5 Although Anthology Film Archives has a print of *Emunah* in their collection, it has not been preserved and thus remains unavailable for public screening and distribution.

6 Most of Dylan's biographers pay scant attention to the singer's friendship with Rubin, who helped nurse Dylan back to health after his devastating motorcycle accident in 1966. Nevertheless, it is rumored that Dylan wrote part of his song "Desolation Row" about Barbara Rubin: "Now Ophelia, she's 'neath the window / For her I feel so afraid / On her twenty-second birthday / She already is an old maid / To her, death is quite romantic / She wears an iron vest / Her profession's her religion / Her sin is her lifelessness / And though her eyes are fixed upon / Noah's great rainbow / She spends her time peeking / Into Desolation Row." See Bob Dylan, *Highway 61 Revisited*, prod. Bob Johnston (Columbia Records, 1965).

7 Bockris, *The Life and Death of Andy Warhol*, 181.

8 Rubin also appears in several other experimental films of the period, including Mekas's *Walden*, and a yet unpreserved sequence of Warhol's *Kiss*. In addition, Rubin's *Screen Test* (Warhol) is available for viewing at the Museum of Modern Art.

9 American experimental film of the period evolved in relation to the changing legal and aesthetic standards of Hollywood, domestic independent and foreign film, stag, exploitation, and hard-core pornography. Characterized by similar struggles over censorship, the history of the American avant-garde nevertheless progressed according to a significantly different trajectory. As with the commercial cinema, experimental film in the 1960s was riddled with legal struggles, including the seizure of film prints by the police, the confiscation of film equipment, the shutting down of theaters, court cases revolving around obscenity, and the arrest of prominent figures from the avant-garde film com-

munity. Nevertheless, due to its relative "invisibility and opacity vis-à-vis public discourse," avant-garde cinema generally enjoyed a greater degree of freedom than the commercial cinema. See Suárez, *Bike Boys*, 298.

10 The caterpillar metaphor is Rubin's own; in 1967, Rubin organized a multimedia performance program at the Cinematheque on 125 W. Forty-first Street, whose title she changed from "Kreeping Kreplach" to "Caterpillar Changes." Although the program featured a range of different performances, from the music of Gato Barbieri, to projection of films by Harry Smith, Andy Warhol, Shirley Clarke, Jack Smith, and Storm de Hirsch on torn sheets, the real caterpillar, as Mekas noted soon after, was Rubin herself ("More on the New Sensibilities in Cinema," 275).

11 Watson, *Factory Made*, 99.

12 Hoberman, "Personal Best," 141.

13 Many experimental films from this period, such as *Christmas on Earth* and Ken Jacobs's *Blonde Cobra* (1959–63) did not include a sound track on the celluloid of the film. Rather, in the projection instructions, the filmmakers specify that the projectionist set an actual radio to certain kinds of stations during different sequences of the film. In this way, filmmakers like Rubin and Jacobs ensured that their films would provoke multiple experiences and different points of view depending on each particular moment of their reception. Regarding *Christmas on Earth*, Rubin also allowed that the different reels of the film could be shown in different orders and enhanced by various color filters. Banes, *Greenwich Village 1963*, 245.

14 Ball, *66 Frames*, 232.

15 See Sally Banes's discussion of *Christmas on Earth* in *Greenwich Village 1963*, as well as David James's analysis in *Allegories of Cinema*.

16 Carol Clover has designated genres such as horror and pornography "body genres" because their aim is to move spectators toward a convulsive response to the images (to jump with fear in horror films, or to shudder in sexual ecstasy in pornographic films). Building upon this notion in her essay "Film Bodies," Linda Williams has argued that pornography aspires to propel the body of the spectator to "an almost involuntary mimicry of the emotion or sensation of the body on screen" (*Hard Core*, 143). For spectators of hard-core pornography, there is an implicit contract between the text and its audience, which stipulates that explicit sexual pleasure will not only be seen, but also be experienced by the viewer.

17 Banes, *Greenwich Village 1963*, 215.

18 See Williams's analysis of the money shot in *Hard Core*.

19 As Williams has argued, Muybridge's chronophotographic studies of the human body are hardly gender neutral. Inextricable from the discourses of power from which they emerge and to which they inevitably respond, Muybridge's photographs do not merely reflect traditional gender stereotypes but

actually impose or "implant" perverse modalities of desire upon the photographed body. For a more in-depth discussion of gender relations in Muybridge, see Williams's chapter "Prehistory" in *Hard Core*.

20 Taubin, "Women Were Out Front, Too," 22.

21 Banes, *Greenwich Village 1963*, 224.

22 See Sigmund Freud's *Three Essays on the Theory of Sexuality* for his account of the relation between perversion and normative sexuality.

23 James, *Allegories of Cinema*, 317.

24 Like Rubin, Ono's first cinema experiments were made with a camera borrowed from an established male figure in the art world—George Maciunas, the leader of the Fluxus movement. For a more thorough discussion of Ono's film work, see Haskell, "Yoko Ono," and Iles, "Erotic Conceptualism." Also see Stiles, "Unbosoming Lennon," for a discussion of the problematic collaboration between Ono and Lennon.

25 Quoted in Stiles, "Unbosoming Lennon," 28.

26 Iles, *Erotic Conceptualism*, 203.

27 For an in-depth discussion of the female masquerade, see Doane, *Femmes Fatales*.

28 Banes, *Greenwich Village 1963*, 224.

29 Melanie Klein explains that the notion of the *vagina dentata* stems from the earliest identifications of the child, in which the child perceives unreal and distorted images of the objects it wishes to incorporate. See "Early Stages of the Oedipus Conflict and of Super-Ego Formation," 136. During this phase, the fantasy of the *vagina dentata* represents the child's unconscious fear that the female genitals are a dangerous opening that threatens to subsume and devour the subject.

30 During this pregenital or infantile sexual phase, satisfaction is primarily associated with the mucous membranes of the mouth, through which the child consumes the breast milk of its mother (Freud, *Three Essays on the Theory of Sexuality*, 48).

31 Ibid., 47.

32 Banes, *Greenwich Village 1963*, 224.

33 Mekas, "Notes on Some New Movies and Happiness," 322–23.

34 Tyler, *Underground Film*, 99.

35 Mekas, "*Flaming Creatures* at Knokke-Le-Zoute," 111–12.

36 Angell, *The Films of Andy Warhol*, 27.

37 Watson, *Factory Made*, 259.

38 Ball, *66 Frames*, 135.

39 According to Callie Angell, many more than thirteen kisses were recorded for Warhol's project, including this still apocryphal smooch between Rubin and Levine. Interestingly, the version of Warhol's *Kiss* distributed through MOMA does not include any female/female kisses, although it does

include other "illicit" kisses, one between two androgynous men as well as an interracial kiss between a black man and a white woman.

40 Rubin was a dear friend of Al Aronowitz's family and acted as a maternal surrogate/babysitter for his children when their mother died.

41 Rubin was also a devoted friend to filmmaker Wendy Clarke and her mother, the avant-garde director Shirley Clarke, with whom Rubin collaborated on several unrealized film projects. In the late 1960s, Rubin and Wendy Clarke opened a hippie clothing store together on Christopher Street between Bleecker and Hudson Streets in New York. Although frequent visits from Bob Dylan and other celebrities transformed the store into a popular Village hangout, it went out of business after approximately one year. Rubin's delight in serving tea and snacks to visitors to the store quickly bankrupted the business.

42 Belasco, "A Note from the Underground," 50.

43 In my extensive research on Rubin, I have come across three different spellings of her taken Hebrew name: Bracha, Brache, and Brucha.

44 Belasco, "A Note from the Underground," 49.

45 Horrigan, "Program Guide" (in awe of).

46 Quoted in Mekas, "Interview with Barbara Rubin," 65.

47 Rimbaud, "Mourning," 101.

ROBERT A. HALLER

Amy Greenfield

Film, Dynamic Movement, and Transformation

◻

Amy Greenfield's cinema is bound up in the dynamism of movement, in the voice of the human body, and the transformation of both through the language of film. Greenfield's thirty-two motion pictures can be divided into three overlapping phases, each building on the previous one. The first period, from 1970 to 1981, can be broadly described as one in which Greenfield (b. 1940) challenged herself with extreme physical trials, developed a personal grammar of cinematic expression, and was the principal performer in her work, as well as its director, editor, and writer. From 1981 to 1996, she became one of several performers in her films and took on increasingly large and complex projects, including a feature film and two live film/video performance events. Since 1996, she has focused on two feature films that have yet to be made, and nine short films or tapes with unusual structures, all performed by dancers other than herself. Some of these later works return to themes and images from her earliest films, but none simply repeat them. Her total work traces a kind of expanding spiral movement. Later works, such as *Wildfire* (2002) and *Dark Sequins* (2004), enlarge, respectively, upon *Dervish* (1974) and *Four Solos for Four Women* (1980), engaging an intricacy in editing that is more visible than in the early tapes. Editing was crucial to *Dervish* and to *Four Solos*, as it is to all of her works, but it is the kind of editing that it is easy to overlook. Indeed, Greenfield's editing is just as important as her direction and performances.

This essay treats Greenfield's cinema in terms of visual concepts and themes, often quoting her. (Many of the quotations are taken from conversations with Greenfield, who has been married to the author since 1980.) It does not attempt to discuss all of her films and tapes. Some of her most awesome works, such as *Corporeal Music, Light of the Body*, and *Saskya* are not mentioned at all, although the use of sound in the first two does parallel the sound in films that are discussed.[1]

Finding a Way to Dynamic Movement

Greenfield turned to film after a decade of studying dance with Robert Cohan at the New England Conservatory, with the Martha Graham Studio, and with Merce Cunningham and Company. She studied choreography with Louis Horst, Robert Cohan, and Lucas Hoving. In 1962 she received her BA from Harvard University. Greenfield made her first film, *Encounter*, in 1970 but had already appeared in several films over the previous three years. One was a conventional documentary of her live choreography, and one was as a nude performer in a short underground film. While performing in other people's films, she wrote about what had been done, and the possibilities of what could be done with the cinematic treatment of human movement. She wanted to explore how film could reveal an interior experience and how it could deepen the inherent dynamism of any kind of movement.

Greenfield's vision of what was possible preceded the making of her own films and is suggested in essays that she published in 1969 and 1984. Her pivotal ideas emerged after she saw films by Maya Deren, Stan Brakhage, Gregory Markopoulos, Carolee Schneemann, Taka Iimura (particularly his film of a *butoh* dancer), and Hilary Harris in the 1960s. As a filmmaker, she watched and learned from her contemporaries, but as a member of the first post-Deren generation of filmmakers, she had few women with whom to consult. Schneemann, Shirley Clarke, Mary Ellen Bute, and Marie Menken were in New York, but Greenfield did not meet them until the 1970s. Yet by the end of the 1960s, she had met the filmmaker Hilary Harris, who became her friend and mentor. Although Greenfield never met Deren, Deren's mother gave Greenfield a bracelet that had belonged to Maya in recognition of the aesthetic kinship

Amy Greenfield directing Hilary Harris. Courtesy of Anthology Film Archives. Photo: Robert Haller.

between the two. In the 1970s, Greenfield worked on developing her own aesthetic and perspective as an artist in film. She was concerned with issues such as bodily energy, the discovery of forms of expression unique to cinema, and equality of visual treatment of women and men.

The ways in which cinema can give meaning to, transform, and enlarge the energy of movement set Greenfield's work apart from most of her contemporaries. In addition, Greenfield consistently works to place us, the spectators, inside her protagonists by bringing us close to them, then skipping across extraneous space and time to revel in movement itself. In her first public declaration about her vision of what film could be, in *Filmmakers Newsletter* (1969), Greenfield wrote that, "Film can still penetrate inward. The camera lens is capable of penetrating the layers of a person's face, body, and movements. It hasn't become dry and removed from blood yet." She continued, "dance as a film language has to be unpostured and unassuming."[2] Although she had not yet seen it, Greenfield was proposing a cinema similar to the live choreography of Yvonne Rainer, which used ordinary movements, like walking and reclining, instead of the traditional dance vocabulary of stylized movements that glide and artfully flow in unison as in ballet. Rainer discussed this new chore-ography in a lecture given in the 1970s that Greenfield attended. Rainer's words, like those of Harris and Brakhage, confirmed the beliefs of the novice film artist, who was exasperated by the work of her bloodless, modern dance contemporaries caught up with hollow, exhibitionistic technique. Greenfield, however, rejected the conceptual postures of Rai-ner's performers, choosing instead to make emotion visible, especially through body contact. Her intention was to speak to widely felt experi-ence by showing how these emotions motivated movements.

From 1970, when she began releasing films, cinematic movement rather than theatrical dance movement has been Greenfield's enduring subject. Dancers are often her performers, and their movements are what she often dwells upon, although she rejects traditional choreography and costuming in favor of the nude human body. In tune with certain feminist aesthetics, she feels that by masking part of the body, clothing frequently eroticizes it. By appearing nude before the camera, or filming other per-formers without the veils of clothing, Greenfield directs attention to no single part of the body, leading the viewer to see the dynamics of the whole organism. Greenfield's work with the body also stemmed from her unhappiness with the passive way in which women appeared nude in most films, including avant-garde films. In all of Greenfield's work, the women, nude or clothed, are active and assertive. They are figures of strength, with a will that sets them apart from the world. Her protago-nists, as portrayed by Greenfield herself or by the dancers/actors she directs, are romantic in that they embody individual consciousness seek-ing ecstatic moments of transcendence. Such use of the active nude was not unprecedented in the work of female filmmakers of this period. Caro-lee Schneemann (*Fuses*, 1967), JoAnne Kelly (*Tilt the Wheel*, 1975), Chris-tine Loizeaux (seven films in the 1970s and 1980s), and Clea T. Waite (*Stella Maris*, 1988) all used strong female nude figures, but none of them have used them so often and with such intensity over several decades.

Movement Transformed

Theatrical dance movement is so far outside Greenfield's interests that it can be misleading to use the word *dance* in describing her work. For lack of a better word, *dance* will be used here, but it needs to be understood as *cinematic* dance. In 1978, discussing her work in holography, another motion picture medium, she wrote that, "the possibilities for dance holography [permitted her] to reveal and transform physical laws of human motion in time and space, while . . . creating a three-dimensional imaginative world which relates to some deep area of the human psyche."[3] Through the envelope of the body she hoped to open up images of the mind. Thus, the movements in Greenfield's films come from internal sources that are less deliberate than autonomic; they are driven by the unconscious, like those that govern the heartbeat. Citing D. H. Lawrence, Greenfield proposed the notion of "a belief in the blood, the flesh, as being wiser than the intellect . . . [that] what our blood feels and believes and says is always true." In 1979, Greenfield wrote of her work that, "the body contains a vast memory of its own . . . basic dreams of both the individual and collective existence . . . which can be uncovered and expressed through a performance of belief and ordeal in the crisis-like, yet suspended process of making cinema."[4]

For Greenfield, the making of cinema means more than directing the performance before the camera lens. Her vision of "basic dreams" realized through expressive physical performance requires filmed or videotaped rehearsals followed by the spontaneity of location filming and, afterward, reshaping the film footage as cinema. Her editing process, which usually takes months or years in comparison to the actual filming, includes incorporating unexpected results. In 1968 she mused on the realm of cinema and dance for a talk given as part of the Film-Makers' Lecture Bureau: "The intense energy of human motion in rhythm . . . is for me the heart of film life—the human being in motion, mysteriously so, sharply defined or defocused into pure energy . . . the body given up to something beyond itself. . . . Dance, which has become too outward, all muscle and exhibitionism, can find a new inwardness through personal cinema."[5] The notion that human motion and energy can become a force, with the body given up "to something beyond itself," echoes through all of her writing. One of the most striking things about her cinema is the degree to which her writings about her intentions have corresponded to her finished work.

Greenfield's first published declarations about what film could be were written in 1968, two years before she finished directing her first film. At this point, she wrote the Lecture Bureau text. In 1968 she also wrote her "Dance as Film" manifesto for *Filmmakers Newsletter*, which appeared in January 1969. Twenty-two months later, in November 1970, that same article was reprinted in the same magazine, with production pictures from the making of *Transport*. In the 1969 *Filmmakers Newsletter* Greenfield cites Brakhage: "I agree with Stan Brakhage that a dance film in the sense of the dancer sensing movement as film hasn't been made. Dancers and choreographers are still committed to theatre, even when it takes radical forms." More pertinent to her own sense of expression, she also cites Brakhage on "human animal necessity," by which she means to abandon "nice clean muscular technique and simply let the body work underneath on its own." This is an explicit declaration "to let the body become itself fully" for the camera, to move "according to the principles of non-chronological (non-physical) time in editing." The ways in which Greenfield began to apply her ideas is described in her memorial tribute to Hilary Harris, her first editing mentor and her principal cinematographer, who died in 1999. In response to his interest in her first edit of *Encounter*, she wrote:

> To me he was a master, which is why I sought him out. . . . I [had] started my own first film, my own cinematic vision and my own process . . . shooting [with] no preconceived dance . . . but rather an image, colors, relationships, emotions, and a desire to communicate through the imprint of human motion on film. In the film frames, how they linked, how motion went from one frame to another. The blur, the rush of red color—these were magical to me.

Working with Harris helped Greenfield grasp the "simplicity of vision in which rhythm and movement themes were unifying factors to make a kind of experience which could move the viewer into a fundamental communication that led to a kinesthetic identification with a core of motion." In addition, she has written that her "intellectual college training worked against a deeper, more fundamental self as artist. Hilary did not—never—imposed his own vision, but somehow he enabled me to let down, and find mine in *Encounter*."[6]

Encounter begins with two women, both dressed alike, reaching toward and across each other, all rendered in very brief shots. The film is eight minutes long, but to get a sense of how different it is from anything else in the "dance cinema," I note that there are twenty-three separate shots in the first forty-five seconds. For an opening sequence, this is a kinesthetic experience unlike any other in dance film. Nor is this all; it is implicitly suggested that the two women, with their similar clothing, may be two facets of one person. The experience of looking at *Encounter* is to question what one has seen, and to feel the reaching gestures of the single or double protagonist.

Transgression and Freedom

Greenfield's embrace of transformation through cinema is described in a 1980 National Endowment for the Arts grant proposal as the "heroic process of symbolic death and renewal." To provide a context for these words about her intentions she pointed to Carl Jung's notions about Faust's desire; like every hero, he yearns for the mystery of rebirth, for immortality. The film that she made in this period shows her rolling down the beach into the sea, nude, submerged within the water, then rising upward in slow motion, and finally striding with confidence through the churning tidal waters. In her 1980 grant proposal, she describes additional images that she wanted to include in the finished film:

> The dancer will seem to "suffer a sea change/Into something rich and strange." This "sea change"—the passage into transformed life, will be accomplished by purely cinematic means. For instance, certain scenes, when filmed upside down facing into the sun will give the impression that the dancer moves on a bejewelled ocean floor. And since the film will be shot at varying speed, from 32–500 frames per second, like the ocean itself, the cine-dance will be timeless. In using the Lo-Cam and fiberglass underwater casing, advanced film technology will be used in new ways.

Although she did not get all of the necessary funding and did not make use of the fiberglass underwater casing, cameraman Harris was able to film at varying speed to transform the sea and the dancer (Greenfield herself) into images out of time. With purely cinematic means, the film slowed down time, reversed its flow, and made the light-illuminated water dance.

Transformation for Greenfield began with her own life. She wrote, "For me to use my body nude was part of the liberation of the times [the 1970s] and a breaking with the confines of the dancified/formalized/ abstracted and stylized dance body, and an acceptance of my totality as a woman."[7] Her creative control in the making of her image with the camera answered a fundamental need in her life. In continuing, she wrote:

> I loved to make imagery and meaning through the body in a new way: the moving image. I wanted to unite psyche, emotion, body. I wanted to experience firsthand the magic of turning flesh into light. I knew I could make meaning through myself on film. I loved the process—more than live dance, more than written poetry. I felt more alive than life when I was naked dancing for the camera. I was happy—powerful and vulnerable both.

I didn't think of myself as beautiful, I wasn't thinking of that, only about the wildness of the experience and the performance to communicate the expression I was possessed by. But now I do realize that I did feel the connection with the tradition of the nude in art. I was surprised that people admired the image of my body as I had always been put down for my body as a child and teenager and young adult learning dance. I'd been admired for my mind.[8]

She discovered that using herself in front of and behind the camera was practical and rewarding. Using herself as material and as a person, was part of 1970s art making as in the work of Yoko Ono, Schneemann, Nam June Paik and Charlotte Moorman, Rainer, and others. In addition to being affected by the transgressive and freeing use of the nude and the environment, Greenfield had trained in a tradition in which the choreographer was her own star.

Element marked Greenfield's first nude appearance, although she was coated in an oozing layer of fine mud. Hilary Harris photographed the film, with Greenfield directing and editing, but he worked from rehearsal sessions so that Greenfield had control of the cinematic image as well as the photographed body in the image. Greenfield has written of the difficulties of working in this way. "*Element* is so complex . . . because the screen movement-image communicates both violent active struggle, with the camera moving in non-synchronous and sometimes opposing [ways] to my movements of sliding, rolling, falling, and languid, sensual flowing . . . so that some find it to be erotic, and others have an 'uck' reaction." But for Greenfield, the film achieved the desired union of "the female nude with [an] extreme action" that energized and communicated a "female—human—experience." Greenfield is fond of citing some of her influences, such as Isadora Duncan in the preface to *Tides* and William Butler Yeats, who wrote that the body is the greatest metaphor. The transformation of the body in *Element* from nude to active human form characterizes her films and videotapes. Greenfield seeks to convey a tangible sense of weight and energy, whether it be the feet sliding against the sandy slope of *Transport*, or the slow motion spray of water droplets in *Tides*, or the abrasive violence of a body being dragged across broken ground in *Dirt*.

The Framed Image

The tactile sense of physical sensation in Greenfield's films is due to the kinetic force of camera movement and proximity, and the framing and angled vision of her work, which give it a palpable tension. In this, her films are comparable to sequences in Deren's work. Like Deren, Greenfield shapes time and space in her films as typified by the leap of Talley Beatty at the end of Deren's *A Study in Choreography for Camera* (1945). In a subjective landscape, Beatty rises into the air in a series of spliced images, stretching across a space that begins in the interior of a building and concludes in a very distant park. Physical distance is collapsed; conceptual space is expanded. At the end of *Videotape for a Woman and a Man* (1974), Greenfield, too, collapses space in order to bring the two protagonists into a condition of ecstatic proximity that is further enhanced by slow motion. Greenfield's means of shrinking the space is not as obvious as Deren's but can be at least as emotionally involving. Just as Deren sets up a duet between Beatty and his environment, Greenfield creates two such spaces (the wave-washed beach in color and a neutral room in black and white). In Greenfield's duet between the man and the woman, she reduces the physical space between the two, using cutting and framing to suggest their growing emotional bonds. Speaking about this film, Greenfield said, "I want to see both the changes in the space between us and a sense of us as whole human beings relating—I wanted [not just the] tension of the bodies against the frame but a sense of the whole of the two, with the focal point the interaction. The whole was interaction as people."

In interviews and in her writings, Greenfield has described *Videotape for a Woman and a Man*, which she began in 1974 with advice on the video process from Shirley Clarke, in terms of her cinematic transformation of time and space. In the Spring 1980 issue of the *Downtown Review*, she described the tape as involving "a nude dance performance by a woman and a man in which they act out a drama of male-female relationships . . . dance tendered and transformed through the . . . video medium." In particular, Greenfield accepted Clarke's suggestion that the videotaping be less structured and formal, and that input from the actors and camera operators be included in the process. This way of working contributed to the spontaneous sense of intimacy that permeates the videotape. In the early part of the tape, which is in black and white, there is a "bumping, teasing, and falling" between the two performers (Greenfield and Ben Dolphin). At the end of the tape their relationship changes, as the tape shifts into color, with what Greenfield accurately calls, "the frenzied last phrase—a kind of abstracted orgasm—which is then repeated in slow motion." In this last phrase the camera approaches close to the bodies and moves with Greenfield and Dolphin, becoming one with them. One of Greenfield's core beliefs is that the distance between spectator and performer is not a barrier. In 1970, when she was just starting to make films, she recognized that the close-up had a transformative effect that cannot be fully rationally explained. "At that time," she told the *New York Times* in 1996, "I was interested in emotion, and the camera seemed to open an area of motion and emotion, coming so close it almost reads thought."[9]

Emotion as the Origin of the Visual Image

For most filmmakers, the personal place where a film is born is not so much an idea as an image or an emotion. For Greenfield this inspiration has often been a sense of the body, or a struggle to enter a different state of being. Her route toward the making of her longest film, *Antigone/Rites of Passion* (1990), gives a sense of how the process has worked. Sophocles's play treats a family that bears a curse, and the consequences that flow from it, especially in terms of the choices, through "free will," made by Oedipus's sons and daughters. As in the revival of all great plays, *Antigone* is used here to dissect contemporaneous issues. Greenfield's Antigone is a character trapped by her origins. In her 1992 *Millennium Film Journal* interview, she describes a character who is resolute yet anguished:

> The film starts with the voice of Antigone over a black screen saying, "The story of Antigone began before she was born." Before she goes into the [death] cave she says, "My birth imprisons me." The beginning narration ends with "Antigone chose to go with him [Oedipus], to lead him in the wilderness." So there are two extremes for her. A path circumscribed horribly by her birth and gigantic choices no one else would make, and once they're made, they lead her to a narrower and narrower sphere within which choice can be made.[10]

Greenfield spoke of her own tangible sense of terror in making the film. She wrote of identifying with being trapped in the coils of destiny, yet overcoming her fear through her choice of action.[11] This victory is part of what makes *Antigone* affecting and, in the end, positive, particularly when Ismene resists destiny, opposes Creon, and then takes up her dead sister's body. Greenfield's emotional investment is what makes so many of her films persuasive, visceral experiences.

Consciousness and the Tactile Image

What we see in a motion picture can represent consciousness, and if the work is successful, it *becomes* consciousness for the period in which we watch. After *Encounter*, Greenfield made three successive films and a videotape that so fully engage the spectator's consciousness that his or her vision is subsumed by Greenfield's images. The analytic dimension of *Encounter* returns in Greenfield's films and videotapes after 1974, but *Dirt*, *Transport*, *Element*, and *Dervish* are, primarily, *experiences* of unusual intensity. In *Dirt* (1971) Greenfield is savagely pulled across broken ground while she struggles against her captors. In *Transport* (1971) she and a man seem to be either unconscious or dead; Greenfield says they were meant to be in a state "between" life and death, their bodies lifted upward. In both films the sound amplifies the actions that the viewer sees.

Greenfield comes from that sector of avant-garde film that is engaged with the politics of vision rather than social action. Her use of the singular mechanism of cinema is intended to challenge the deadening conventions of popular narrative. In sound and silence, Greenfield's world is always on the fringes of our own. Her spaces are not ours, but they are not fully apart either. What, one wonders, is happening in *Transport* with its very physical struggling to elevate the two bodies, and then the suddenly serene ending when the bodies and the men who carry them appear to skim or float over the ground? For all the mystery of her films, protest and the pain of the oppressed of our time, are visible in at least two of her works. *Dirt* evokes the abuse of political protesters, and her 1990 *Antigone* treats the conflicting imperatives of loyalty to family, the state, and the gods, addressing especially the restricted roles of women.

Although Greenfield's films are not overtly feminist, the women in her work do not submit to external forces, whether they be gravity in *Element*, destiny in *Antigone*, childhood training in *Dialogue for Cameraman and Dancer*, or gender roles in her 2005 film, *Club Midnight* (where the women "become" the male narrative voice of poet Charles Simic). As a choreographer, Greenfield's protagonist women take on the forces of nature as well as of culture. For example, in *Dervish*, the struggle is with

From Amy Greenfield's *Transport*, 1971. Courtesy of Anthology
Film Archives. Photo: Sam Robbins.

the limits of the body's endurance and the inevitability of exhaustion. In
Wildfire, which involves similar movements, there is no struggle within,
but rather a surmounting of the direction of time and of weight and of
space. *Tides*, with Greenfield's immersion and embrace of the ocean, like
Wildfire, speaks to a kind of cosmic transcendence through the body as
an ultimate liberation. This liberation in *Wildfire* has two notable historical sources. The four nude women who whirl through *Wildfire*, pulling
large sheets of fabric behind them, are modeled on Loie Fuller and her
imitator, the 1894 Edison Company film dancer Annabelle (who appears
at the opening and closing of Greenfield's film). The women are also
modeled on figures in another turn-of-the-century hand-painted film. In
this brief, unidentified film a sorcerer liberates a number of "butterfly
women" from captivity, who rush about in their new state of liberty and

From Amy Greenfield's *Light of the Body*, 1998. Courtesy of Anthology Film Archives.

then refuse to return to his control. Greenfield described this early film to her dancers, giving them this condition of liberation as the reason for their exultant locomotion.

The film *Element* speaks to Greenfield's belief that sound or its absence is not a matter of realism but a means of evoking the world beyond the present. The film depicts a woman coated in mud and struggling against the force of gravity and the use of silence emphasizes the film's dreamlike sense. In *Four Solos for Four Women* (1980) there is another potent silence, not of a dream but of an anguish unspoken until the videotape completes its first cycle of mourning and joy. The "missing" sound of *Four Solos* (featuring nineteenth-century lieder for female voice) is heard in the second phase of the tape, confirming what our eyes alone have grasped in the first, silent phase of the identical visual footage. In another aural variation, *Wildfire* has a minimal, repetitious score by Philip Glass, which conveys general emotion but does not attempt to speak to specific visual moments. For Greenfield, silence is not the absence of sound, but a kind of sound. So, too, are darkness and light.

In the opening chapter of her 2004 tape, *Dark Sequins: Dance of the Seventh Veil*, Greenfield speaks of "my body wielding the knife edge of light." In the most literal, direct sense this can be understood as referring to dancer Andrea Beeman, who wields a sword in the second half of the tape. Holding the sword upright, she bisects the film frame and then whirls the blade, all the time catching the slash of light. But at the time Greenfield utters these words in the film, the sword sequence is at least five minutes away. Rather, her words seem to refer to the edge lighting that defines Beeman's half-naked body on the stage of a club where she is performing an erotic dance—not for the one spectator in the onscreen audience, but for the camera, for us, and in a mythic sense, for her own empowerment. Greenfield speaks to the mythic context she has set for Beeman, that of Ishtar (the Babylonian goddess of both love and war) and Salome, both of whom used their bodies to wield power in the under-world and in the royal court of Judea, respectively. At the end of *Dark Sequins*, the last titles declare that Ishtar departs the underworld, return-ing light to our world.

But of course the ultimate interpretation of "my body wielding the knife edge of light" refers to that of the filmmaker, Greenfield herself, who composes and shapes her motion pictures. In *Dark Sequins* we have another transformation, an orgasmic whirling invocation of energy in which the knife edge of light, Beeman's—and Greenfield's—sword, criss-crosses the film frame, drawing down from above and from the sides bolts of the luminescent energy that lights up all of cinema.

Filmography

Encounter, 1970 (8 min.): si., col.; 16mm
For God While Sleeping, 1970 (8 min.): sd., col.; 16mm
Dirt, 1971 (3 min.): sd., col.; 16mm
Transport, 1971 (8 min.): sd., col.; 16mm
Element, 1973 (11 1/2 min.): si., col.; 16mm
Dervish, 1974 (15 min.): sd., col.; video
Dialogue for Cameraman and Dancer, 1974 (25 min.): sd., col.; video
Fragments: Mat/Glass, 1975 (8 min.): sd., b&w; two-channel video
One-O-One, 1976 (11 min.): sd., col.; 16mm
Saskya, 1977: 120-degree hologram
Fine Step, 1977: 360-degree "doubled" hologram
Videotape for a Woman and a Man, 1978 (30 min.): sd., col.; video
The Wave I, 1978: 360-degree hologram
The Wave II, 1979: 360-degree hologram
Four Solos for Four Women, 1980 (28 min./15 min.): sd., col.; video
Tides, 1982 (12 min.): sd., col.; 16mm
Bertram Ross, 1988/2004 (12 min.): sd., col.; video

MAJORCA/fantasia (collaboration with Nam June Paik and Paul Garrin), 1989 (5 min.): sd., col.; video

Antigone/Rites of Passion, 1990 (90 min.): sd., col.; 16mm, video, DVD

Elements, 1992 (2 min.): sd., col.; video

Bodysong, 1992 (1 min.): sd., col.; videotape for multimonitor installation

Tribute to Charlotte Moorman, 1994: sd., col.; multivideo projector live performance conceived with Nam June Paik

Corporeal Music, 1995 (7 min.): sd., col.; video

Downtown Goddess, 1996/2003 (10 min.): sd., col.; video

Raw-Edged Women, 1996–98: sd., col.; film/video/slide live performance

Light of the Body, 1998 (10 min.): sd., col.; 35mm

Dark, 1998 (4 min.): sd., col.; video

Wildfire, 2002 (11 min.): sd., col.; 35mm and video

Bodysong, 1978/2003 (8 min.): sd., b&w; video

Bodysong: The Burning Lovers, 1978/2003 (3 min.): sd., col.; video

Club Midnight, 2005 (8 1/2 min.): sd., col.; 35mm and video

Dark Sequins: Dance of the Seventh Veil, 2005 (12 min.): sd., col.; 35mm and video

Notes

1 I treat each of the works in my forthcoming book, *Body of Light*.
2 Greenfield, "Dance as Film," 1–2.
3 Greenfield, personal communication, 1978.
4 Haller, "Amy Greenfield," 106.
5 Film-Makers' Lecture Bureau, 1968 catalog, unpaginated.
6 Greenfield, "Hilary Harris," unpaginated.
7 Greenfield, personal communication, n.d.
8 Ibid.
9 Dunning, "Free-Spirited Progeny," 15.
10 Pipolo, "Making *Antigone/Rites of Passion*," 38.
11 Ibid., 36–37.

CHUCK KLEINHANS

Barbara Hammer

Lyrics and History

◻

Barbara Hammer (b. 1939) is a remarkably productive and innovative filmmaker. These admirable qualities result in a peculiar way in limiting critical perceptions of her work. She is both prolific and unafraid to try new forms and new topics. Those who know her primarily from her initial fame as a lesbian feminist experimental filmmaker would hardly expect her to have done a long piece on the career of a famous male Japanese maker of realist documentaries and his filmmaking collective. But she has, and she has taken on topics ranging from love and sexuality to intense landscape explorations. She has made film and video meditations on death that are deeply personal, but also films about large issues of war and social justice. She has made polemical pieces on AIDS, and also challenging representations of the female body. Throughout her career, she has sought new technologies, new forms of expression, and new adventures. But as a result, there is not the kind of obvious continuity of theme and topic, or style and execution that is often noticed and then endorsed by critics. It is not easy to characterize the corpus of her work. But this is also part of who she is as an artist, and a mark of her stubborn independence; she has never held back.

For those new to experimental film and video or unfamiliar with the range of Barbara Hammer's career work, a chronological organization provides the opportunity to see the complex development of a major media artist. With this arrangement the viewer easily traces the evolution from a simple lyricism to a dense referentiality, from technically elementary means to elaborate production and postproduction, from spontaneity and celebration to self-reflection and critique, from silence or a simple sound track to richly elaborated and layered audio, from the screen as window on the world to screen as site for changing layers of consciousness and reflection.

At the same time, a chronological survey presents a potential problem. Inattentive or superficially sophisticated viewers may be puzzled with some work for not matching the canonical expectations of the avant-garde or feminist establishments, and Hammer has always been a disturbing presence for both.[1] A too hasty labeling of her work characterizes much of the critical response to it. But her most significant work of the past three decades demonstrates the mind and talent of a major North American artist who must be assessed and understood on her own terms. Understanding her originality demands breaking some of the easy commonplaces of current media criticism.

Hammer's work in the 1980s gained depth from her technical mastery in the service of a deepened vision and understanding of life's possibilities and limits. In *Sanctus* (1990) she achieved a celebration of the body that is corporal and spiritual, presenting the amazement and joy of life simultaneously with the body's inevitable temporality. In *Still Point* (1989) she accomplished a fusion of the personal and the political that maintains visual and aural contradiction in the service of a heightened sense of her own, and our own, practical and moral situations in the Reagan-Bush era. In *Vital Signs* (1991) she wove postmodern media fragments with her own image in a *danse macabre* that recalls the unity of life and death in medieval art while updating the metaphor for the age of AIDS.

In retrospect, the continuity of cinematic exploration and personal embodiment of her concerns stands clear. The pairing of natural and social worlds mediated by individual vision and camera technology, the layering of images and their repeated reconsideration, the fracturing of consciousness by using the material alteration of film, the obsession with altering light as a fulcrum point between vision in consciousness and sight of the world; these are also major themes in the U.S. experimental film tradition, particularly as found in the history of "visionary film" described by critic P. Adams Sitney. Yet Barbara Hammer's work remains little known in that context, so much a male preserve.

From the perspective of her predecessors in women's experimental film work, however, Barbara Hammer clearly belongs at the center of

Portrait of
Barbara Hammer.
Courtesy of www
.barbarahammerfilms
.com.

tradition. Like Mary Ellen Bute's pioneering work in abstract lightpieces in the 1930s, often filming from cathode-ray tube patterns, Hammer freely works visual rhythms and moves back and forth from film to video to computer in production and editing. Hammer has also followed Marie Menken's film strategies from the 1940s and 1950s with lyrical examinations of gardens and places, using paint to animate still images and creating drastic satiric juxtapositions by optically printing images and appropriating scientific documentary and found sound. In the context of Hammer's work, other films by women experimentalists come to mind: Sara Arledge's deadpan mock exposition in the pre-Beat *What Is a Man?* (1958), Shirley Clarke's intense optical printing in *Bridges Go Round* (1958), the visual romanticism of Storm de Hirsch's lyrics and Chick Strand's documentaries, the wacky humor about women's bodies and lives in Gunvor Nelson and Dorothy Wiley's *Schmeerguntz* (1966), the exploration of the filmmaker's own body and unruly sexuality through alterations of film material and layered printing in Carolee Schneemann's *Fuses* (1964–67), and Joyce Wieland's examination of her body and domestic environment in *Water Sark* (1964–65). In this context Hammer's handcrafted, visually dense, wildly romantic, disarmingly autobiographical, slyly satiric, and comically celebratory concerns find a congenial place.

Placing Hammer within a tradition of North American women's experimental film makes much more sense than an earlier approach, which tried to fit her into an essentialist "lesbian feminist aesthetic."[2] Time and experience have shown that the push to a we-are-all-alike politics of identity served unity and celebration at the expense of paying attention to crucial differences of race, class, age, experience, and lifestyle. Hammer's *Still Point* serves as her definitive reassessment of 1970s cultural feminism. She literally places side by side the romantic image of her companion walking and stretching under the sun in a landscape and the gritty realism of a methodical garbage picker on the streets of New York City, pushing a shopping cart and moving on to the next waste container. The film indicates that our worldview must encompass both realities. Privilege cannot obscure vision.

Hammer's role as a feminist and lesbian media maker in the 1970s needs to be understood in a historical context. For many years, she was almost alone as an out-of-the-closet lesbian filmmaker. Virtually excluded from the boys' club of the film avant-garde, she showed her own work in feminist bookstores, women's coffeehouses, and women's studies classrooms, often organizing the event and carting the equipment as well. Determined to promote women's media, she organized weekend workshops and classes to teach women filmmaking skills and set up screenings of women avant-gardists from the past. She created her own distribution company, Goddess Films, to reach the audience. At the same time she produced film after film, taking every opportunity to make new work, learn new skills, and try new techniques.

The mid-1970s works represent women's bodies as physical, gendered, and sexual, existing within a lesbian community. Some function primarily as filmed skits, such as *Superdyke* (1975), which shows groups of women appearing in public space carrying shields emblazoned with "Amazon" or dancing in the street in front of San Francisco's city hall. Simply showing young, out lesbians in public provided empowering imagery for a group that had been denied filmic representation from their own point of view and free access to public space (precisely why annual Lesbian/Gay Pride parades were originally so important). The film tends to directly illustrate ideas, and those ideas are not necessarily shared by everyone in the intended audience. Fantasies of running through parks with bows and arrows like ancient Amazons are not universal among homosexual women. At the same time, the film succeeds best in documenting guerrilla theater fun, such as finding a display of massage vibrators in a crowded department store and publicly appropriating the demonstration model for erotic joy.

The more private films of this period set in domestic space or rural retreat remain personal and compelling while revealing the artist trying to find new forms for representing women's bodies as objects of desire. *Dyketactics* (1974) presents a now-classic lovemaking film, with the camera not a distant voyeur or blunt close-up recorder as in so much pornography, but a living and moving presence capturing, framing, and reframing caresses and touching. *Women I Love* (1976) presents a series of portraits which show women in nature or in intimate settings in an often magical way. Opening a dishwasher reveals daffodils in bloom, and the flower reappears in a plastic speculum, being actively kissed by one of the lovers. A lover appears on a motorcycle trip, another in a forest glen. Lovemaking appears not isolated, but as part of a continuum of nature and intimacy.

For some feminist critics, the romanticism of Hammer's work in the 1970s created a disturbing undercurrent. Some rejected what they viewed as her ideology of a separate mythic goddess spirituality or Amazon culture. Some found images of naked women in pastoral nature a flight from reality and her autobiographical depictions of her own body and those of her lovers a recapitulation of masculine patterns of looking. Yet the abruptness of the critique fails to address other questions. Clearly, as we see repeatedly in election seasons, the issue of queer sexuality can be used to mobilize voters. In 2004, it was "defense of marriage," while a decade earlier the depiction of homosexuals in media art became a rallying cry for the presidential campaign of Patrick Buchanan and led to Senator Jesse Helms decrying Marlon Riggs's video *Tongues Untied* (1989) for showing "naked dancing black homosexual men" on PBS. Hammer herself has mocked such hysteria in *No No Nooky T.V.* (1987), an animation created on the Amiga computer, in which a machine speaks and draws naughty words and, in a bit of cybernetic cross-dressing, wears a bra and underpants while sexually cavorting with the animator who smears the machine's face with paint.

To some extent Hammer's work overlapped with debates in the movement between universal biological and essentialist positions on the one hand and social-historical explanations for female and lesbian difference on the other,[3] not that the filmmaker did not have something to add to the discussion. *Synch Touch* provides an argument that touch is an earlier and more primary sense than sight, but that the two are closely related, and it emphasizes the corporeality of visual perception. The film also wryly contradicts the argument of much psychoanalytic-semiotic film theory that verbal language provides the master model for consciousness —a position often favored by academic feminists who either ignored her work, which hardly fit the heterosexual bias of their theorizing, or who distained Hammer's "essentialism." Her indirect response: the tongue can be used for more than talking.

By positioning Hammer's work as simply romantic, critics often inhibited appreciation of her remarkably different group of films and tapes in the 1980s when she turned from the female body set in romantic nature to a series of what she called "perceptual landscapes," that made her own investigation of the world's spatial and temporal dimension a key element. *Pond and Waterfall* (1982) puts woman in nature, but in a wet suit with an underwater housing around her camera. Air and water form a changing fluid boundary as changes of scale and distance, light and color, shape and reshape perception. *Pools* (1981) takes the viewer through a liquid (literally and figuratively) exploration of the early-twentieth-century American architect Julia Morgan's swimming pools.

Hammer's understanding of the body itself changed and deepened in the 1980s. The body's social nature came to be represented no longer as a circle of women cavorting in Northern California, but a body imbedded in contradiction and complication through the impact of government censorship and right-wing repression, of AIDS hysteria in the media, of disease and dying, of aging, and of environmental decay. *Optic Nerve* (1985) represents visiting her grandmother in a nursing home, and *Endangered* (1988), vanishing animal species. With *Sanctus* Hammer reworks pioneering X-ray medical motion picture footage of bodies by elaborate optical printing and the use of color and an intense music track. The result provides a dense and awe-producing view of the body as simultaneously concrete and physical and spiritual. At the end of the 1980s, when she reentered her film and video work by again presenting her image, Hammer moved with a maturity that deepened the irony of her comedy, opened the wonder and fear of the body and its often precarious life, and made the filmmaker's personal quest for loving relations deeply grounded in the social and historical moment.

The field of feminist film studies grants overwhelming attention to the dramatic feature film, either in critiquing the dominant, looking for subversive subtexts in Hollywood representations, or trying to find feminist

From Barbara Hammer's *Sanctus*, 1990. Courtesy of Barbara Hammer.

alternative narrative strategies. A second order of critical attention considers the substantial body of women's realist documentaries on social issues. Concern for the lyrical avant-garde mode and its complex intersection of the personal and the political, of perception and cognition, feeling and knowing, lags far behind. Yet Hammer's work deserves attention for addressing personal, aesthetic, and social issues with a complexity and density rare in fictional narrative or social documentary forms. From such an understanding, much of her earlier work can be taken in a fresher way, beyond some simplifications found in previous criticism.

In the 1990s Hammer began to pursue longer form works. In interviews she attributed some of her motivation to the problems of establishing a media career on the basis of short works, which are often assumed as "minor" in stature in film and video festival events. Having become a regular on the women's and queer festival circuits, Hammer had the opportunity to show feature-length work, often with a personal appearance. In some arenas, funding for longer work is easier to find. Related to this decision are historical changes in the festival ethos. Originally begun as countercultural celebrations of media work that was often speaking directly from the movement and concerns of the subcultural pioneers, in many places festivals have moved from almost improvised grassroots fringe events to well-established institutions supported by local business sponsors and national retailers aiming at a chic lifestyle market rather than highlighting alternative and outlaw social groups.

Given this historical shift, Hammer's actual production of longer projects in the last decade underlines some provocative inconsistencies. A case in point is *My Babushka: Searching Ukrainian Identities* (2001), a documentary record of a trip to the Ukraine, where her grandmother was born early in the twentieth century and which she subsequently left at about age fourteen. In the video, Hammer, accompanied by other local and diasporic filmmakers and sponsored by a Soros grant, visits with a range of people, searching for the grandmother's village and any remaining relatives. It seems that an elderly woman is found who is her grandmother's niece and apparently the closest remaining relative. The visual style combines documentary reportage with abstractions (such as an extreme close-up of a glass of tea), footage of looking in and through old churches, a close-up of dough being made, or blurred and distorted images such as one of people in an urban space, apparently taken from a reflective surface that gives a slightly irregular mirror effect.

As the journey begins, the trip is clearly important to Hammer, but the audience soon wonders how it matters to us. The video tends toward the "my travel film about my ancestor's home" genre. For example, the family members do not seem to be significant as sources of information; in fact they seem so vague that one might even wonder if perhaps they are imposters, glad to fake being a relative to the visiting American tourist, in hope that some material benefit might emerge. I do not want to be cynical, but the fact that Hammer parachuted into the scene with no previous research or correspondence, in addition to the local people's vagueness, invites it. A local male journalist tells (through a female translator who seems to be changing his first-person story into a third-person narrative) of discrimination against Jews, both locally by Ukrainians and Russians, and then during the Second World War by Germans who massacred thousands at Babi Yar, enthusiastically aided by some Ukrainian and Russian anti-Semites.

Yet the question that Hammer initially asks, "Why did they have pogroms?" (something that could be cogently discussed in terms of the history of East European Jews for hundreds of years), is never answered. Instead, examples are presented: discriminations from the Soviet and post-Soviet era, the monument to Babi Yar and gravestones of the perished (some defaced), a building that was a large synagogue from which Jews were expelled at some time in the past, and of which they have now reclaimed a small section. We see mostly elderly people at a meal in the synagogue, but see neither religious practices, a rabbi, a cantor, nor people in worship. This absence and lack of specificity is frustrating, or irritating, depending on one's basic level of interest in the subject. One also senses that Hammer does not know much about Eastern European Jews and their history, something perhaps not so unusual for a third-generation American, but odd for anyone who is going to make an on-location documentary on the subject.

The video could be contrasted with Susan Mogul's *Prosaic Portraits, Ironies, and Other Intimacies: A Travel Diary* (1991), another personal journey to the past (this time Poland and Polish Nazi concentration camps), which is organized around a single female artist enjoying an adventure and meeting interesting local people while establishing personal as well as professional relations. The stigma of the implied imperial tourist perspective whenever Americans go abroad can be overcome when counterweighted with a personable engagement with native informants or, as in Mogul's case, with showing the heroine-maker's vulnerabilities (in her case, a bit lonely or lovelorn). But Hammer's personal work seldom gives any hint of self-questioning or doubt, and in her earliest travel work such as *Our Trip* (1981), an animation of a backpack trip in the Andes, the mood is one of celebration of the North American couple on an adventure abroad, oblivious to local people, histories, or customs.

Hammer's more documentary and essayistic long-form work tends to be organized around the assemblage of shorter materials. This process allows her to continue her lyrical strengths in short passages but it also introduces the problem of inconsistency in constructing an overall through-line argument. Typically, feature documentary uses a narrative structure that builds tension into a conflict that is then resolved (a pattern easily found in documentaries ranging from *Primary* [1960] to contemporary reality television's *Survivor*). This is usually cued by a timeline or an inexorable unfolding of events. Even the essayistic personal documentary tends to a journeylike structure in which there is a movement to discovery and/or enlightenment. The underlying problem in Hammer's later work is a slippery notion of history and what historical investigation is or could be. In her earlier short films, even when a history was stated (the six former lovers in *Women I Love* [1976], or the record of a disintegrating love relation in *Double Strength* [1978]), there was no burning need for a fuller context. The former lovers appear in footage that maintains an eternal now when screened later, snapshots of the way it was, the way they were. But as she has taken up historical topics in her later years, the understanding of history becomes more of an issue. In *Tender Fictions* (1995), a general autobiography is mixed with fictional interventions and diverse appropriations from mass culture to create a "might be true" story of Barbara Hammer's life. While strong on jokey claims, the piece also leaves deeper questions open and deeper emotions unexamined.[4]

Although Hammer's work is always substantially experimental in form and approach, some of her 1990s documentary essays offer clearer paths for the audience than others. *Nitrate Kisses* (1992) provides an initial framing with a quotation from Adrienne Rich about lost histories and a sound track with conversational recollections by older lesbians (apparently gathered at a celebration event of senior dykes), as well as the more analytic voice of a female historian providing context and elaboration. Photos are frequently used (for example, an image of Willa Cather appears while the audio track discusses the writer's actual life, in which she usually dressed as a man, versus her literary reputation, which erased any mention of her sexuality).[5] We see titillating covers of lesbian pulp fiction in the 1940s and 1950s while women recall their lives in the same era.[6] Also running through the piece are images of abandoned buildings in ruins, which are identified by Hammer elsewhere as standing for "public space" (if so, why damaged?). The old ruins may function as a crutch to cover the paucity of past images with a metaphoric statement about the passage of time and physical decay, as do her images of the wrinkled skin of older women, which is itself a more prominent theme in Hammer's work in the 1990s.

In the major second section, *Nitrate Kisses* includes outtakes of the pioneering silent film *Lot in Sodom* (James Sibley Watson and Melville Webber, 1933), which reproduces the Bible story with considerable theatrical exaggeration. Hammer adds a voice-over explanation of the silent film original, which is itself intercut with other footage—some of it from silent film comedies showing prissy or hysteric male actors and other footage from a contemporary male couple engaged in a caressing type of lovemaking. Voice-overs comment on changes in gay male life, both repressed and closeted in the past, and the sound track includes blues songs about "sissy men" in the black community. There is a kind of estrangement about the whole section, as cuts take the viewer from the theatricalized biblical story to fast-paced and exaggerated physical comedy to languid close-up lovemaking. The most intimate sex passage includes a superimposed scroll-up of the 1933 Hollywood production code

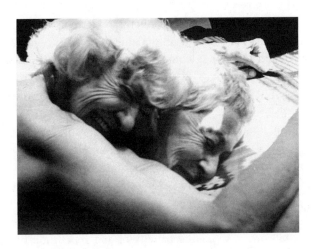

From Barbara Hammer's *Nitrate Kisses*, 1992.
Courtesy of www.barbarahammerfilms.com.

while a narrator explains that Hollywood officially eliminated gay representations for thirty years.[7] In the last section, a German woman, interviewed by Hammer, discusses lesbians in concentration camps in which the authorized historical version is that Jewish and "political" female prisoners had "platonic" lesbian loves, while the criminal, prostitute, and "asocial" ones had "disgusting" physical relations. This voice-over is cut with footage shot under a boardwalk with striking shadow patterns on the ground, of which the possible or metaphoric significance is unclear or unknown, and depictions of two stylish tattooed and pierced leather-women undressing each other and making love. The film ends with credits revealing it was funded in part with National Endowment for the Arts money at the very time the "culture wars" contestation was at a height.

The strength of *Nitrate Kisses* is in part due to its recurring ability to ground the image material in explanations on the sound track. Experts are present but detached from bodies, and they seem less "authoritative" for not being granted a face and body. The assembled shots of disparate material at times work associatively (for example, shots from a gay pride parade in Paris, marking a present continuation of queer life) and at other times seem to have no connection (the boardwalk and beach shots). There is a daring willingness to take risks, and yet at other times the fragments seem simply puzzling (for example, shots of a tablet memorializing Gertrude Stein and Alice B. Toklas in Paris) when contained in a section on lesbian history that has been lost in the concentration camps and the subsequent stigmatization that erased continuity and community. At another point a bizarre pun appears when the German lesbian feminist historian says of the loss of lesbian documentation: "We have only our oral history," and the image cuts to the lovemaking leather-women with a close-up of cunnilingus. It is unclear if this is intended to produce smutty hilarity, but in any case, it rather undercuts the narrator's substantive point.

A direct juxtaposition of found footage and comic intent runs through the adventurous *History Lessons* (2000), which builds on appropriation without the same discourse of sobriety that underlines *Nitrate Kisses*. *History Lessons* has good intentions: to consider lesbian images from the beginning of film until the Stonewall uprising, including popular culture examples, and also marking the legal, medical, and scientific discourses of control. This is a tall order, given the paucity of and repression of women-generated materials (often available today only in snapshots, personal journals, and interviews with elderly dykes) and given the situation of film, in which scattered home movies are barely archived. Hammer solves the problem by inserting commercial materials ranging from "girl-girl" porn to lurid covers of lesbian-themed pulp fiction to 1950s scandal sheets in popular culture, and dramatic recreations of Kinsey-like "scientific measurement" of lesbians in more serious arenas. The result, according to the video box, is "radical sexual politics in a jester's surprise package of impudent humor and Situationist-style found-footage monkeyshines." Yet the results are definitely uneven, undercut by remarkably sappy feminist folksongs and clumsy dramatic restagings of past events that invite us to laugh at rather than with the film.

Given the pioneering work of lesbian historians, both academic and amateur, today's queer audience knows a great deal about many aspects of the past revolving around visual misrepresentation and the way the community itself appropriated and reinterpreted mass culture. We know from the extant histories and personal stories that the situation was more complex than Hammer shows. First of all, butch/femme did not encompass the whole of lesbian experiences, and when role-playing is considered, it raises questions that go far beyond the surface of appearance to inner psychology, the pleasures of imaginative performance, and the social functions of sharply stereotyped roles. By appropriating extant image materials, such as a World War II news documentary about women serving in the Army Air Corps (transporting planes, not participating in combat), the film signals a simple rereading through context. These women, in their various activities, can be read as an Amazon Nation outpost. But staying on the surface, the "hidden history" of lesbians in the

From Barbara Hammer's *History Lessons*, 2000. Courtesy of www .barbarahammerfilms .com.

armed forces remains a one-line joke. "Could be" is a fantasy, not a reflection of real lived lives.

This sort of tension exists as a fundamental problem of historical analysis. The modernist gay and lesbian stance sought affirmation in identity. Thus the act of "coming out" was finding and declaring one's true identity against explicit social and political repression. The postmodern queer stance seeks affirmation in diverse and fluid performance. The performance of queer is a constant restaging and acting out always open to another way (and often regarded as a retreat from politics and commitment by those in a more modernist-activist framework). In a real sense, the film diminishes what these depicted women were doing for a complex set of reasons. The Army Air Corps women who became pilots had worthy goals and motives beyond a playhouse lesbian romp: they mastered aviation, responded to patriotism, rose to a challenge, had the reward of physical and mental achievement, and showed that they could do "a man's job." Some were even heterosexuals.

By working primarily with image material as her inspiration, Hammer clearly intends to "expose" repressive and policing discourses in *History Lessons*. But she actually reproduces one of the major errors of the "scientific" discourse. Researchers like Kinsey, trained in empirical science, thought that photographic documentation could actually reveal certain truths (for example, a film of a woman masturbating to orgasm) without taking into account acting (either for the camera or faking an orgasm) or the utter failure of empirical external observation to record and account for internal bodily states. Hammer, using archive material or recreating little mimed dramas with today's lesbians, misses the difference between living as a butch in the post–Second World War United States, and 1990s "drag kings" whimsically dressing up in costume and impersonating people from an earlier era. The cases are similar on the surface, but the contemporary image alone cannot capture the lived truth of the past; for that we need voice, memory, words.

As complex as these issues are, it is doubtful that Situationist appropriation can actually provide any analytic reference point. In a much more sober vein, *Resisting Paradise* reimagines France during the German occupation. Granted a Camargo Foundation fellowship year to do a 1999 residency in Cassis in southern France, and inspired by the region's landscape and light, Hammer began the film with a vigorous revival of her technique of painting on film and creating a bright plastic expression. But disturbed by images of suffering in news reports of events in Kosovo, she wanted to leave and film the battle area. Told that the fellowship requires residency, she deflected her attention to the World War II historical moment when Matisse and Bonnard continued to paint in the same area, apparently oblivious to the war. Having found stories of the French Resistance and a woman who used her government post to create false papers for refugees, Hammer reflects on landscape, art, light, and color, personal choices in politics, and herself and history. In its best passages this is ambitious and vigorous experimental filmmaking, recasting the lyricism of light and landscape into an ethical drama. At its weakest, the judgmental point seems lost: yes, Matisse was seemingly totally unconcerned with the war and just continued making his art. But he was an old man, seventy-five in 1944; pragmatically, what could he have done?[8] Or is it that he did not voice his opposition, feel uncomfortable, make more political art? The implicit comparison is with Hammer, who does not give up her fellowship, follow her ideals and desires, and run off to war, but who articulates her discomfort. While praising little-known Resistance heroism, perhaps the most banal moment in the film is a "dramatic recreation" of Walter Benjamin's crossing the Pyrenees.[9]

From Barbara Hammer's *Resisting Paradise*, 2003. Courtesy of
www.barbarahammerfilms.com.

Often falling between an innovative eclecticism of form and theme on the
one hand and an underdeveloped thoughtfulness and pathetic restaging
on the other, overall the film intrigues and aggravates.

Given Hammer's uneven struggles with finding an effective long form
for the documentary essay, one might anticipate that *Devotion: A Film
about Ogawa Productions* (2000), an intense examination of a famous
Japanese documentary film collective, would harbor serious problems,
and it does. Ogawa Productions, lead by Ogawa Shinsuke, began filming
student activism and continued with documenting the fight by peasant
farmers to resist the government confiscation of their land to build the
Narita International Airport. Their landmark political documentary,
Narita: Peasants of the Second Fortress (1971), achieved an intense power
from the film collective living in close relation to the farmers. Lead by a
charismatic and difficult leader, the collective consumed itself in internal
tensions until and after Ogawa Shinsuke's death in 1992. *Devotion* played
at the Yamagata International Documentary Film Festival in 2001. Hammer was to be an invited guest, but the events of September 11 prevented
her travel. As a result, what would have been a celebratory hosting of the
director and her new film was replaced by a roundtable discussion by
Hong Kong feminist director Ann Hui (*Boat People* [1982], *Song of the
Exile* [1990]), Japanese documentary director Sato Makoto, and U.S.-
based academic Abé Mark Nornes, who is writing a critical study of
Ogawa Productions. The record of the discussion is remarkable. Ham-

mer, coming to the subject as an outsider, faced the project with predictable problems: she had to work with translators throughout the making of the film; she had no previous familiarity with Japanese film or culture; and while she had unparalleled access to photos and footage of the collective shot over many years, she had to rely on personal testimony in the present to make sense of the past history. The roundtable pinpoints key problems, such as talking-head interviews with cutaways to films and outtakes of Ogawa films but without explanation of the source. The result for those familiar with the original situation is confusion. But, counterintuitively, Hammer's limits actually potentiate the results, and her interest in the internal dynamics of the collective include bluntly addressing questions that Japanese critics would typically avoid, such as sexual relations and patriarchal patterns in the group. As a result, according to the roundtable, *Devotion* is inaccurate and misleading, but also able to explore the complex and hidden side of the Ogawa collective: the pathology of its erratic leader, the repression of women, and the deeply neurotic interpersonal relations within the collective.

Given the trajectory of Barbara Hammer's entire body of work to date, her persistent concern with perception, her sharp critical wit, and her longstanding work in animation and related techniques, her work must be considered as an analytically sophisticated development of forms and themes that begin in a romantic tradition but which have increasingly evolved into an intellectually critical while visually pleasurable experience. Hammer's films and tapes move beyond a naive response to the body and the natural environment. At the same time, her work sometimes seems limited by her own framework of extreme individual and personal media making. Throughout her career there is a racial sameness in the women who appear in her work, which is not remarked on, however reflexive the form. When footage of African American lesbians enters *History Lessons*, it seems last-minute and token in its presence. As the Yamagata roundtable on *Devotion* indicates, Hammer's individualist take allows for both refreshing originality and also idiosyncratic limits and a loss of historical and contextual understanding.

Hammer's major shift from short lyrics to long-form experimental documentary produced work that is strongest in its plastic visual episodes, building on her accomplished style of using paint, film, and optical printing. Assembling her films and videos from a wide variety of sources and materials, Hammer maintains change and variety despite temporal length. But the long form breaks down in areas such as dramatic reenactment, where amateurish skits appear rather than the work of skillfully directed, talented actors. Similarly, while mainstream documentary has a deadly predictable presentation of old photographs, films, and print materials (encapsulated in the "Ken Burns Effect" available in all levels of computer video editing),[10] typically Hammer employs a rapid handheld movement and quick cutting, which creates what could be called a "Barbara Hammer Effect." While visually stimulating, the style also undercuts the opportunity to examine, study, even savor, the original image. Those experiences are subordinated to the maker's control of our vision. While Hammer quotes from many and varied sources, such as feminist writers and theorists, explaining the quotes in interviews as postmodern appropriations, she also changes them with audio manipulation and selective contextualing. By heavily using visual variety, Hammer maintains immediate interest but can also sacrifice a clearer through-line argument or development. In interviews, Hammer explains her working method as collecting and assembling from the storehouse of visual materials, but she does not seem to go through the same kind of background historical research that informs most long-form documentaries.[11] An experiential present overtakes a dialogue with the past. In contrast, appropriating the scientific X-ray movies for *Sanctus* did not need an explanation of the original footage since the lyrical reuse rests on phenomenological awe at the body in motion, not on calling on the medical dimension of the source.

Barbara Hammer's evolving accomplishment in film and video art does what the best experimental work always does. It challenges the audience to new ways of thinking and feeling, new kinds of experience. It moves the boundaries for thinking of media art as well, creating space for a reevaluation of the past and new issues for the future. In this it is profoundly optimistic. It assumes we can learn and change, even when facing death, environmental disaster, and social decay. Art is then not a retreat from the world but an active engagement with it. The filmmaker faces the world and challenges it, not simply recording life but provoking the audience and changing it.

Filmography

Schizy, 1968 (15 min.): si., col.; Super 8
Barbara Ward Will Never Die, 1969 (6 min.): si., col.; Super 8
Traveling: Marie and Me, 1970 (20 min.): si., col.; Super 8
The Song of the Clinking Cup, 1972 (3 min.): si., col.; Super 8

I Was/I Am, 1973 (7 1/2 min.): sd., b&w; 16mm

Sisters!, 1974 (8 min.): sd., col.; 16mm

A Gay Day, 1974 (3 min.): sd., col.; 16mm

Dyketactics, 1974 (4 min.): sd., col.; 16mm

X, 1974 (9 min.): sd., col.; 16mm

Women's Rites, or Truth Is the Daughter of Time, 1974 (10 min.): sd., col.; 16mm

Menses, 1974 (4 min.): sd., col.; 16mm

Jane Brakhage, 1975 (10 min.): sd., b&w; 16mm

Superdyke, 1975 (20 min.): sd., col.; 16mm

Psychosynthesis, 1975 (9 min.): sd., col.; 16mm

Superdyke Meets Madame X., 1975 (28 min.): sd., col.; video

Moon Goddess (with G. Churchman), 1976 (15 min.): sd., col.; 16mm

Eggs, 1976 (12 min.): sd., col.; 16mm

Multiple Orgasm, 1976 (6 min.): si., col.; 16mm

Women I Love, 1976 (27 min.): sd., b&w; 16mm

Stress Scars and Pleasure Wrinkles, 1976 (20 min.): sd., col.; video

The Great Goddess, 1977 (25 min.): sd., b&w; 16mm

Double Strength, 1978 (16 min.): sd., col., b&w; 16mm

Home, 1978 (12 min.): sd., col.; 16mm

Haircut, 1978 (6 min.): si., col.; 16mm

Available Space, 1978 (20 min.): sd., col.; 16mm, film performance

Sappho, 1978 (7 min.): sd., col.; 16mm

Dream Age, 1979 (12 min.): sd., col.; 16mm

Pictures for Barbara, 1980 (12 min.): sd., col.; 16mm

Machu Picchu, 1980 (15 min.): sd., col.; 16mm

Natura Erotica, 1980 (12 min.): si., col.; 16mm

See What You Hear What You See, 1980 (3 min.): si., b&w; 16mm

Our Trip, 1981 (4 min.): sd., col., b&w; 16mm

Arequipa, 1981 (12 min.): si., col., b&w; 16mm

Pools (with B. Klutinis), 1981 (6 1/2 min.): sd., col., b&w; 16mm

Synch-Touch, 1981 (12 min.): sd., col., b&w; 16mm

The Lesbos Film, 1981 (30 min.): sd., col.; 16mm

Pond and Waterfall, 1982 (15 min.): si., col.; 16mm

Audience, 1983 (33 min.): sd., b&w; 16mm

Stone Circles, 1983 (10 min.): sd., col., b&w; 16mm

New York Loft, 1983 (9 min.): sd., col., b&w; 16mm

Bamboo Xerox, 1984 (6 min.): si., b&w; 16mm, film installation

Pearl Diver, 1984 (6 min.): sd., col.; 16mm

Bent Time, 1984 (20 min.): sd., col.; 16mm

Doll House, 1984 (4 min.): sd., col., b&w; 16mm

Parisian Blinds, 1984 (6 min.): si., col., b&w; 16mm

Tourist, 1984–85 (3 min.): sd., col., b&w; 16mm

Optic Nerve, 1985 (16 min.): sd., col., b&w; 16mm

Hot Flash, 1985 (20 min.): sd., col.; video

Would You Like To Meet Your Neighbor? A New York Subway Tape, 1985 (20 min.): sd., col.; video

Bedtime Stories, 1986 (20 min.): sd., col.; video

The History of the World According to a Lesbian, 1986 (25 min.): sd., col.; video

Snow Job: The Media Hysteria of AIDS, 1986 (8 min.): sd., col.; video

No No Nooky T.V., 1987 (12 min.): sd., col., b&w; 16mm

Place Mattes, 1987 (8 min.): sd., col., b&w; 16mm

No No Nooky T.V., 1987 (12 min.): sd., col.; video

Endangered, 1988 (18 min.): sd., col., b&w; 16mm

Two Bad Daughters, 1988 (12 min.): sd., col.; video

Still Point, 1989 (9 min.): sd., col., b&w; 16mm

T.V. Tart, 1989 (12 min.): sd., col.; video

Sanctus, 1990 (19 min.): sd., col., b&w; 16mm

Vital Signs, 1991 (9 min.): sd., col., b&w; 16mm

Dr. Watson's X-Rays, 1991 (20 min.): sd., col.; video

Nitrate Kisses, 1992 (67 min.): sd., b&w; 16mm

Out in South Africa, 1994 (55 min.): sd., col.; video

Tender Fictions, 1995 (58 min.): sd., col.; 16mm

The Female Closet, 1997 (60 min.): sd., col.; 16mm and video

Devotion: A Film about Ogawa Productions, 2000 (84 min.): sd., col.; video

History Lessons, 2000 (65 min.): sd., col.; 16mm

My Babushka: Searching Ukrainian Identities, 2001 (53 min.): sd., col.; video

Resisting Paradise, 2003 (80 min.): sd., col.; 16mm

Lover/Other, 2005 (55 min.): sd., col., b&w; video

Notes

An earlier version of a part of this essay was commissioned as an exhibition brochure by the Mary Ripma Ross Film Theater at the Sheldon Memorial Art Gallery, University of Nebraska, Lincoln. Discussions with Barbara Hammer over the years inform my knowledge of her work. Discussions with Martha Vicinus, Linda Dittmar, Jeffrey Skoller, Michelle Citron, Julia Lesage, and Robin Blaetz were invaluable in shaping this project.

1 She has been most often ignored by the experimental film establishment, such as it is, and pigeonholed as a lesbian feminist, or faulted as a counter-cultural feminist by others. A new critical anthology, Petrolle and Wexman's *Women and Experimental Filmmaking*, includes her films in the filmography, but Hammer is not among the twenty-three mostly U.S. filmmakers given featured essays. In the one substantive mention of her work, she is mistakenly

claimed as a member of the new generation of the 1980s and 1990s who "began using formal radicalism to explore lesbian themes" (10), missing the fact that she had been producing work since the early 1970s.

2   Essentialist thought in feminist circles of the late 1960s and 1970s assumed that all women were basically identical, thus eliminating any considerations of history, nation, culture, class, or race. Within a cultural lesbian orientation, often combined with New Age thought and countercultural practice, this conceptual singularity tended to activism in terms of cultural separatism and a focus on issues of women's bodies, health, art, and spirituality. A themed issue of *Heresies: A Feminist Publication on Art and Politics* (Spring 1978), "The Great Goddess," provides an excellent introduction. Within second-wave feminism, liberal and socialist feminisms argued against essentialism and for political, institutional, and structural change rather than separatism. Within the lesbian community, essentialism was particularly inept at dealing with issues of race, class, cultural background, age, and relations with hetero- and homosexual men.

The most sophisticated elaboration of Hammer's early work in terms of a lesbian feminist aesthetic is by Jacqueline Zita ("Films of Barbara Hammer"). In contrast, Andrea Weiss offers a critique of Hammer as a lesbian feminist (*Vampires and Violets*; "*Women I Love* and *Double Strength*"), while both Claudia Gorbman ("Body Displaced, Body Discovered") and Alex Juhasz (*Women of Vision*) have also considered her work.

3   An academic and theoretical discussion continues among queer thinkers. Christopher Reed summarizes a 1998 international conference in Amsterdam: "In brief, the essentialist view, arising out of 19th century medical discourse, assumes that homosexuality is an innate, historically continuous, biological phenomenon. The constructivist approach arises primarily out of 20th century anthropological research into incidence and attitudes toward same-sex sexuality in so-called non-western cultures. This analysis suggests that the concept of homosexuality—indeed the whole notion of sexual orientation—is specific to our time and place and cannot be assumed to be mappable onto other cultures" (6).

4   For example, Hammer refers to having being born in Hollywood, crosscuts her childhood image with that of Shirley Temple, and presents herself dancing on the Walk of Stars commemorative tile for Temple, giving the impression that she was a Hollywood brat or L.A. aspirant. Yet she elides high school years in upper-middle-class suburban Westchester County, New York, and zips past a nine-year marriage, sublimating the teen and twentysomething years that most autobiographies explore as foundational for later life experiences.

5   Hammer's critique can seem simplistic. As a teenager Cather did crossdress and had crushes on women. But driven to pursue her career as a writer, she hid her private life from public scrutiny. She clearly placed her professional

goal of gaining respect and position as a serious author above personal lifestyle expression. In this framework, critics and historians are not totally at fault for interpreting the art without reference to her sexuality. Foster's interview provides Hammer's point of view on the issues.

6 This technique is also used in *Forbidden Love* (Aerlyn Weissman and Lynne Fernie, Canada, 1992).

7 True enough, but the statement does not take into account the work of contemporary scholars, such as Alexander Doty and Matthew Tinkcom, who read a gay history and spectatorship back into classic Hollywood and examine specific gay production practices.

8 "During the war [Matisse] was old and ill with cardiovascular, renal, and abdominal disorders; he underwent a colostomy in 1941 and, a year later, almost died" (Schjeldahl, "Art as Life").

9 This now well-known event has been told by various biographers and commentators with more attention to historical and biographical complexity than the film's clumsy recreation. Its representation in the film comes off as painfully opportunistic rather than thoughtful, with "Benjamin" walking down a Pyrenees road being more reminiscent of Chaplin's Little Tramp shuffling than a German Jew after months of desperate anxiety seeking escape from annihilation.

10 The Ken Burns Effect, named after the famous PBS historical documentary producer who uses it so extensively in his work such as *The Civil War*, allows for easy panning over scanned two-dimensional images.

11 For example, Connie Field's feminist classic *Rosie the Riveter* (1980) was based on background interviews with hundreds of women. An interesting contemporary case is Michelle Citron's *Mixed Greens* (2005), an interactive DVD with extensive sampling from collected archival materials, interviews, home movies, and dramatic recreations that examines interwoven themes of family history, Irish Jews, and lesbian lives.

MARIA PRAMAGGIORE

Chick Strand's Experimental Ethnography

□

I am a believer that art can always be tampered with.—Chick Strand

At a retrospective held at the Los Angeles Film Forum in 2000 on the work of West Coast experimental filmmaker Chick Strand (b. 1931), David James described her as a "radically original pioneer in feminist, ethnographic and in compilation filmmaking," and one whose work has maintained its integrity "somewhat aslant of prevailing fashions."[1] This essay endorses and extends those observations by examining several of Chick Strand's films that not only confirm her status as a radically original pioneer but also help to suggest some of the reasons the significance of her work, as James notes, has not always been apparent.

Strand's work must be framed by—but cannot be fully contained within—the aesthetic and political milieu of the 1960s and 1970s. Her embrace of anarchy, hippiedom, and drug counterculture played out in her filmmaking and her long professional collaboration and personal relationship with pop artist Neon Park (Martin Muller, 1940–93), best known for his Hollywood duck series and colorful, surreal album covers for Frank Zappa and Little Feat. Strand and Park's long marriage—they lived and worked together from the late 1960s until Park's death from ALS (Lou Gehrig's disease) in 1993—included annual forays into Mexico to shoot footage that Strand used in her films. They were "too young to be beatniks and too old to be hippies," Park told one interviewer.[2] That statement reflects their attraction to the political and aesthetic movements of the 1950s and 1960s yet also manages to assert their iconoclasm and resistance to labels.

In a similar balancing act, Strand's filmmaking encompasses documentary and experimental cinema. With a background in anthropology, combined with an interest in assemblage form, Strand produced a body of work during the 1960s, 1970s, and 1980s that anticipated the radical theories of subjectivity that became prominent during the 1990s. This fact may account for a renewed interest in her work in the 1990s and 2000s.[3] She has written about her approach to ethnographic film as "liberal and radical in terms of the accepted methods of anthropology."[4] The most distinctive feature of her work is the complex layering of visual and sound elements, accomplished through techniques such as superimposition and the juxtaposition of found footage and sound with original images.

Film scholars have focused on Strand's compilation films (which rely on the assemblage aesthetic, specifically associated with the San Francisco Bay Area in the 1950s) and her interest in giving voice and image to women's stories on film. Strand's work addresses one key issue in feminist and postcolonial film studies: the power of the gaze. Yet "aslant of prevailing fashions," as James writes, her films reject the prevailing orthodoxy of feminist cinema of the 1970s and 1980s: the necessity of undermining the power of the (male) gaze. Strand steadfastly refuses to relinquish the objectifying power of the camera, asserting her aesthetic activity (as both the maker of images and the compiler of existing images and sounds) as a legitimate process through which to explore sensual states and subjective visions. As Irina Leimbacher, curator of the Pacific Film Archives, puts it, in Strand's films, "an intensely personal vision merges with concerns (whether 'intended' or not) to deconstruct fixed notions of objectivity, identity, narrative, and female sensuality."[5] But Strand does not deconstruct the process of filmmaking; rather, she sees her work in terms of the people and processes caught up in making art. She has written, "Ethnographic films can and should be works of art, symphonies about the fabric of a people."[6]

Several film histories and studies of experimental cinema include a brief account of Strand's work. James Peterson's *Dreams of Chaos, Visions of Order* (1994) offers the most extensive engagement in a reading of *Loose Ends* (1979) as an exemplary and enigmatic compilation film. David James's *Allegories of Cinema: American Film in the Sixties* (1989) more generally describes Strand's work as part of a "classically modernist collage tradition."[7] By contrast, Kristin Thompson and David Bordwell's *Film History: An Introduction* (2003) briefly mentions Strand's *Mujer de Milefuegos* (*Woman of a Thousand Faces*, 1976) as part of a tradition of alternative ethnography that they associate with Godfrey Reggio (*Koyaanisqatsi* [1983], *Powaqqatsi* [1988], and *Naqoykatsi* [2002]), and Issac Julien (*Looking for Langston* [1989], *Young Soul Rebels* [1991], *The Attendant* [1992], and *Frantz Fanon* [1995]). In a 1998 issue of *Wide Angle* devoted to women's experimental film, Kate Haug's interview and Irina Leimbacher's essay locate Strand firmly within women's experimental cinema. The *Wide Angle* issue also contains a filmography and a bibliography of Strand's writing on film.

In assessing Strand's work, I join Thompson and Bordwell in focusing on experimental ethnography, but I incorporate James's and Peterson's emphasis on the West Coast assemblage aesthetic. In extending the useful observations of these scholars, I characterize Strand's style as a fusion of poetic imagery with the critical distance that the assemblage approach compels: a merger that generates a productive tension between lyricism and irony.

This tension, ubiquitous in her work, may provide another explanation for the current reappraisal of Strand's work. David James writes that, "with the increased currency of quotation and the nonorganic representation of already-existing images in postmodernism, compilation films have acquired a fresh eminence."[8] One example is the work of pop-punk artist Winston Smith, whose collages—composed of advertising images gleaned from old magazines—served as illustrations on posters for nonexistent clubs and graced Dead Kennedy album covers in the 1980s and 1990s. Smith's work recalls Neon Park's colorful, surreal compositions. Yet Smith (who chose as a pseudonym the name of the protagonist in George Orwell's *1984*) argues that his outsider sensibility has become commonplace in politics and advertising: "What used to be my little ironic joke is now the mainstream," he says. "Shows how low the mainstream has sunk."[9]

Although hardly well known, Chick Strand's films endure because, like Smith's collages, they suggest that the significance of images derives from their cultural context (hence her frequent use of preexisting images and sound) and from the personal context of filmmaking. As such, her films refuse to obey the conventional distinctions between traditional documentary realism, with its implicit promise to present rather than represent reality, and avant-garde film, as a highly personal art form that creates an aesthetic experience wholly distinct from everyday concerns. Her work speaks two languages, refusing to observe the distinction between an "objective" examination of the real world and the expanded consciousness of the visual artist. As each of her films suggests, Strand's work draws upon the real world—a source for found objects and for her connections with other people—and transforms that world at the same time.

Before turning to a discussion of the way four of Strand's films use poetic images and ironic structure to produce experimental ethnography, I briefly summarize relevant biographical and historical information.

Chick Strand and Assemblage Art: Life in Three Dimensions

A native northern Californian born Mildred and nicknamed Chick by her father, Strand grew up a free spirit and anarchist in the San Francisco Bay Area. She studied anthropology at Berkeley and became involved in the free speech movement, which shaped her outlook and political approach (she first embraced but later rejected anarchy). Her lifelong interest in collage as an aesthetic form developed from a photography course and early experiments in two-dimensional photographic collage. In 1961, Strand and Bruce Baillie (b. 1931) organized film happenings, setting up makeshift film screenings at restaurants, local colleges, and at Strand and Baillie's homes. They shared an interest in film collage: Baillie's celebrated *Castro Street* (1966), for example, "layer[s] or combine[s] multiple images" and exhibits "an unusual sensitivity to texture, color, and light."[10] On any given evening, the group screened a variety of films, including popular features, animation, newsreels, and experimental films. According to Strand, they knew they had to entice viewers not accustomed to the esoteric demands of avant-garde cinema. The carnival atmosphere made the screenings themselves into performance art, where Strand and others wore costumes and passed a sewing basket for donations.

Along with Baillie and Ernest Callenbach (b. 1929, founding editor of *Film Quarterly*), Strand began editing and distributing *Canyon Cinemanews*, a journal that became a focal point for the independent film movement on the West Coast. In 1967, Bruce Baillie, Lenny Lipton, Robert Nelson, Larry Jordan, and Ben Van Meter founded Canyon Cinema, a collective that describes itself on its Web site as "synonymous with Bay Area independent and experimental film." The still thriving Canyon collective distributes the films of a number of important experimental

Chick Strand in 2004. Courtesy of Chick Strand.

filmmakers such as Kenneth Anger, Peggy Ahwesh, Bruce Baillie, Stan Brakhage, James Broughton, Shirley Clarke, Bruce Conner, Les Blank, Storm de Hirsch, Valie Export, Ernie Gehr, Barbara Hammer, Peter Kubelka, Jack Smith, Paul Sharits, and Chick Strand.

Strand left Northern California in the early 1960s, abandoning her second marriage and "running off" to Mexico (as she put it) with pop-surrealist visual artist Neon Park. In 1966, they moved to Los Angeles and Strand began studying ethnographic film at UCLA. She experienced anger and frustration, however, because the films she saw were "made with cold indifference to living, breathing people. . . . In a scientific attempt to present what is perceived only by what the anthropologist sees, all nuances, sensibilities, aesthetics, emotions and human drama in the culture are lost. . . . The films lack intimacy, dimension, heart and soul."[11]

Seeing anthropology as a "dead end," Strand committed herself to avant-garde film, as well as to paying the bills. A collaboration with Patrick O'Neill, another Los Angeles–based filmmaker interested in multiple, layered images, included a commercial for Sears where they "did irreverent things with their back to school fashions."[12]

She directed the film arts program at Occidental College until her retirement in 1996. Throughout the 1970s and 1980s, she and Park divided their time between Los Angeles and San Miguel de Allende, Mexico, where Strand often shot footage. "To me," she states in an interview, "Mexico is surrealism."[13] In 1989, Park was diagnosed with ALS and Strand turned from films to painting so that she could take care of him at home. Since his death and her retirement in 1996, Strand continues to paint and make films at her home in Tujunga, California. She is working on four films based upon footage shot in Mexico with Park in the late 1980s.

Chick Strand and Experimental Ethnography

Strand's film work is based upon the principles of assemblage, an art form that depends on tensions arising from the juxtaposition of seemingly unrelated objects. Her films always use assemblage: she incorporates found footage and sound even in films such as *Anselmo* (1967), *Mosori Monika* (1970), and *Mujer de Milefuegos* (1976), which are organized primarily around footage that Strand herself shot. But assemblage is more than merely a structural element of individual films; it acts as a conceptual framework that defines Strand's entire oeuvre. While allowing her camera to explore her subject with great intimacy, Strand invariably tempers that potential immersion in the seductive image with the ironic, distanced, intellectual element that arises from juxtaposing her own images with found footage and sound.

In other words, not only does her work fuse avant-garde and documentary, but it also merges two seemingly irreconcilable traditions within avant-garde cinema: the film poem and the compilation film. P. Adams Sitney and James Peterson characterize the film poem as a modern form that represents subjectivity through metaphor. Sitney has further described these films as trance, architectonic, and mythopoeic films. The film poem uses techniques such as slow motion, repetition, voice-over, and associational editing to establish subjective psychological states. They evoke sensual and emotional responses through symbolism and metaphor, where meaning derives from the abstract or subconscious similarities evoked between two images in a sequence or two sounds.

By contrast, assemblage art—a major influence on West Coast experimental cinema—is a postmodern bricolage that relies on ironic distance. Assemblage highlights the aesthetic process of imposing form on a collection of disparate, often unrelated elements and thus calls into question the purity, unity, and coherence of the art object. In the assemblage film, form is imposed through a temporal chain that joins unrelated images. The juxtaposition of found objects (in the form of written, visual, and aural texts) distances the audience because it highlights the processes of citation (combining preexisting images) rather than inviting viewers to immerse themselves in the content and flow of images. Assemblage films thus depend less on metaphor—the deep structural similarities brought to the surface by comparing two images—than on metonymy, where meaning arises from spatial or temporal proximity along a chain of images. Metonymy is based on closeness or contiguity; it does not assert any transfer of qualities shared by the two represented objects or images (as metaphor does) but, rather, stirs up associations less central to any essential significance of the two images or objects.[14]

Peterson writes that any work of assemblage "maintains a tension between its incorporated elements and the new composition that comprises them."[15] In Strand's films, that tension highlights the synthetic quality of the artwork and emphasizes the transformation of raw materials (from animals to musical instruments to film footage) into shared and meaningful cultural and aesthetic experiences. Strand addresses the topic of "making" in her interview with Haug, where she talks about her work as "a handmade anything, which I think is really fun." For Strand, the process of making films involves being in the transcendent moment at every step along the way. She views working as going to "some other area that is not of this world. It is that meditative kind of thing."[16]

An especially distinctive combination of the personal, the poetic, and the ironic flavors Strand's work. For example, films such as *Waterfall* (1967), *Elasticity* (1976), and *Fake Fruit* (1986) combine found footage and sound with the motion poetics of dancer-filmmakers like Maya Deren, Yvonne Rainer, and Carolee Schneemann. At Occidental College, Strand instructed her students to dance with the camera in their hands, a practice that resonates with the work of many feminist artists and critics of the 1960s and 1970s who devised strategies to intervene in the camera's processes of objectification. Strand's dancing camera is apparent in *Angel Blue Sweet Wings* (1966), *Anselmo*, and *Mujer de Milefuegos*.

In emphasizing the vibrant tension between poetry and irony in Strand's films, I want to avoid the suggestion that the poetic and assemblage strains stand in radical opposition to one another. As Peterson observes, similarities exist between the general approaches of the film poem and the compilation film: namely, that the relations between shots are characterized by a "wide range of associations" (both metaphorical and metonymic) and that the two forms share an emphasis on local effects, often at the expense of overall structural coherence.[17]

Strand's experimental ethnography grows precisely from this combination of poetic and assemblage aesthetics. Because Strand imbues her work with a personal vision (grounded in the emotional texture of people and places) and the critical distance of assemblage, they should be read within the tradition of surrealist ethnography. The surrealist movement's focus on dream states, radical juxtaposition, and the logic of the absurd has been important to experimental filmmaking throughout the twentieth century and into the twenty-first. In *Experimental Ethnography*, Catherine Russell considers the work of Spanish filmmaker Luis Buñuel (1900–1983) and observes that "experimental ethnography . . . apprehends otherness as fundamentally uncanny" by combining the surrealist fascination with the bizarre and absurd with the spectatorial practices of ethnography.[18]

Buñuel's sensibility is a useful paradigm for Strand's work, because of his attraction to the grotesque and focus on collections of objects and practices that resist marketplace logic.[19] *Las Hurdes* (*Land without Bread*, 1932) is particularly instructive because of its form: it juxtaposes images and narration in startling ways.[20] In this documentary, Buñuel pairs images of extreme poverty among the Hurdanos, a group of people in remote Spain, with a narration whose tone is conventionally neutral and distanced, but whose content is shocking. The callousness of the narrator's words makes it difficult to adopt the same position (as outsider), yet the images provide little access to the subjective humanity of the Hurdanos. An incongruous and unidentified presence (which may be attributed to the filmmaker himself) endows the film with grim irony. A much-cited example is a scene where a boy, shown to have little prospect of ever owning anything, learns to write the phrase "Respect the property of others" on a chalkboard in school.

Because Strand's films suggest both extreme subjectivity and distanced irony, they, like Buñuel's, circumvent ethnographic objectification, not by posing otherness as uncanny, but, instead, by destabilizing self and other, highlighting the uncanny character of those fixed categories. Unlike the work of Trinh T. Minh-ha, a Vietnamese experimental ethnographer who critiques ethnographic filmmaking as an ideological apparatus through which Western eyes apprehend cultural others, Strand acknowledges, even embraces, her singular vision. "I make movies about people I know and places I've been," she stated in a May 2004 interview with the author. Her films do not pursue a *deconstructive* ethnography, exposing the way

the Western gaze constructs Native Americans as others or the patriarchal gaze objectifies women. Instead, they acknowledge the fact of
colonial encounters and male dominance, but linger on moments when
individuals momentarily relinquish fixed identity positions and foreground the process of assemblage (collection and combination) to shape
the material of life (including personal relationships, stories, objects,
animals, and found footage/sound) into art.

   Below, I examine four of Strand's films as examples of an experimental
ethnography that combines the metaphorical and highly subjective images of the poetic film with the surreal irony and fragmentation of assemblage art. Because James Peterson and Marsha Kinder have provided
definitive readings of *Loose Ends* and *Soft Fiction*, I focus here on *Anselmo*, *Mosori Monika*, *Cartoon le Mousse*, and *Mujer de Milefuegos*,
describing the way these four films draw upon poetic and assemblage
traditions, encouraging viewers to apprehend self and other as uncanny
constructs.

Experimental Ethnographies

Anselmo (1967)

Anselmo represents an early example of Chick Strand's abiding interest in
documenting people, objects, animals, and events through a heightened
and poetic subjectivity, while at the same time using assemblage techniques that allow her to incorporate disparate, sometimes jarring elements. She has described this film on the Canyon Cinema web site as "a
symbolic reenactment of a real event," when she and Neon Park smuggled
a tuba into Mexico to give to her musician friend Anselmo. The film's
layered quality forces the viewer to reevaluate and, perhaps, to resist the
sensual invitation the images offer.

   The film begins with a superimposition of a biplane over the Mexican
desert, flocks of birds, and negative archival images of horses running in
undulating slow motion. The film documents the gift exchange through
superimposition as well: Anselmo walks across the empty desert toward a
woman at screen left holding the tuba. But these images are intercut and
superimposed with images of him carrying and playing the tuba. As
music begins to play, negative images of a group of brightly dressed
musicians and dancers are intercut with and superimposed over images
of the desert. The dancers' bright costumes, which take on a saturated

From Chick Strand's *Anselmo*, 1967. Courtesy of Chick Strand.

metallic quality in negative, endow the image with a velvety, luminous, and solarized surface. The camera moves among them as if it is dancing, too, recalling the undulating motions of the horses in the earlier scene. The camera moves in toward the curve of the tuba, where light plays off the metallic surface. In the concluding moments of the film, celebratory fireworks are superimposed over the dancers, tuba, and desert to conclude the festivities. The crescent shape of the spray of fireworks rhymes with and wraps around the tuba. The closing moments of the film repeat the images of the horses and the biplane. Finally, a simple color image of Anselmo appears, taken with a static camera, as he walks into the vast, empty desert with the tuba.

Several signature Strand elements emerge in this film and reappear through several decades of filmmaking: images of animals (especially birds, horses, and fish), beautiful barren landscapes, and a focus on organic movement (in camera movement as well as motion-filled imagery). The techniques Strand returns to again and again include asynchronous sound, found footage, superimpositions, negative images, and distorting close-ups.

Anselmo embodies the tensions in Strand's experimental ethnography. Its velvety, colorful images document the events and emotions of a highly personal moment among friends and draw viewers into the sensual kinetics of poetic motion and visual metaphors (for example, the horses and dancers, and the fireworks and the tuba). Yet several elements also mark the film as a work of ironic assemblage and raise questions about the relationship between Americans and Mexicans, between the natural world and the manufactured world of art, and between authenticity and performance.

For example, the opening depicts ambiguous images: the biplane is a technological achievement that simultaneously allows humans to experience the freedom of birds (the next image in the metonymic chain) but also serves as a technology of surveillance and military conquest. The plane alludes to General John "Blackjack" Pershing's 1916 punitive expedition into Mexico in search of the guerrilla Pancho Villa, which was seen in part as an occasion for testing new military equipment, including armored cars and airplanes. Like the mechanized plane, the horses move laterally across the landscape, yet they may also evoke associations with Cortes's conquest of indigenous people, aided by horses. Furthermore, because the plane, birds, and horses appear on film in a clearly manipulated manner, they also represent manufactured, human technologies that attempt to harness the beauty and power of the natural world, for better and for worse.

In this film, art emerges as a process that combines preexisting spaces and objects (the desert, the animals, and the people) and technology (the plane, the tuba, the fireworks, and the dancers' costuming). The shimmering clothing and languorous dance moves attest to the fact that both "raw materials" and human connections are required to produce art. Several dancers wear masks, calling attention to the dance as an exuberant performance, not a statement of authenticity. The closing image of Anselmo in the desert contrasts sharply with the highly decorative superimpositions, juxtapositions, and mobile camera shots, emphasizing the fact that filmmaker has *chosen* to document the world not through indexical realism but through sensual, poetic images and thought-provoking assemblage.

Rather than presenting Anselmo as a grateful recipient of the Western cultural artifact in the form of the tuba, *Anselmo* privileges a circuit of gift-giving wherein a shared moment of exchange functions as a point of departure for a perpetual motion machine where bodies and the camera dance. Anselmo's music and Strand's film flow out of relationships. The images extend the joy of motion, yet the exuberance of the moment is tempered by a critical distance that situates the exchange within history and human-made technology. This momentary performance is contextual and fleeting, rather than an expression of permanent roles and identities.

Mosori Monika (1970)

Mosori Monika is Strand's first overtly ethnographic film. The Strand film that is most reminiscent of Buñuel's *Las Hurdes*, it was screened at the Robert Flaherty Film Seminar in 1971.[21] While studying ethnographic film at UCLA, Strand was asked to participate in the project documenting the lives of Warao Indians in Venezuela with little prior knowledge of the culture. She immediately turned her focus to the cultural encounter between the Warao and recently arrived Spanish missionaries. She describes the finished project on the Canyon Cinema web site as "an expressive documentary . . . an ethnographic film about two cultures that have encountered one another. The Spanish Franciscan Missionaries went to Venezuela in 1945 to 'civilize' the Warao Indians."

As is usual in Strand's work, a central tension—in this case, between the Indians and the missionaries—is revealed through the film's form: "The acculturation is presented from two viewpoints . . . structured in counterpoint so that the deeper aspects of the juxtaposition of the modern culture over the old becomes apparent through the revelations." Those two viewpoints assume the form of a dialogue of sorts between the narration of Sister Isabel, a missionary in the Orinoco River delta, and Carmelita, an indigenous woman. Asynchronous voice-overs offer access to the thoughts of these two women. In these first-person monologues, they seem to take the implied listener (Strand and the film's viewers) as confidantes, sharing feelings that they might not share with others. Close-ups and personal narratives immerse viewers in the two women's subjective experiences as sister Isabel proudly comments on the civilization the Spanish have brought to the Indians and Carmelita describes her upbringing, marriage, and motherhood.

Here again, however, the lyrical seductiveness of the two women's "voices" is undermined by Strand's strategic juxtaposition of images and sound. As Ernest Callenbach wrote about the film in 1972, "the images . . . are cast by the sound track into a double and conflicting perspective."[22] This technique introduces ironic discrepancies when paired statements and images undermine the women's discourse. When Sister Isabel claims that the Warao lacked civilization before the missionaries' arrival, she states, "They didn't have *anything*." This comment is belied by the images Strand pairs with it: the Warao eating from wooden bowls and paddling across the river in boats they have clearly made (another instance where film art proceeds from the technological transformation of preexisting objects).

Another juxtaposition questions the imposition of European culture. When Sister Isabel proudly proclaims, "We civilized them," Strand inserts a poignant image of a naked Warao boy sitting on a train track wearing a shoe on one of his feet. The shot, which might well be at home in *Las Hurdes* (or the later *Los Olvidados*, 1950), is poetic in its design, with a camera that slowly moves up from the shoe to encompass the boy's entire body. It is also wickedly ironic. The worn, laceless shoe dangles off the boy's foot, a useless object that attests to the absurdity of transporting Western technologies and cultural values to the Warao.

Carmelita's first-person narrative presents a counter discourse to that of Sister Isabel, yet the film refuses to privilege her viewpoint as more authentic than or superior to that of the missionary. Her description of her traditional life reveals a world circumscribed by her duties to her husband and family, as taught to her by her mother. "Your daughter has remembered all you have taught her. We live very well." A sound cut moves from Carmelita's story back to Sister Isabel's narrative, where she recounts the process of teaching Warao children to cook and clean, suggesting the ways that the missionaries are usurping traditional maternal roles.

Moving between the two women's stories probes the complexity of the cultural encounter between missionaries and the Warao without idealizing or demonizing either the Europeans or the indigenous Warao. Although Richard Eder, in a 1976 *New York Times* review, argues that "[Strand's] thesis is that primitive cultures are good and that developed cultures come in and spoil them," the irony of assemblage refuses this simple dichotomy.[23] Juxtaposing the commentary from a Christian wedding ceremony that instructs women to obey their husbands highlights the patriarchal rules that, albeit unspoken, govern Carmelita's life as well. She describes first providing her husband with food and then dividing what is left among her ten children. These juxtapositions imply that both cultures are organized according to rules that advantage some individuals over others, specifically focusing on gender and power.

The film also examines the two cultures' treatment of sickness and health in a way that counters a *Village Voice* critic's charge that Strand's perspective is "Rousseauist, sometimes tritely so."[24] Far from ennobling the "primitives," *Mosori Monika* explores medical practices, revealing them to be cultural institutions that, like art, rely on individuals to transform the natural world for the benefit of the larger group. Whereas Carmelita talks about a shaman saving her brother, Sister Isabel describes modern medicines preventing death in childbirth (a commentary made double-edged because it is accompanied by close-ups of needles). Carmelita's reply expresses her feeling of helplessness when her husband dies because she could not afford to bring a shaman. Here, maintaining good health in both Warao and Spanish cultures is shown to depend on the responsiveness of male experts and their ability to transform elements in the world around them into vehicles for curing human diseases. In both cases, faith, resources, and commitment to the community are required for healing to occur. The film thus moves social practices away from individual politics and scrutinizes them in an analytical and abstract manner, underlining common elements of human existence.

Finally, the film again moves toward abstraction and away from the personal resonance of these two women's stories when the credits reveal that others read the English language voice-overs. Richard Eder calls the two voices "invented."[25] While the reasons for making this choice may well have depended upon pragmatic concerns such as the film's intended audience, the effect is to distance viewers from any notion of authenticity in Carmelita and Sister Isabel's first-person accounts. The thoughts and emotions of the two women remain compelling and clearly help the viewer to understand something about the two cultures, yet they also call into question the notion of any objective or truthful account of Warao and Spanish missionary societies.

Cartoon le Mousse (1979)

If *Mosori Monika* represents Strand's most conventional documentary—an intensive study of two women's stories that also distances viewers from those first-person accounts—then, at first glance, *Cartoon le Mousse* seems to occupy a position on the other end of the spectrum, much closer to the sheer intellectual abstraction of the compilation film. *Cartoon le Mousse* is a rigorous experiment in assemblage that, nevertheless, manages to involve the viewer's emotions through oddly evocative images. According to Gene Youngblood on the Canyon Cinema web site, the film creates "a surreal and sublime universe beyond reason." In other words, playing against type as usual, Strand highlights a formal structure of metonymy, where meaning arises from the proximity of images, to emphasize metaphor, a deeper symbolic or emotional resonance that connects disparate images.

As the title suggests, Strand draws together footage from old cartoons and educational films, redeploying the images in an investigation

From Chick Strand's *Mosori Monika*, 1970. Courtesy of Chick Strand.

(below) From Chick Strand's *Cartoon le Mousse*, 1979. Courtesy of Chick Strand.

of Western culture and, most particularly, the disciplinary practices of looking. The film opens with an absurd narration in French, delivered by a woman dressed like a dance-hall performer. The film later depicts scenes of a cartoon character who sings "Someday My Prince Will Come" as she swings through space alone. The editing suggests that her cartoon lover languishes in prison. Darkening shadows serve as precursors to a thunderstorm. The separation of the lovers is echoed in original footage Strand shot that recalls B-films of the 1940s in its depiction of solitude and secrets in the darkened rooms of empty houses at night.

The "surreal and sublime universe" that Youngblood describes emanates from the emotional texture of these ominous and apocalyptic images. In Western popular culture, a sad cartoon image functions as an oddly affecting oxymoron. And the noirish scenes of individuals alone at home at night are discomfiting in part because they are difficult to locate generically. The images hint at a detective plot while the music suggests horror-film suspense and 1950s science fiction. Because the film is an assemblage, a viewer might expect that an important key to meaning should rest in the metonymic connection between images—the chain of proximity that builds meaning. Yet the metaphorical significance of the elegiac tone and disturbing notes of solitude and abandonment overwhelm the metonymic chain. The temporal sequence—the linear metonymic chain that combines these disparate elements—is less important to the film's meaning than the mournful feeling of impending dark days that permeates the images.

Metonymic and metaphoric connections form the basis for meaning in a later sequence and, in so doing, point to one possible ethnographic frame for the film. The sequence focuses on the materials and practices of Western science and art. Strand follows images that make reference to early cinematic representation (animal locomotion studies, the zoetrope, and Muybridge's horse experiments) with educational footage that defines the rules of photographic representation and a partially clothed human torso on which another person draws a circular mark. Here Strand exposes Western cultural notions of objectivity and subjectivity to scrutiny by linking science and technology to the human body. That link is formed through practices of looking: the metonymic link between the images is the human gaze, including that of the spectator, following linear and circular patterns in the images. Metaphorically, the elements of the sequence all imply that cultural practices—not natural capacities—teach people how to form coherent ideas about objects in the world (including animal and human bodies) and a sequence of images.

An ironic and layered moment arises when the educational footage presents a definition of the circle of confusion. "Circle of confusion" seems to bear the name of an emotional conundrum (linking it to the earlier images of sadness and loss), but, in fact, it has a highly technical definition: it is an artifact produced by the reflection of a lens that itself limits the degree to which an image is in sharp focus.[26] The circular shape drawn over the heart of the human torso earlier in the sequence adds another level of significance: the confusion of human emotions. Finally, however, this linguistic and visual metaphor may suggest the dilemma faced by the ethnographic filmmaker, whose presence in the process of art making (serving as the lens through which images are filtered) inevitably affects the outcome. Strand's own reflections are captured in her films, just as any camera lens creates a blur because its rays cannot render a point of focus perfectly. In both cases, no scientific or aesthetic practice has yet been established that eliminates that representational dilemma.

Mujer de Milefuegos (Woman of a Thousand Fires) (1976)

Mujer de Milefuegos offers an excellent example of Strand's penchant for using distancing irony as Buñuel did, to structure poetic images, rendering them absurd, surreal, and ultimately grotesque. The film traces the eerie, solitary daily rituals of a woman dressed in black who wanders through a Mexican landscape that is part ruined castle and part barren desert.

Like contemporary *Village Voice* critic Jake Gaffrey, I view the film as a rejoinder to Maya Deren's now-iconic short dream film, *Meshes of the Afternoon* (1943), although my grounds for comparison are vastly different from his. After a 1976 screening of the film, Gaffrey wrote, "There are moments that border on being as dumb as the worst of Maya Deren, yet the film has a strong erotic undertow that keeps one fascinated."[27] I also depart from Thompson and Bordwell, who state that the film "presents a Latin American woman's housekeeping as a ritual that becomes ecstatically joyful."[28] After a brief description of the film, I will develop the formal and thematic connections between *Mujer* and *Meshes*, focusing on the way both films link sexuality and violence while distinguishing Deren's subjectivism from Strand's more distanced approach to the surreal.

Mujer opens with natural images of tall stalks of grain accompanied by an electronic sound track, immediately merging nature and technology.

From Chick
Strand's *Mujer de
Milfuegos*, 1976.
Courtesy of Chick
Strand.

A woman, dressed in a long black gown, strides across a vacant, rock-
filled landscape, finally arriving at a huge Spanish-style villa. The woman's black costume, the camera's focus on her feet, and the empty villa in
which she wanders all recall the repeated scenes of entry into the house in
Meshes. Yet, whereas *Meshes* establishes a distinction between inner
thoughts and outer reality after the woman is inside the modern domestic space, Strand's film situates the solitary woman in an otherworldly
external landscape whose doors, patios, and open stairways make it difficult to distinguish inside from outside. In *Meshes*, the woman seems to
be distinguishable from an ominous, hostile setting, but in *Mujer* the
woman's subjectivity is conterminous with the setting. She engages in
oddly misplaced domestic labor, such as sweeping rocks. Sounds of sexual ecstasy accompany an image of the woman killing a rooster by swinging the bird in the air. As she caresses the dead bird, the image dissolves
into one where the woman caresses her own body, clad in the black gown.

The next sequence suggests cycles of sex, birth, and death. The sounds
associated with the woman's sexual caresses—moaning and breathing—

carry over into new images of hands disemboweling an animal, tearing into its entrails. A baby's wail is heard as hands and knife cut into fat and fibrous tissue. Metaphors arise from the semantic links between and among sex, reproduction, and death, while the metonymic chain of events implies a causal physical process that leads from pleasurable caresses to the painful separation of flesh in childbirth and the cutting of an umbilical cord.

In the film's closing moments, this woman dances on the rocky landscape while wearing a brightly painted face mask, which offers a startling visual shift between animate and inanimate. Finally, two masks efface the woman and the sound of wailing wind returns the film to images of waving grain stalks that opened the film.

Images of a woman engaging in disturbing and surreal domestic work and sexual activities while wearing a long black gown certainly evoke Deren's *Meshes* on a surface level, but I would argue that the film engages more profoundly with the Deren film, although it differs from it in important ways. The films share an interest in exploring surreal moments of subjectivity and the violence of women's sexuality. In one scene, the camera tracks alongside the woman as she slowly ascends a staircase and becomes involved in an unusual, disembodied caress that reveals hands on her black dress—possibly hers, possibly those of her lover. The camera moves in to capture extreme close-ups of the woman's face while the hands and the sound track features her breathing and her moans. During the scene, the subtitle "and at my throat the hand of love slowly tightening like snake skin" is visible and, during the scene of violent stabbing: "another obscure poet dreams." The moment of sexual ecstasy yields to a moment of violence involving the woman stabbing something off-screen repeatedly with a long knife, then the camera cuts to images of hands immersed in a basin, accompanied by a theremin (an electronic instrument known for its use in science fiction film), which provides an absurdly modernist touch to this primal mise-en-scène. The sequence culminates with the woman's light-skinned hand grasping a tiny dark hand, revealed to be a door knocker.

Whereas a subjective camera invites viewers to participate in the protagonist's dreams and experiences in Deren's film (the woman walks up stairs, engages in a sexual caress, and stabs her lover and a mirror), in Strand's films that process of identification is interrupted by subtitles that pull the viewer away and by the absurd juxtaposition of images. Strand incorporates elements of the uncanny through proportion (the door knocker hand is tiny) and the interplay between animate and inanimate objects (having witnessed so many moving hands in the previous scenes, the viewer may be startled upon realizing the tiny hand is inert). Yet the uncanny is not located *within* the subjectivity of the protagonist but exists already as an objective feature of the world she inhabits, a situation that Deren arrives at in the conclusion of *Meshes*.

Whether or not Strand intended the film as a sublime or grotesque homage to Deren, *Mujer* shares a number of the same concerns as *Meshes*. The "erotic undertow" Gaffrey mentions derives from the way both films link sexuality to violence, emphasizing the ambiguity of ecstasy. Both films rely on the techniques of experimental film to evoke the way that women experience sensuality, eroticism, danger, and death. Unlike *Meshes*, where surreal elements are located in a dream state that manages to penetrate a stable reality, the world that the woman inhabits in *Mujer* is already an unstable, ironic, and distancing assemblage of a surreal worldview that focuses on the relation of fleshly materiality (which encompasses sex, life, and death) and the prosaic, repetitive rituals of everyday life.

Conclusion

Catherine Russell writes, "The question of distance is raised by ethnography and the avant-garde in many overlapping ways,"[29] and this essay argues that Chick Strand's work—situated at the intersection of these two filmmaking modes—negotiates the question of distance in striking ways. She uses the visual language of documentary films to undermine the notion of easy access to other cultures or fixed identities; she examines the conjunction of the natural and the artificial in the world and in art; and she blends the subjective mode of the film poem with the irony of assemblage. Her films express her marked passion for the process of creating new experiences and new works of art by reassembling materials the world presents.

Like a number of other experimental ethnographers, Strand harbors suspicions regarding film as a mode of truth telling by, for, or about cultural others, unless those truths are understood to be a new experience that arises from the intimate engagement of filmmaker and subject. That same suspicion has provided the impetus for vastly different choices among documentary and experimental filmmakers. Trinh T. Minh-ha, for example, seeks to deconstruct the process of film representation in order to destabilize the viewer's apprehension of images, whereas Errol Morris addresses the same problem by developing an elaborate system for conducting interviews. His Interrotron (later the Megatron) is a system intended to take advantage of the fact that "technology makes possible a different kind of intimacy."[30] All three of these filmmakers combine poetic images, subjective visions, and the irony of found or historical footage. More so than these other two filmmakers, Strand's work is dominated by the implicit and pervasive tension between moments of heightened subjectivity—which provide for the erotic undertow of her films—and a distancing irony. This characteristic tension among filmic elements embodies Strand's commitment to the assemblage aesthetic, while her unique orchestration of sensual pleasure and intellectual abstraction reveals her fascination with the sublime aspects of the encounter between the filmmaker's subjectivity and the world.

Filmography

Angel Blue Sweet Wings, 1966 (3 min.): sd., col.; 16mm
Anselmo, 1967 (4 min.): sd., col.; 16mm
Waterfall, 1967 (3 min.): sd., col.; 16mm
Mosori Monika, 1970 (20 min.): sd., col.; 16mm
Cosas de Mi Vida, 1976 (25 min.): sd., col.; 16mm
Elasticity, 1976 (25 min.): sd., col.; 16mm
Guacamole, 1976 (10 min.): sd., col.; 16mm
Mujer de Milefuegos, 1976 (15 min.): sd., col.; 16mm
Cartoon le Mousse, 1979 (15 min.): sd., b&w; 16mm
Fever Dream, 1979 (7 min.): sd., b&w; 16mm
Kristallnacht, 1979 (7 min.): sd., b&w; 16mm
Loose Ends, 1979 (25 min.): sd., b&w; 16mm
Soft Fiction, 1979 (54 min.): sd., b&w; 16mm
Anselmo and the Women, 1986 (35 min.): sd., col.; 16mm
Artificial Paradise, 1986 (12 1/2 min.): sd., col.; 16mm
By the Lake, 1986 (9 min.): sd., col.; 16mm
Coming Up for Air, 1986 (26 1/2 min.): sd., col.; 16mm
Fake Fruit, 1986 (22 min.): sd., col.; 16mm
Tierra Incognita, 1986 (6 min.)

Notes

1 James, "Notes from Los Angeles Film Forum Retrospective."
2 Squire, "Why Did the Palette Cross the Road?"
3 No mention is made of Strand's work in the books by Scott MacDonald,

Rees, Sitney, Wees, and Russell listed in the bibliography. Despite critical neglect, Strand's work continues to be shown and discussed. The first public exhibit of her paintings was at the La Luz Gallery in Los Angeles in 2000. Her films were screened in the 1990s and early 2000s at the Pacific Film Archive (1994), the Whitney Museum of Art (2000), Los Angeles Film Forum (2000), Portland's Four Wall Cinema (2001), and at the San Francisco Museum of Modern Art (2003). The renewed interest in her work is only one reason for a more comprehensive scholarly engagement with her films than is currently available.

4   Strand, "Notes on Ethnographic Film by a Film Artist," 50.

5   Leimbacher, "Chick Strand," 143. I put forward interpretations of Strand's work that she herself may not endorse. In an interview in May 2004, she encouraged wide-ranging interpretations of her films rather than declaring any intention on her part. She listened carefully and discussed particular details of filmmaking contexts with vivid clarity. When I asked about a person (or object, or animal) that appears in one of her films, Strand responded not with explication or analysis, but with a story about how she first encountered the person, made a connection, and perceived that individual's situation in the world. At first, I was frustrated at her approach, but I ultimately found the exchange liberating, as it highlights Strand's commitment to the filmmaking process as well as the product and also makes explicit my responsibility for interpreting her works.

6   Strand, "Notes on Ethnographic Film by a Film Artist," 51.

7   James, *Allegories of Cinema*, 143.

8   James, "Notes from Los Angeles Film Forum Retrospective."

9   Sullivan, "Punk Master of the Absurd Winston Smith Shows His Art."

10   MacDonald, *A Critical Cinema*, 2:110.

11   Strand, "Notes on Ethnographic Film by a Film Artist," 47–48.

12   James, "An Interview with Pat O'Neill," 1997.

13   Strand, "Chick Strand at the Cinematheque," 14.

14   In the rhetorical terminology of tenor, vehicle, and ground (all associated with metaphor), metonymy does not presume or assert a ground between the two items that are related.

15   Peterson, *Dreams of Chaos, Visions of Order*, 145.

16   Haug, "An Interview with Chick Strand," 109.

17   Peterson, *Dreams of Chaos, Visions of Order*, 145.

18   Russell, *Experimental Ethnography*, 25.

19   Ibid., 27.

20   In "Chick Strand at the Cinematheque," the unnamed interviewer specifically compares Strand's *Loose Ends* to Buñuel's *Las Hurdes* (*Land without Bread*), and the filmmaker replies, "I've had that attitude too. And I like Buñuel a lot." After making *Las Hurdes*, Buñuel went on to produce compilation films for the Museum of Modern Art during the 1930s.

21 This annual gathering, named after the documentary film pioneer Robert Flaherty, has, since 1955, devoted itself to the contemplation of film in all its forms.

22 Callenbach, "*Mosori Monika*," 57.

23 Eder, "The Screen."

24 Gaffrey, "Off the Beaten Tracks with Chick Strand," 47.

25 Eder, "The Screen."

26 The title of Hollis Frampton's important essay collection *Circles of Confusion* is another example of the metaphorical use of this technical term by an avant-garde photographer and filmmaker.

27 Gaffrey, "Off the Beaten Tracks with Chick Strand," 47.

28 Thompson and Bordwell, *Film History*, 601.

29 Russell, *Experimental Ethnography*, 24.

30 Kaufman, "War! What Is It Good For? Errol Morris Finds Out With *Fog of War*."

ROBIN BLAETZ

Amnesis Time

The Films of Marjorie Keller

□

Marjorie Keller (1950–94) was one of very few experimental filmmakers as active in scholarship and teaching as in artistic production. Keller received a doctorate from the cinema studies department of New York University in 1983 and taught at the University of Rhode Island until her death in 1994. Throughout this period and earlier, she was active as both a filmmaker and as a participant in the cooperative avant-garde film communities in Chicago and New York. Despite the widespread recognition of her more than twenty-five films and the fact that her body of work is now complete, Keller has received little critical attention. This oversight is partially the result of the neglect of avant-garde film practice in general, particularly the work of most women artists. However, the more intriguing and unsettling cause for Keller's obscurity concerns her informed refusal to work within the paradigms established by feminist film theory in the mid-1970s. Having studied with the likes of Annette Michelson, she was not unaware of the significance of Laura Mulvey's groundbreaking essay "Visual Pleasure and Narrative Cinema," which introduced the precepts of Lacanian psychoanalysis into film studies and called for a countercinema in reaction to classical Hollywood structures. Rather, Keller rejected film practice based on feminist theory because she believed, as she said in a review of E. Ann Kaplan's 1983 book *Women and Film*, that theory "obfuscates women's filmmaking in the name of feminism."[1]

Marjorie Keller in 1987.
Courtesy of Anthology Film
Archives. Photo: Robert Haller.

In the context of the heightened emotions that characterized debates in the 1970s and 1980s about varieties of feminism, Keller's status as an outcast was assured.[2] Not only did she reject the structural demands on her work made in the name of feminist film theory, but she also declared openly that her primary influences were the maligned lyrical and diarist filmmakers Marie Menken, Gregory Markopoulos, and Stan Brakhage. Added into this mix is the fact that Keller was not just a practitioner of poetic cinema but also a committed activist in the politics of her day. Thus she was not one to accept passively the decree that her work was nonfeminist simply because her films did not follow a trajectory put in place by people who were not, for the most part, practitioners.

Keller's convictions as a filmmaker were not swayed by the rejection of her work by the feminist critical community, but she was inspired in the late 1980s to write a book that covered those filmmakers who traced their roots to Maya Deren rather than to theory. Instead of writing about Yvonne Rainer, Chantal Akerman, or Sally Potter, all filmmakers who overtly deconstructed the Hollywood gaze, Keller set out to write about filmmakers less known at the time—including Abigail Child, Leslie Thornton, and Su Friedrich—whose work was not as easily analyzed under the rubric of feminist theory. The notes for the book, which was left unwritten at the time of her death, provide a useful entry into Keller's own concerns.[3] She writes of this group of filmmakers as manifesting a derangement of classical cinema through what she called "a radical distortion of values and perception . . . often associated with insanity." Reprocessing imagery from Hollywood, home movies, educational film, and instructional film, these films see "old forms . . . as if through an anamorphic lens." The reference to the lens is crucial here. Keller was concerned with the film artifact not on the level of character and story, but at the level of the image: in the image of woman and the self-image of the filmmaker "from the ground up: as film emulsion struck by light, as domestic shadows of their male cameraman counterparts, as edited out of the picture." Keller sought new strategies of cinematography, editing, and sound, but she refused to accept the notion that there was only one road available to the feminist filmmaker.

Like many filmmakers of the American avant-garde, as well as the earliest documentary filmmakers of the feminist consciousness-raising movement of the 1960s, Marjorie Keller used the raw material of her life for both the images and the themes of her films. From her earliest film diaries, which weave fragments of the faces and bodies of family and friends with images from the suburban, pastoral, or foreign-travel contexts in which she saw them—for example, *Objection* (1974) or *Superimposition* (1975)—to her final film exploration in *Herein* (1991) of the physical space in which she lived much of her adult life, Keller drew from her rich domestic world to fashion gemlike renderings of the conflicts and challenges facing a feminist in the second half of the twentieth century. The problem at the heart of her visual and aural explorations involves the psychological adjustments demanded of women who were born and raised in the traditional domesticity of upper-middle-class America in the 1950s but who came of age in the unsettled social and political seas of feminism.

Keller was born in 1950 in Yorktown, New York, the youngest of seven children and the daughter of the chief executive of a large lighting company. She grew up in a prosperous, mostly conservative, Protestant family.[4] As many who knew her have attested, she was beautifully trained by her mother in traditional feminine arts such as cooking, entertaining, and gardening. Unlike many feminists of her generation, she never rejected these skills and their pleasures but instead used them both in her life and as the basis of her work. Keller graduated from Tufts University in 1972, although she completed her coursework at the School of the Art Institute of Chicago after she was expelled from Tufts for participating in a protest over the racially motivated firing of a departmental secretary. This kind of political activism was typical of Keller and her close friend and companion at the time, Saul Levine, who had been Keller's first film instructor at Tufts. Levine and Keller settled in Chicago, where Keller enrolled in and coordinated Stan Brakhage's film courses at the Art Institute, worked side by side with B. Ruby Rich, and became part of the growing film community there. During these years Keller became interested in the artisanal mode of filmmaking practiced by Brakhage and, like Rich, was involved in the programming and discussion of women's cinema.[5]

Keller left Chicago in 1974 to attend graduate school at New York University, where she received a master's degree in 1975 and a doctorate in 1983. During these years she lived at 100 Forsyth Street on the Lower East Side of Manhattan, a derelict neighborhood that became symbolically important in her films (particularly *Herein*) and was a literal center for many of the filmmakers and scholars nourished by her dynamic presence and warm home. In 1986 Keller married P. Adams Sitney, one of the founders of Anthology Film Archives and one of the first major proponents of American avant-garde cinema; they became the parents of twin girls in 1991.

During her years in Boston and Chicago, Keller was a committed social activist. During the 1960s she was a member of the central committee of the Students for a Democratic Society; she resigned only as the movement began to dissolve in reaction to the violence of the Weather Underground, the faction that had become dominant by the end of the decade.[6] In Chicago she worked with Levine on several of his political films, including *Note to Patty* (1968–69), *The Big Stick* (1967–73), and *New Left Note* (1968–82). More famously, she was arrested at the White House in a protest over the Nixon administration's price control policies, and she participated in the demonstrations at the 1972 Republican National Convention in Miami. A photograph of her at that event—where she disrupted a fashion show for politicians' wives to model the typical outfit of a poor working woman—appeared on the front page of her hometown newspaper.[7]

In the early 1970s Keller made a documentary film about the welfare system and racism called *Hell No: No Cuts!* The film was flawed by intrusive camerawork and was successful, according to Levine, only to the extent that it provided Keller with a model of an ineffectual film.[8] Like many filmmakers, Keller came to understand the difficulty of making a political film that is interesting, unpedantic, and clear enough for a general audience, not just an audience of the converted. Although she considered all of her work to be documentary in nature, she never again made an explicitly activist film. Instead, she directed her political energies toward local problems, working throughout her life on issues such as welfare reform, labor union rights, and AIDS activism. Committed as she was to real political practice, she had little tolerance for theoretical leftists whose involvement with race, class, or gender issues never strayed from the page or screen.

Both at NYU and later, Keller was an indispensable part of the New York experimental film community. Between 1984 and 1987 she served on the board of directors of the Collective for Living Cinema, and between 1985 and 1988 she was the founding editor of the collective's journal, *Motion Picture*. During this time (1984–85), she was also the managing editor of the film journal *Idiolects*. At the end of the 1980s, during an embittered period of reorganization, she took over the helm of the major East Coast distribution house for experimental filmmaking, Film-Makers' Cooperative in New York. Considered the voice of reason and an endless font of common sense and good humor, she was what J. Hoberman called "an unselfish champion of the American Avant-Garde."[9] In 1975 she began teaching occasional film production courses in the art department of the University of Rhode Island. Eventually she developed an entire interdisciplinary film studies program there and became a professor of filmmaking and film history.

Over the course of her career Keller made more than twenty-five 8mm and 16mm films of from one to sixty minutes, which were exhibited at film festivals and in museums internationally. A revised version of her dissertation, *The Untutored Eye: Childhood in the Films of Cocteau, Cornell, and Brakhage*, was published in 1986, as was an exquisite and charming children's pop-up book written and illustrated by Keller called *The Moon on the Porch*. Her book on women experimental filmmakers, as well as three films, remained incomplete at the time of her sudden death in 1994. Of particular interest was a film about her young daughters learning the alphabet, tentatively called "Learning to Write," and described by Keller as a feminist film about the creation of the female voice and the interaction between drawing and writing.[10] As the many people whom Keller touched both professionally and personally over the course of her life have attested, her greatest accomplishment may have been the warm, gracious world she created for her family and friends, a milieu that both inspired and served as the source for her cinematic legacy.

Amnesis and the "Lost Object"

The driving force behind Keller's films can be described as an exploration of the repercussions of being born in one era and coming of age in another. The most obvious manifestation of this phenomenon in Keller's life was the rupture experienced by women raised in the 1950s to be homemakers in the mold of their mothers who found themselves functioning in the professional world of their fathers. However, if Keller had explored this notion only in terms of personal experience, and the difficulty of finding role models for the integration of personal and professional life, her body of work would not carry the weight that it does. She was able to see that this disjunction, involving problems of time and absence, is not limited to a particular historical situation but is common to much of human experience in general.

Many poets and critics speak of memory in relation to time passed and the recalling, or recapturing, of what came before. Even modernist art and poetry, which value indeterminacy and acknowledge the role of invention and confabulation in memory, envision the past to be retrievable through searching the unconscious or creating concrete symbols that connect the present to the past. Visual and verbal images, in this sense, are created as dikes against a sea of forgetting.[11] Keller's work, however, manifests more of an interest in ruptures of history and in the absence of a usable past. To approach this absence—or this amnesia—I turn to the work of Nicomedes Suarez-Araùz, a poet of the Amazonian jungle, where all traces of human life are continually eradicated in the tides of nature and political upheaval. Suarez describes what he calls "amnesis time" as multiple, non-linear, fragmentary, and inclusive of past, present, and future. He says, "We are, in large measure, what we have lost and can never recover or recall."[12] According to Suarez, memory is a kind of a lie, since it offers as history what inevitably is the work of the imagination. The notion of amnesis offers a different model for aesthetic representation, replacing recall with invention. Amnesis art overtly intimates absence through images that represent what Suarez calls the "lost object." It points to a space that is empty of images and disconnected from chronology, and it erodes the logical connections between conventional meanings of signifiers to create "a tangled world of surprising and shifting meanings."[13] The work of amnesis art represents, but does not recover, what has been lost both personally and collectively and reveals history to be a series of fragments. Rather than simply acknowledging this "underlying oblivion," it celebrates the freedom inherent in a rejection of history.[14]

Many modernist artists have alluded to concepts akin to amnesis. Suarez points to Stéphane Mallarmé's mystical, creativity-heightening silence, to Samuel Becket's preoccupation with the void, to John Cage's work with relative levels of sound, and of course to Marcel Proust's unexpected recall through sensory experience.[15] However, none of these ideas reaches as far as Suarez's metaphor of amnesia, which is applicable to all communication and experience; the dispersion of meaning functions everywhere, at all levels of discourse. In art this absence appears as what philosopher John Rajchman calls "the world it is not yet possible to see or to foresee. For as it occurs, it changes what we can and cannot see."[16] The absence at the heart of amnesis might fruitfully be compared to Michel Foucault's countermemory—a transformation of history into a different form of time, in which the narratives of history are made to reveal the hidden contradictions that in turn uncover the workings of power.[17] In discussing the work of the genealogist, Foucault returns again and again to the words and images of profusion and entanglement—elements that are particularly suggestive of Keller's films. Both Suarez's amnesis and the films approach the world and experience in this mode, using the surface of the world to suggest all that has been forgotten and unspoken. Like Foucault's genealogist, the artist looks for myriad beginnings, "whose faint traces and hints of color are readily seen by the historical eye" in order to "[liberate] a profusion of lost events."[18]

At first glance, film—a photographic medium—would not seem an ideal mode for capturing the ephemera of lost time. Indeed, in its most conventional formats, film follows in the long line of recording technologies that have sought to contain the past ever more accurately through indexical images and recorded observations. In fact, Keller's choice of such a medium involved the embracing of such a paradox, since her project was, in film scholar Paul Arthur's words, to express not only "what is 'beyond' the powers of representation," but also "what is 'inadequate' or 'impossible' for film." Keller was fascinated by the mystery of the image; according to Arthur, she intended specifically to examine the "material/psychic/metaphysical continuities of cinema."[19] In her dialogue with the medium of film, Keller concentrated on the spaces between images. She found in editing not the means to seamlessly join images from the world, but a space in which to suggest the lacunae of memory.

Keller's editing practice was modeled on the work of Gregory Markopoulos, particularly the blinking or strobe format, in which an image either fades or turns to black or a solid color to create a rhythm and to stress the integrity of its form. Markopoulos, for his part, had credited the filmmaker Robert Beavers with suggesting "the invisible image between the frames which is seemingly never photographed, and that other invisible image between film frames which is never projected."[20] Keller's complex editing created puzzlelike films in which images and blank leader produce an ahistorical collage of discontinuities, resonances, and ambiguity. In Foucault's terms, the films reveal that things that are not seeable at a given time may be invisible but are not hidden. They present us with what Foucault might call a "polyhedron of intelligibility"—images and sounds that surround the "lost object" with multiple ways of comprehending it. In the mode of the genealogist of the absent world, Keller encourages the viewer to ask how things are given to us to be seen, how they are seen, and what is not seeable at a given moment.[21] Her films contain "scattered and fragmented images, suspended figures, ghost-like shapes, objects at the edge of cognition, negative forms, multiplane perspectives, impossible architectures, topological forms suggestive of absence, [and] indeterminate narratives."[22] Nevertheless, while these descriptive terms suggest an esoteric practice and indecipherable texts, Keller's work is fully accessible. By means of, rather than in spite of, all the visual and aural fragmentation, and through the surfaces of the world she records and the internal reality she creates, her films achieve a reintegration of that world.

Like Foucault, Keller directed her gaze and exploration "in the most unpromising places, in what we tend to feel is without history—in sentiments, love, conscience, instincts."[23] While her material is composed of the recorded visual and aural artifacts of her everyday life, the films, as shaped and edited constructions, evoke the lost and unspoken and thus defy narrative readings. The films that one might examine in this regard include *Superimposition* (1975), in which Keller worked with the images and sounds of a couple's car trip, *On the Verge of an Image of Christmas*

(1978), a portrait of a family's holiday celebration, *Six Windows* (1979), a study of the windows of a home, and *The Fallen World* (1983), a rendering of the rippling effects of a dog's death.

The first of the two films that I will discuss is *The Fallen World*, which Keller described for the Film-Makers' Cooperative catalogue as "an elegy for a Newfoundland dog named Melville and a portrait of his owner" (P. Adams Sitney). The film offers, in both black and white and color, images from many different angles: close-ups of Roman monumental statues, grave stones, Venetian buildings, canals, and gardens; images of Sitney riding in a gondola, visiting the grave of Percy Bysshe Shelley, and in the Melville Memorial Room in the Berkshire Atheneum; a large, black dog running on a half-frozen pond; a leaf-covered deck in the rain; and a section of film resembling Brakhage's 1965 *Pasht* (his quasi-abstract portrait of the bodily surfaces of a cat) in which Sitney seems to be playing with the dog by a fire. These thematically and visually disparate elements are edited rapidly so that they do not tell a story but rather evoke a sense of the connectedness of all things and the ways in which we incorporate a life-altering death into lived experience.

Keller's tools for this task are simple. Her carefully framed but loosely filmed images are cut elliptically to highlight texture, color, and movement, and then they are rejoined to create rhymes, gaps, and flow. Blank frames are intercut between images to create rhythm and pace, to prevent the search for narrative, and to assure the integrity of each image. An interesting reading of *The Fallen World* can be derived from studying the presence of water and the images of fluidity throughout the film. The film opens with and returns often to a close-up pan of a monumental stone foot, an image of the cultural attempt to hold onto the past in all its detail and at all costs. But its first sound is a sea chantey evoking the passing centuries and, in connection with later frames, the themes of Herman Melville. Water connects the fragmented images of Sitney's tightly framed profile floating down a canal, snow covering the world over the drowned Shelley's grave, and then, in a key image, the dog playing on a surface that is at once solid and liquefying. A requiem is sounded, and then an image of the dog in the snow viewed from above flashes into a high-angle shot of a fountain in an Italian garden, rain drenching the deck above the dog, and empty Venetian canals. The overall emphasis is on flux and on the ties between the past and the present. The monuments, grave markers, and memorabilia in the Melville archive are opposed to the flowing water of the ever-changing present, expressed finally by the sequence of fur, teeth, movement, and fragments of faces that formally present the experience of life with the dog, now gone. The film is both an elegy for the dog, Melville, and a commentary on the ways in which we search through the past to understand present losses. While Paul Arthur's brilliant analysis of the film suggests that death is represented in the film,[24] I would argue that *The Fallen World* gives the viewer a sense of life itself as it flows through all forgotten objects, events, and beings, and through all time. With its sensual camerawork, which both frames and manipulates the surfaces of the world, and painstaking editing, which forces us through unlikely juxtapositions, to see the world anew, Keller's film connects the viewer to all that history makes invisible.

Besides their complex editing, the blinking format using solid leader, the play with focus, and the fragmentation of the body, Keller's films are characterized by a layering of images. Like Brakhage and Markopoulos, Keller sought to go beyond the chronology that inevitably remains with even the most rapidly shifting images. Following the solution elaborated by Maya Deren in her search for a poetic, vertical cinema rather than a narrative one, she adopted the practice of showing multiple images on a single plane.[25] The early 8mm film *Superimposition* is, as its title indicates, a study in layering. The film centers on a couple's journey to places that are at times recognizable—San Francisco landmarks, city streets, beaches, a carnival—but are more often indeterminate. In typical Keller fashion, the man and woman are introduced as fragments, with the top of the woman's head seen at far left and then the torso and the head of the man seen from below. Although one of the film's actual locations is a carnival, the entire film's quick cutting, deliriously panning camera, and shifting focus create the sense of an endless Tilt-a-Whirl ride. Particularly striking are the superimposed images, which allow day/night and interiors/exteriors to penetrate each other so that the boundaries of time and space are erased. In a particularly evocative image, the screen is filled by the torso of a woman wearing a white sweater and gold necklace, over which is layered a series of events that she seems to be emitting. They represent both what she perceives in the world and what she projects outward; the journey is both exterior and interior, and the lost object is imaginatively constructed rather than remembered as a series of discrete episodes. At the end of the film, a sequence of images of a woman cooking and the couple eating in a kitchen is layered over images of people walking and playing on a beach and a pan across the sea to a rock jetty. First one set of images dominates, then the other, so that the man and woman seem to rise out of and then sink back into the ocean as they engage in the most mundane of activities. Here the film formally captures the sense of life lived and all the thoroughly forgotten moments that are, in the end, life itself.

The Notebook and Images of Childhood

In his discussion of Keller's *The Answering Furrow* (1985), film scholar Scott MacDonald notes Keller's indebtedness to the work of Marie Menken and her home movie aesthetic.[26] Both women documented the world around them in a spontaneous, carefree fashion with a handheld, often swinging or quickly panning camera. The looseness of the shooting style allowed for poetry free of symbolism and also made clear that the films did not depict, for example, a garden or a home. Rather, they used everyday objects as markers of time passed and as fragments to be reintegrated into a more intentional kind of documentary than is possible with the in-camera edit of a home movie. As her early collaborator Helene Kaplan Wright noted in an interview, Keller shot film and recorded sound freely and continually in the midst of her domestic life. The familiar imagery and sounds of children, family, and friends provided the material, just as they would in the writing of a journal or notebook. She shaped these through meticulous and ruthless cutting of the images and the desynchronizing of the sound in order to evoke a particular place, person, or mood. While *The Answering Furrow* and *Objection* (1974) both highlight Keller's "notebook aesthetic" in their use of the nonintrusive camera and the highly flexible manipulation of sound, I will discuss *Ancient Parts* (1979), *Foreign Parts* (1979), and *Private Parts* (1988) in order to simultaneously discuss Keller's scholarly work.[27]

In *The Untutored Eye: Childhood in the Films of Cocteau, Cornell, and Brakhage*, the published version of her doctoral dissertation, Keller examines the work of three filmmakers known for their representation of children and for their romantic sense of childhood as a privileged, visionary period of life. Jean Cocteau's films were formally and conceptually intriguing to Keller for their faith in the power of photography and editing to confer plausibility on the most supernatural of events and to make these alternative realities believable, even to an uninitiated audience. By using similar textures of light, movement, and sound to unite the realistic and the purely imagined, and by avoiding the soft focus or slow motion often used to mark the improbable, Cocteau created, according to Keller, a "complex layering of simultaneous realities."[28] Cocteau was not a surrealist, Keller points out, and he rejected Freudian thought because of its concern with analyzing and explaining the often mysterious and tenuous worlds created in art. For Cocteau, as for Keller, the aesthetic achievement of art was the very point of the endeavor, not the content to be explained via symbolic or psychoanalytic readings.[29]

In Cocteau's films, as in those of Joseph Cornell and Stan Brakhage, a child protagonist is particularly able to seduce the viewer into entering and believing in alternative worlds. Children are portrayed as fully and ecstatically aware of the universe in all its fullness, and childhood itself is understood as a mode of perception gradually destroyed with age and experience. Cocteau's androgynous young heroes seek to escape the debilitating effects of institutionalized education and the onslaught of adulthood. His primary motif is the child as voyeur, someone who visually and psychologically absorbs the sensory world while remaining unseen. His films are based on what Keller called a "hierarchy of seeing," in which the filmmaker reformulates his childhood relation to his parents by allowing his adult self the privilege of the child's all-encompassing vision, including its illusion of omnipotence.[30]

In several ways, Keller's first two notebook films in the "Parts" series explore this "hierarchy of seeing" as well. In both, the placement of the camera identifies the filmmaker as a voyeuristic presence that organizes the world at the moment of seeing it. *Foreign Parts* is most notable in this regard. The film consists of a rapid alteration, with some repetition, of scenes of children playing on a lawn that slopes down to a beach, of a woman walking on the lawn and a man cutting the grass, and images from nature (flowers, water, birds, cows) as well as from a more mechanical world (lawn mower, sliding glass doors, cars in a distance across a concrete driveway). Of particular note are a large, elaborate birdhouse on a pole in the yard and the cutting on movement that equates the birds darting back and forth with the running children. Keller described the film in the Film-Makers' Cooperative catalogue as "portraying the poetics of family life in an unfamiliar context." It charts how we make sense of the new through what we already know, and likewise, how what we know is changed by a new environment. The film's central images consist of the filmmaker's voyeuristic framings of familiar figures in a different space. In one instance, the person behind the camera seems to be crouching indoors as she looks out through the lens at an older man riding a lawn mower; the door slides shut in the middle of the shot, so that the glass

From Marjorie
Keller's *Foreign
Parts*, 1979.
Courtesy of
Anthology Film
Archives.

distorts the world and calls attention to the importance of seeing and
how conscious looking changes what is seen. Near the end of the film,
from the same crouched position, the filmmaker looks through the space
created by the arm, back, and seat of an aluminum lawn chair to see a
woman walking along the beachfront lawn where children previously had
been playing. The camera pans right to remove the woman from the
space, then back again to include her in its intentional framing. The
filmmaker, having placed herself at a child's height, creates an image of a
threatening parental world in which she alone controls what is seen and
thus assumes power over the adults.

Like Cocteau, Cornell was interested in portraying simultaneous realities. However, while Cocteau embedded his alternative universes in conventional cinematic narratives, placing them on the same phenomenological plane as everyday reality, Cornell was bolder. In both his films and
the three-dimensional collage boxes for which he is famous, Cornell
worked with the objects that entranced him, including found footage; his
particular vocabulary consisted of stellar imagery, birds, printed words,
scientific paraphernalia, and children, all grouped in such a way as to
show them in a new light. His method as a filmmaker was characterized
by what Keller called "visual equation"—the rearrangement of apparently ephemeral, disconnected images according to a rhythmic or graphic
logic. Each image is connected to the previous and subsequent ones in a
"complex of simultaneities," in which meaning is subtly shifted in a non-
sequential, nonnarrative way. Throughout her career, Keller remained
interested in the child psychologist Jean Piaget's notion of a natural order
in which things and events in the world are understood by children
without being explicitly stated.[31] The practice common to Cornell and

Keller of using bits and pieces of the present world to suggest a natural order and to evoke that which is absent, taboo, or unsayable calls to mind once more the importance of amnesis as a model of artistic creation.

Like Cocteau, Cornell used children in his films to signal to his viewers that he was operating from the child's untainted and all-encompassing mode of perception, in which reality is shaped in conformance to a private vision. Like Brakhage, his films are based on the logic of children's prerational game playing; they feature repetition, nonrealistic space, and an absence of narrative flow, as well as a childlike attachment to certain images that carry magical significance. Cornell's films resemble his boxes more than they resemble other people's films; their meaning depends on one's holding all the images and iconography in mind and integrating them into the distinctly Cornellian system.[32] The viewer, rather than remembering specific images and connections, retains evanescent visual ideas in which children, birds, stars, and all the other forms become disembodied and recreated in a mysterious and charming new world.

Keller too used fragmentary images and motifs in a cyclical, nonnarrative structure, although her goal was not to disembody childhood and children, but rather to embody them. Keller's films do not reduce the complexity of adult life by returning to childhood's magic. They present the layers of simultaneities in order to speak about the transition from childhood to adulthood and all that is lost. A case in point is the brief single-roll film *Ancient Parts*, which more than any of Keller's films resembles a Joseph Cornell box. *Ancient Parts* consists of minimal action in a tiny room that includes a small boy, a mirror, a bed, and a mother in a nightgown. These iconic elements are united by the golden, grainy quality of the film and the tilting, ever-shifting camera work. Most important is the fact that most of the film was shot into the mirror, so that visually it resembles a box within a box. As the boy gazes upon and touches parts of his body, with the filmmaker and the mother as audience, he almost enacts the psychoanalyst Jacques Lacan's mirror phase of development, in which the child conceives an idealized sense of the body's functional wholeness, or ego ideal. The toddler attempts to climb into the imagined mirror space, an action that is echoed by the filmmaker's recording of the reflected scene as she and her camera assume the same gaze as the boy. Like the three filmmakers she analyzed in her book, Keller literalizes the process whereby a filmmaker shows the world through the child's superior perception. But she also reveals her adult consciousness of what the child is experiencing. Twice in the film the boy turns away from the mirror and climbs onto his mother's lap, sequences that are filmed without the mirror's mediation. As the camera moves to a close-up, the boy's face is seen to be scraped and scratched, as if to indicate that the task of separating from the mother is not without pain. Unlike her predecessors, Keller is interested in infusing an image with a certain amount of humor and an indication of her adult awareness.

Keller's focus on the difficulty of crossing from childhood innocence to adult experience suggests a stronger resemblance to Brakhage than to Cocteau or Cornell, although the final film in the "Parts" series also manifests the ways in which she learned from, and then moved beyond, her teacher. *Private Parts*, as the title indicates, is about the filmmaker's private life, and it features her family and friends in uncharacteristic long takes that make their identities clear. Keller took to heart Brakhage's admonition to work within the sphere of daily life, as well as his Emersonian belief that the deeper one looks inside oneself, the more universal one's observations become.[33] The setting of this film—on another lawn, in front of yet another house on the water—also reflects the indirect influence of one of Brakhage's mentors, the poet Charles Olson, who advised artists to fix themselves in a particular place in relation to the world and examine that place in terms of a larger history, from the geological and archeological to the anthropological and the mythological.[34] Whereas Brakhage placed himself in the Rocky Mountains near Boulder, Colorado, Keller worked at the shore of the Atlantic Ocean in Rhode Island. In *Foreign Parts*, as in many of her films, shots of the water (with or without boats), the horizon, and the rocky or sandy shoreline are powerful representations of places where the particular textures of daily life meet the flow of time. People foraging for clams among the rocks show the same intuitiveness and deliberation as the filmmaker using her handheld camera to record the textures and forms of their bodies. This mundane search for dinner is alternated rapidly with shots of the ocean, allowing the filmmaker to connect the daily world with the larger one encompassing all of human relations as well as the connections between human beings and nature.

Like many experimental filmmakers, Keller was indebted to Brakhage's well-known text "Metaphors on Vision," in which he asks the reader to imagine the world as it would appear to a child who has not learned language. According to Keller, Brakhage thought of a child as both "a being and a metaphor" and he urged filmmakers to see the most common of life's events as if for the first time, in close up and with attention.[35] In truly seeing the world as it was before it disappeared behind linguistic markers, the filmmaker makes available for his camera the raw material of creation. Keller believed that Brakhage had a more honest relation to childhood than that of either Cocteau or Cornell, who used this stage of life mostly as a rhetorical guise to approach forbidden truths. Brakhage's films, on the other hand, chart a deeply felt search for personal mysteries that are painful and finally insolvable.[36] Keller learned from Brakhage how to rigorously structure the material gained from the search as recorded in sketchlike bits of film, then how to use repetition and the serial presentation and visual rhyming of key imagery (water, gardens, horizons, birds, vacant spaces, fragments of bodies) to give the viewer multiple points of view. As Keller wrote, "one sees the child and alternately sees how a child might."[37]

Where Keller differs from Brakhage is in her intentionality. She wrote of her mentor that he was part of a Romantic tradition that allowed him to think of his films as "given" to him to make, just as his children were given to him by his wives. In line with this prophetic tradition, his films were revelations that he shared with his audience.[38] Keller also approached the world nonintrusively, recording it with an eye tuned to whatever was present. But she structured her films to illustrate what lies under the surface and also to provide a commentary on those observations. The title of *Private Parts*, for example, refers clearly to the people and places that it shows. But it also alludes to the dominant event of the film, the three firings of a phallic-formed rocket by a boy and his father. The rocket, which disappears into the sky or the ocean, celebrates some elemental bond between father and son, and the launching also unites the people scattered across the lawn, who are all excited by it. Eventually they gather around a table, and a young girl who has been peripheral to but interested in the main event walks back and forth from the house to the guests, transporting food. Throughout the film, this girl had been shown along with other women holding small children, thus suggesting, as a parallel to the male rocket sequence, the gendered division of labor and pleasure. Intercut with these scenes are fragments of an episode in which the father hands a manuscript to another man, who is shown reading it. This image is captured from over the reader's right shoulder in a fairly tight shot, which flashes into red at the end of the film reel. One feels here that Keller is commenting on the very process of constructing meaning— of turning the particulars of life into art—with the manuscript a metaphor for the work of the film and the red beneath the film's emulsion a metaphor for complexity beneath appearances. *Private Parts* may give the appearance of a home movie, revealed to its maker in the shooting, but like all of Keller's work it is a carefully constructed film that must be read and interpreted.

Politics and Feminist Film Theory

In the early 1980s, a hostile interview with Keller in the feminist film journal *Camera Obscura* and Keller's dismissive review of E. Ann Kaplan's 1983 book *Women and Film* solidified Keller's alienation from feminist psychoanalytic film criticism.[39] Linda Reisman, the interviewer, had the clear and reductive agenda of proving that Keller was not a feminist filmmaker because she was too close to the male-dominated American avant-garde, particularly Brakhage, with its personal filmmaking and what Reisman perceived as its refusal to engage in the critique of ideology. *Camera Obscura* took the position that Keller's poetic documentary practice could not be feminist because it failed to clearly and logically uncover the constraints imposed by patriarchal discourse. One could look at Sally Potter's 1981 film *Thriller* to find an ideal of feminist countercinema practice during this period. With its meticulous archeology of the myriad, arbitrary-seeming systems of repression underlying Giacomo Puccini's eternally popular nineteenth-century opera *La Bohème*, the film contains an unambiguous message.

But while Potter and other filmmakers such as Yvonne Rainer and Laura Mulvey worked deliberately to reveal the unconscious rules guiding patriarchy and particularly classical Hollywood cinema, Keller was more interested in dissolving conventions. In the tradition of Foucault's genealogy and Suarez's amnesis art, Keller traced and suggested what has been forgotten or repressed in female experience in order to provide some of the missing pieces of the puzzle of human experience. Her films do not seek specific historical roots or announce essential truths but instead force the viewer to see and thus to think differently. Two of the early films, *She/Va* (1973) and *The Outer Circle* (1973), as well as her two best-known films, *Daughters of Chaos* (1980) and *Misconception* (1974–77), exemplify her artistic response to these issues. This section will cover *Daughters of Chaos*, which is particularly interesting when viewed as Keller's rejoinder to Kaplan's psychoanalytic feminism, and *Misconception*, which, on the other hand, may be seen as Keller's feminist response to the version of female experience presented by her teacher Stan Brakhage.

Saul Levine has noted that Keller was both "bothered and amused" that feminist film critics ignored her work.[40] She was amused because she was well aware of the integrity of her work. But she was bothered by what she saw as single-mindedness on the part of feminist theoreticians, who overlooked not only her own work but also that of filmmakers such as Deren, Schneemann, Menken, and Friedrich simply because they were not feminist "in our contemporary sense."[41] In her review of Kaplan's *Women and Film: Both Sides of the Camera*, Keller suggests that the book's feminism—as well as one of Kaplan's own sources, Laura Mulvey's enormously influential essay "Visual Pleasure and Narrative Cinema"— was based on a narrow interpretation of psychoanalytic theory that neglected and obscured some of feminist film history's most complex and influential work.[42] In particular, Keller was irritated by the wholesale acceptance of Roland Barthes's assertion that "visual pleasure is narrative pleasure," as well as what that notion meant for filmmakers whose films were not narrative or whose narratives were not scripted or dependent on mise-en-scène. The narrowness and reductionism of theorists like Kaplan were captured, for Keller, in statements such as Kaplan's assertion that "narrative at its most hysterical, melodrama, is the form proposed for the fullest achievement of women's aesthetic or political potential." It seemed to Keller arbitrary, confining, and downright antifeminist to engage so fully with the work of a single male theoretician so that only those filmmakers who fit the paradigm were worthy of attention by the feminist film community. Since Rainer and Potter, both dancers, were explicitly engaged with issues of the body, performance, and the relation between the spectator's gaze and the image, their work fit easily with the theory.[43] Keller, on the other hand, worked from a much broader knowledge of film history and film theory, and she had more complex intentions and ambitions.

Daughters of Chaos is probably Keller's best-known film. As she told an interviewer for *Camera Obscura*, it is about a particular wedding and all that the event evokes about memories of girlhood and the place of weddings in the fantasy life of girls in much of Western culture. To the questioner's comment that the film is filled with mere "decoration," Keller responded that there is no such thing because everything in the visual and aural track works to create and shift mood. Keller did not apologize for the personal and demanding nature of her films, and she insisted that poetry and feminism were not necessarily at odds.[44] Like all of her films, the thirty-minute *Daughters of Chaos* consists of a quickly edited set of her usual sorts of images recorded with differing focuses and from various distances: girls performing, water, boats, gardens, flowers, animals,

From Marjorie
Keller's *Daughters
of Chaos*, 1980.
Courtesy of
Film-Makers'
Cooperative.

and the like. In this case, the images are used in the context of a wedding
filmed through the windows of a contemporary church (with the filmmaker's reflection sometimes visible) and several segments of young girls
in boats moving across the water or stopping to visit the Statue of Liberty
and other New York landmarks. Some of the images were taken from old
home movies, and some were recorded for this film, with the latter serving as its core. As they travel in the boat, outside the church and beyond
the city, the girls examine a set of photographs of their mothers and
respond with hearty laughter and ironic commentary. In her notes for the
film, Keller described them as "narrators, foreigners."[45] The sound from
this scene is often used over other shots in the film, particularly those of
the wedding.

In this complex film, other key images and juxtapositions emerge. The
wedding itself, with its fragments of traditional hymns and its bouquet of
bridesmaids in all shades of pastel chiffon and long, flowing hair, is intercut with other images: an empty lawn chair in the garden, which comes to
represent the bride's mother; shots of the Statue of Liberty and the girls
gazing up at her impossible height; the muscular body of a horse; a young
girl in a red bathing suit entering the ocean; and a naked woman leaving a
pond. While the meaning of these images seems obscure at first, Keller's
tropes and the ways in which they are used are fairly straightforward. The
performing girls in the home movies are preparing to wear the costume
of the bride in order to execute their roles and assume their places in the
world modeled by the mother. The same message is transmitted by the
rear view of the adolescent girl in red entering the sea and the naked
woman leaving the water. In the midst of these images, shots of flowers
and the sky, the color red, and swish pans of water from a boat shift the

mood and tone from the sentimental to the ironic to the analytic. More pointedly, fragments of sentences spoken by the two girls studying the photographs (which are never shown) comment implicitly on other parts of the film. After a voice-over of the minister at the wedding declaring, "Time will come when I shall know," the girls are heard to say, "Not true." Later, after the minister speaks of love, the girls burst into laughter. A different tone is created by a series of images—the horse's leg and its eye in close-up, the bride, the naked woman at water's edge, the wedding, a girl in the boat looking over her shoulder, and the color red—accompanied by other sounds: the voice of the minister speaking of ideal marriage, the girls saying that "everyone wants to get married," the minister saying "never to be seen again," and then dead silence. All of these fragments convey the sense that the internal reality of the girls in the boat challenges assumptions about the world shared by those in the church.

Dominated as it is by nonlinear, prismatic editing featuring the color red, unfocused close-ups of multi-hued flowers, and glinting water, Daughters of Chaos is like a jewel-encrusted box that both represents and responds to the confusing process of becoming a woman in a patriarchal culture. The film shows the outside of the box, as it were, but calls attention to what is inside and cannot be seen. Absence is present in the concealed images in the photographs perused by the girls and in the empty chair in the garden, which is marked by a sign saying "Keep Out." The mothers' lives have not been recorded since their weddings, although their presence remains powerful in the continuation of the rituals they enacted as they, themselves, left girlhood for marriage. This film is both poetic and personal, but it is also feminist in its acknowledgment of the complexity of female adolescence and its critique of the seductive institutions that thwart women's development. Daughters of Chaos is balanced between what Keller referred to as "irony and sincerity [that are] internalized and organic."[46] The film is the work of a woman bred to look forward to a wedding but educated to understand all that such an event represents and destined to live within the contradictions so created. In an optimistic gesture, Keller gave this film (which happened to be of her niece's wedding) to her stepdaughter, who is the girl in red entering the sea. Perhaps she meant to encourage her to keep swimming.

Clearly, Keller was openly indebted to the work of the American avant-garde and particularly to Brakhage. As a student of Annette Michelson as well, she understood that these filmmakers were "deeply transgressive" in their rejection of industrial modes of production and in the representation of eroticism.[47] She learned from Brakhage in particular the value of the domestic environment as subject matter and the means of creating a subjective vision through quick cuts, the use of the textures of the film itself, the freely moving camera, and the full range of exposure and focus. But she was also fully aware of the weakness of the male-dominated American avant-garde, and she engaged this problem primarily through the use of sound. While Brakhage's films are largely silent, Keller experimented with the effect of sound on image and the way in which sound, with all of its potential for humor and irony, is able to deidealize and deromanticize the world. Her most explicit commentary on Brakhage—and his problematic relation to women and the female body—is *Misconception*, a film that was made at the very time that the feminist critique of woman as muse and bearer of meaning for the male artist was beginning to be articulated in film theory.[48]

Ann Friedberg has called *Misconception* a "loving critique" of Brakhage's 1959 film, *Window Water Baby Moving*, in which the filmmaker's wife is shown before and during the birth of the couple's first child.[49] Like Brakhage, Keller approached childbirth with awe and was determined to convey the experience on film. Keller said, "I challenged childbirth to see if I could come up with a film that would be as strong as if I asked an audience to experience a childbirth in person."[50] Both *Misconception* and *Window Water Baby Moving* are heavily edited, and both feature a searching camera that marks the filmmakers' active involvement in the process and lack of a preconceived design. Keller, in fact, never even filmed the actual birth of the baby, irresistibly drawn as she was to the mother's face. Where Keller differed from Brakhage was in her desire to explore the difficulties of pregnancy and childbirth from a woman's point of view. Her film is divided into six numbered sections, each of which features a dialogue in both sound and image about the subject in question. Discussions take place about topics as diverse as the difficulty of raising children, pain control in childbirth, and the validity of Pavlov's experiments, while imagistic polarities are created through the juxtaposition of indoor and outdoor shots as well as alternating views of a house being demolished and a woman receiving an internal medical exam. The most obvious response to Brakhage occurs in the second section, in which the pregnant woman takes a bath with her toddler son. Whereas Brakhage's film features rosy close-ups of his wife's belly as it emerges from a bath, flecked with drops of water and lit by twilight to resemble a planet coming into being, Keller's sister-in-law is fully present in a mildew-rimmed tub in a brightly lit bathroom, hoisting her heavy body around as she splashes water on her child and later struggles to bend over to pick up discarded towels. Intercut are scenes of labor, in the full meaning of the word, and the sounds of screaming, male doctors giving directions, the mother laughing and singing with her child in the bath, and silence. To Brakhage's silent romanticizing of the birth process, Keller responds with something close to the real thing, and the viewer feels bodily the experience that Brakhage reduced and mythologized beyond recognition.

Misconception is more than a dialogue with an earlier film, however, and more than the presentation of the many ways in which men and women differ in their conceptions of pregnancy and childbirth. The film formally elaborates the sensual experience of birth and, more importantly, foregrounds the way in which its own cinematic form transforms the experience and presents it as if for the first time. *Misconception* evokes perhaps the most profound of lost objects by conveying the inability of language to describe birth, the most central of human experiences. The film's fourth, elliptically edited section consists of a father and son navigating a waterfall in soft focus, accompanied by sound that is reduced to static, fragments of imagery suggesting the woman in labor, and finally by silence. The segment, which begins with the father lecturing the child about birth, ends in total abstraction. At the end of the film, in which the woman giving birth is shown with extremely quick editing, swish pans, and soft focus, the mother speaks to her own mother on the telephone and tells her that the baby is a girl. She says, "It wasn't nothing, but right now it seems as if it was." Absolute silence then accompanies an extreme close-up of her vibrant, active eyes as she continues the now unheard conversation. Keller's film gives the viewer something of the experience of childbirth and at the same time, manifests the degree to which patriarchal culture, by failing to find the language to describe childbirth, has elided it from representation and thus from human experience.

Conclusion

Keller referred to her final film, *Herein* (1991), as a "reinvention of documentary film form from a personal and feminist view point."[51] The film was motivated by Keller's acquisition of the FBI files detailing her activities in the SDS in the 1960s and 1970s and her observation that everything important had been deleted. The governing image in the film is the multipage document in negative, with the erased material appearing as empty rectangles scattered throughout the text. The film is a search for what these holes represent, for what has been lost over time of all that Keller was and all that she did during her period of social activism. The focus of the film is her youthful home—the apartment and the building in New York City that she described as "a kind of background to my life."[52] This building, in a poor and neglected urban neighborhood, is juxtaposed against her later middle-class home in Rhode Island, which represented her entry into a new phase of adulthood. The film of the building, and the building that becomes the film, reflect Keller's longtime fascination with the work of Cornell and the ways in which he adapted his box structure to filmmaking. *Herein* begins and ends with images of windows; the opening shot looks out at a wintry park at dusk, with bare trees forming lacy patterns on white, while the final shot through a barred window reveals the green of springtime. In between, Keller's roaming camera searches the cluttered, tight interiors that contain the lives lived in the building.

The film, like the building, is dominated by a bearded storyteller, an Orthodox Jewish cantor who was known for befriending the neighborhood's prostitutes and pimps, and who relates anecdotes about the people who have passed through the site. His voice, chanting in Hebrew, accompanies the opening images of the FBI document; various parts of his body are filmed with the same tight close-ups and tracking shots that the filmmaker uses to reveal the building's peeling, cracked, and broken walls. The camerawork signals her distrust of the man's appropriation of these stories, the way in which his questionable personal relations with the women compromise his social activism, and the filmmaker's determination to frame and film her own versions. The film opens with a voice reading a text by Emma Goldman in which the early-twentieth-century feminist describes her anxieties about supporting herself as a prostitute. Goldman speaks, in a sense, for Keller herself: for the filmmaker's youthful decision to live among the prostitutes on Forsyth Street as a political act and a repudiation of middle-class society, and her eventual rejection of these convictions as naive.[53] The rest of the film explores, through a cinematic investigation of the literal space that once was so important to her activist self, the psychic space she occupied at the time.

The film is composed largely of close-up pans and tracking shots of dirty, dilapidated hallways; glimpses through doors into small, disorderly, sometimes occupied rooms; and the interior of a well-maintained apartment featuring plants, books, a cat, and a window that further divides the space into a self-reflexive series of boxes within boxes. The sound track is reminiscent of Leslie Thornton's work, with its layering and overlapping of bland Asian music, Hebrew chants, unidentified film sound tracks, and voices reading from anarchist texts. But the most significant footage consists of images from or references to other filmed scenes—which are shown in the process of being shot in and around the building and also as they appear on a television inside the building. These scenes both contain the building and are contained within it, "dissolving like dioramas" into one another, just as *Herein* both creates the building of Keller's youth and is created by it.[54]

The film contains excerpts from at least two films from 1985 that were shot in and around the apartment building: segments from *Almost You* (Adam Brooks), a love story about a less-than-successful actor and a visiting nurse, and a sequence from *Evergreen* (Fielder Cook) showing Hasidim pushing carts to market. Old footage recording the production of *Evergreen*—in which the neighborhood was returned to the early twentieth century by way of set and costume—are used in *Herein* as a marker of any film's flexible relation to time. As a film within the present film, the *Evergreen* material allows the Forsyth Street building to be present in three times simultaneously: the past of *Evergreen*'s fiction, the moment of *Herein*'s reflexive shooting, and the eternal present in which all the films are viewed. The films within the film are held up against the male storyteller's self-centered and often cruel invention of the building, on one hand, and Keller's cinematic version, on the other. The former, resembling Hollywood films, exploits both facades and interiors in order to arrange the past in a historical mode, with a single point of view. The women's films, both Keller's and two from which she quotes (Su Friedrich's *The Ties That Bind* [1984], and Mary Filippo's *Who Do You Think You Are* [1987]), suggest an alternative mode of creating an image of a place and all that it contains of time. The images that flash and are superimposed on the screen defy the controlling orderliness of conventional narrative. Keller does not eliminate the dark corners that do not fit a predetermined story. She includes, rather, all the contradictory, obscure, and mysterious images and sounds in a prismatic structure that documents her own experience of the place that formed her.

One of the last images in *Herein* is a televised version of a negative of the FBI document that inspired the film. As a challenge to the institutional attempt to erase the difficult parts of her life, Keller's film has literally filled in the empty spaces of the text with the sounds and images of the building that housed her radical self. She has made a "palimpsest" (as spoken at the end of the film), one that does not retrieve the irrecoverable past but forms a layered image that speaks of her personal history in relation to her present concerns. *Herein* can thus be understood as a lost object that helps to reconcile ongoing conflicts in the lives of women: the sexual politics that affected the women of her generation and complicated their relation to organized politics; and the contradictory constraints, ambitions, and desires that continue to plague them in relation to family and labor. Keller's final film is similar to all of her work in its use of sensual handheld camera movement; heavy editing, quick cuts, and flashes of color and light; play with exposure, focus, angle, and shot distance; and flexible, ambiguous sound. The film differs, however, in both its overt political intentions and in its imagery, for Keller has moved here from the natural and familial world to one in which found footage plays an important role. Just as her unfinished book project sought to examine women's films that deranged patriarchal constructs by manipulating media manifestations of them, this last film contrasts two versions of a world she knows well: the narrow descriptions of women's lives offered by Hollywood and a dominating male voice, as opposed to the far richer version created by the wide-open eyes of the experimental artist fully aware of cinema's potential.

Although Keller's premature death ended her intriguing and stimulating career as a filmmaker and a scholar, her body of films forms a bridge linking the concerns and aesthetics of the American avant-garde of the 1960s and 1970s with feminism. Her reconsideration and revision of Brakhage's themes and approaches in light of feminism, along with her challenge to feminist film theory to pay attention to women's experience and to the variety of female voices, makes Marjorie Keller a unique figure in the history of experimental cinema.

Filmography

Hell No: No Cuts!, ca. 1972 (25 min.): si., b&w; 8mm
Backsection, ca. 1972 (4 1/2 min.): si., col.; 8mm
History of Art 3939, ca. 1972 (2 1/2 min.): si., col.; 8mm
Part IV: Green Hill, ca. 1972 (3 min.): sd., col.; 8mm
Turtle, ca. 1972 (2 1/2 min.): si., col.; 8mm
Untitled, ca. 1972 (7 1/2 min.): si., b&w; 8mm
Pieces of Eight, 1973 (3 min.): si., b&w; 8mm
Duck Fuck/Rube in Galena, 1973 (4 min.): si., col.; 16mm
Swept, 1973 (3 min.): si., col.; 16mm
The Outer Circle, 1973 (6 3/4 min.): sd., col.; 16mm
She/Va, 1973 (3 min.): si., col.; 16mm
Objection, 1974 (18 1/4 min.): sd., col.; 16mm

Film Notebook: Part 1, 1975 (12 1/4 min.): si., col.; 8mm

Superimposition (1), 1975 (14 3/4 min.): si., col.; 16mm

By Two's & Three's: Women, 1976 (7 min.): si., col.; 8mm

Film Notebook: 1969–76; Part 2, Some of Us in the Mechanical Age, 1977 (27 min.): si., col.; 8mm

Misconception, 1977 (43 min.): sd., col.; 16mm

The Web, 1977 (10 min.): si., col.; 8mm

On the Verge of an Image of Christmas, 1978 (10 1/2 min.): si., col.; 8mm

Ancient Parts/Foreign Parts, 1979 (6 min.): si., col.; 16mm

Six Windows, 1979 (7 min): sd., col.; 16mm

Daughters of Chaos, 1980 (20 min.): sd., col.; 16mm

The Fallen World, 1983 (9 1/2 min.): sd., b&w, col.; 16mm

Lyrics, 1983 (9 min.): sd., col.; Super 8

The Answering Furrow, 1985 (27 min.): sd., col.; 16mm

Private Parts, 1988 (12 3/4 min.): si., col.; 16mm

Herein, 1991 (35 min.): sd., col.; 16mm

Notes

I extend my gratitude to several people for their help in the writing of this essay, including P. Adams Sitney, Saul Levine, Helene Kaplan Wright, Sky Sitney, B. Ruby Rich, Joan Braderman, M. M. Serra, and Ann Steuernagel. I also note that a fuller version of this essay has been published in the *New England Review* 26, no. 4 (2005): 135–60.

1 Keller, "Review of E. Ann Kaplan's *Women and Film*," 46.

2 See Rich's lively and informative book about this period, *Chick Flicks*.

3 The notes for the proposed book, tentatively to be titled *What Do Women Want?*, are found in Keller's personal files, currently in the possession of P. Adams Sitney, Keller's widower. All references to the book are taken from notes in these files. The book was to begin with an introduction covering the work of Germaine Dulac, Deren, Menken, and Schneemann and then cover the films of Abigail Child, Mary Filippo, Nina Fonoroff, Su Friedrich, Heather McAdams, Ester Shatavsky, Leslie Thornton, and Sokhi Wagner.

4 Most information about Keller's life is taken from personal interviews with P. Adams Sitney, Saul Levine, and Helene Kaplan Wright in March 2003. I have attempted to cross-check both facts and impressions and apologize in advance for any perceived misinterpretations.

5 See Rich, *Chick Flicks*, 116–20. In a personal interview in July 2003, Rich noted that Keller was not particularly interested in feminist women's cinema at this time and became so only once she started teaching film. In the late 1970s, Keller was one of the organizers of the national Women's Studies Association's meetings at the University of Rhode Island, at which Rich was invited to speak.

6   The SDS was a radical student group formed in 1960 from the youth organization of the socialist League for Industrial Democracy. In the Port Huron Statement, written in 1962, the group advocated nonviolent protest against racism, poverty, and war and called for a fully participatory democracy. After the 1965 march on Washington, D.C., against the Vietnam War, the group became increasingly militant and ever more present and disruptive on U.S. college campuses. With the police reaction to the student protests at the 1968 Democratic Convention in Chicago and the killing of four students at Kent State University in Ohio in 1970, the factions of the movement that advocated violence, particularly the Weather Underground, began to dominate and by the mid-1970s, the movement was over.

7   Interview with Saul Levine, March 2003.

8   The filmmaker Jeff Kreines worked on this film for several days and remembers it as an agit-prop film with nothing in common with Keller's later work (correspondence with the author, August 12, 2003).

9   Hoberman, obituary for Marjorie Keller. Other obituaries appear in the *New York Times* (February 19, 1994) and the *Providence Sunday Journal* (April 10, 1994).

10 A thirty-second digital film that was part of this project, called *Gust*, was produced during a winter intercession in January 1994 at Middlebury College.

11 Suarez-Araùz, *Amnesis Art*, 29.

12 Ibid., 93.

13 Ibid., 8.

14 Ibid., 29.

15 Ibid., 5.

16 Rajchman, "Foucault's Art of Seeing," 141.

17 Foucault, "Nietzsche, Genealogy, History," 93.

18 Ibid., 89, 76, 81.

19 Arthur, "Letter to Marjorie Keller," 66.

20 Markopoulos, "The Intuition of Space," 73.

21 See Rajchman, "Foucault's Art of Seeing," 119–21, 133.

22 Suarez-Araùz, *Amnesis Art*, 57.

23 Foucault, "Nietzsche, Genealogy, History," 76.

24 Arthur, "Letter to Marjorie Keller," 64. Arthur's argument is based on the notion found in both Siegfried Kracauer and André Bazin that film is a death mask that represents eternally what is dead and gone.

25 See Deren, "An Anagram of Ideas on Art, Form and Film," 267–322.

26 S. MacDonald, *The Garden in the Machine*, 58, 73.

27 I note that Keller made several 8mm films early in her career in the notebook mode, some of which are titled as such.

28 Keller, *The Untutored Eye*, 69.

29 Ibid., 78.

30 Ibid., 15.

31   Ibid., 100–111.

32   Ibid., 105.

33   Ibid., 183. Keller notes that Brakhage was influenced by Ezra Pound's demand to "make it new," by Gertrude Stein's belief that one need not look farther than the things in one's own milieu to find subject matter, and by Emerson's valorization of the sights of daily life and children (181).

34   Ibid., 184. See R. Elder, *The Films of Stan Brakhage.*

35   Ibid., 179. See Brakhage, "Metaphors on Vision."

36   Pruitt, "Review of *The Untutored Eye,*" 82.

37   Keller, *The Untutored Eye,* 204.

38   Ibid., 192.

39   Reisman, "Personal Film/Feminist Film," 60–85, and Keller, "Review of *Women and Film,*" 43–47.

40   Levine interview, March 2003.

41   Keller, "Review of *Women and Film,*" 45, referring to E. Kaplan, *Women and Film,* 87.

42   Keller, "Review of *Women and Film,*" 44–46. See Mulvey, "Visual Pleasure and Narrative Cinema."

43   See Bruno, "Women in Avant-Garde Film," 141–48.

44   Reisman, "Personal Film/Feminist Film," 78–79.

45   Keller files.

46   Ibid.

47   Michelson quoted in Bruno, "Women in Avant-Garde Film," 147.

48   Friedberg, "*Misconception* = the 'Division of Labor' in the Childbirth Film," 64–65.

49   Ibid., 64.

50   Keller in Reisman, "Personal Film/Feminist Film," 74.

51   Keller files.

52   Ibid.

53   Ibid.

54   Ibid.

MARY ANN DOANE

In the Ruins of the Image

The Work of Leslie Thornton

◻

Every passion borders on the chaotic, but the collector's passion borders on the chaos of memories.—Walter Benjamin

Toward the beginning of *Let Me Count the Ways* (2004), there is a series of images of Leslie Thornton's father and his fellow workers, lounging, playing, working, with intertitles locating the activities "outside Los Alamos, New Mexico 1945" or on "Tinian Island, in the South Pacific," or in relation to "Project Alberta, delivery of the bomb." The shakiness of the camera, the slightly washed-out quality of the image, and the jerkiness of the pans signal that we are in the presence of old amateur or home movie images. Intermittently, typed over the images of one of the men, is the simple word "Dad." The terseness, the abruptness of that simple indicator—"Dad"—collides with what the spectator must acknowledge as the image's production on the margins of, but also in causal relation to, a major historical trauma. The sound track, an untranslated War Department recording of a Hiroshima survivor's story, is a trace of how one person's home movie constitutes another's nightmare. At the time of this writing, this section, "Minus 10, 9, 8, 7 . . . ," of *Let Me Count the Ways* constitutes the first foray into a new project for Thornton, one which, like much of her previous work, is ongoing, potentially boundaryless, and subject to reworking and revision. As short as it is, it encapsulates many of the concerns and formal obsessions that are present in Thornton's earlier work: the recycling of images, the pathos of language and its limitations, the activation of anecdote as a quasi-narrative device, the concern with historicity and the archive of images and sounds, the legibility of the image, and the obscene fragility of biography and autobiography.

Thornton's father and grandfather (a nuclear physicist/engineer and an electrical engineer, respectively) both worked on the Manhattan Project during the Second World War and contributed in different ways to the development of the atomic bomb, later dropped on Hiroshima.[1] A certain genealogy of horror hence resides within the familial for Thornton and manifests itself in a fascination with explosiveness (the recurring shot of a tremendous explosion within a tunnel, debris flung toward the camera in *The Last Time I Saw Ron* and *Strange Space*) and science (the use of found footage of NASA, the moon walk, and laboratory experiments in *Adynata* and *Peggy and Fred in Hell*). The terse "Dad," typewritten over the image in a vain attempt to localize and constrain identity, thus carries within it a surplus of affect, extending beyond the limited circle of the family and tinged by historical trauma. The "Minus 10, 9, 8, 7 . . ." section of *Let Me Count the Ways* traces the effects of Hiroshima at a number of levels and in startlingly different forms. The home movie footage of Thornton's father is succeeded by a less readable section of images—footage of a foggy day in Brooklyn, images taken from a train in Connecticut and Brussels as well as from a plane over New York City in 2001, test footage of tanks and a jet engine, and images from *Operation Hardtack*'s atomic bomb tests taken from the National Archive, all accompanied by the voice-over of an English-speaking Hiroshima survivor responding to congressmen's questions and describing the aftermath of the bombing. All of these images are barely decipherable beneath a flashing blue circle that dominates the center of the frame, present either in its sheer intensity (and recalling the flash of light associated with the Hiroshima bomb) or as a fainter afterimage. If this film is "about" anything it is precisely the afterimage of Hiroshima— the afterimage impressing itself upon the retina as the trace of the violence of seeing.

The last two sections of the film ("Minus 8" and "Minus 7") use typewritten text (together with the faintly metallic sounds of typing) to describe the paradoxically lush growth of vegetation that blanketed the site after the bombing. An excerpt from John Hersey's *Hiroshima* chronicling a survivor's astonishment at seeing flowers and rich green plant life covering the otherwise dead and deadly landscape followed by a rigorously technical scientific text about a plant mutation linked to the radioactivity are inscribed over the graceful and undulatory movements of plants growing in "slow motion" as conveyed by time-lapse photography. The scientific discourse scrolls by at an increasingly rapid rate until it reaches the point of illegibility, the ghostly plants still swaying and extending in a fascinating dance in the background. The film exposes both the persistence and the inadequacy of the scientific and legislative attempts to comprehend. What can a congressional hearing tell us about the measure of pain or shock? Can the discourse of science trace the precise forms of mutation inscribed by radioactivity in the genes? Both discourses nevertheless subject the event to an epistemological demand and incarnate the strength of the desire to know in the face of extraordinary violence. *Let Me Count the Ways* as a whole is concerned with the relations between war and language, with a focus on World War II, the Cold War, and the post-9/11 present, and, according to Thornton, will consider such topics as "the deployment of propaganda and disinformation, media commentary, eyewitness accounts, war stories, as well as what is unspoken (secrecy), and what is unspeakable (horror, awe, uncertainty . . .)."[2] These are topics that are not new for Thornton but take on a particular urgency in the current sociopolitical context.

A concern with the contours and limits of language in both its written and spoken forms and with "unspeakability" is evident very early in Thornton's career and often coincides with a feminist reflection on sexual difference, a crucial aspect of her work. In *Jennifer, Where Are You?* (1981), a man's voice, incessantly repeating the film's title in various tones and inflections, with connotations of appeal, command, and anger, accompanies an image of a little girl playing with lipstick and matches. His voice is all the more terrorizing insofar as it remains unseen, an echo of the traditional, disembodied, anonymous, and powerful male voice-over of documentary.[3] She is all image; he is all voice. In an excerpt from *Peggy and Fred in Hell* (1985), a close-up of vibrating vocal cords is accompanied by Handel's opera *Rinaldo* (a bricolage of earlier operatic pieces), superimposed over pop Latin music by Yma Sumac from Peru (alias Amy Camus from Brooklyn), known for the range of her voice (seven octaves). The black-and-white image of quivering vocal cords is from a classic science film and, taken out of context, it is almost unrecognizable. The vocal cords' resemblance to female genitalia is inescapable, and one gets the strange sense that we are witness to the body producing speech—a singing vulva.[4] Documentary is investigated as a site for the "scientific" dissection and analysis of the voice in its minutest bodily movements.

Fragments of intertitles relating pitch to the rapidity of movement under-line the fact that this is a discourse that strives to be scientific. Yet it is a "science" that constantly returns us to questions of sexual differ-ence, the cultural construction of femininity and masculinity. In her film work, Thornton has consistently been interested in elaborating the way in which sexual difference is a matter of sound as well as image. In this excerpt from *Peggy and Fred in Hell*, an image of the lower half of a television set is presented along with a voice that is reminiscent of "edu-cational" voices associated with "learning by rote." The voice tells us: "Listen to the two voices which follow and decide which is the higher in pitch." The sentence produced by the two voices whose pitch we are to decide is: "The pitch most people prefer for the female voice is about A-flat below middle C." Later, the multiple-choice test activates a male voice that informs us, "The pitch most people prefer for the male voice is around low C." The second, "preferable" male voice is recognizable as the overly familiar "neutral" voice-over of the documentary—the voice that inhabits the space outside the image, a space of reserve, authority, tran-scendental otherness, in short—knowledge. In Thornton's work, one gets the sense that the most oppressive site of patriarchal authority is the sound track rather than the image. In *Adynata* (1983), "maleness" on the sound track is evidenced not in a voice but as heavy measured footsteps that contrast with the image of simultaneous deformation and delicacy associated with the bound female foot. In another section of *Peggy and Fred in Hell*, Peggy sings a Michael Jackson song, "Billie Jean," convo-luting the gender positions marked out by its lyrics: "Billie Jean is not my lover; she's just a girl who says that I am the one; but the kid is not my son."

Yet the haunting of language by sexual difference is not its only prob-lematic feature. Language is deficient but must, nevertheless, be used. *adynata* is a rhetorical term meaning the expression of the impossibility of expression or a confession that words fail us. Words fail us, not be-cause they are inadequate for the expression of a full interiority, but be-cause meaning leaks out, cannot be contained by a logic of morphemes; it contaminates the gaps and absences language depends on for the very differentiating power of their emptiness. On the sound track of the early *X-Tracts* (1975), Thornton *cuts* language differently, producing alterna-tive minimal units and hence different differences. One is tempted to compare her endeavor to Julia Kristeva's emphasis upon *echolalia* or Roland Barthes's "grain of the voice" (both pointing toward the otherness that inhabits language). These are theories of asignification or, perhaps more accurately, the signification that escapes the constraints of socio-symbolic ordering. Yet, Thornton's choice of sounds and images often has less to do with any otherness in relation to the symbolic than with an over- or hypercodification, hence the constant recourse to found footage as well as the icons of popular culture. Still, one does get the sense that there is an investment here in something beyond, beneath, or outside of language, if only in the putting into play of classically and hauntingly beautiful images and sounds. However, *adynata* is not only the confession that words fail us but also, and more primarily, a stringing together of impossibilities. Language fails us only if we expect it to deliver the perfect clarity of a machine; the fact that it is inhabited by impossibility opens up a space for the play of fantasy, otherness, the *ab*normal. The syntax of Thornton's films often suggests that very "stringing together of impossibilities."

A description of Thornton's working process would seem to be in order here. *Jennifer, Where Are You?* and *Adynata* are anomalies within her corpus because they exist as discrete texts, classically finished works whose identity is set, unalterable. From a critic's point of view, these are easier works to deal with since they are limited, contained, with stable boundaries. More typical of her filmmaking practice is the extended, long-term project—works such as *Peggy and Fred in Hell* (1985–), *The Great Invisible* (1997–), and most recently, *Let Me Count the Ways* (2004–). Thornton works in sections, honing a particular piece or sequence of a larger project, releasing it as an independent work, and then returning to it to revise and rework so that the context is continually mutating. The same images—her own or found footage—are recycled and reused in different films. It is as if she were continually striving to "get it right," the trajectory of her work nevertheless revealing an insistent distrust of the idea of the static art object or the definitive version of a film.

These reworkings sometimes cross or combine different media, joining video, film, and digital media and even deploying film or video footage in the context of a museum installation. Despite Thornton's sensitivity to the specific aesthetic properties of film, she has never been fully invested in the defense of a particular medium and was one of the first filmmakers to enthusiastically engage with video. Sections of *Peggy and Fred in Hell* (described by Thornton herself as a lifetime project) have been released in various formats since 1985, including black-and-white 16mm films such as *Peggy and Fred in Hell: The Prologue* (1985) and *Whirling* (1996); black-and-white videos—*Peggy and Fred in Kansas*

Leslie Thornton filming in Kenadsa, Algeria, in 1991 at the madrassa where Isabelle Eberhardt studied. Courtesy of Leslie Thornton. Photo: Susan Slyomovics.

(1987) and *Introduction to the So-Called Duck Factory* (1993); and combinations of 16mm film and video such as *[Dung Smoke Enters the Palace]* (1989) and *The Problem So Far* (1996). Thornton has continued to work on the *Peggy and Fred in Hell* series, editing a new form of the project that foregrounds the narrative aspects of the material. Since 2000, she has completed three new episodes: *Bedtime* (2000), *Have a Nice Day Alone* (2001), and *The Splendor* (2002). Thornton has also taken the material for this project into a new realm—that of the multimedia installation. In 1999, she was invited to do an installation for a major exhibition, "Presumed Innocent" (on images of children in various art forms) at the Musée d'Art Contemporain de Bordeaux. This installation, *Quickly, Yet Too Slowly*, situates footage from *Peggy and Fred in Hell* and new material in a space designed for the intermittent and open-ended time of museum viewing. Thornton is currently using some of these elements in a more ambitious installation, *The Ten Thousand Hills of Language*, which deals with the conjunction of language, technology, and childhood. Similarly, *The Great Invisible* is a work that has spanned the last seven years, the material documenting Thornton's fascination with the figure of Isabelle Eberhardt first emerging as a "complete" video, *There*

Was an Unseen Cloud Moving, in 1988. Two short sections of *The Great Invisible* were distributed in 1997 and 1998 (. . . *or lost* and *The Haunted Swing*) and a one-hour work-in-progress of the film was released in 2002. The borders of a work, for Thornton, are permeable and the fate of the image resides in its very repeatability—at its heart lies the phenomenon of technical reproducibility. The incorrigible incompletion characterizing her work is intimately linked to the use and recycling (within her own oeuvre) of found footage, the tendency to implant it within varying contexts and syntaxes, extending the life of an image as though it were a word in some fantastic and obscure vocabulary that she is trying to make legible.

Leslie Thornton was born in 1951 in Knoxville, Tennessee, and grew up in a defense-industry family not far from Oakridge, where methods of refining radioactive materials used in the bomb were developed. Outside of Oakridge, there is a highway sign that reads:

What you see here,
What you do here,
What you hear here,
When you leave here,
Let it stay here.

Thornton's filmmaking practice might be situated as the transgression of that sign's injunction not to allow visual and auditory images to travel, both within and across the boundaries of her own works and against the limits of the "unspeakable." She began as a painter, not a filmmaker, and, according to Thomas Zummer, "Thornton's paintings organized a sensual, expressionist hand into strict formal geometric mappings. These works begin with a painterly sensuality set within and against a series of structural grids, so that there is a constant tension between expressivity and the ineffable. As the physicality of painting is diminished, sensuality is reduced to a minimal mark, a trace, a spectral remainder holding place before the sublime, unrepresentable, unspeakable."[5] Painting, however, did not leave room for Thornton's obsession with language, with event, with contingency. At SUNY-Buffalo, she studied with avant-garde filmmakers Hollis Frampton, Stan Brakhage, Paul Sharits, and Peter Kubelka, and at MIT with practitioners of cinema verité Richard Leacock and Ed Pincus. Although she rejected both the formalism and ascetic structuralism of the Buffalo filmmakers and the blind faith in the transparency/legibility of the image and minimization of editing characteristic of cinema verité, these filmmakers have nevertheless had an effect upon her work. This is visible in the sheer aesthetic pleasure of the image (Brakhage and Frampton), the commitment to the intricacies and complexities of editing as a process (Kubelka and Frampton), and the deployment of the image as shock (Sharits, Brakhage). While skeptical of cinema verité's activation of the camera as mute witness to the event, Thornton nevertheless is fascinated by historical and scientific claims about the image's evidentiary status and by the idea of an archive of images and sounds, traces of something, if not of truth.

The mise-en-scène of *Peggy and Fred in Hell* is that of a postapocalyptic era, although it is not entirely clear what that apocalypse was. Two children play in a world devoid of adults, indeed of any other humans, traces of whom persist only in lyrics and references drawn from popular culture. Peggy and Fred appropriate cultural and technological objects in different and unexpected ways, play at being adults, and generally search for a language that would be adequate to their experience. We are faced with the solipsism of children in an empty world, playing next to each other with only a slight awareness of each other's existence. In the dystopia of *Peggy and Fred in Hell*, the subjects are overwhelmed by a kind of technological clutter and a mise-en-scène of dysfunctional objects, out of place. In one fairly sustained shot of a television set, wires fall from the ceiling and eventually fill the space in front of the television. Before the eyes of the spectator, the cinematic image is disemboweled, its technological substrate exposed. The only interiority, however, is a technological one—there is no attempt to psychologize the children. Across the series of films, Peggy and Fred intermittently grow older, but they remain children, fascinated with their environment, investigating a mise-en-scène that contains only highly mediated glimpses of the "natural" order. They are left to the device of others—telephones, toasters, televisions, wires, clothes that do not fit. As Linda Peckham points out, "there is a certain black humor in the notion of a future in which technology simply accumulates rather than progresses and a Hell that is not so apocalyptic so much as untidy. . . . Peggy and Fred are condemned to occupy an unrelieved dis/continuity, for there is no history to give time any meaning, only the sedimentation of objects around them."[6]

Yet, there is a history that makes itself felt across the various installments (twelve so far) of *Peggy and Fred in Hell*—that of imaging systems themselves, their decay and replacement by different technologies. The first episode is characterized by a pristine and polished black-and-white image that is carefully framed and lit to enhance all the clarity and

Peggy and Fred dancing, from *The Splendor*, 2001. Courtesy of Leslie Thornton. Photo: Thomas Zummer.

Peggy, from *[Dung Smoke Enters the Palace]*, 1989. Courtesy of Leslie Thornton. Photo: Leslie Thornton.

resolution classically associated with the film image. Within it, Peggy and Fred dance and play, sing and exhort, inside a mise-en-scène diligently designed as overflowing with unimaginable combinations of things. Later episodes have recourse to the less-crafted video image with all its connotations of presence and spontaneity. In *Introduction to the Duck Factory*, a stark video close-up of an older and slightly unkempt Peggy presenting a monologue about cutting up worms and feeding fish seems to suddenly leap out of the screen as pure presence. Yet, video also more readily allows a form of manipulation of the image: as Peggy and Fred wade through the water the huge and haunting forms of ducks seem to swim by them, each species oblivious to the other. A glow or halo envelopes the bodies of Peggy and Fred, further separating them as entities from their environment. Within the later episodes of the series, Thornton also makes use of the possibilities opened up by digitization. In *Have a Nice Day Alone*, the image seems to shimmer and assume the liquid quality of molten metal beneath the typewritten statement: "Gesture reflects the making of word choice before the word itself is available." At one point, Fred lies on a sofa explaining the necessity of speaking slowly and clearly in a frame dominated by a large table with a telephone on it. The scene is gradually distorted as the corner of the table seems to mutate, opening a circle within the image that contains the image itself. A computer or robotlike, purely mechanical voice seems to respond to Fred from some unknown extradiegetic space. Most recently, Thornton has begun to experiment with multimedia installations for the exhibition of material from *Peggy and Fred in Hell*. It is not that the medium does not matter—on the contrary, it matters very much—but it takes on the same traits of instability and disequilibrium that contaminate Peggy and Fred's world. With an archive of more than thirty hours of images for the project, and Thornton's tendency to continually revise her approach to the material, the possible permutations are staggering.

In *Peggy and Fred in Hell*, even nature emerges as unrecognizable, foreign, other, not because we are witnessing a postapocalyptic landscape after some unthinkable nuclear holocaust but because we are forced to look at it differently. Throughout her career, Thornton has been intrigued by the foreign and the exotic, by the epistemological catastrophe constituted by cultural otherness. This fascination is most strikingly delineated in *Adynata*, in which she investigates the mise-en-scène of orientalism—the conglomeration of sounds and images that connote the Orient for a Western viewer/auditor. The images in this film are lush, unlike those in *Peggy and Fred*, and one consistently gets the sense of an overwhelming surplus of the signifier: a rippling piece of bright red silk that fills the frame; jewelry, ornamentation, and clothing designed to connote the otherness of the "Oriental"; exotic flowers and grasses in lavish botanical gardens; a close-up of bright blue undulating waves of water; silk slippers against wicker edged by peacock feathers and deep green leaves of tropical plants. The colors are extremely vivid and work to amplify what at first glance appears to be an unruly fetishism of the exotic object. There is *too much* for the eye—the film seemingly capitulates to the seductive force of visual pleasure. But this richness of the image is somewhat deceptive. It is itself already a second-order signifier of an exoticism associated with the discourse of orientalism, which is both quoted and criticized by the film. For Thornton, the discourse of orientalism is precisely a discourse of excess, of hyperbole, of the absurd. Perhaps this is why the film was initially misunderstood by a number of audiences as itself an instance of orientalism. It seemed to them to be a form of mockery or ridicule. The tone of the film, in its ironies and ambivalences, does seem to posit that the risk of such a misunderstanding is inevitable, just as the risk of misunderstanding inhabits all attempts to engage with difference in representation, just as risk is inseparable from discourse.

In *Adynata*, Thornton's work converged with the theoretical explorations of such figures as Edward Said (*Orientalism*), Roland Barthes (*Empire of Signs*), and Julia Kristeva (*About Chinese Women*). The film's organizing image is a formal portrait of a Chinese Mandarin and his wife taken in 1861, its fascination a function of both its age and its evocation of the faraway, the inaccessible. The portrait seems to authorize a sustained meditation on the iconography and the morphology of orientalism. The obsessive and seductive "That has been," which Barthes associates with the photograph, is translated into the inescapable "Here it is" of the cinematic image when Thornton herself assumes the position, pose, and dress of first the Mandarin's wife and then the Mandarin.[7] The cinematic image mimes the photographic image and acts out the perverted analogical gesture of orientalism whereby the Orient comes to mirror the underside of the Western subject's own desire. Putting herself in the picture, Thornton embodies identificatory procedures by means of which the lure of representation is revealed to reside in its relation to the subject rather than to the referent. Orientalism functions both to insure the coherent, cohesive identity of the Western subject and to sustain desire in representation.

The excesses of orientalism are even more visible and audible in the sound track than in the image. Rare ethnographic recordings of Chinese opera from the 1920s are combined with the "Hartz Mountain Canary Orchestra," recurrent "pings" associated with an Oriental musical instrument, old 78-rpm love songs and blues, television-style background music that connotes "Pacific island-ness" and the suspense associated with police dramas; microphone hum (the "noise" of the apparatus); "nature" sounds, including crickets, birds, and thunderstorms; and dialogue from a Korean soap opera. The relation of sound to image is often contentious rather than supplementary, producing ruptures and disjunctive moments that force the discourse of orientalism to stutter and falter. In its insistence upon making problematic the relation of sound to image, *Adynata* finds its greatest affinity with Barthes's approach in *Empire of Signs*. In a short prologue to the series of essays that constitute the book, Barthes explains the alignment or misalignment of text with photographs, paintings, and drawings: "The text does not 'gloss' the images, which do not 'illustrate' the text. For me, each has been no more than the onset of a kind of visual uncertainty, analogous perhaps to that *loss of meaning* Zen calls a *satori*. Text and image, interlacing, seek to ensure the circulation and exchange of these signifiers: body, face, writing; and in them to read the retreat of signs."[8]

For Thornton, as well, the cinematic sign is dismantled through the mismatch, the asynchronism of sound and image. But in many crucial respects, Thornton's project differs markedly from that of Barthes. If the sign "retreats" in *Adynata*, it does not get very far. Barthes, on the other hand, would like "to 'entertain' the idea of an unheard-of symbolic system, one altogether detached from our own."[9] Barthes's writing about his trip to Japan is evidence of an impossible desire for absolute and irreducible otherness—with no point of contact with the West. One gets the sense that he finds the Western episteme constraining, if not suffocating, in its insistence upon the ideological hold and closure of meaning. Barthes's search is therefore for an outside—and the Japanese test seems to offer him a material order of signifiers that never coagulate in the production of a signified. What he looks for is, in effect, something pre-Symbolic. Barthes travels to Japan in some sense to experience the originary. In contrast, there is nothing originary in *Adynata*; everything articulated about the Orient has already been respoken. The film delineates a representation of the Orient that flaunts its own inadequacy, its status as a cliché. As Jonathan Rosenbaum points out, spectatorial engagement with such a discourse reveals "all sorts of ideological positions and forms of ignorance about the Orient," demonstrating that "one's misconceptions and uncertainties about what one sees and hears are not a distraction from the film's focus but part of its subject."[10] Orientalism is hence a kind of continuous misreading that does not, however, presuppose a "correct" or "accurate" reading. Rather, the discourse of orientalism is a perpetual deviation without a norm.

Thornton consistently uses sounds that are difficult to recognize or place, often situating dialogue from an untranslated Asian language next to images that are also opaque. This thwarting of the invocatory drive is paralleled by a scene that aligns orientalism with scopophilia or a desire to see that is similarly blocked. A figure in an ornate red robe (echoing Thornton's earlier "reproduction" of the subjects of the photograph) is glimpsed at the edge of the frame, in a walking point-of-view shot through a sculptured Oriental garden. The image is fogged and the point of view always fails to "catch up" with its object, to achieve a secure and stable relation with it. Any fixing of the object is quite literally its death, and it is clear that the film's project entails an investigation of the murderous tendencies of representation. Toward the end of *Adynata*, there is a long section that is constituted by a distorted refilming of the final scene of François Truffaut's *Shoot the Piano Player* (1960). The images are almost illegible—a shaky camera traces the movements of pencil-thin dark figures (in the compressed anamorphic image), themselves out of focus, against a blurry and snowy background. The most recognizable image in this context is that of the dead woman's face toward the end of the scene, accompanied by the familiar gesture of closing the eyes of the dead. The original subtitle of *Adynata* was "Murder Is Not a Story"—death is more compatible with the still image (for example, the photograph of the Mandarin and his wife and, later, the stiff poses of the entire family) than with the narrative procedures of Truffaut's film. Here, photography becomes a form of murder (in line with both Bazin's and Barthes's theories of the relation between photography and death), particularly when it concerns the representation of the woman.[11] In a description of the formal portrait of the Mandarin and his wife, Thornton points out that "while the man appears wholesome and animated, the woman seems quite lifeless by comparison, her features made up in the stylized manner of a 'china doll.' "[12]

Hence, one of the most prominent aims of *Adynata* is comparable to that of Sally Potter's *Thriller* (1979)—to investigate the determinants of the woman's murder in and through representation. Part of that endeavor involves the examination of the "deathly" discomfort of the pose. In front of an expanse of silver cloth that fills the frame, two hands join, clasp, fidget, and rejoin, unable to find and maintain a comfortable position. Their maneuvers are accompanied by a strained and off-key humming. The thick white makeup, ornate headwear, beads, and jewelry that constitute the costume of German filmmaker Karen Luner (who also masquerades as the Mandarin's wife) clearly inhibit movement. The fact that she is seated in front of a movie light establishes her position as, precisely, a pose. In a walking point-of-view shot of the ground, bound feet in Oriental slippers shuffle in and out of the frame. In its Western representation, the Oriental body displays a perpetual awkwardness and lack of fluidity. It is constrained, constricted, regulated; the bound foot is its most telling image. Eroticism is the rigidly ornate. The pose—"being" for the camera—forcefully orchestrates and arranges the body just as the botanical garden organizes and controls the vicissitudes of nature for the purposes of aestheticization.

In *Adynata*, the references to the Far East, to the Orient, are of necessity unspecified, dehistoricized, precisely because this vague and nebulous notion of the Orient is subject to critique. The slippers, the robes, the jewelry, the ornate boxes are elusively "oriental," but one would be hard-put to specify their exact nationality or historical genealogy. Because the film deals entirely with the discourse of orientalism and its heavily inflected stereotypical representations, it remains vulnerable to criticisms that it simply continues, and in a way sanctions, the mystification. Thornton's major project on Isabelle Eberhardt seems designed to counter that critique through its focus on a specific and idiosyncratic individual, whose mimicry is put into play and puts her at risk in a specific situation, in a quite specific historical, political, and religious context. Thornton herself discusses the differences between an early video on Eberhardt, *There Was an Unseen Cloud Moving*, and the later work on the still-in-progress *The Great Invisible*:

> The first piece, *Unseen Cloud*, was a kind of anti-biography—working from the premise that historical reconstruction is based on pretty arbitrary, chance data, and interpretation. It was an attempt to foreground the arbitrary by not going for one coherent image of Isabelle Eberhardt. That's mostly what it's about. Later on I felt it wasn't enough, staying on the surface. I felt I was getting off a lot of hooks and avoiding difficult material. Like learning something about Islam, for example. It wasn't enough in the long run to say, well, we can't really talk about that, because it's not part of our world and we can't know anything. Because we weren't there, we aren't them. All of the authenticity issues. I decided to keep going with Isabelle Eberhardt because I wanted to learn more about her historical context, and to experiment more with narrative structure.[13]

Thornton took lessons in Arabic and researched Islam and Sufi mysticism as well as the historical background of Isabelle Eberhardt and of Algerian politics in the late nineteenth century. She consistently points to *The Great Invisible* as her attempt to engage with narrative and historicity, but it is a narrative and a historicity that are barely recognizable and do not assume the sedimented traditional forms that we usually associate with these frameworks. Bits and pieces of Eberhardt's biography are deployed but the emphasis seems to be on the detail, the tangential, the marginal rather than on building a coherent story that attempts to grasp and encapsulate a life.

Isabelle Eberhardt (1877–1904), born in Geneva, Switzerland, traveled extensively in North Africa, particularly Algeria, dressed as a man, calling

Leslie Thornton and Abdelrahman Hellal, a merchant and the village storyteller, in Tolga, Algeria, in 1991. Courtesy of Leslie Thornton. Photo: Susan Slyomovics.

herself Si Mahmoud Essadi. She converted to Islam and was revered as a saint by a number of tribes in Algeria and Tangiers. Eberhardt was a writer and kept diaries and notebooks as well as contributing columns to French newspapers. Ironically, in the middle of the desert, she died mysteriously in a flash flood in 1904. Thornton is no doubt attracted to Eberhardt's idiosyncracies and aberrations, her resistance to the sexually and the politically conventional, her unexpected and seemingly strange behaviors. Her life span also coincides with the emergence of various technologies for the mechanical reproduction of images and sounds, most especially cinema, and *The Great Invisible* is very much about the reproduction and transmissibility of images and voices—it begins and ends with references to Thomas Edison and his invention of the phonograph (in 1877, the year that Eberhardt was born). There is a strange conjunction, in this project, of a fascination with the auratic, the ineffable, and the implications of mechanical reproducibility. Thornton engages with modernity as a moment that brings together issues of image-making and sound reproduction, the violence of colonialism, and perturbations in sexual identity and the role of women.

In *The Great Invisible*, Thornton is concerned with the competing and contradictory nature of the traces/documents/artifacts that are usually activated to produce a coherent narrative in the writing or filming of biography. Isabelle's story is coincident with the emergence of technologies of representation (photography, phonography, cinema), which have been instrumental in the rendering of "history." What would usually be treated as pure coincidence by the traditional historian—the fact that 1877 marked the year of the birth of both Isabelle and the phonograph—is given a much stronger inflection in Thornton's film, inscribed within some exorbitant or unutterable cause-effect relation. A voice-over in the beginning of the film recounts the unlikely and awkward meeting of Thomas Edison and Sarah Bernhardt (who asks to be recorded reading lines from Racine's *Phaedre*), and this anecdote is followed by found footage, documentary images of a man demonstrating Edison's invention of "a machine that will give you back the voice of the dead." An intertitle, "12 Years Later," precedes a scene of a young Isabelle flamboyantly acting to a recording of Sarah Bernhardt in *Phaedre*. It is as though the phonograph, the fantastic recording machine, initiated the history of miming that was so central to Isabelle's story. The penultimate shot of the film,[14] after Isabelle's death, is preceded by the intertitle, "Mr. Edison speaks." It is indeed found footage of Edison speaking, but no sound emerges from his lips; he is mute. The sound is drained from the image, no longer anchored to the body, and replaced by the unfamiliar music of an Arabian instrument. Edison, the inventor of a machine to preserve the voices of the dead, is silenced.

The industrial revolution and mechanical reproduction defining Western modernity are imbricated with Isabelle's history in different ways throughout the film. In a recurring scene, a French photographer directs Arab women to assume the poses of an orientalist pornography popular in the late nineteenth century; he returns in scenes where he photographs young Caucasian women in Arab dress. A woman introduced as Rebecca Eyo of the Université Nanterre presents an academic slide show in 1924 chronicling Eberhardt's life. She is intermittently shown pushing huge glass slides into the projection machine. In response to a question, she points out that Isabelle's father was an avid photographer, often taking images of his wife and daughter in the nude. Isabelle's mother's death, represented by a shot of her in a coffin with pennies on her eyes, is punctuated by the flash of a photographic camera. André Bazin links cinematic specificity to a scandal—that of the repeatability of the unique, a repetition that is particularly obscene in the case of death and sexuality (two moments that are, for him, more intensely unique, less acceptable as subject to repetition).[15] Finally, trains and views from trains are omnipresent in *The Great Invisible*. The fact that Isabelle's mother was said to suffer from railroad spine, a nineteenth-century illness that specified a pathological relation to trains, afflicting primarily women and "sensitive men," occasions a digression on the relation between the cinema and trains. Accompanying found footage of a train traveling through a tunnel is a voice-over recounting the probably apocryphal story about the first cinema audiences who fled at the sight of a train on the screen apparently approaching them directly. The trauma associated with railroad spine together with a fear of the cinematic image signal a pathological relation to modernity. For Wolfgang Schivelbusch, the train, the cinema, and the department store all colluded to produce a historical change in perception: "Panoramic perception, in contrast to traditional perception, no longer belonged to the same space as the perceived objects: the traveler saw the objects, landscapes, etc. *through* the apparatus which moved him through the world. . . . This vision no longer experienced evanescence: evanescent reality had become the new reality."[16] For Thornton, there is something fascinating about this new vision of mechanical reproduction that goes beyond its seemingly infinitely accurate iconicity. When the train enters the tunnel in her found footage, it produces an illegible but bewitching gestalt pattern of black-and-white splashes as a response to the changed exposure context of the tunnel. Inadequacies of the image, its limitations, are activated intermittently throughout the film as flash frames, shakiness, poor exposure, and lack of focus. If the cinematic image's predilection for realism has been linked with its indexicality, that indexicality for Thornton is the trace of the historicity of the image and of its material limitations.[17]

These constant references to technologies of reproduction and to the idiosyncrasies of the medium operate as a resistance to what might often be seen as a conventional, linear narrative that respects the constraints of a customary chronology. Instances of apparent linearity are contained primarily in the sound track, in a plurality of voice-overs, none of them the authoritative male voice-over of documentary but instead hesitant, wavering, accented female voices. Nevertheless, they recount the story of Isabelle's mother's flight from Russia with the tutor of one of her children, Alexandre Nicolaïevitch Trofimovsky, called Vava, an ex-priest, an anarchist, and a convert to Islam. They recount the circumstances of Isabelle's birth and describe the unorthodox education provided by her strange father. The voices trace the trajectory of her travels to North Africa, the death of her mother, the death of her father, and, ultimately, her own death in a flash flood. The academic slide show also presents an opportunity to narrate coherently various aspects of Isabelle's biography. Yet the coherency of that narrative is shattered from within by the improbabilities and impossibilities of its representation and the syntax of its images. Sepia tinted scenes are juxtaposed to color home-movie footage documenting Thornton's travel to North Africa; found footage of camels, the desert, documentary images of mystic practices such as piling snakes on one's head, coaxing bugs into one's mouth, and sticking needles through one's neck are interspersed with reenacted scenes of Isabelle's life. There is one scene involving a tense conversation between Isabelle, her mother, and her father, which is shot in color but accompanied by intertitles reminiscent of a silent film rather than synchronous dialogue. Rebecca Eyo's slide show contains both still photographic images and, inexplicably, film clips. Even the images in the reenacted scenes shot by Thornton are aged, somehow evidencing historicity and decay. There is a predilection for the close-up, providing a vision too intimate to assure legibility and too partial to suggest comprehension.

Nevertheless, there is a biography here, and perhaps one that is inseparable from the notion of autobiography. How are the contingencies, the accidents, the tangents of a life—the images of which are recorded intermittently, accidentally, and often fall victim to loss, destruction, or sheer neglect—somehow sutured together into a harmonious, cohesive discourse? In *The Great Invisible*, they do not resolve into a unified whole, but the fragments are there, insistent in their opacity, demanding that we ponder them. They are the markers of a loss, but one that we are doomed to incessantly attempt to retrieve, to make good. Thornton's response to the challenge of narrativity is a certain predilection for the anecdote, as a kind of microcosm of narrative. The anecdote is often viewed as the illegitimate rival of history—as, indeed, antihistorical. For it is situated as deficient in terms of its status as compelling evidence ("anecdotal evidence" is maligned). The anecdote is a little story, one that cannot be sustained and hence expires prematurely, before it can achieve the fullness and clarity of knowledge usually associated with both narrative and history. On the other hand, its brevity and condensation are also signifiers of a rich or dense meaning, one that is evocative rather than definitive. The anecdote is saturated with a signification that exceeds its size. In *The Great Invisible*, Isabelle Eberhardt's biography is composed of a series of anecdotes about herself, her family, but also about railroad spine, the cinema, the phonograph, Thomas Edison, Sarah Bernhardt, photography, camels, and about the very process of recording or constituting history. Her biography perceptibly merges with the autobiography of Thornton, as the film's author. Thornton's tendency to incarnate figures in her films, to inhabit their mise-en-scènes (this is a characteristic of *Adynata* as well as *The Great Invisible*), is less an attempt to experience the lives of characters than to inscribe herself within the ecology of images and sounds, to verify her complicity with the possessiveness of narrative, to demonstrate the inseparability of biography and autobiography. Playing Isabelle's mother, Thornton acts the neurasthenia that has become the reductive marker of her existence in the official histories. Suffering from a speech disorder called quietism, the mother dies quickly in the film, the illness preceding her death signified by a single image of Thornton gagging while attempting to speak. Speech and language in general have consistently occupied a problematic position in Thornton's work (the challenge of "the unspeakable"), from the use of the voice in *Jennifer, Where Are You?* to the scientific images of the vocal cords in *Peggy and Fred*, to the very choice of the title of *Adynata*. In an interview, Thornton has traced her relation to language to a childhood in which, "Language [was] something outside. Speech was like an object, an enemy, a barrier. It was externalized. Language was overwhelming, inadequate to describe or convey many things." In *The Great Invisible*, the early vicissitudes of the technological attempt to inscribe speech—Edison's staticky voice reciting "Mary Had a Little Lamb," Sarah Bernhardt's relation to the phonograph—are inextricable from Isabelle Eberhardt's history, which is in a sense the trace of a modernity gone awry, become unspeakable.

Toward the end of *The Great Invisible*, found footage documents an absurd ritual: a line of cars drive over the desert terrain and toward the camera, their tires leaving deep gouges in the sand, the final car, quite ridiculously, pulling a skier. Images of an orderly line of young girls, parading over the desert, their long shadows preceding them and marking out a pattern over the sand, follow. The colonization of Northern Africa is both visual (in documentary as well as in pornography) and material, culminating in the absurdity of Western Europe's attempt to appropriate the desert as its own private playground. The industrial revolution facilitates travel—by railroad or steamship, later the airplane—but also what might be understood as the travel, the reproduction, the dissemination of the image. The pathology of railroad spine is more than matched by the perverse documentation of otherness, the possessive ethnography of the documentary form. This is a theme also taken up in *Old Worldy* (1996) and *Another Worldy* (1999). The first of these films, with a single cut matching sound to image, aligns a reel of film made up of

1940s line dances and a belly dance to techno-pop music. The seren-dipitous nature of this production (Thornton and her friends simply put on some music while watching a reel of film she had purchased from a junk dealer and were struck by the effects of the chance synchronization) does not detract from the forcefulness of its dismantling of the ritualized forms of movement we know as dance. According to Thornton, she was interested in the collision of two pop-cultural moments, from the 1940s and the 1990s. Other sources of archival footage were added in *Another Worldy* and the editing is more extensive and strategically critical.

Another Worldy is a surreal ethnography of dance, which locates rhythmic movement as always already foreign, as ritualized excess. It is a compilation film made up of footage from musicals of the 1940s, eth-nographic documentaries about the role of dance in "primitive" cultures, and various markers of the filmic including titles, leader with a syn-chronizing countdown, copyright notices, and scratches and marks on black leader. The estrangement effect of the film is largely a function of the subtraction of most of the original sound tracks and the resyn-chronization (through editing) of the dance movements to techno-pop music (selections from *The Tyranny off the Beat* produced by Cleopatra and OFF BEAT, 1995). The movements of the dancers appear to uncan-nily and anachronistically match the rhythms of the techno-pop music and the constant juxtaposition of Hollywood musicals with ethnographic footage of native dances works to denaturalize and exoticize all gesture. A description of the montage in one section of *Another Worldy* gives a sense of the extent to which movement begins to function as a citation from elsewhere: a sequence of a Hollywood version of a Middle East-ern belly dance, an ethnographic documentary scene of bare-breasted women pounding the ground with large sticks, a series of markings on film leader, a backward title for a film titled *Daddy*, another Holly-wood scene of a waitress and a busboy dancing, an 1894 Edison Kineto-scope film of Eugene Sandow, a famous Austrian bodybuilder, three men dressed in seventeenth-century costume dancing rather stiffly, a title—"Strange rhythms of trained bodies"—preceding ethnographic documen-tary footage of two very young dancers in traditional costume in what was then called Ceylon, a shot of a bare-breasted woman from an ethno-graphic film, a title reading "Mystic Movements," a return to the two Ceylonese dancers, interspersed with another title—"Erotic music." All of these are set to the techno-pop selection "Why Me?" by the band Dorsetshire.

Most of the Western musicals already invest in the lure of the foreign and exotic (the Middle Eastern belly dance, a Polynesian show, women in white Cossack-like uniforms in *"Russian Revels* with the Lucky Girls"). It is as if some supplemental significance were required to rationalize a fascination with movement. Through its disconcerting juxtapositions, the film effects a leveling or flattening of strangeness so that what are presented as norms of Western movement become invested with the pathological. Movement, which in the Hollywood cinema normalizes the representation of time through anchoring it to the body, becomes disengaged, a sight to behold.

The use of found footage is, of course, not unique to Thornton's work. A long line of avant-garde filmmakers have redeployed film footage, including Bruce Conner, Ken Jacobs, Martin Arnold, Douglas Gordon, Abigail Child, and Malcolm LeGrice. Yet there is something different about Thornton's practices, particularly when found footage is juxtaposed to her own in films like *Peggy and Fred in Hell*, *Adynata*, and *The Great Invisible*. Found footage signals the fragility of the image, its historicity, the very fact that it is subject to decay, ruin, and the vicissitudes of time. Found footage, juxtaposed to "made" footage, anticipates the historicity of the latter, the inevitability that it will stand as a marker or trace of a specific historical moment and of a particular stage in the transformation of media. As Paolo Cherchi Usai has pointed out, there would be no history of the image if it were not subject to decay.[18] Thornton has become something of a collector of marvelous images, both her own and those she discovers in the debris of film history, subjecting them to a working and reworking which seems to be without limit, and which reveals the aspirations of intermediality. In her film work, it is tempting to see the return of Benjamin's aura, but in a form that embraces rather than resists technical reproducibility. Technically reproduced images and sounds have an aura, not only that of their apparently easily readable indexical link to a singular historical moment (which confirms us in the fantasy that we own it, if only briefly), but that of their simultaneous strangeness, their inaccessibility, and their illegibility. Thornton spends a good deal of time searching through junk and antique shops, attics, and archives for images and sounds. The footage for *Peggy and Fred* constitutes her own private archive of images that can be used and reused, recycled in a potentially never-ending series of permutations that resist a final ordering. In a short essay on collecting, Benjamin claims that "there is in the life of a collector a dialectical tension between the poles of disorder and order."[19] It is hard to imagine a greater potential for disorder than that of the vast array of images and sounds made available for circulation and transmission by mechanical and electronic reproduction, each bearing with it the marks of its own historicity. Benjamin also specifies in the collector "a relationship to objects which does not emphasize their functional, utilitarian value—that is, their usefulness—but studies and loves them as the scene, the stage, of their fate."[20] Benjamin is discussing the book collector here but the description seems even more appropriate to the collector of images. One gets the sense that Thornton studies and loves these images and sounds as the scene, the stage, of their fate. This is why Isabelle Eberhardt's story is intertwined with that of the phonograph, the photograph, and the cinema. Like Thornton's own work, the concept of an archive is both that of a set with material limits and boundaries and that of an infinite project, continually redefined. But while archival desire is usually about the singularity and uniqueness of an object (Benjamin's priceless and historical editions of books), what Thornton collects are objects that are defined by their very reproducibility, their ability to be deployed and redeployed far from their original context, while retaining traces of their historical trajectory. The image is defined by its travels. This, for Thornton, is the charm and the passion of archival desire.

Filmography

Face, 1974 (10 min.): si., col.; Super 8mm
X-TRACTS, 1975 (9 min.): sd., b&w; 16mm
All Right You Guys, 1976 (16 min.): sd., b&w; 16mm
Howard, 1977 (30 min.): sd., b&w; 16mm
Fiddlers in May (documentary produced for Connecticut Public
   Television/CPTV), 1977 (28 min.): sd., col.; 16mm
Minutiae, 1979 (55 min.): sd., col.; 16mm
Noexitkiddo, 1981 (30 min.): sd., col.; 16mm
Jennifer, Where Are You?, 1981 (10 min.): sd., col.; 16mm
Adynata, 1983 (30 min.): sd., col.; 16mm
Oh, China, Oh, 1983 (3 min.): sd., b&w; 16mm
*Peggy and Fred in Hell: The Prologue***, 1985 (21 min.): sd., b&w; 16mm
1,001 Eyes, 1987, multimedia installation
She Had He So He Do He to Her, 1987 (5 min.): sd., col.; 16mm
*Peggy and Fred in Kansas***, 1987 (11 min.): sd., b&w; video
There Was an Unseen Cloud Moving, 1988 (60 min.): sd., col.; video
*Peggy and Fred and Pete***, 1988 (23 min.): sd., sepia; video
*[Dung Smoke Enters the Palace]***, 1989 (16 min.): sd., b&w; 16mm and video

Introduction to the So-Called Duck Factory**, 1993 (7 min.): sd., b&w; video

Strange Space (coproduced with Ron Vawter), 1993 (4 min.): sd., col.; video

The Last Time I Saw Ron, 1994 (12 min.): sd., col.; video

Whirling**, 1996 (2 min.): sd., b&w; 16mm

The Problem So Far**, 1996 (7 min.): sd., b&w; 16mm and video

Old Worldy, 1996 (30 min.): sd., b&w; video

. . . or lost***, 1997 (7 min.): sd., col.; 16mm

The Haunted Swing***, 1998 (16 min.): sd., col.; video

Another Worldy, 1999 (24 min.): sd., col., b&w; 16mm

Chimp for Normal Short**, 1999 (7 min.): sd., sepia; 16mm

Quickly, yet Too Slowly, 2000, multimedia installation, A *Peggy and Fred in Hell* environment in *Presumés Innocent*, Musée d'Art Contemporain de Bordeaux, France

Have a Nice Day Alone**, 2001 (7 min.): sd., b&w; video and 16mm versions

The Splendor**, 2001 (2 min.): sd., b&w; video

Document of an Installation, 2002 (6 min.): sd., col., b&w; video

Bedtime**, 2000–2002 (11 min.): sd., b&w; video

Paradise Crushed**, 2002 (12 min.): sd., b&w; video

Peggy and Fred on Television, 2002* (105 min.): sd., b&w, sepia, col.; video, single channel variant

The Great Invisible, 2002* (90 min.): sd., col.; 16mm

The 10,000 Hills of Language, 2002*, multimedia installation, A *Peggy and Fred in Hell* environment

Let Me Count the Ways, Minus 10, 9, 8, 7 . . . , 2004 (20 min.): sd., col.; video

Minus 9: Actinic Blue, 2005, multimedia surround-sound installation based on an episode from the series *Let Me Count the Ways*

Key: * work currently in progress; ** a section of *Peggy and Fred in Hell*; *** an episode of *The Great Invisible*.

Notes

1   Given the top-secret status of the enterprise, Thornton's father and her grandfather were unaware that they both worked on the Manhattan Project until after the war, when a local Boston newspaper published the information. See Zummer, *Leslie Thornton*.

2   Thornton, written communication with the author over several years.

3   For a provocative analysis of *Jennifer, Where Are You?*, see Su Friedrich's essay "*Jennifer, Where Are You?*"

4   It is difficult to avoid a reference here to the work of Luce Irigaray, particularly her two essays, "When Our Lips Speak Together" and "This Sex Which Is Not One" in *This Sex Which Is Not One*, 23–33; 205–18. Irigaray's

project is the extended development of a morpho-logic whereby a psychical sexuality mimics a bodily sexuality and in which the phallus is no longer the supreme arbiter of sexual difference.

5   Zummer, "Leslie Thornton."

6   Peckham, "Total Indiscriminate Recall."

7   See Barthes, *Camera Lucida*, 76–77.

8   Barthes, *Empire of Signs*, xi.

9   Ibid., 3.

10   Rosenbaum, *Film*, 206.

11   See Bazin, "The Ontology of the Photographic Image," 9–10, and Barthes, *Camera Lucida*, 92–94.

12   Quoted in Rosenbaum, *Film*, 206.

13   Borger, "An Interview with Leslie Thornton."

14   It should be kept in mind that I am analyzing a work in progress and there is no guarantee that the order of scenes or shots will remain the same as Thornton continues to work on the project.

15   Bazin, "Death Every Afternoon," 30.

16   Schivelbusch, *The Railway Journey*, 64.

17   The notion of indexicality is derived from Charles Sanders Peirce and his primary tripartite division of all signs into the categories of icon, index, and symbol. The relation of an icon to its object is that of resemblance or similarity (a painting, for example); the relation of the index to its object is an existential or physical one (a footprint, a weathervane); and the relation of symbol to object represented is arbitrary (e.g., language). A photograph or film (excluding animation) has both an iconic and an indexical relation with its object. Its indexical aspect transforms it into a kind of historical trace. For more, see Peirce, *Peirce on Signs*.

18   Cherchi Usai, *The Death of Cinema*, 41.

19   Benjamin, "Unpacking My Library," 60.

20   Ibid.

MAUREEN TURIM

Sounds, Intervals, and Startling Images in the Films of Abigail Child

□

Abigail Child (b. 1948) has been making films for over twenty years. She is also a poet—the kind of poet who gives one the impression that she listens for fragments. In truth she listens, and samples, but the fragments are just as often her own. She has an exquisite ear for rhythms and meanings. Just as her ears are sensitive, her eyes are sharp and subtle. She uses repetition and variation as honed tools of a precise montage, a montage that is attuned to intervallic structures and associative irony. She is a postmodern constructivist, with new angles on the ways in which words and images come together to make meaning. She is a semiotic poet of the fragment, a gatherer of treasured shards. Her films are like her poetry, a distilled collection of images and sounds.

This essay will provide an overview of Child's development as an artist. Her film work is not directly autobiographical, nor her poetry lyrical or confessional, even to the extent that one finds personal revelation in Yvonne Rainer's *MURDER and murder* (1996). One of the striking aspects of her films, poetry, and critical writing is her bold look at sexuality and female desire. Her journeys with desire call for a theoretically informed close reading/viewing of the films to understand how this creative feminist engages with both the history of film and art making in general.

For Abigail Child is a feminist, as well as being politically engaged in everyday life on the Left. Here again, though, direct expression of her

Abigail Child.
Courtesy of Abigail
Child. Photo: Fred
Rochlin.

heartfelt positions may not necessarily be evident to those who read her poetry or see her films. Devoted to abstract ways of expressing herself and of making meaning, Abigail Child's works and her comments on these works sometimes are misunderstood at public screenings. Some audience members react viscerally to the energetic rhythms of her films as aggression directed against them or dismiss her work as formalist play, even as entirely nihilistic. Such reactions are not uncommon to audiences of avant-gardes; Dziga Vertov once was chastised for his "formalist jack-straws and unmotivated camera mischief"[1] by none other than his close contemporary, Sergei Eisenstein, who later found more to praise in *Three Songs about Lenin* than he had in *Man with a Movie Camera*, the film that engendered Eisenstein's critique. It is not by chance that I evoke in this reference Vertov and Eisenstein, for as we shall see shortly, the work of both filmmakers provides key intertexts for Child's works, particularly as concerns their notion of the interval.

Child also has a unique place within a subgenre of the avant-garde, the found-footage film. While the best-known practitioner of this subgenre remains Bruce Conner, whose montage of cataclysmic, explosive images in *A Movie* (1958) forms another significant intertext with Child's films, much variation exists in approach to found footage. Work ranges from the saccadic frame repetitions and variations of Martin Arnold in *Pièce Touché* (1989) to work that analyzes home movies such as Alan Berliner's *The Family Album* (1988) to Peter Tscherkassky's cinemascope trilogy of the 1990s that turns found footage into a highly abstracted visual montage. Child's weave of diverse found footage sources characteristically combines the rapidity of staccato inscription and great contrast between elements. Sometimes she combines the found footage with footage she shoots and composes, creating a fascinating correspondence between the found and the self-generated.

Sound always plays an enormous role, granted autonomy in the Eisensteinian sense of contrast as well as correspondence. Her sound tracks form their own complex montage of both found and invented sound, as we shall see. Child's 2005 book *This Is Called Moving* includes a long interview with sound poet Charles Bernstein in which Child lays out her theory of montage: "I was interested in how far I could go to have things not match up, but have them still fit together. So it became a corner of a building, corners of linkages. . . . I'm attempting to compose elements that are out-of-step, create a time corner, a bending, instead of an adjacency. I'm trying to break the adjacencies."[2] Her metaphors here are spatial. Indeed, she evokes walking a city block, only to turn the corner to another space and time altogether. Reimagined urban spaces and pliant, folded temporalities characterize several of her films. Child reimagines space through a multifaceted approach to temporality. Her work, as we shall later examine in more depth, thus moves onto the terrain laid out by Gilles Deleuze in *Cinema II Image-Temps*, in which cinematic composition instates what he terms "the fold" and the crystal of images, concepts of imbrications and refraction of a multiply threaded and complexly designed textuality.

First though, let us take a look at the development of Child's films by focusing on the seven-part group of films with the collective title *Is This What You Were Born For?* The twelfth plate of Francisco Goya's lithograph series "The Disaster of War" serves as source of this title. Goya in this series of images directly comments on the political upheavals of his time. Rather than pursue as direct a course in her work, Child instead begs us to let his image of nausea at a battlefield scene of slaughter and purification float over her work.

Child's borrowing of Goya's rhetorical question also allows the phrase to garner additional, quite different, connotations. Her use of the title reworks the "born to be wild, born to ride, born to be free" claims of American mythic consciousness. What were post–World War II generations born for? The implied answers may constitute a lament over the limitations of any clear purpose other than those dictated by systems and institutions that have become increasingly difficult to escape or even meaningfully protest. In another sense, this rhetorical question, when interpreted reflexively as pertaining to the art work itself suggests that one can be born into an exploration of new forms, a discovery of aesthetic possibilities, even as a reanimation of the detritus of abandoned imagery. On a more hopeful note, one can also imagine a generation born to revive feminism, and to make significant strides in expressing and accepting queer sexualities. Her films suggest the possibility that we may still explore and claim urban environments as generative of cultural resistance. Child offers her explanation:

> *Is This What You Were Born For?* is conceived as a way to bracket my ongoing film investigations in the context of the aggressions of the late Twentieth Century. . . . The work is in seven detachable parts, each of which can be viewed by itself for its own qualities. The films don't form a single line, or even an expanding line, but rather map a series of concerns in relation to mind, to how one processes material, how it gets investigated, how it gets cut apart, how something else (inevitably) comes up.[3]

The films were shot and completed in a different order than they figure in the finished series, as the film *Both* was the last to be finished in 1988, but is inserted in the series as the second film, between *Prefaces* (1981) and *Mutiny* (1981–82). *Mercy*, which serves as the final part 7, was made in 1986 between *Perils* (1985–86) and *Mayhem* (1987). These placements into an order discrepant from historical production compel us to imagine the films obtaining special nuances when ideally screened in the order of series placement, but since they are rarely all viewed by audiences as an ordered ensemble, our access to any such nuances becomes a conceptual project. Unlike artworks that can be assembled in a series order in a gallery or in reproduction, a series of films, as Child and, notably, Hollis Frampton (in the *Magellan* cycle) have made, speaks to a larger conceptual project. The film series holds a place in our memory, comparatively.

There is of course every point to thinking of *Prefaces* (1981) as the opening notes of a much longer work. More abstract than many of the subsequent parts of *Is This What You Were Born For?*, the fragments that compose *Prefaces* lay out elements of the montage patterns to follow. Images of flows, water, and molten rock establish the rhythmic flow of images. In the midst of this flow, a contrary impulse, a circle appears dead center in the frame. Negative images and X-rays suggest a world whose dimensions are not those of everyday vision, and a beating heart visible through clamped-back flesh intrudes to pulsate with the suggestion that even the organic is oddly displaced in this collage, appearing as both unusual vision and abstract vibration, before we quickly cut to the next move. For the punctuation tends toward sharp swish pans, sharp movements left then right, to be echoed later by reverse motion and inverted steps backward that follow ethnic dancing footage. Black-and-white images predominate, but a rust color flows through the midst of the images. A sound collage is ornamented by operatic high notes. Single words, short phrases, often voiced as *sprechgesang*, at one point add up to a longer phrase, but mostly extreme fragmentation dominates. Human motion presents itself as the gestures of work, hands typing, a bat swung. Black frames punctuate.

Both, the shortest part of the series, is also the only silent section. Writing about the film in 1989 for the Frameline Film Festival in San Francisco, Cecilia Dougherty remarked, "Child's camera creates . . . a richly textured film that is simultaneously revealing and mysterious as a study of the nude in light and movement." Certainly this formal appreciation reminds us of Child's links to earlier photographic avant-gardes, here particularly Man Ray's photos of Kiki. Whereas in the 1920s and 1930s such formal studies also refracted Montparnasse's bohemian sexuality, Child's return to the nude as light machine in motion comes after much feminist debate about female representation as muse, object of desire, and emblem of the privilege granted male artists to possess their female models. *Both* introduces the way *Mutiny*, *Perils*, *Mayhem*, and *Mercy* will revisit female representation as the province of the female filmmaker. Females as objects within images and subjects within minor narratives of desire will dominate much of *Is This What You Were Born For?* In addition, the silence recalls Child's earliest films, *Peripeteia 1* (1977), *Peripeteia 2* (1979), and *Ornamentals* (1979).

Women dance, perform as athletes, play violin, and pound trampolines throughout *Mutiny* (1982–83). Achieved as a mixture of footage shot largely in downtown Manhattan featuring Polly Bradfield (violinist), Sally Silvers (dancer), Erica Hunt (poet), and Shelley Hirsch (singer) with footage Child culled from her early documentaries (*Game* [1972], *Savage Streets* [1974], and *Between Times* [1976]) and some found footage, the film highlights gesture and repetitive motion. Again singing and guttural sounds contrast to verbal voicing throughout, as wild female articulations engage with and depart from the images, in a play of sync and non-sync sound. Rust and red continue to appear sporadically, now against blue tones. In fact, a pool splashes with red in an expressionist wash of color. A black woman appears in a nearly black frame. The street dominates as scenes of dancing, performing, and everyday motion constitute, by suggestion of the title, an artistic mutiny. The phoneme "ay" echoes, perhaps suggesting the personal pronoun beginning to enunciate a phrase never finished, or perhaps the eye. When the sound is followed by the plural, "eyes," we guess that we have perhaps been hearing *I, eye, eyes*, as a sort of declension of the possibilities (Child's transcript bears this out). "This is called moving" emerges on the sound track at the very end, providing a closure of sorts and offering the poetic phrase that Child will give to her later volume of her writings about film, *This Is Called Moving.*

Child writes of the genesis of the film:

> *Mutiny* incorporates documentary and performance film in a complex staccato structure. The film was originally planned as a montage of out-takes (those images not used) from a documentary I had directed seven years previously for a Public Broadcasting national television series, *Women Alive!*, on teenage girls in Minneapolis before their senior year in high school. Ultimately, the high school material felt limiting, and the need to get out of suburban alienation, albeit multicultural and class reve-latory, proved imperative. I scavenged my early documentaries, including *Game* (1972) about a prostitute and a pimp in downtown Manhattan, and *Savage Streets* (1974), a portrait of South Bronx street gangs, to add to the mosaic that was becoming *Mutiny*. I filmed downtown colleagues: Sally Silvers dancing in a Manhattan office, Polly Bradfield playing violin in Chinatown, Shelley Hirsch singing in Little Italy at the Sullivan Street Fair. Combining the materials, usually with their synchronous sound attached, I wanted to create a dissonant percussive *musique concrete*.[4]

Child's reference to concrete music interests me here, as the filmic sound track historically seems to be an influence in the foundation of concrete music; in addition, film composers such as Toru Takemitsu infuse their sound tracks with a musical use of sound learned from con-crete music (both as performance and as recordings). For a sound poet like Child to evoke concrete music points to the composition of the sound track out of fragments of noise and speech treated as notes inter-vening against silences. In other words, all sound materials, music, noise, and voice, are scored, articulated in time and in relationship to each other, rather than simply edited or collaged, though of course they are edited and collaged as well. What does this difference of verbs tell us? How do we conceive of "to score" as different from "to edit" or "to collage," given that all three mean to compose? As I have tried to indicate, the difference lies in how we think of sound in time, in sequence, and in overlay, and whether or not we can fully embrace the most radical gestures of avant-garde composition, as it rethinks its work, ignoring easy intelligibility in favor of the innovative, creative reconceptualization of its very project.

The film leaves me with many questions. Does Child mean to suggest a solidarity between the struggles of the Hispanic and black women retained from the documentary sources with the artistic gestures of the other women artists who perform for her film? Are they all part of the same mutiny? Perhaps we need not answer this right away, and perhaps it is too linear a question. A close look at the phrases of the sound track will provide, however, some clues. Early in the film we hear:

The pictures aren't linear, and that
automatically—
bongo
you know?

The direct phrase, "The pictures aren't linear," becomes undone by an additional and derivative phrase introduced by "and that," which remains, however, cut off and absent. Augmented with the insertions that follow— "automatically—/bongo/you know?"—linearity has been pulled apart. But much later the notion of linearity returns, though it follows from a negation as equivocation, to be similarly disrupted by what succeeds it:

no
alright. it doesn't go linearly
a deedle dee
what?
sticky.
whoa

Clearly Child's pictures and her sounds are not simply linear, but for all their paradigmatic resonances, they do have a linear aspect to their trajectory. Yet she seems to imply that the negation of the linear is not nearly as disruptive as the incompossibility—the mutual presence of contradictory possibilities—of being simultaneously both linear and nonlinear, even while one is disorderly, a far more sticky problem, to which she calls a halt.[5]

The rapid cutting of Child's *Covert Action* (1984) continues, in extremis, the path established in *Prefaces*. The images are taken primarily from home movie footage, which one eventually understands to be the chronicles two men made of their amorous encounters with various women at their vacation house. Although consisting of found footage, the composition of the images themselves seems at ease with Child's signature cinematography as seen in *Mutiny* and *Mayhem*, as if by selection one can compose as surely as if one were behind the camera. Mainly the personages are seen cavorting in the backyard, but there are also a number of close-ups, many of them shots of kisses. Child fragments the shots to an extreme—some are only a few frames long—then systematically repeats, varies, interweaves them, matching or contrasting the motion, or the graphic dominants involved. The frenzied pace is augmented by an autonomous and equally rapid sound track montage of musical clips, conversational fragments, random phrases, periodic announcements.

Montage patterns are the driving mechanism of the film. Once an image fragment is introduced, it is submitted to variations such as a flipping of the frame from left to right, which inverts the graphic elements of the image. Thus a close-up of a woman turning left will be followed by the same shot with the direction of the movement inverted, in a manner that recalls the interval montage of Fernand Leger's 1924 *Ballet mécanique*, a film made in collaboration with Man Ray. However, unlike the topically or spatially oriented series in *Ballet mécanique* devoted to object types or actions, the series here are even more pronouncedly determined by kinetic or graphic patterns. In *Covert Action* each shot migrates into new montage contexts, becoming a part of many different heterogeneously ordered series.

Over the course of a screening, one begins to recognize the shots through their repetitions. One begins to know the image of a woman in the cloche hat and distinguish it from the woman in the fedora, or the one in the bandanna, or from the close-up face in soft focus, or the young girl in the Eskimo jacket. The images gradually accrue the weight of referentiality, and we can reconstruct the individual women, the events of each visit. Thus a walk by a stream, acrobatics on a lawn, a game of leapfrog, drinks by the beehive, an embrace on a wicker chair, become events through the sum of their fragmented parts, dispersed throughout the body of the film. Women's faces and their bodies dominate the imagery, creating a swirl of sensuality, of performance for the camera, alternately self-aware or captured in unsuspecting innocence. This ambiguity of the means through which these images were taken (complicity or naive abandon) adds to the violence built by graphic contrasts and fast pace. The sounds accentuate this violence, especially the screams and screeches,

From Abigail Child's
Covert Action, 1984.
Courtesy of Anthology
Film Archives.

and the words comment upon it with such intertitles as, "He had to be eliminated"/"She had to be bitten," "Ending with a rupture of the hypnosis," and "My goal is to disarm my movie."

Found footage of a different sort also circulates throughout the home movie footage; these images are fragments of documentary footage including a hula dance, a waterfall, a tree being uprooted, Chinese junks in a harbor, a masquerade ball, and a bathing suit competition. As such they are reminiscent of the documentary views produced by primitive cinema such as the films of the Lumière brothers. This cinematic reference is even embedded in one of the fragments, an image cabinet displayed as an attraction on a sidewalk by an oriental showman. A tracking shot explores this popular entertainment, allowing us to appreciate it as a paracinematic sculpture. Another of these images, a whirling merry-go-round, forms a visual metaphor for the montage of this film.

What then, to make of this kinetic puzzle, this dazzling onslaught? *Covert Action* is a film composed of frenetic gestures, repeated for our scrutiny. Its deconstruction and repetition reveals the gestural, without really fixing a commentary on what it shows of gestures. Spying is ambiguously inscribed in the title—are we, as spectators, spies, or are we analysts of the covert elements of the social geste? Who are these women, and how do we feel about them as elements of a double spectacle—the one constituted by the home movie and the one reconstituted by the deconstructive montage of the home movies in the context of a speculation on image, motion, and pacing? Abigail Child has left her film whirling beyond itself. She has not fixed the answers to her image dilemma within the framework of the film. The film poses its women as questions.

Perils risks stagy action for the camera against a sound track composed entirely of orchestrated noise. It evinces comparison to silent cinema through many of its gestures. First are the series of highly stylized close-ups of all actors, similar to the introductions of casts in certain silent film traditions. Performance art makes an intriguing cross-reference, for the posing Child's cast adopts in static tableaux shots give us boxing, for example, not as action, but as stopped posing of action. The film complicates what we might call moving, to paraphrase the title of Child's book *This Is Called Moving*, as the still invades the moving picture. Heightened by mugging characteristic of home movies, the action displayed is once again posed differently by a 16mm camera on a tripod appearing in the frame. An architectonic corner of Rivington Street becomes the movie set, allowing us to imagine all the connections of this postmodern movie crew with performers and film crews from the earliest days of cinema, especially those of D. W. Griffith's *Musketeers of Pig Alley* of 1912, a film shot at this location.

Musketeers of Pig Alley, written by Anita Loos and starring Dorothy and Lilian Gish, is evoked by both Child's back-alley setting and her use of women among the male street combatants. It features a young musician and his wife struggling to survive in the mean streets (and most significantly the back alleys) of a gangster-ridden New York, culminating with a gangster shoot out. Yet in Child's rendition, the stripes and patterned clothes that one associates with the textures of French silent films meet both the antics of Keystone comedy and the exaggeration imagined by the melodramatic serial. The title, *Perils*, might seem to evoke the great serial melodramas of the 1910s, especially *Perils of Pauline*. The intertitle "Earlier" that intervenes after other intertitles enumerating sections 1 and 2, yet offers no distinct structural narrative difference, reminds us perhaps of Luis Buñuel's surrealistic temporal delineations through such intertitles in *Un chien andalou* (1928). However, the intertitle "To Be Continued" that ends the film more clearly cites the serial's structure and famous tagline, here referring perhaps to this film's place in the seven-part series. The references to silent film seem less specific than the serials of the 1910s per se, as these spread back to include films from the first decade of film history, even if the fainting of one of the female characters mocks that melodramatic mode. It also underscores the postmodern play with gendered roles that has the women writhing with the men in shots composed to recall Jack Smith's *Flaming Creatures*, the often-banned 1963 avant-garde film notorious for its posing of a male homosexual orgy including drag queens whose state of undress did not foreclose flamboyant traces of their femininity.

In fact, the early 1960s avant-garde characterized by the films of Jack Smith (*Normal Love* [1963]) and the work of Ken Jacobs (*Little Stabs at Happiness* [1960] and *Blonde Cobra* [1963]) seems equally relevant as intertextual reference here. Child seems to be creating an homage to those who filmed in the streets and on the rooftops of lower Manhattan decades before she sent her troupe into their perilously self-conscious actions on the Lower East Side. One of her ironies will be to highlight the similarities of generations of artists filming fictions emanating from similar neighborhoods—even as the real estate transformations of the Village, Soho, Tribeca, and Chelsea shift, leaving only the East Village, once home to the immigrants of silent cinema nickelodeon, exposed to the energy of a not-yet-entirely-arrived artist colony.

The following description of Jack Smith's work helps us see the similarities *Perils* sustains: "Much of his work is about the importance of style and, specifically, *the pose*; he practically rubs our noses in the idea that logic and progress and movement are always secondary to experience and stasis."[6]

Performative DJ-inspired sampling techniques on the sound track earn Christian Marclay a film credit for "turntables," along with Charles Noyes's credit for percussion. As a result, sounds often mimic a slide whistle and other percussive comic effects, creating unique sound envelopes; sometimes sounds seem to collapse into a hole, like breath being sucked in. The animated sound track adds to this most humorous of the sections of Child's *Is This What You Were Born For?*

I have written previously about how Child's *Mayhem* (1987) and her prose poem, "A Motive for Mayhem," may be thought in the conjunction of cutting as montage and collage practice, as well as a coping strategy whose psychoanalytic interpretation includes acting out the release of pain:

> The cuts that her cinema brings to imagery and sound pose sharply drawn questions. The very title, "Mayhem," historically meant mutilation of the body, though a more common "wreaking havoc" or "creating disorder" still retains the meaning of a violent dispersal. *Mayhem* strews the shards of a broken order into a new configuration. Certainly Child's cutting strives to maximize our appreciation of disorderly conduct, giving us the playful gestures in odd retakes on film history cut with found footage. She emphasizes the display of the female body and the edge of danger that seems to emanate from or be assigned to such display.[7]

In this essay, I make the comparison of Child's film imagery to the "portraits, dancers, and coquettes" that Maud Lavin has analyzed in the Weimar photomontages of Hannah Höch.[8] In particular, I address two of Höch's collages, her "Deutches Madchen" (1930), displaying the mismatched features of the German woman, and "Cut with a Kitchen Knife," whose full title is "Schnitt mit dem Kuchenmesser Dada durch die letzte weimarer Birbauchkulturepoche Deutschlandes" ("Cut with a Kitchen Knife Dada through the Last Weimar Beer Belly Cultural Epoch of Germany). Comparing Child's film to Höch's collages allowed me to show how Child's film might be taken as social protest, even if that social reading is not as clearly demarcated as it is in Höch.

An equally compelling comparison might be drawn to Cindy Sherman's series *Untitled Film Stills* (1977–80) of black-and-white photographs of Sherman impersonating various female poses that appear to be

From Abigail Child's
Mayhem, 1987. Courtesy
of Abigail Child.

stills from imaginary but prototypical 1960s films to eventually comprise sixty-nine images. Unlike the later Cibachrome images that reconfigure fairy tales through elaborate costumes, Sherman's earlier disguises were relatively simple, focusing on the codes of mise-en-scène and cinematography of various film styles as they might be emblematized by an individual film still. Similarly, Child poses her actresses in *Mayhem* in an exaggerated version of film noir mise-en-scène; most notably, the shot of a woman on the phone, the phone cord stretched by her spread legs. Once one sees the various characters of *Mayhem* as enacting poses from film noir so that the shots in which they figure appear to be found footage, the link between the montage praxis of Child in found-footage films like *Prefaces*, *Mutiny*, and *Covert Action* and that of *Mayhem* becomes clearer. Child treats her composed fragments as if they were found footage. To complicate matters, found footage is added to this mixture. What remains to clarify is the intervallic structure of the montage.

Mayhem divides into sections of montage intervals. It seems to roughly approximate narrative developments in its intervallic structure, but to convey them through such a paradigmatic choice of elements as to disperse the narrative event into a combination of fragments of its possible depictions. In part this is accomplished through the film's mixture of stylistic references: shots referring to the Hollywood films of the teens are cut with shots evoking the avant-garde of the 1920s on one hand, and 1940s noir traces on the other. Diverse elements of film history are replayed through scenes set in Soho and the Lower East Side of New York, then cut as intervals roughly corresponding to narrative categories. These types of narrative sequences here remain virtually overtonal, rather than forming a dominant,[9] to use terms introduced by Eisenstein: connotation becomes more central, while characteristically narrative denotative meanings become only a step toward connotation, emptied of other purpose or value. Action supplies a ground against which coloristic elements are articulated, such as the graphic matching of glances or a particular element of composition. Categories of action provide the ground for the film's montage: interrogation, escape, chases, stairways, seductions, sexual couplings, bondage, and dancing. Street scenes interlace with interior scenes.

One scene in particular is subject to a number of recurrences and variations, as a woman places a phone between her spread legs to telephone. Each repetition portrays slightly different points in the action each time from slightly different angles. Such treatment emphasizes the image as performance space. It also places the image in a tight relationship to montage, recalling the editing used by Fernand Léger and Man Ray in presenting the woman ascending the stairs in *Ballet mécanique*, which in turn becomes articulated against the conceptual backdrop of cubism and futurism. In this context the event becomes an icon. A woman sprawled on the bed becomes an emblem of film noir, portending danger.

Throughout these visually delineated sequences loosely organized as narrative threads, an active, independent sound montage further cuts into the images. A combination of "improvised" sound and sampling from different musical traditions, the sound track variously underscores and highlights, mocks or interrupts. In the recombined found footage, in the staged footage, and in the cuts we are made aware that the onslaught of imagery, its pace and density, is part of the furious fun. Such effects of montage are never more evident than when Latin rhythms conform to and undercut sexual activities by deliberate excesses.

Verbal articulations, left fragmentary and detached from any source in the action, often correspond to gestures in ironic ways. A voice posing such questions as "Why do you ask?" floats over the interrogation scene, and a softly—even sweetly—asked, "Do you want me to be more violent?" comes in the midst of the seduction and bondage images. A scream of terror marks a rhythmic climax, without the simple logic of causality that one associates with the scream on a sound track. Denaturalized from any incipient cause, the scream that heralds mayhem here is generalized, hovering over the cuts this film makes in narrative consequence.

Stripes and dots that adorn the clothing of various characters form graphic oppositions and matches. Through these graphic flourishes, the film develops a style that borrows from both European avant-garde films of the 1920s and film noir. They are part of an overall compositional style that unifies the fragmentary footage and integrates found footage with newly acted footage, in much the same way as in *Peril*.

Toward the end of *Mayhem*, found footage of a pornographic film retrospectively invites a rereading of earlier images. The footage of a Japanese lesbian encounter seems at first to be crosscut with a cat burglar sequence from another film. Yet once the cat burglar voyeur enters the scene of the Japanese lesbians, we realize that crosscutting we were assuming to be a collage effect was actually a narrative development. The pornography has a joke ending as the burglar intervenes to assume a role of male sex partner to the women. Breaking the contact between the women, the burglar seals heterosexuality securely in place, but *Mayhem* as film has already thoroughly undercut any such resolution. The women chasing, telephoning, stretched out on a bed, or engaged in sex become, like the dots and stripes, compositional elements that connect across the cuts, assuming the film's very energy and connecting their voices to their powerful representations.

Mercy, as part seven, closes the series *Is This What You Were Born For?* with a montage of color with black-and-white found footage, which recapitulates the blending of fragments that we have already come to expect. Yet it charts new territory in the attention to the body and to technologies of U.S. popular culture. Parades, a Ferris wheel, and midway fairground rides in brilliant color whirl rapidly, compared to factory assembly lines, whose orderly perspectives to diagonal vanishing points form their own fascinating motions. Winding threads join pouring liquids, including bright molten reds, to create both a sense of abstract flow and further reference to the manufacture celebrated in the mid-twentieth century (when this vintage footage was first shot) as characterizing the energy of the United States. This film uses more superimpositions than any of the others, overlaying images and evoking memories. Laboratory images become visually linked to images of bees, but also to underwater snorkeling; discrepancies between the images are woven together by the sound montage, as when the crosscutting between bees and ocean are held as a series by the intermittent buzzing. An orange in a young black girl's hands serves as homage to the color cinematography that this film highlights.

Athletes and dancers introduce a preoccupation with the body that soon takes more chilling forms. A shivering man and the body submitted to medical imaging provide the context for perhaps the strangest moment in the film, an inserted clip in sync sound from a propaganda film extolling a family's pride in having a son in combat. No sooner given than repeated, the voice-over commentator intones in Rod Sterling's characteristic voice, leaving us wondering which twilight zone we have entered. A dog in close-up moves back rapidly and at a diagonal, repositioning his body within the frame. Color footage of waterskiing formations seen earlier now link to a shot from a boat traveling slowly through a southern U.S. swamp, high-speed performance ceding to a more contemplative trajectory. This image gives way across a montage to couples exchanging kisses, which in turn builds toward a final black-and-white image of roots growing.

A hopeful ending, perhaps, to the *Is This What You Were Born For?* series, these roots suggest energies stretching out toward survival. The word *mercy* may suggest divine or legal forgiveness, but neither of those notions is evoked by Child's film. In fact, the propaganda film extolling sacrificial offerings of children to unstated causes positions us as subject to no mercy, bound in a system of obligation and loss. Haunted by melancholia, Child's films abound with images of tortured existence or stress, with mercy coming through one's own making, one's own creative release, one's own navigating of tensions to cull generative tensions, rather than any simpler peace.

Child's work of the 1990s continues her sound track innovations, most prominently in the film that names her play with sound/image relationships, *Surface Noise* (2000), but also in *8 million* (1992), *Dark, Dark* (2001), *Cake and Steak* (2004), and *The Future Is Behind You* (2004). In addition, she returns to the documentary impulses that began her foray into film in *Below the New* (1999) and *B/Side* (1996). I will discuss this renewed documentary tendency, then sum up Child's project by examining her latest montage work.

Below the New (1999) takes on the Russian city of St. Petersburg in transition to market capitalism, and in some ways is parallel to Chantal Ackerman's earlier *D'Est* (*From the East*, 1993), although Ackerman films not only in Russia, but throughout Eastern Europe. Ackerman's more meditative film consists of seventy scenes in ambient sound, and has since been used to generate her installation piece *Bordering on Fiction*, which displays segments of the film simultaneously on different monitors. Its politics are left implicit, for there are few direct political references in either sound or image.

Child's film has an entirely different montage strategy for both image and sound. Her title evokes *Staroe i novoe* (*The Old and the New*, 1929), Eisenstein's celebration of collective farming, and its introduction of technology, which he portrays sensuously by the joyous addition of a cream separator. The new technological advances associated with Lenin's Soviet Union have in Child's film become the haunting images of the past, as in the memorable image of the beautiful, deep escalators of St. Petersburg's subway. It is also the cacophony of a punk band playing, in montage with footage of the Russians floating in a space capsule and on a space walk.

Heterogeneity rules the imagery here more than might be apparent at first, signaled at the beginning through found footage of a young boy blowing a bubble from a long straw to illustrate "surface tension." The entrance of this educational film footage into the interlaced montage prepares us not only for the children seen amusing themselves climbing on statuary both in the film's present and in found footage of the past, but also the metaphorical formation of and bursting of bubbles in the pipe-dreams of politics.

Two voices, one female, one male describe the present state of Russia with its "disappeared middle class" and broken dreams. They belong to Olessia Tourkina, a curator at the Russian Museum and coeditor of *Art/ Science Kabinet*, and to Sergei Bugayev, a conceptual artist also known as "Afrika," who are elegant, astute, and poetic observers of present-day St. Petersburg. "You are living in an imaginary space," Tourkina comments, adding that phobias cut one off from the real. Found footage from the revolutionary years and from World War II intercuts with contemporary scenes. Brutal war imagery from the three-year Nazi siege of the city that was then Leningrad echoes with contemporary street scenes. "What does it mean to be unequal? What does it mean postponed life?" are the questions voiced by Tourkina that haunt a trip to palace grounds outside the city; the first question refers to the emergence of new wealth in a Russia of present poverty, the second refers to the way utopian societies such as those envisioned by revolutionary communism postpone life in favor of imagined futures.

The crossed borderlines of world history are what Bugayev voices over images of a group dinner notably marked by a television broadcast visible just beyond the table. Child's film, in evoking Soviet film of the Leninist period through found footage, continues an implied comparison between her montage and that of her hallowed predecessors, Eisenstein and Vertov. Unlike their utopian dreams, her film documents loss and unease in a present weighted by the past and suspicious of any futurity; in doing so it perhaps asks us to remember the more ironic moments in Vertov that already prefigure this unease.

B/Side (1996) can be seen as the U.S. parallel to *Beneath the New*. This film looks at a tent city of the homeless who occupied a corner of New York's Lower East Side. In "Being a Witness: Notes for *B/Side*," Child explains the genesis of the film: "In June of 1991, the police descended into Tompkins Square Park in Lower Manhattan to oust 150 homeless squatters from the park. The park, a creation of the renowned landscape architect Frederic Olmsted, who designed Central Park, had housed hippies and Ukrainians for years in an uneasy truce aggravated by the increasing poverty and lack of city services across the 1970s and early 1980s."[10]

As Child documents an aspect of her neighborhood, she as an apartment dweller and artist knows that she is observer and commentator on the struggles of the homeless in her midst. Her solution to the dilemmas her status poses is found in her observation that the onlooker's place becomes inscribed in the architechtonics of New York's neighborhoods: "On a number of levels New York is the most *local* town in which I have lived. The scale is that of the human body, the streets are human sized. It is a city designed for the foot walker, the jaywalker, the cross walker and the onlooker."[11]

Taking her cue from the people around her, Child looks particularly at a black woman's daily life in the tent city, capturing survival strategies that mark this extraordinary squatting with the rituals of daily life, washing, cooking, relationships, sex. Seemingly inspired by Jean Rouch's cinema verité, but shot and edited in Child's characteristically rhythmic style, the film never apologizes for its onlooker observation, instead seeing its deep look at this scene as its own form of respect.

The title *Surface Noise* forms Child's audiophilic salute to phonograph records and, in fact, all sound recording, named for the term denoting the noise created by the friction of the stylus as it moves over the grooves of a record. *Surface noise* implies wear, age, decay, and environments, as it may be increased by dirt, damage to the record, or static electricity. Now the term is used to describe extraneous noise that contaminates any sound signal. The term has specific resonance with film sound tracks, both in their magnetic and optical-printed states; nuisance sounds may result from dirt, dust, scratches, and emulsified particles present on the sound track, though increasingly technologies have provided filters to rid us of these noises.

Child's title points to the reversal of filtering aesthetics. We are asked to listen to the strange rhythms and the patterns and the random outbursts of what are usually considered undesirable and detrimental sounds. Child uses what she calls "additional music" by Zeena Parkins (synthesizer), Christian Marclay (turntables), Shelley Hirsch (vocals), and Jim Black (drums).

"Willful heterogeneity," a poetic line in the film, could serve as its motto, as it alternates black and white, vivid color, and earth tones punctuated by black frames, bringing together a wide variety of textures and representations. Often there is an all-over glistening of elements in a frame, as when sparks shoot out, or a jellyfish glows against a dark ground. Although associative editing is characteristic of much of Child's film work, here the associations are more abstract than in Child's other found footage montages. There are clusters of suggestive meanings associated with the images, but they are strewn paradigmatically across the film's unfolding. The film opens on a sharp red diagonal, tempting us to read it as an ode to constructivist composition; Child has spoken about its connection to Vertov's *Enthusiasm* (1930), itself an ode to sound recording, and a continuance of Vertov's constructivist image composition.

An image of a black woman wearing headphones echoes that film's preoccupation with the newness of sound technology later echoed in an image of a television control booth. Another cluster of images connects to sight and the technologies of sight: girls in white dresses play blind-man's bluff; veins in an eye, as would be seen in a medical eye exam, and the eye of a storm as seen in tracking radar. Yet other images describe energy flows, as we see water flowing, a salmon run, a waterfall, the casting of lines in fly fishing. Heroic marches include both religious ceremonials as parades and a communist political demonstration. Those rituals are compared to children's games: the girls' game of blindman's bluff mentioned earlier reverberates with a high-angle shot of boys staging a mock bullfight. A number of images in the film, such as dyeing vats and drying colored cloth, depict labor, particularly labor marked in its global, ethnographic dimension. Parades, games, work: the resonances of Vertov's way of capturing the daily life of his world here find their postmodern iteration as elements traced through the archive of found images. This secondarization of experience—images one degree removed from the world—seems placed in tension in Child's films with images gathered directly as in *B/Side*, and with another reading of found footage that looks at it as verité, as its own moment of temporal and spatial actuality. *Surface Noise* is part 1 of a new series, *How the World Works*, and its epistological argument concerning a secondary aspect of postmodern imagery is taken up again in the second part of this series, *Dark Dark* (2001).

Comprised of outtakes from several B movies of entirely different genres—a film noir–influenced mystery titled *Crystal Ball*, a western, and a romance—*Dark Dark* pays attention to the melding together of gestures in its collage of images selected from these films. Fragments of narratives, hints of conflicts seep through the images: a card game, a box delivered, a fortune read in a crystal ball. The crystal ball becomes a dominant mysterious icon, enclosing flashbacks or perhaps flash-forwards to other scenes, while identities seem open to transformation. In a risky move, the film inverts certain images horizontally, which are especially poetic as characters walk through a space now defamiliarized by its upside-down vanishing points. Because of this risk taken by the film, like a bet in a card game that could end in gunshots, the film attains the poetics of a death drive that haunts the viewer across genres. The sound track, appropriated music of Ennio Morricone, attains a fresh listening divorced from the narratives it was composed to embody. The haunting, repeating tones and extended crescendos work well with the uncanny, floating, detached, mysterious elements swirling in *Dark Dark*. As did *Perils* and, in an entirely different sense, *Surface Noise*, *Dark Dark* metacritically addresses cinema, displacing a hermeneutics of cause and effect, initiation, conflict, resolution, and closure. As its film installation version, *The Milky Way* (2003), underscores, *Dark Dark* takes its poetics from the tone poem, concentrating on how elements form a mood, an atmosphere, containing its own mysteries, delights, and surprises.

A different sort of play with a musical baseline on which to compose images is offered by *8 million* (1996). Ikue Mori's music seems to call this video work into being. The collaboration between musician and video artist seems to venture into the terrain of music video as its most avant-garde alternative. In an essay titled "Art/Music/Video.com," I explore how commercial music videos have tapped the historical avant-gardes for inspiration; this work exemplifies another cross-fertilization between popular culture and the avant-garde, as it addresses the question, What kind of creative image montage will work in consort with avant-garde music?[12]

In *8 million*, an early, slow montage of Ikue Mori's group performing gives way to Child's montage clips linked to each separate song. The video ensemble of these clips gains its name from the population of the five boroughs of New York City as recorded in the 2000 census, as well as from one of Mori's compositions, "8 Million Ways to Die."

"Fishtank," the first "number," fuses mirrors on a nighttime merry-go-round ride in high-contrast black and white to a close-up on a white moth against a black ground. The imagery moves toward color with a seahorse in an aquarium intercut with now colored images of the merry-go-round, ending with firecrackers on the streets of New York's Chinatown. "Shiver" connects a light-box abstraction effect to images of young women on display in what appears to be footage from soft-core pornography. Yet the images shift to a forest in snow. The contrasting imagery provides entirely different associations for Mori's grinding percussive musical work.

"Kiss of Fire" sets a rock riff over images of an urban park where women meet and dally. The women kiss, as *fire* corresponds to painterly effects of image manipulation, a play with after imaging, and flowers. "8 million ways to die" uses silvered black and white to explore street construction. An accordion plays as slight washes of color in superimposition accompany images of streets, the homeless, and the Brooklyn Bridge in the background. "Faint Clue" places Mori's experimentation with chimes and voice in a montage of close-ups of polka dots and Venetian blinds, reminiscent of motifs in Child's *Mutiny* and *Mayhem*. *8 million* ends by returning to Mori's performance ensemble finishing their set at the Kitchen Performance Space.

"Kiss of Fire" joins *Cake and Steak* as recent works Child devotes to females. What do the glamorous and amorous lesbians of "Kiss of Fire" have to do with the adolescent girls cheerleading themselves into adulthood in the suburbs of the late 1950s? The buoyant color of home movies that exude self-satisfaction is echoed by the exuberant colors that adorn

From Abigail Child's *Dark, Dark,* 2001. Courtesy of Abigail Child.

From Abigail Child's *8 Million,* 1992. Courtesy of Abigail Child.

Child's women kissing in their urban glen, a color pattern set off by their bright red lipstick. The sensuality of female adornment on one hand, and of female athleticism even in its strangest cultural manifestation, the baton twirler, on the other, seem to highlight the eroticism of the everyday. Yet *Cake and Steak* wavers between camp reinvigoration and satirical judgment. Its montage of rituals, which include Ferris wheel rides and lines of children preparing for communion in angelic costumes, performs a strange ethnography.

Cake and Steak was also shown as two installations: *Where the Girls Are,* with its focus on adolescence, and *Blond Fur,* which frames the social dance of striving for glamour and luxury that marked a middle-class, middle-aged arrival to a self-fashioned suburbia in the late 1950s. Again it is the sound track that frames these images, giving them an advertising "barker" tape loop repetition, coupled with musical rhythms that highlight their dance. "Kiss of Fire" and *Cake and Steak* taken together suggest a fascination with women, some celebration, but, as in *B/Side*, a kind of ethnographic gaze that is self-consciously aware of ironies of reception of any such images. Does Child mean to wrench these women from the context of male voyeurism and cultural control to explore the place they occupy in the culture?

If there is a certain thoughtful ambivalence to making and redeploying these images of women, this tension can be traced back through Child's earlier work, back through all the women's images that circulate in the series of film forming *Is This What You Were Born For?* Ambivalent, because these images inspire great attachment, even while we can never know exactly what they will mean to an audience the next time the film is shown, or the next time they arrive in the collage or film installation loop. Here is where the manifold daring of earlier avant-gardes reverberates in Child's films. Man Ray, Dimitri Kirsanov, and Dziga Vertov grabbed their indelible images of women, indeed all their characters, with the fascination of artists who delighted in their cameras (and their editing tables) as tools of description, transformation, and possession. Child operates knowing this history, knowing its power, and its gendered significance. She plays with reengaging it as a woman looking back from a postmodern vantage point in which filmmaking, to be anything like avant-garde, seems to quake as it ruptures any too-straight a discourse. Formal montage tensions, then, become isomorphic with tensions at the level of signification.

This high-tension high-wire act, charged and fraught, is further exemplified by *The Future Is Behind You* (2004), which creates an entirely fictional narration to accompany a montage of home movie footage from a family in a 1930s Bavaria. In the narration, two sisters puzzle their way through family ideology, learning to see a fascist heritage for what it is. The video begins with the younger sister dancing the Charleston in a Bavarian folk costume with her older sister, who wears a white dress. After posing in constant cavorting motion, the two sisters walk forward to take bows for their performance. Elfrieda and Elenore Grunig (fictional names) appears as text over this image of the two sisters, as they bow and kiss one another's hand, as if acknowledging this introduction. A family hiking trip illustrates a first-person narration marked by its retrospection; Elfrieda tells us her mother initiated these walks, she would later realize, as an outgrowth of her youthful affiliation in the German Wandervogel hiking movement. Intimated in this phrasing is the child's later realization of the pre-Nazi anti-Semitic aspects of parts of the Wandervogel movement, the film's first framing of these found images as a coming of age in the time of fascism. A grandmother shown gathering flowers is introduced in a third-person title as a convert from Judaism. Moments later, Elfrieda's voice returns in a title that says, "We never thought of ourselves as Jewish."

The film continues its family chronicle inserting titles for the years 1933, 1935, and 1939 over images of the girls. Images of them participating in a physical culture dance group; a party at which lots of kissing occurs; a highly erotic, partially nude summertime bath in the spray of a garden hose; and a wintertime ski trip are used as a background. However, the images do not necessarily inherently indicate the precise temporal progression they are assigned by the titles that carry the narration, a dual narration of the girls' sexual coming of age (the first kiss from another girl, one being jealous of another, Elenore's betrothal), and the parallel narration of the imposition of fascist laws, an uncle's deportation to Dachau, and the grandmother's suicide. Emigration to the United States for Elfrieda and to Israel for Elenore allows for the retrospective voices to be grounded in survival.

Yet a series of interwoven questions in an entirely different voice than either the first- or third-person narrations gives us a clue to the fictional, and therefore philosophical aspect of this film's narrative ploy: "Why does the camera invite good-byes?" "Are memories only reliable when they serve as explanation?" "What is omitted?" "Another picture that is not shown." These enunciations, poetic and metacritical, point to a strategy beyond documentary, a strategy that is sealed by an end title that lists as texts credited the works of W. G. Sebald, Victor Kemporer, Walter Abish, Abigail Child, and the U.S. Patriot Act. Of course, we realize retrospectively that the archival images do tell a story of Bavaria slipping into fascism, even if the Jewish secret of this family remains fictional. Part of the story they tell all by themselves is that the everyday life of young girls had its own energy and sexuality that cannot be entirely enclosed within a prelude to fascism that in other ways the images do contextually predict. The Jewish fiction then gives the sweetness of these young girls a historical out, retrospectively framing their sensual beings by their difference and their escape from the oppression that would have been aimed at them. Finally the film's collage of fictions is a technique for defamiliarizing and therefore thinking about the ironies of history, especially as personal histories intersect with larger social histories.

This film tips its hand toward Child's claim on the postmodern, born through its homage to previous avant-gardes, but aiming at a heterogeneity and textuality that finds its place in our moment. Theoretically, this means that Child may seem to have evaded critical categories through which feminist filmmaking was channeled beginning in the 1970s, as she followed a poetics that eschewed the discursive functions easier for feminists to champion. Time seems to have caught up with Child's game, and she seems to have made a large body of work now that finds sufficient intertextual resonance that the postmodern direction of her work echoes for all its strange beauty.

Filmography

Except the People, 1970 (20 min.): sd., col.; 16mm

Game, 1972 (40 min.): sd., b&w; 16mm

Mother Movie, 1973 (5 min.): sd., col.; 16mm

Tar Garden, 1975 (50 min.): sd., col.; 16mm

Some Exterior Presence, 1977 (10 min.): si., col.; 16mm

Peripeteia I, 1977 (10 min.): si., col.; 16mm

Daylight Test Section, 1978 (4 min.): si., col.; 16mm

Peripeteia II, 1978 (11 min.): si., col.; 16mm

Pacific Far East Line, 1979 (15 min.): si., col., b&w; 16mm

Ornamentals, 1979 (10 min.): si., col., b&w; 16mm

Prefaces, 1981 (10 min.): sd., col., b&w; 16mm. Part 1 of *Is This What You Were Born For?*

Mutiny, 1983 (11 min.): sd., col., b&w; 16mm. Part 2 of *Is This What You Were Born For?*

Covert Action, 1984 (10 min.): sd., b&w; 16mm. Part 5 of *Is This What You Were Born For?*

Perils, 1986 (5 min.): sd., b&w; 16mm. Part 4 of *Is This What You Were Born For?*

Mayhem, 1987 (20 min.): sd., b&w; 16mm. Part 6 of *Is This What You Were Born For?*

Both, 1988 (3 1/2 min.): si., b&w; 16mm. Part 3 of *Is This What You Were Born For?*

Mercy, 1989 (10 min.): sd., col.; 16mm. Part 7 of *Is This What You Were Born For?*

Swamp (with Sarah Schulman), 1990 (25 min.): sd., col.; High 8, video

8 million (music by Ikue Mori), 1992 (24 min.): sd., col., b&w; Super 8 and High 8 original, video

Through the Looking Lass (with Lenora Champagne), 1993 (12 min.): sd., col.; video

B/Side, 1996 (40 min.): sd., col., b&w; 16mm

Her Thirteenth Year (with Melissa Ragona), 1998: script

Below the New, 1999 (25 min.): sd., col., b&w; High 8 and 16mm original, video

Surface Noise, 2000 (18 min.): sd., col., b&w; 16mm. Part 1 of *How the World Works*

Dark Dark, 2001 (16 1/2 min.): sd., b&w; 16mm. Part 2 of *How the World Works*

Subtalk (with Eric Rosenzvieg and Benton Bainbridge), 2002 (4 min.): sd., col.; digital video

The Milky Way, 2003: projected film installation of *Dark, Dark*

Cake and Steak, 2004 (20 min.): sd., col.; single channel and multiple screen projections of *Where the Girls Are* and *Blond Fur*, 16mm transferred to video

The Future Is Behind You, 2004 (20 min.): sd., col.; 16mm transferred to video

The Party, 2004 (21 min.): sd., col.; video

By Desire, 2004 (in progress)

To and No Fro, 2005 (4 1/2 min.): sd., col.; 16mm

Mirror World, 2006 (13 min.): sd., col.; 16mm

Notes

1 I am indebted to Vladimir Padunov for his help in tracing the original Russian phrasing in "Za kadrom" (1929), roughly, "behind the image." The passage occurs on page 295 of volume 2 of the six-volume edition of *Izbrannye Proizvedeniia Sergeia Eizenshteina* (1964). The exact Russian wording is "prosto formal'nye biriul'ki i nemotivirovannoe ozornichan'e kameroi (*Chelovek S Kinoapparatom*)."

2 Child, *This Is Called Moving*, 183.

3 Child quoted in the *Canyon Cinema Catalogue* at www.canyoncinema .com/C/Child.html.

4 Child, *This Is Called Moving*, 200.

5 "Incompossibility" is the translation of a neologism coined by Liebniz that indicates the coexistence of logically impossible propositions. It has been revitalized by both Jean-François Lyotard and Gilles Deleuze. Beyond paradox, incompossibility becomes an aspect of postmodern structures of thought. See Gurwitsch, *Compossibility and Incompossibility in Leibniz*; Deleuze, *Difference and Repetition*; Lyotard, *The Libidinal Economy*.

6   Morris, "Raging and Flaming."

7   Turim, "A Look at the Violence of Female Desire in Avant-Garde Films."
Some of the discussion of *Mayhem* here reworks points I made in that essay.

8   Lavin, *Cut with a Kitchen Knife.*

9   Eisenstein, "Methods of Montage," 72–83.

10 Child, *This Is Called Moving*, 245.

11 Ibid., 241.

12 Turim, "Art/Music/Video.com."

WILLIAM C. WEES

Peggy's Playhouse

Contesting the Modernist Paradigm

◻

I like it when a work involves the viewer in some kind of dilemma about how to read its meaning. I don't do it as a punishment, but it's a very exciting, ethical, and philosophical place for me. My work is not supposed to be comfort food.—Peggy Ahwesh

Born in 1954, Peggy Ahwesh grew up in Canonsburg, Pennsylvania. She started making conceptual art, photographs, and Super 8 films while attending Antioch College. After she received a BFA in 1978, she moved to Pittsburgh. There she continued working in the arts and met a number of filmmakers, musicians, and photographers. "The punk scene was us and various hangers-on," she says. "We would document the bands, and the bands would play at the clubs where we showed our movies—we were our own on-going entertainment."[1] She programmed screenings for an art center called the Mattress Factory and, subsequently, for Pittsburgh Filmmakers. In 1982 she was a production assistant for George Romero's *Creepshow* and soon after moved to New York, where she still lives and actively participates in the avant-garde film scene. During the 1980s, she began to work in video as well as Super 8, and her first 16mm film, *The Deadman* (made with Keith Sanborn), appeared in 1990. In 1991 she joined the faculty of Bard College, where she is now an associate professor of film and electronic arts.

In a 1991 essay, Manohla Dargis offered Ahwesh's films as "exemplary of a battle against what French feminist theorist Luce Irigaray calls 'phallic imperialism.' "[2] She might have added that Ahwesh conducts her "battle" through indirection and subversion, rather than direct confrontation. Taking a hint from the title of Ahwesh's film *Martina's Playhouse*, I suggest that a playhouse might be a more appropriate metaphor than a battlefield for the site of Ahwesh's assaults on "phallic imperialism." Certainly, her films and videos are notable for their improvisation and experimentation, their juggling of genres, and their lack of formal markers announcing, "Serious Artist at Work."

In fact, Ahwesh has referred to her Super 8 films as "little playgrounds" and admitted that her work has "an under-achiever, self-deprecating quality," although she is quick to add that, "maybe that's deceptive in some sense."[3] Dargis refers to a "deceptively thrown-together feel" in *Martina's Playhouse* and the Super 8 films that preceded it,[4] and Lia Gangitano has noted that Ahwesh's techniques "could be viewed as indulgent, undisciplined, pointless," though, in fact, they serve "an aggressive feminist aim that demands a form that does not comply with existing authoritative narrative structures."[5] Ahwesh offers an instructive example of an avant-garde filmmaker whose serious intentions are disguised (at least in part) by a playfulness that is also a genuine form of critique, as well as a constructive alternative to "phallic imperialism" and "authoritative narrative structures."

Her films and videos also reflect a major change in the interests and intentions of North American avant-garde filmmakers who, like Ahwesh, came to prominence in the 1980s. Particularly notable is a reorientation of the oppositional stance traditionally associated with the avant-garde. Post-1980 avant-garde filmmakers not only stand in opposition to mainstream, commercial cinema, as have most avant-grade filmmakers since the 1920s, but most also oppose, to varying degrees, the aesthetics of modernism that dominated avant-garde film discourse until the 1980s, especially in North America. That discourse is based on (1) the concept of the autonomy of art, (2) the drive to discover and exploit the unique properties of each medium of artistic expression, (3) the moral and aesthetic superiority of "high" art over popular culture, and (4) the imperative to create innovative works that express the maker's unique sensibility, but, at the same time, are endowed with "universal" and "timeless" (that is, apolitical and ahistorical) significance.

The new avant-garde discourse encouraged an open and creative engagement with all levels of cultural production, and presumed that art should not—indeed, *could not*—be isolated from its historical and political contexts. By the 1980s those contexts included feminism, lesbian and gay activism, multiculturalism, poststructuralism, postmodernism, and the pervasive influence of the mass media. As P. Adams Sitney has noted, "Younger artists were energized by the issues the older generation sidestepped,"[6] and Tom Gunning announced that "avant-garde filmmaking has suddenly gained a new influx of energy" leading to the production of films notable for "their freshness, their distance from the dominant [avant-garde] films of the last two decades." This new cinema, Gunning insisted, "calls into question the terms in which the future of the avant-garde has been theorized in recent decades."[7] Those terms, as I have already suggested, derive from a modernist paradigm unsuited to the aims and accomplishments of many younger avant-garde filmmakers.

Indicative of the new frame of mind among younger avant-garde filmmakers was an open letter protesting the predominance of older avant-garde filmmakers in the programming of the International Experimental Film Congress held in Toronto in spring 1989. Widely circulated and discussed in avant-garde film circles at the time, the open letter proposed that due to changing historical conditions, the "old masters" of avant-garde filmmaking had lost their relevance. "The time is long overdue to unwrite the Institutional Canon of Masterworks of the Avant-Garde," its authors announced and concluded by declaring, "The Avant-Garde is dead; long live the avant-garde."[8] More recently, Ahwesh (who not only signed but also helped to write the open letter) remarked that in light of "the dying out of a certain kind of high modernism that reached its peak in the late Sixties . . . , the issue is not innovation, not how innovative you can be, but how you can contextualize," and that realization, Ahwesh says, marked "a seismic shift, a really big break" in how avant-garde filmmakers regarded their mission as visual artists.[9]

Contextualizing her own interests as an artist, Ahwesh says, "Intellectually, I was formed by the '70s. I come out of feminism and the anti-art sensibility of punk."[10] As far as a specifically cinematic context for her work is concerned: "For me it is in terms of genre: melodrama, home movies, faux documentaries, ethnographic films, horror movies," to which I would add pornographic films and video games.[11] Working within those parameters, Ahwesh makes her own distinctive contribution to the dismantling of "the Institutional Canon of Masterworks of the Avant-Garde."

As evidence I offer three quite different works: a Super 8 film, *Martina's Playhouse* (1989), a 16mm film, *The Color of Love* (1994), and a video, *She Puppet* (2001), all of which are worth examining for their intrinsic interest, their demonstration of Ahwesh's command of different media, and their contextualizing of avant-garde work within contemporary issues of gender and sexuality, art and popular culture. Moreover, to illustrate some of the consequences of "the really big break" in avant-garde film aesthetics, I will contrast *Martina's Playhouse* with Gunvor Nelson's *My Name Is Oona* (1969), *The Color of Love* with Carolee Schneemann's *Fuses* (1967), and *She Puppet* with Maya Deren and Alexander Hammid's *Meshes of the Afternoon* (1943). In this way I hope to highlight Ahwesh's contribution to recent avant-garde film discourse while, at the same time, setting up a kind of intergenerational discourse involving Ahwesh and three of her predecessors in the history of avant-garde filmmaking by women.

Martina's Playhouse

In my Super 8 movies I don't stage things. I have no idea what I'm going to do, but I *like* not knowing.—Peggy Ahwesh

Although a number of film artists have worked in Super 8, the format still signifies "home movies" and consequently, as Catherine Russell notes, "constitutes a challenge to the aesthetics of mastery implicit in more high-tech film forms."[12] For Ahwesh, rejecting an "aesthetics of mastery" is in keeping with her rebellion against "authoritative narrative structures" and (given the masculinist connotations of "mastery") "phallic imperialism." It is also a pragmatic decision, arising from what she has called "the ethos of Super 8 production and the low budget movie aesthetic based on daily life. . . . None of the planning pertains to what actually happens. Nobody does what's expected. Everybody's a star. Nobody gets paid. Everybody performs themselves in some exaggerated form."[13] As in home movies, the performances usually take place in ordinary, everyday living spaces, and as Russell observes, this "contributes to the aura of authenticity and, ironically, to the overall sense of playacting."[14]

The dialectic of "authenticity" and "playacting" can undermine viewers' confidence in their ability to understand exactly what is going on and why. A prime example in *Martina's Playhouse* is a sequence in which Martina's mother (performance artist Diane Toll) pretends to be a baby asking for milk. The four-year-old Martina undoes the shoulder straps of her dress and "breastfeeds" her mother. Of this reversal of roles, Russell remarks, "The effect of substitution and displacement is that much

Martine Torr in
Peggy Ahwesh's
Martina's Playhouse,
1989. Courtesy of
Peggy Ahwesh.

stronger because of the home-movie framework of their performances."[15] The effect is not only stronger but also potentially more unsettling for the viewer, which is a difficulty that Ahwesh recognizes:

> When you make something that seems sort of unauthorized, or is not authoritarian, it's hard to figure out who's responsible and how, as a viewer, you should take it. In most movies, the plan of the producers is *there*, the directorial position of the filmmaker is *there*. Whereas with experimental film that's the thing people *can't* figure out. But all the material I've shot with Martina . . . I could never have suggested in a million years. . . . And that "nursing" footage sat on my shelf for two years, because I had *no* idea what to make of it or how to incorporate it.[16]

Such are the consequences of making films with what you *get*, rather than what you *want*.

It is hardly surprising to find Ahwesh declaring, "I *never* get footage in the can that edits easily. I always have an ornate, complicated pastiche relationship to my editing. I'm always reinventing the work as the process goes along."[17] On another occasion, she explained, "You make the movie in the editing. . . . I want the linkage to be tight, but I always want the people [in the film] to be able to present themselves. . . . I don't want to cut it up too much. It becomes a little game of making all those pieces connect in an interesting way."[18] To edit the footage so that her subjects are "able to present themselves" indicates Ahwesh's interest in, and respect for, the people she films, many of whom are friends; it is also evidence of a kind of anthropological impulse to keep the record of their performances "authentic" and unaltered by intrusive editing. As a result her films commonly include many long takes that, nevertheless, "connect in an interesting way."

As Manohla Dargis's reference to the "deceptively thrown-together feel" of *Martina's Playhouse* suggests, the underlying logic of those connections is not always apparent, even to astute and experienced viewers of avant-garde films. One such viewer is Scott MacDonald, who admitted to Ahwesh, "I couldn't figure out what I was supposed to be doing with this film, what sort of pleasure I was supposed to take from it."[19] He speculated that at least part of the reason was that the film seemed "so open." To which Ahwesh responded, "Is it possible that the problem is that it's so *much* a female point of view—which includes that openness? There are people who don't like the film because there's no explicit authority telling them how to think about the images or structuring the material in a way that reduces it to a formality. I *refuse* to do both those things. I just refuse."[20]

Ahwesh's response is instructive in at least two ways. It helps to contextualize the film by insisting on its "female point of view" (though one might challenge her seemingly "essentialist" equation of "a female point of view" with "openness"), and it reaffirms her refusal to adopt what she regards as authoritarian methods of structuring films and signaling how they should be read. "I'm not playing by the rules of experimental film-making you expect," she says to MacDonald. "The work is not regulated by the formal devices of modernism—but what better way to address sexuality, girlhood, desire, and mothering than in a provocative home movie?"[21]

To pursue the implications of that rhetorical question, let us begin with a brief examination of a film that addresses some of the same issues and has some of the same qualities of a home movie, but is "regulated by the formal devices of modernism": Gunvor Nelson's *My Name Is Oona*. Those devices include fluid, handheld camera movement, slow motion, negative images, superimposition, extensive use of close-ups, and intricate patterns of light and dark (emphasized by black-and-white film stock), especially in shots with bright sunlight and deep shadows, or with strong backlighting from the sun that outlines dark forms with a magical glow and, in some cases, transforms them into rhythmically flowing abstract shapes. Enhancing these powerful visual effects is a chantlike sound track composed of loops of Nelson's daughter saying "My name is Oona" or simply "Oona." Midway through the film, the sound mix also includes Oona's attempt to recite the days of the week, and near the end of the film, as the endlessly repeated "Oona Oona Oona" reaches a climax of overlapping waves of pulsating sound and then gradually fades out, a lovely, gentle ballad sung by Nelson in Swedish (her mother tongue) gradually fades in.

Both the images and the sounds come from ordinary, everyday events in the life of a young girl who is looking at her mother looking at *her* through a camera; running around; playfully wrestling with a boy (both of them naked to the waist); leading a horse into a stable, grooming it and then riding it while wearing a long silken cape; pronouncing her name; learning the days of the week; hearing her mother singing. But these home movie elements are refined and molded into a tightly structured and thematically rich evocation of childhood. It is the cinematic equivalent of a well-crafted modernist poem.

Accordingly, in a review of the film when it first appeared, Amos Vogel called *My Name Is Oona* "one of the most perfect recent examples of poetic cinema."[22] In the same vein, though many years later, Scott MacDonald captioned a still of Oona riding her horse, "Oona Nelson as mythic child."[23] Such comments are indicative of the degree to which the material, social, and psychological specificity of those sources has been subsumed by a rarefied, ahistorical, mythic significance of the kind prized in modernist discourse. Even Oona's act of enunciating her name, which Vogel regards as "a magic incantation of self-realization,"[24] becomes progressively detached from its real-life referent until it functions primarily as another of the "formal devices of modernism" that give the film its shape and meaning.

In *Martina's Playhouse*, on the other hand, the precocious and very verbal Martina always speaks for herself, thanks to the filmmaker's consistent use of unmanipulated, synchronized sound. We first see Martina standing on the roof of an apartment building, eating a sandwich and staring silently at the camera. After some intervening shots (to which I will return), she suddenly announces, "I am M-a-r-t-i-n-a," and asks, "What does that spell?" Offscreen, Ahwesh responds, "Martina." Instead of beginning with an informative "my name is," Martina assertively challenges *us* to name *her* by saying what "M-a-r-t-i-n-a" spells (which Ahwesh does on our behalf). If Martina's unconventional introduction of herself highlights her individuality, it also alludes to the social context of names and naming—not to mention of language itself—and suggests that subjectivity, too, is a series of ongoing negotiations between individuals and their cultural contexts. The consequences, as Ahwesh's film demonstrates, may take surprising and even contradictory forms.

The "nursing" scene is one of these surprising turns. Others include a naked Martina holding up a diaper and asking her mother to put it on her so she can "be a baby." When her mother does not do it, Martina, with some difficulty, puts it on herself. When her mother pretends to be a baby, she lies on her back, fully clothed, kicking her feet, waving her arms and babbling in a high-pitched voice while Martina tries to put a diaper on her. A different sort of reversal occurs early in the film when Martina puts a dress on a large stuffed frog. Her mother says, "I thought Froggie was a boy." Martina replies, "No, he was a girl. He was a girl. I thought he was a boy, but he was a girl." And to her mother's response, "You changed him into a girl?" Martina answers simply, "Yeah."

Gender issues reemerge when Martina holds up a page from a magazine showing a smiling bride and groom, and says, "Once upon a time, there was a marry girl. They was marrying each other, and they were being married. The end." When she notices that the camera is still running, Martina shouts, "The end, the end, the end, it's the end!" Martina's version of marriage alludes directly to the woman (her use of "girl" revealing, perhaps, her identification with the bride), but not to the man, except vaguely and indirectly in the non-gender-specific pronouns *they* and *each*. While Martina intends her insistent and repeated "the end" to mean her brief narration is over, the fact that Ahwesh keeps the camera running suggests a subtle critique of one of our culture's most familiar "authoritative narrative structures": the equation of marriage with narrative closure. In Martina's rendition, that closure sounds purely formulaic, which could be taken as an unintentional comment on its problematic application to real life, just as Ahwesh, in keeping her camera running, seems to be saying, "No, it is *not* 'the end.'"

There are many such moments in the film, due in part to Martina's uninhibited presentation of herself and Ahwesh's openness to whatever takes place in front of her camera. But they are also due to the combination of the Martina footage with other, quite different material, including an intimate session with the filmmaker Jennifer Montgomery and extensive close-ups of flowers. In addition, running through much of the film is a kind of "visual noise" created by flares and moments of black; fluctuations in exposure and color saturation; colored inks, scratches, hair, specks of dirt, and visible bits of splicing tape on the film; all of which augment the film's low-tech look and "deceptively thrown-together feel."

The coherence of *Martina's Playhouse* depends on associations, parallels, comparisons, contrasts, resonances, and allusions among the diverse materials Ahwesh assembled for her film. For example, separating the first and second appearances of Martina are two brief close-ups of flowers followed by a much longer shot of hands manipulating a snapdragon blossom to make its "mouth" move as a male voice on the sound track reads from Georges Bataille's essay "The Language of Flowers" in his *Visions of Excess: Selected Writings, 1927–1939.* The gist of the passage is that there is a disjunction between the function and the symbolic significance of parts of flowers: "If one expresses love with the aid of a flower, it is the corolla, rather than the useful organs that becomes the sign of desire." (An earlier passage in Bataille's essay—not included in the voice-over—identifies the snapdragon as "the emblem of desire.")

A close-up of a flower also accompanies an extract from Jacques Lacan's *The Four Fundamental Concepts of Psychoanalysis.* It begins in midsentence and is read haltingly and with some mistakes by an uncomprehending Martina, and again, later in the film, by Ahwesh herself. Only viewers thoroughly versed in Lacan are likely to grasp that, as Ahwesh has explained, "The text is about the law of the father regarding sexuality,"[25] but certain key words—"desire," "lack," "the first Other" (which Lacan modifies by adding, "let us say, by way of illustration, the mother")—resonate with the mother-daughter relationship in the film and with many direct and indirect evocations of desire: from Bataille's reference to the corolla as "the sign of desire," to the photo of bride and groom and Martina's narration of the legal sanctioning of their desire in marriage. Jennifer Montgomery acts out desire by playing with a slender, phallic microphone as if it were a sex toy. Later, referring to her appearance in front of the camera, she says to Ahwesh, "So this is all, like, this substitute, right? A substitute for me coming here, like, getting down on my knees and begging you to go to bed with me."

If a kind of circulating current of desire is one source of connections in the film, another is alluded to in Montgomery's reference to "a substitute." "The substitution of juxtaposed elements for essential elements," the voice reading Bataille says, "is consistent with all that we spontaneously know about the emotions that motivate us." Being filmed substitutes for

Jennifer
Montgomery in
Peggy Ahwesh's
*Martina's
Playhouse*, 1989.
Courtesy of Peggy
Ahwesh.

sex. A microphone substitutes for a dildo. Froggie substitutes for a girl substituting for a boy. Images of flowers substitute for Bataille and Lacan. In one striking graphic match in the film's montage, Martina's round face filling the frame substitutes for a round yellow flower filling the frame of the previous shot. And in the funniest moments of the film, Martina substitutes her own words for Lacan's, as Ahwesh tries to correct her:

> Martina: . . . it is this
> Ahwesh: in
> Martina: in this part of the luck
> Ahwesh: no, point
> Martina: point of luck
> Ahwesh: lack
> Martina: lack . . . meaning it is insofar as his desire is unknown that it is in this point of *lack* that the desire of the subject is considered
> Ahwesh: con-
> Martina: con-
> Ahwesh: -sti-
> Martina: -sti-
> Ahwesh: -tuted
> Martina and Ahwesh (together): constituted
> Martina: *con*stituted.

Ahwesh regards Martina's misreading of Lacan as "so freeing and enabling; it has so much agency."[26] At the same time, her efforts to correct Martina's reading produces a little dialogue/drama illustrating the kind of verbal intercourse between adult and child that assures the latter's place in the symbolic realm of language. After Martina's labored effort to master the complex, jargon-laden lines from the English translation of Lacan's lecture on psychoanalysis, the repetition of the same passage, competently and coherently read by Ahwesh, suggests that *this* is what Martina will be able to accomplish when she grows up.

As Martina's mother demonstrates, however, grown-ups can regress to infantile babbling and monosyllabic whining for "milk." And something like a prelinguistic "primal scream" introduces Jennifer Montgomery. In contrast to the silent stare Martina gives the camera the first time we see her, Montgomery, in her first appearance, lunges forward and roars at the camera. Then, responding to a nearly inaudible Ahwesh behind the camera, she says, "No, it didn't feel good at all. I didn't feel comfortable with it," but she does it again anyway, though less aggressively. Cut to Martina in underpants sitting on the floor, saying repeatedly

"I'm not ready!" as she puts a dress on Froggie. This connection via montage establishes Martina and Montgomery as the principal reference points for the various issues raised in the film, one of which is how a little girl and a grown woman present themselves to Ahwesh's camera and relate to Ahwesh herself—which is pretty much the same thing.[27]

Perhaps the strongest unifying element in the film is the invisible presence of the filmmaker, made apparent by Martina's and Montgomery's constant awareness of the camera and the person behind it. And while we do not see her, we hear Ahwesh on the sound track saying what "M-a-r-t-i-n-a" spells; responding to Martina's repeated "I'm not ready!" with, "That's okay"; laughing with Montgomery after the latter's not very subtle invitation to go to bed with her. The hand-held camera signifies the presence of Ahwesh as a participant-observer, and the colored inks, scratches, flares, and so on call attention to Ahwesh as hands-on manipulator of the film image. While these techniques were adopted by a number of artists working in the modernist tradition of avant-garde filmmaking, in this case they seem to come out of what Ahwesh called "the anti-art sensibility of punk" that powerfully influenced her intellectual development generally, and her Super 8 filmmaking in particular.

The Color of Love

I think of it as a menstruation film first and following that, I like to think of it as a lesbian vampire film.—Peggy Ahwesh

Made from a reel of damaged, decomposing Super 8 pornography found by a friend of Ahwesh, *The Color of Love* belongs to a subcategory of avant-garde film usually labeled "found footage films" or "recycled cinema," films composed principally or entirely of footage the filmmaker did not *make*, but bought, borrowed, stole, was given, or simply happened upon and appropriated for her or his own work. Among these sources, pornography is one of the most problematic because, as Liz Kotz writes in her contribution to the anthology *Dirty Looks: Women, Pornography, Power*: "Pornography represents a place where distance breaks down, where subjectivity is insistently engaged, even uncomfortably so. Even its incorporation into a project of critique is notoriously unstable, since even the most determined efforts to reframe pornographic representations as objects of a politically motivated examination can go deeply awry, subverting authorial intention in fascinating if problematic ways."[28]

The Color of Love, however, opens pornographic images to readings that Kotz does not take into account. Moreover, because it shares with Carolee Schneemann's *Fuses* the presentation of explicit representations of sexuality integrated with scratches, colors, and textures applied to the film's surface or embedded in its emulsion, it offers another opportunity to delineate characteristics of Ahwesh's work that distinguish it from the modernist practices of the preceding generation of avant-garde filmmakers.

Daringly candid, for its time, and notable for its emphasis on female sexuality, *Fuses* is an intimate, autobiographical account of sexual relations between Schneemann and her partner at the time, James Tenney. Yet, despite its direct, unembarrassed, and graphic depictions of male and female genitalia, cunnilingus and fellatio, foreplay and intercourse, the film is suffused with a romantic eroticism that celebrates heterosexual lovemaking in the visual language of avant-garde film.

Schneemann makes extensive use of chiaroscuro lighting, shoots with both handheld and fixed cameras, and presents the lovemaking in a montage of separate moments of passion and repose. She also paints and scratches on the film. This direct intervention in the imagery of her film produces several mutually reinforcing effects. It imparts tactility to the image, metaphorically linking the physical strip of film and flesh, seeing and touching, the energetic play of light, color, and texture and the psychosexual dynamics of lovemaking. In keeping with one of modernism's tenets, it asserts the materiality of the medium and the "flatness" of the projected film image. It is also an indexical sign of the filmmaker's presence in the filmmaking process and an expression of the personal, artisanal relationship of the filmmaker to her film. Thus, in form as well as content, *Fuses* epitomizes the avant-garde film discourse of the 1960s by expressing its maker's unique, personal vision through unconventional cinematic techniques. At the same time, as David James notes, it implicitly placed "the site of sexual performance . . . outside the historical and political conditions of women."[29]

In *The Color of Love*, Peggy Ahwesh places "the site of sexual performance" inside those "historical and political conditions"—though in a way some viewers might find more than a little perverse. In the footage Ahwesh appropriates, two women happily engage in various sexual activities with each other, but fail to arouse a man who seems to have passed out, or possibly is dead. He makes no response when one of the women cuts his chest, leg, and genitals, nor when the women, with the man's blood smeared on their bodies, try to mount his flaccid penis. Frequently,

From Peggy
Ahwesh's *The
Color of Love*,
1994. Courtesy
of Peggy
Ahwesh.

dirt, scratches, and decomposing emulsion produce a kind of accidental censorship that replaces sex organs and sex acts with pulsating abstract patterns and vibrant colors. Ahwesh enhanced these effects by reframing, step-printing, and rearranging some of the original footage. The result is as visually stunning as it is sexually transgressive, and it prompted one critic to exclaim, "Through lurid poetics of film composition, the tawdry is transformed into the sublime."[30]

"Sublime" may be an overstatement and "tawdry" an understatement, but the emphasis on transformation is correct. Ahwesh successfully avoids the pitfalls Kotz warned about when attempting "to reframe pornographic representations as objects of a politically motivated examination." One way she transforms or reframes pornographic representations is by subverting conventional wisdom about mainstream pornography. Christian Hansen, Catherine Needham, and Bill Nichols have written: "Mainstream pornography represents a phallocentric order symbolized by male desire and a universal masculinist order, naturalized as a given. The phallus stands in for sexuality and power. . . . The phallus provides an index or standard of power and authority. The penis as phallus—symbol of sexual potency—is the 'true star,' celebrated in countless close-ups."[31] While "lesbian" sex scenes do appear in pornography aimed at heterosexual males, unresponsive penises do not. Hence the subversiveness of Ahwesh's choice of found footage in which the erect phallus has been reduced to a flaccid penis and mere prop in scenes of the women's vigorous lovemaking.

Another kind of reframing of pornography results from the original film's deterioration. By frequently obscuring part or all of the actors and their interactions, it works against the kind of clear and unambiguous representation of sexual organs and sexual acts that producers of pornography strive for and consumers of pornography expect. In Laura Marks's provocative reading of *The Color of Love*, "the film's emulsion flowers and evaporates, giving itself up to bliss and to death."[32] As well, the textures and colors produced by the passage of time and the unstable chemistry of film emulsion complement and expand upon the film's substitution of the vagina and female sexuality for the phallus and male sexuality. As the densely textured, brilliantly colored, fluid, fluctuating patterns of decay flow in and out of the frame, they become tropes for the intricately layered tissues of the vagina, and as they expand and contract, they literally reframe the mise-en-scène and action. Assisted by Ahwesh's step-printing (and tango music by Astor Piazzolla on the sound track), they endow the film with rhythms, shapes, and textures that are the antithesis of the rigid, erect, penetrating and ejaculating phallus of mainstream pornography. It is almost as if, in a metamorphosis more bizarre than anything David Cronenberg has concocted, the actual, physical strip of film is turning into a vagina.

Ahwesh's critique of phallocentric pornography is not all that brings out the differences between *The Color of Love* and *Fuses* and between the avant-garde film discourses they exemplify. Ahwesh's images come from anonymous found footage rather than from the filmmaker's camera aimed at her own and her lover's bodies. The "added" textures and colors in *The Color of Love* are the result of processes in which the filmmaker had no hand (except to emphasize them through optical printing), in contrast to *Fuses*, where they derive from the filmmaker's handmade marks on the film, complementing her performance within the film. Although Schneemann bravely opened a space in North American avant-garde film for explicit (hetero)sexual representations, and the significance of her film for the emerging counterculture of the 1960s cannot be discounted, she does not offer the kind of "critical perspective on cultural production" that Ahwesh achieves by distancing herself from her film's content and formal techniques. That distance allows her to address a range of topics of interest to her generation of avant-garde filmmakers: from pornography and phallocentrism to lesbianism and "the historical and political conditions of women," from revisionist challenges to theories of "visual pleasure" and the "male gaze" to the exploitation of un-fixed, non-gender-specific signifiers of desire in visual representations of sexuality. *The Color of Love* was made for a gaze that encompasses both pleasure and critique in its subversion of "phallic imperialism."

She Puppet

Over the years, I've usually worked with ordinary people, family members, neighbors, "nobodies." But *She Puppet* is a whole different thing: I worked with a superstar!—Peggy Ahwesh

Ahwesh appropriated images from the video game *Tomb Raider* to make her video *She Puppet*. She has said of the original *Tomb Raider*, "It's like, bang-bang, run-run, bang-bang, run-run. I had hours of this material. . . . It took a long time for the piece to flip over to *my* use of the material, as opposed to what the material wanted you to do."[33] By resisting what the material "wanted [her] to do," Ahwesh made something of her own that is *about* that material: about, in the first instance, *Tomb Raider*'s protagonist Lara Croft, described by Ahwesh as "the girl-doll of the late 20th century gaming world . . . a collection of cones and cylinders—not a human at all—most worthy as a repository for our post-feminist fantasies of adventure, sex and violence without consequences."[34] In Ahwesh's view, "[Lara] holds out the promise of transcendent wish-fulfillment. . . . She remains a forever-accommodating and private fantasy ideal facilitated by clever computer programmers."[35] But in *She Puppet*, she says, "I make Lara a vehicle for my thoughts on what I see as the triad of her personas: the alien, the orphan and the clone."[36] *She Puppet* is also about *Tomb Raider*'s low-resolution look, its computerized rendering of space and movement, its narrative structure of "bang-bang, run-run," and the relationship between its form and the gratification it offers video game players: "a repetition compulsion of sorts, offering some kind of cyber-agency and cyberprowess for the player."[37]

To make her video be *about* all these things, Ahwesh deconstructed *Tomb Raider*'s version of video game conventions of unmotivated malevolence, uninhibited acts of derring-do, and unending violence without permanent consequences (for the hero or heroine, who can always be brought back to life). At the same time, her video engages in a kind of defamiliarization of the mise-en-scène, dramatis personae, and action of *Tomb Raider*. The two strategies, deconstruction and defamiliarization, work together to produce a revisionist, postmodernist, and, arguably, postfeminist treatment of subject matter that, from a modernist point of view is, at best, banal, and at worst, another example of the corrupting, alienating influence of popular culture, and from a feminist point of view is an excuse to place a virtual (in more than one sense) caricature of a

Lara Croft, from Peggy Ahwesh's *She Puppet*, 2001. Courtesy of Peggy Ahwesh.

large-breasted, narrow-waisted, shapely-bottomed, long-legged young woman under the control of the video game player (presumably male, although anecdotal evidence suggests that many females have been drawn to the game as well). As Ahwesh puts it, "You put her through her paces, practicing the moves over and over without her ever getting impatient. You stare at her body with impunity—mainly her butt—and you get to kill her off in any number of sadistic and pleasurable ways."[38]

In *She Puppet*, things are different. In the first place, Ahwesh augmented the video game's sound effects with voice-over readings from Fernando Pessoa's *The Book of Disquiet*, Joanna Russ's *The Female Man*, and writings of the jazz guru Sun Ra.[39] All the passages are read by women, and all use the first-person singular, so that the "I" of the texts becomes associated with Lara Croft's thoughts about herself and the world she inhabits. Interspersed with the game's sound effects and some added music and effects, the voice-overs help to convey Ahwesh's sense of Lara Croft as "the alien, the orphan and the clone" (for example: "I'm not a human. I never called anybody mother. . . . I don't know about being born. I just happened" [Sun Ra]) and as a kind of female counterpart of Camus's Meursault in *L'Étranger* or any number of Samuel Beckett's characters, with whom she shares a bleak worldview and a stoic lack of self-pity: "Although I walked among them a stranger, no one even noticed." "Why did they give me a kingdom to rule over, if there is no better kingdom than this hour, in which I exist between what I was not and what I will not be?" "Tomorrow I will return home to set down coldly further thoughts on my lack of conviction. Let the players continue just as they are. When the last domino is played and the game is won or lost, all the pieces are turned over, and the game ends in darkness." (All three quotes are from Pessoa.) The last extract accompanies the video's final shot of a nighttime cityscape, after which the screen goes black. "The game" alludes to both the video game and Ahwesh's video as a game played with the *Tomb Raider* material. "Darkness" refers, literally, to the dark screen at the film's conclusion and, figuratively, to death and the dark vision of life Ahwesh discovered in and imposed on her source material.

Another significant difference between *Tomb Raider* and *She Puppet* is that the interactive element of the video game has been replaced by the fixed and final decisions of the artist. "I made Lara Croft do things that normally you wouldn't do to play the game," Ahwesh has said. Furthermore, *She Puppet* is, in her words, "a conceptual piece in some ways, because it's not my footage. The look was completely created by some programmer guys."[40] The look, yes, but not how we look at it or think about it in its new context. By interrupting and rearranging sequences of action in the original video game, Ahwesh subverts its goal-directed, "authoritative narrative structures" and replaces them with patterns of repetition and theme-and-variation that work against the game's linear, "bang-bang, run-run" organization. The most striking example is a series of images of Lara Croft dying. The same soft gasp accompanies the same way of falling to her knees and then face-forward with her arms flung out. The variations in these repetitions are in the settings, costumes, evil antagonists who kill her, and points of view from which her demise is seen.

Of course, the video game itself is based on a kind of theme-and-variation structure of pursuit, engagement, and (temporary) resolution that, presumably, those playing the game take for granted. But Ahwesh makes this structure strange by extracting and juxtaposing sequences that reveal a fascinating interplay of shifting perspectives, misleading distances, and unpredictable movements through ambiguous spaces. The result is a dreamlike mise-en-scène for equally dreamlike events: guns fired point-blank miss their targets; tigers prowl but do not pounce; vicious dogs and rapacious, vulturelike birds attack, but without visible effect; enigmatic figures appear and disappear; scenes change unexpectedly; some actions remain uncompleted, while others are repeated for no apparent reason. *She Puppet* could be the dream of someone who has spent too much time playing *Tomb Raider*, and having lost the "cyber-agency and cyberprowess" to influence the game's events, must let the dream take its own course.

Or, looked at differently, *She Puppet* could be Lara Croft's dream—just as *Meshes of the Afternoon* could be the dream of that film's protagonist. Like Lara Croft in *She Puppet*, Maya Deren in *Meshes of the Afternoon* finds herself in an environment of shifting, ambiguous spaces. As Maureen Turim points out, "The house space is magical . . . ; its architecture includes an infinite staircase, a second-story window that one can leap into from the outside, a picture window that becomes a telescopic tunnel into the space of dreams."[41] Dreamlike, too, are the many repeated actions of the protagonist, most notably her fruitless pursuit of a black-robed figure with a mirror face. The film as a whole, as P. Adams Sitney observes, "has an intricate spiral structure based on . . . repetition, with variation."[42] In addition to repetition-with-variation and dreamlike spaces and events, *Meshes of the Afternoon* and *She Puppet* have in common a female protagonist who must negotiate strange, threatening environments and hostile confrontations, and whose body is nearly always on display. Although the two works look very different, and the conclusion of each is also different (Maya dead and draped in seaweed in the chair where she had settled in for an afternoon nap; Lara wide-eyed, as always, and posed in her gun-slinger stance), the most significant differences between the two lie in their adherence to different avant-garde film discourses.

Renata Jackson has convincingly argued that Deren's film aesthetics belong "within the tradition of modernist film theory," and, specifically, the modernist dedication to "medium-specificity."[43] For Deren, film is a time-based art whose essence is the manipulation of movements in time and space through the creative use of camera and editing. While *Meshes of the Afternoon* was shot and edited for powerful rhythmic and visual effects, it is also laden with allusive, ambiguous images inviting multi-layered interpretations in the best tradition of modernist poetry. The film's imagery can be read as dreamlike visualizations of invisible energies —aggression, fear, desire—emanating from the unconscious. While at various times Deren tried to distance herself from surrealism and psycho-analytic interpretations of art, as well as from "confessional" and auto-biographical motivations for making her films, it is hard to disagree with P. Adam Sitney's judgment that *Meshes of the Afternoon* "was made possible through a Freudian insight into the processes of the surrealist film,"[44] or Maureen Turim's much more recent description of the film as "at once a home movie (a biography inside the home, inside the artist's mind, inside the unconscious) and a formally realized work of art."[45] Deren herself wrote in an early program note that the film, "is concerned with the interior experiences of an individual, and reproduces the way in which the sub-conscious will develop, interpret and elaborate an apparently simple and casual occurrence into a critical emotional experience."[46]

If Deren finds inspiration in the prelogical workings of the sub- or unconscious—the terrain of psychoanalysis and surrealism—Ahwesh finds her inspiration in the pleasures offered by a shallow, computer-generated video game—the terrain of producers and consumers of popular culture. If *Meshes of the Afternoon* is intended to achieve a kind of timeless relevance to the inner workings of the mind (although now it looks to be very much of its time and place), *She Puppet* clearly derives from, and refers to, the here and now. As far as the politics of gender is concerned, if *Meshes of the Afternoon* is prefeminist (which is not to say it cannot be given a feminist reading), *She Puppet* is defiantly postfeminist. In sum, if Deren is the mother of North American avant-garde film,[47] Ahwesh is one of her particularly rebellious daughters.

Filmography

The Pittsburgh Trilogy, 1982–83 (35 min.): sd., col.; Super 8

From Romance to Ritual, 1985 (20 min.): sd., col.; Super 8

Ode to the New PreHistory, 1984–87 (25 min.): sd., col.; Super 8

I Ride a Pony Named Flame, 1988 (5 min.): sd., col.; video

Martina's Playhouse, 1989 (20 min.): sd., col.; Super 8

The Deadman (with Keith Sanborn), 1990 (40 min.): sd., b&w; 16mm

Philosophy in the Bedroom, parts 1 and 2, 1987–93 (15 min.): sd., col.; Super 8

The Scary Movie, 1993 (9 min.): sd., b&w; 16mm

Strange Weather (with Margie Strosser), 1993 (50 min.): sd., b&w; video

The Color of Love, 1994 (10 min.): sd., col.; 16mm

The Fragments Project, 1985–95 (55–60 min.): sd., col.; Super 8

Trick Film, 1996 (6 min.): sd., b&w; 16mm

Magnetism, Attraction and Repulsion, Deep Sleep, Auto Suggestion, Animal Magnetism, Mesmerism, and Fascination, 1996 (15 min.): sd., col.; video, QuickTime

The Vision Machine, 1997 (20 min.): sd., col.; 16mm, available on video

Nocturne, 1998 (30 min.): sd., b&w; 16mm

73 Suspect Words and Heaven's Gate, 2001 (7 min.): sd., b&w; video

She Puppet, 2001 (15 min.): sd., col.; video

The Star Eaters, 2003 (24 min.): sd., col.; video

Certain Women (with Bobby Abate), 2004 (72 min.): sd., col.; video

Pistolary! Film and Video by Peggy Ahwesh, 2005 (195 min.): sd., col., b&w; DVD

Notes

1 MacDonald, "Peggy Ahwesh" (interview), hereafter cited as MacDonald interview, 3.

2 Dargis, "Beyond Brakhage," 66.

3 MacDonald interview, 12–13.

4 Dargis, "Beyond Brakhage," 66.

5 Gangitano, "Warhol's Grave," 66.

6 Sitney, *Visionary Film*, 409.

7 Gunning, "Toward a Minor Cinema," 2–3. Although Ahwesh's name appears in the title, none of her work is discussed in the article.

8 The full text of the open letter and other documents related to the International Experimental Film Congress can be found in Wees, "'Let's Set the Record Straight.'"

9 William C. Wees, interview with Peggy Ahwesh, October 12, 2002; hereafter cited as Wees interview.

10 MacDonald interview, 10.

11 Wees interview.

12 Russell, "Culture as Fiction," 368.

13 Ahwesh, "Film, Baby," 80.

14 Russell, "Culture as Fiction," 367. "Authenticity" in conjunction with "playacting" also characterizes some of Ahwesh's more recent works, like *Strange Weather* (1993), a fifty-minute video that includes professional actors and began with a script the performers quickly discarded, and the seventy-minute minifeature on video, *Certain Women* (2004), based on short stories by Erskine Caldwell.

15 Ibid.

16 MacDonald interview, 9–10.

17 Ibid., 20.

18 Wees interview.

19 MacDonald interview, 7.

20 Ibid., 12–13.

21 Ibid., 8.

22 Amos Vogel, quoted in *Canyon Cinema Film/Video Catalogue 2000* (San Francisco: Canyon Cinema, 2000), 313.

23 MacDonald, *A Critical Cinema*, 3: 189.

24 Vogel, *Canyon Cinema Film/Video Catalogue 2000*, 313.

25 MacDonald interview, 12.

26 Ibid.

27 A somewhat older Martina Torr appears in Ahwesh's *A Scary Movie* (1993), in which she and another girl act out horror movie scenes. Jennifer Montgomery returns as the uninhibited protagonist of Ahwesh and Sanborn's *The Dead Man*.

28 Liz Kotz, "Complicity," 107.

29 James, *Allegories of Cinema*, 321.

30 Smith, "The Way of All Flesh," 18.

31 Hansen, Needham, and Nichols, "Pornography, Ethnography and the Discourse of Power," 211–12.

32 Marks, *Touch*, 101.

33 Wees interview.

34 Peggy Ahwesh, program note, www.ps1.org/cut/animations/install/ahwesh.html.

35 Ahwesh, "Lara Croft," 77.

36 Ahwesh, program note.

37 Peggy Ahwesh, e-mail to the author, February 1, 2002.

38 Ahwesh, "Lara Croft," 77.

39 The quotes from Sun Ra come from fan sites Ahwesh accessed through the Internet (e-mail to the author, August 31, 2003).

40 Peggy Ahwesh, quoted in Halter, "Festivals."

41 Turim, "The Ethics of Form," 92.

42 Sitney, *Visionary Film*, 7.

43 Jackson, "The Modernist Poetics of Maya Deren," 47.

44 Sitney, *Visionary Film*, 11.

45 Turim, "The Ethics of Form," 84.

46 Deren, "Program Notes on Three Early Films," 1.

47 Starr, "Maya."

JANET CUTLER

Su Friedrich

Breaking the Rules

◻

New York–based filmmaker Su Friedrich (b. 1954) has created a rich body of work that has established her as a major figure in contemporary avant-garde cinema. The maker of formally elegant and emotionally evocative films, Friedrich has produced Super 8 films, videotapes, and a dozen 16mm films, most notably *Cool Hands, Warm Heart* (1979), *Gently Down the Stream* (1981), *The Ties That Bind* (1984), *Damned If You Don't* (1987), *Sink or Swim* (1990), *First Comes Love* (1991), *Rules of the Road* (1993), *Hide and Seek* (1996), and *The Odds of Recovery* (2002). For all but *Hide and Seek*, she served as writer, director, editor, and cinematographer.

Friedrich's personal, provocative films are finely woven tapestries of disparate materials: text scratched onto film stock, intertitles, black-and-white leader, still photographs, home movies, found footage, television broadcasts, and original images; ambient sound, spoken word, popular music, and silence. Seen and heard together, Friedrich's juxtapositions of images, words, and music lend her films great intensity and power. Watching Friedrich's films is like watching a person's mind working: you can sense the filmmaker thinking through the possible ways to proceed, drawing parallels and making connections between otherwise unrelated images and sounds, encouraging the viewer to follow a line of thought to the point at which a new idea or a new understanding emerges.

Part of what makes Friedrich's work compelling is the way that it resists simple explication. Her films characteristically address highly charged, interrelated issues and explore them in all their complexity—past and present, personal and political, daily life and dream. The intelligence of Friedrich's work is linked to a sense of urgency. Her most satisfying films are driven by a need to look closely at disturbing, personal experiences, including vivid dreams, childhood traumas, emerging sexuality, turbulent romances, and medical problems. The films bravely lay bare her most intimate concerns, examine her darkest fears and strongest desires, and prompt viewers to address their own sexual identity, family history, religious upbringing, and mortality.

Friedrich lends her works emotional resonance and intellectual clarity through a variety of strategies. She carefully structures intensely private material, maintaining its raw power while giving it lyricism and poignancy. She blends the past and the present, offering insights into the significance of memory. She displaces painful experiences onto ironic tales, using humor to balance difficult material. She mixes intimate recollections with elements of popular culture and gender politics, placing her own experience in a broader social context. She makes use of the conventions of melodrama, allowing her audiences some of the pleasures of narrative filmmaking and attaining a degree of accessibility unusual for experimental filmmakers.

Friedrich's quirky, self-conscious works defy conventional definition. Experimental in form, they are driven by storytelling. Autobiographical in content, they incorporate social and cultural criticism. Mixed genre in nature, they juxtapose avant-garde, documentary, and narrative modes. Breaking the rules, or rather making them up as she goes along, Friedrich crafts a surprising, unique cinema. At once angry and droll, wounded and analytic, Friedrich embraces and critiques her chosen subjects: the film medium and her own life.

Because Friedrich's films overlap genres, scholars have taken different approaches to her work. For example, Chris Holmlund calls *Rules of the Road* "autobiography" and *First Comes Love* "ethnography."[1] Holmlund's analysis of *Damned If You Don't* asserts that the film is in part a "remake" or a "makeover" of *Black Narcissus* (Michael Powell and Emeric Pressburger, 1947), a kind of revisionist melodrama that "reconstructs a narrative of heterosexual desire giving it a happy ending for lesbians."[2] In a book that examines intersections between the avant-garde and ethnography, Catherine Russell calls *Hide and Seek* "an experimental documentary about adolescent lesbian identity . . . to think of queer filmmaking as ethnographic is to recognize the problem of representation as self-representation, in which the self is socially and sexually configured." Russell sees Friedrich as the maker of "new autobiography" or "auto-ethnography" in that Friedrich "understands . . . her personal history to be implicated in larger social formations and historical processes."[3] Michael Renov classifies *Sink or Swim* as "domestic ethnography," asserting that in assembling a portrait of her father as other, Friedrich is also representing the self. According to Renov, "*Sink or Swim* functions as a kind of ethnography—instructive and generalizable—for the ways it exceeds the bounds of family portraiture. The film is structured by a series of generic elements that reinforce the universality of the subject matter."[4] The fact that Friedrich's work invites a variety of critical perspectives is evidence of both its hybridity and its unique sensibility.

While Friedrich's films are distinctly her own, they also have precedents in subgenres of avant-garde practice: the psychodrama (*Damned If You Don't*), the trance film (*Gently Down the Stream*), the structural film (*Sink or Swim*), and the diary film (*Rules of the Road*).[5] Yet Friedrich both inherits and rebels against the idioms of avant-garde cinema. Film scholars and critics like Bruce Jenkins credit Friedrich with reworking the traditions of the avant-garde, turning existing film practices to her own purposes. Jenkins notes that "*Gently Down the Stream* demonstrates Friedrich's considerable technical talents and formal creativity as well as her canny historical sense in reappropriating the formal strategies . . . generally associated with the 'structural film.' " While Jenkins cites Friedrich's singular talents as a filmmaker, he also points out that "Friedrich's work is unimaginable without the artistic precedents of such films as [Hollis] Frampton's *Surface Tension* (1968), [Tony] Conrad's *The Flicker* (1966) or [Paul] Sharits's *STREAM:S:S:ECTION:S:ECTION:S:S:ECTIONED* (1968–71). *Gently Down the Stream* resurrects these historic texts, absorbing their lessons and moving on."[6] Liz Kotz writes, "Working to reopen and expand the traditions of American avant-garde filmmaking, Friedrich's work has brought a deeply lyrical style to questions of lesbian identity and lesbian desire. . . . she refuses to fetishize 'the personal' as the locus of meaning in the heavily codified manner of much American 'personal' filmmaking of the 1960s and 1970s."[7] Scott MacDonald explains that, "By the 1980s, Friedrich was becoming convinced that the rejection of personal filmmaking, structural filmmaking, or other approaches did not 'liberate' cinema in any practical sense; it simply narrowed the options. The issue was not to avoid the personal or the systemic, but to reappropriate and reenergize as many useful dimensions of the previous film-critical practices as possible."[8] At a time when subjectivity and interiority were no longer sovereign, and when the cultural politics of feminism and gay activism gave rise to a new wave of socially engaged filmmaking, Friedrich's work constituted an important intervention. It redefined personal filmmaking in formal and thematic terms.

Film historians have also noted that, in appropriating and reinventing elements of experimental practice, Friedrich helped to reinvigorate American avant-garde cinema at a moment when the movement seemed played out.[9] While acknowledging that her work may have served that function, Friedrich clearly regards her filmmaking as instinctive and reactive. She cites others—Peggy Ahwesh and Leslie Thornton—who in the 1980s also embraced and reacted against dominant avant-garde practices, and in so doing conceived a new generation of avant-garde film: "So I think in some crazy way in my early films I was reacting against both psychodramas and structural films, and trying to do something different. But mostly I was just pissed off and thought, 'Some of these films are really boring, and some of them have potential but they're really badly crafted, and *where are all the women?*' "[10]

Friedrich's films challenge the modes of what was at the time a predominantly male enterprise, both in mainstream and independent filmmaking, and add a feminist perspective. As Laura Rabinowitz points out, the world of avant-garde filmmaking, partly because of its marginal status, initially provided women with access to media but eventually reaffirmed their marginalization.[11] Friedrich is among a new generation of women experimental filmmakers who took advantage of screenings at the Millennium Film Workshop and the Collective for Living Cinema, honed their skills with equipment available through the cooperative workshops, and emerged as artists eager to make films that provide a passionate critique of patriarchy.

Women's Bodies, Bodies of Water: *Hot Water* (1978)

I took a three-night filmmaking class at the Millennium that was taught by David Lee. On the first day of the class, he made us write a list of the ten things that for us were the most important or powerful in our lives. And then he made us read the list out loud (I now make my students do this at the beginning of every class—which they hate).[12] It was such a revelation for me. My list probably included "riding my bike" and "eating ice cream," but the last thing on the list was "fear." And when I wrote that I thought, "O.K., that's the thing for me— fear."—Su Friedrich

When Friedrich turned from photography to filmmaking, her first effort was striking and revealing. In a Super 8 sound film called *Hot Water* (1978), Friedrich clearly and unselfconsciously introduces concerns she addressed in later films. Initially inspired by her childhood fear of and fascination with water (a topic most richly explored in *Sink or Swim*), *Hot Water* rhythmically patterns images of water in its several forms: a gymnasium swimming pool (a young woman enters the water and swims away); a bubbling potful of boiling water (a woman drops a brick of frozen vegetables into the pot and recoils when, as she pushes the floating brick under water, her fingertips are burned); and snow blanketing a car's windshield and hood (someone brushes it away in three separate shots using three distinct, sweeping arm movements). Another image simply evokes water: a woman exercises on the gymnasium's rowing machine, energetically pumping oars as if she were speeding across the surface of a lake. The film begins with a dedication to bodies of water: the Swanee River, the River Styx, and the Red Sea.

As in Friedrich's later works, the female body is a central motif in *Hot Water*, and the film's main setting, the gymnasium, is an ideal place in which to take pleasure in observing the female protagonist in motion and repose. The film's footage includes the woman's nude back in the changing room and in the massage sequences, her crouched body in the rowing equipment sequences, her sleek body in the swimming sequences, and her feet crossing the deck and entering the pool or being fitted into the loops of the rowing machine. Friedrich's lingering shots caress the woman's body: camera movements glide down the protagonist's nude back during the massage, down her backstroke-swimming body from face to feet as the splashing water churns around her like the boiling water on the stove, down her torso on the rowing equipment from her shoulders to the space between her legs. The filmmaker celebrates the strength and fluid motions of the woman's body rowing and swimming, seeking out its sensuous qualities.

Hot Water is emblematic of Friedrich's work in that its title constitutes a puzzle for the viewer to solve, with numerous possible meanings to entertain. Most immediately, the phrase "hot water" suggests "getting into hot water," or getting into trouble. But what sort of trouble? Is the filmmaker courting danger? In over her head? Considering a sexual encounter bound to end badly? Characteristically, Friedrich's titles are drawn from simple childhood songs and games (*Gently Down the Stream, Hide and Seek, First Comes Love*) and colloquial expressions (*Sink or Swim, Odds of Recovery, Rules of the Road*) that take on multiple associations in her hands. In addition, *Hot Water* employs a back-and-forth rhythm that elicits an open-ended consideration of pain and pleasure, fear and desire. The film marks the beginning of Friedrich's attempts to express in poetic rather than literal terms topics she returns to in *Gently Down the Stream* and *Damned If You Don't*, including the multifaceted tensions between eroticism and repression, pleasure and guilt. In fact, *Hot Water* signals an ambivalence that exists in all her films—a conflict between denying and facing up to fears, repressing and expressing sexuality.

Friedrich's overriding themes are present in her earliest film, but her mastery of technique grew over time. With limited experience and means, Friedrich made films that necessarily resembled a reinvention of the cinema. She began with simply edited, silent black-and-white exercises before moving on to complex sound-and-color works (except for *Hot Water*, with a sound track improvised on toy recorders and drums, Friedrich's first half-dozen films are silent). The course of her career, full of false starts[13] and great leaps forward, was not simply a passage from apprentice to accomplished filmmaker, but rather a series of steps taken in order to discover a cinematic language to convey a growing and deepening set of concerns. As she says, "In some cases, I do the thing when it *needs* to be done rather than because it *should* be done." As she conceptualizes each new project, Friedrich expands her filmmaking skill to accommodate her aspirations, extending the length of her films, scratching words onto the filmstrip so that the viewer reads as well as watches a work, drafting text, or adding music. In this way, Friedrich's work progresses simultaneously in thematic and formal ways.

Film and Feminism:
Cool Hands, Warm Heart (1979) and *Scar Tissue* (1979)

Friedrich's involvement in the women's movement informs her work in the late 1970s and resurfaces in the more recent *The Lesbian Avengers Eat Fire Too* (1994), made with Janet Baus. This documentary celebrates the political activism of members of "The Lesbian Avengers," including Friedrich, and depicts the first year of the group's activities. In her own work, Friedrich's feminism is most evident in early, relatively didactic films like *Cool Hands, Warm Heart* and *Scar Tissue*.

Cool Hands, Warm Heart depicts women performing private rituals, such as shaving their legs and their armpits, in public streets, on a makeshift wooden stage before a gathering crowd. In each episode a woman makes her way through the crowd to the stage and challenges the performers. A performer shaves her legs, and the woman wipes shaving cream from a leg and applies it to the performer's face as a man would before shaving his beard. A performer cuts open her shirt to shave her armpits, and the woman places a flower on the performer's lap. A performer braids her hair, and the woman hands her scissors, with which the performer cuts off her braid and loops it around the woman's neck. At one point, the woman stops to look in a mirror and puts on eyeliner. The film's written text reads, "Can I stop them if I can't stop?" The woman is shown to be both critical of and complicit in the rituals compulsively performed to meet socially constructed definitions of femininity. Eventually, the woman becomes an onstage performer, peeling an apple with a knife.

Toward the end of the film, the woman is pulled offstage by another woman, who accompanies her to an arcade where they shoot rifles, play video games, and compete at table hockey. The fun the two women have together, engaging in aggressive entertainments away from the crowd's watchful eyes, suggests an alternative to the violence they do to themselves daily with razors and scissors. In a magical moment, the women play an arcade driving game, and then are seen riding a bicycle together.

Cool Hands, Warm Heart is grounded in the gritty reality of Manhattan's rough-and-tumble Lower East Side, which Friedrich's film transforms into a kind of dreamscape. Its freeze frames poeticize candid footage of the watching men and the women's bicycle ride, as does its poetic text filled with disturbing imagery, implying that film and fantasy overlap. One segment relates:

IN A HOUSE A TREE GREW

IT TOOK ROOT

IT SHATTERED THE WINDOWS

IMPALED THE INHABITANTS

ROCKED THE FOUNDATION

BUT AS IT TORE THROUGH THE ROOF

I WOKE MYSELF UP

By transferring the daily routines of women to the realm of public spectacle, the filmmaker asks us to consider the meaning of and motivation for the activities she documents. As Friedrich calls them, "these things we do out of fear—we shave the hair off our legs and our armpits—because otherwise we think we won't look like women."

Like *Cool Hands, Warm Heart*, but in a more concise way, *Scar Tissue* addresses the dangers women face in a male-dominated world. In *Scar Tissue*, Friedrich cuts between shots of women's feet in high-heeled shoes and shots of men's midsections to comment on gender roles and power relationships in what seems to be the business world. The film has an ominous quality, its men aggressively poking cigars at each other, standing belly to belly and briefcase to briefcase. Toward the end of the film, the women run, while the men walk in a purposeful, menacing way. Friedrich addresses issues of gender coding in her simple depictions of postures and gestures. Would the women rest their arms confidently across their midsections or stuff their hands into their pockets? Would the men balance themselves uncomfortably on high heels? Limiting her film to contrasting views of men and women, Friedrich suggests ways in which women in the workplace necessarily build "scar tissue."

Early in her career, however, Friedrich made a dramatic turn from social criticism to autobiography, as did other avant-garde filmmakers in the 1960s and 1970s. Examining that earlier wave of autobiographical films, P. Adams Sitney catalogues important differences between autobiography in film and in literature. He argues that "what makes autobiography one of the most vital developments in the cinema of the late Sixties and early Seventies is that the very making of an autobiography constitutes a reflection on the nature of the cinema, and often on its ambiguous association with language."[14] Su Friedrich's early 1980s autobiographical work reflects and elaborates on this dictum. Centering on her dream life, Friedrich's films use visual fragments and scratched text to call attention to the filmmaking process and the written word.

Film and the Evocation of Dreams:
Gently Down the Stream (1981) and *But No One* (1982)

Gently Down the Stream is Friedrich's first fully realized silent film, one in which she demonstrates a determination to depart from earlier, more "rigid" films. The film incorporates narratives taken from Friedrich's journal of ninety-six dreams. In planning the film, Friedrich narrowed down the number of dreams to forty, then thirteen. Abbreviated dream plots scratched onto the filmstrip allow the viewer entry into the world of the film. Friedrich's program notes explain that "you hear your own voice as

Marty Pottenger
in Su Friedrich's
*Gently Down the
Stream*, 1981.
Courtesy of Su
Friedrich.

you read." Because the film is silent, the scratched words, which have a
strong graphic quality, work both as a visual component and as the film's
dominant voice. At times, the words tremble, suggesting a less stable
element than the concrete images of religious icons, gymnasium activities, views from the Staten Island Ferry, abstract flashes of light and dark,
and the surface of the sea.

One of the most interesting aspects of Friedrich's work is the complex
relationship between words and images.[15] In *Gently Down the Stream*, the
poetic rather than literal images have a mysterious, yet powerful relationship to each other and to language. Thus, as Friedrich writes in her
program notes, images of "animals, saints, water and women are chosen
for their indirect but potent correspondence to the text." For example,
recycled images of *Hot Water*'s rowing machine accompany the dream
text:

WALK INTO CHURCH
MY MOTHER TREMBLES
TRANCES
RECITING A PRAYER ABOUT ORGASM
I START TO WEEP.

The images of *Gently Down the Stream* are not meant to illustrate the
dreams. Rather, Friedrich establishes "metaphoric and metonymic relationships" between words and images. In this way, she uses film technique to approximate dream mechanisms like condensation and displacement, which transform literal meaning into symbolic narratives.
However, the film does not invite specific dream analysis. Instead, it

suggests the evocative way dreams trigger images that work together and against one another.[16]

In discussing the film's stories, which focus on two relationships (one involving a man, the other a woman), Friedrich acknowledges that she relied entirely on her own vision, rather than a feminist agenda, in shaping the film, a decision she's made many times since: "At first it seemed that if I was going to be a 'good' feminist I should show the relationship with the woman to be a good one as compared to the relationship with the man. But the dreams revealed that both relationships were pretty much failures, and that seemed more realistic than trying to show some theory about how relationships *should* be."[17]

Friedrich's subsequent works are never doctrinaire. In *First Comes Love*, she was attracted to the ritual quality of weddings, even while decrying the fact that (at the time) lesbians and gays were allowed to marry in only one country—Denmark. In making *Damned If You Don't*, she began the film fully intending to launch an attack on the Catholic Church but found herself moved by its attempts to convince individuals to lead moral lives.[18] Her expression of these tensions and ambiguities—her following the uncertain path—enlivens her thinking and technique, adding surprise and depth to her films.

A related film, *But No One*, includes material that Friedrich could not fit into *Gently Down the Stream*. Unlike that earlier film, *But No One* addresses a single dream and employs a limited set of images: a construction site with workers and a dump truck, prostitutes walking the streets and approaching cars, fish at market, a woman who removes her robe and enters a bathtub, and abstract lines. These images are juxtaposed with words scratched onto the surface of the film. The visual material of *But No One* corresponds to the waking world of the filmmaker—the view in and around her bathtub, through her window, on her block, at her neighborhood market—but it is cast in the form of a dream. Thus, Friedrich establishes a contrast between her relatively banal daily life and her rich inner life. Yet it is clear that the images in her real world, like her dreams, are troubling: again and again the prostitutes approach the cars, the construction workers destroy and rebuild, and the fish are dumped from tanks of water onto market shelves and gasp open-mouthed, in an eerie, soundless way.

Friedrich establishes links between the bathing woman, construction workers, sex workers, and marketed fish. The fish are removed from water, while the woman enters water. Faces on the fabric of the woman's discarded kimono echo the faces of the fish. Here there is a more literal relationship between elements than in *Gently Down the Stream:* the shots of a man on a fire escape are accompanied by text that reads "fat boy stands on a ledge"; shots of the gaping fish are accompanied by "babies of all races float by in colorful clothes, all dead and dying, little mouths crying above the water." However, its compact constellation of repeated images is satisfying, an important part of Friedrich's ongoing exploration of film's ability to work like dreams and convey a unique, personal vision.

Film and Memory:
The Ties That Bind (1984) and *Sink or Swim* (1990)

The Ties That Bind and *Sink or Swim* both address the importance of the past by structuring disparate materials to evoke memory. *The Ties That Bind*[19] is a significant departure from the films that came before. It is fifty-five minutes long, it has sound, and it features Friedrich's mother, Lore Bucher Friedrich, talking about her life in Germany during the 1930s and 1940s. Friedrich interviews her mother, and the viewer hears her mother's answers but never the filmmaker's questions (although they occasionally appear as scratched text). Lore Bucher and her family experienced the rise of the Third Reich and the war, and while otherwise conventional, they were staunchly unsympathetic to Hitler. Bucher later came to the United States with her American husband, Friedrich's father. This is not a traditional documentary portrait; while Friedrich's mother speaks on the sound track, the accompanying images rarely correspond to her words. Instead, the film presents a rich mix of material: various nonsynchronous images of the mother; footage Friedrich shot on a trip to Ulm, Germany, to see where her mother grew up; archival footage of the war; home movie footage taken after the war; an early cinema single-shot film of a woman dancing while holding an American flag; and footage of Friedrich participating in political protests in the present. In keeping with Friedrich's original impulse to make a film about uprooted people without a home, the film features shots of hands constructing a model of a German house and then destroying it.

The primary tension comes from the filmmaker's uncertainty about what her mother might reveal about the past: how her mother's family was affected by Hitler's rise to power, whether her mother should have done more to resist, what means her mother employed to survive the war and the subsequent liberation, whether she herself would have behaved differently in her mother's place, whether the filmmaker should be more politically engaged in the present. In spite of the charged nature of the interview (summed up by Bucher, speaking of the shame in being German: "It is a persecution to the end of my life and I don't deserve it"), only one overt conflict emerges:

> The thing that was most difficult for me to figure out was how to deal with the part when my mother is talking about Dachau and she says, "Nobody was killed there." I felt I had to find a way to say "No, actually . . ." so I scratched the facts about deaths at Dachau onto the film. When I showed her the finished film, I thought she was going to say, "How dare you undermine me," but she didn't say anything about that part of the film. What she said, which was bizarre, was that she could prove she wasn't in the Hitler Youth, and in order to do that she showed me a document that was signed with her then-married name. At that point, she revealed to me that she had been married in Germany to another man prior to marrying my father. I was probably thirty-five years old at the time, and I never knew that she'd been married before, so that was a completely unexpected revelation for me.

Sink or Swim, which expresses Friedrich's profound ambivalence toward her father, is her "classic" film, the one that best represents her work; it is most often rented and sold, included in academic courses, and written about by scholars.[20] Friedrich establishes a rigorous structure—twenty-six scenes, each corresponding to a letter of a reversed alphabet from Z to A—to address painful but ultimately liberating childhood memories. Some scenes are silent and others are accompanied by Friedrich's stories about her childhood, recounted in a matter-of-fact tone by a young girl. The film chronicles Friedrich's life with her father, a linguist and anthropologist who left the family in 1965. Unlike *The Ties That Bind*, this film is about the filmmaker's memories, rather than those of a parent. Over the course of *Sink or Swim*, Friedrich provides damning anecdotes about a father who taught her the mechanics of swimming before throwing her into the water so she could "sink or swim." He told her about deadly water moccasins waiting in nests at the bottom of the lake for unsuspecting swimmers; he held her and her sister's heads under water in the bathtub to punish them; he taught her to play chess and then refused to play again after her first win; he sent her home from a trip to Mexico to punish her for being out too late with a boy.

Sink or Swim contains Friedrich's most complex interweaving of sounds and images and includes an extraordinarily nuanced, many-faceted relationship between past and present, reportage and poetry. The film's materials include home movie footage, images from television sitcoms like *Father Knows Best*, educational films about reproduction, documentary footage of women bodybuilders, and newly shot images.

> In *Sink or Swim*, some stories are illustrated with completely unrelated images—like the story about my father writing the poem and the images of me putting roses in a vase—and at other times there's a more direct correspondence—like the story about writing in my diary combined with the images of Catholic schoolchildren, which I used because as a child I went to Catholic school. But I consciously wanted *Sink or Swim* to include both direct and indirect correspondences. I wanted to give the viewer's imagination room to play, not just provide them with illustrations of the voiceover stories.

As with many of her films, Friedrich first intended to denounce her subject but ultimately abandoned a one-sided approach. Although many of *Sink or Swim*'s stories reveal Friedrich's father to be surprisingly cruel and distant, others acknowledge that he too is a victim of his past—he lost his sister to drowning in childhood and experienced cultural pressures to behave in an unemotional, authoritarian manner.[21] Although Friedrich's father initially refused to see the film, his reaction upon seeing it shocked the filmmaker.

> My father had a remarkable response to *Sink or Swim*. He sent me a letter and the gist of it was, "Like all your other work, *Sink or Swim* was technically brilliant, but I won't give you an *explication du texte* . . . I don't know whether you remember, but in Otto's book . . ."—he had a brother named Otto who was a writer—" . . . he used me as an example, and so I find that I am pleased once again to have provided someone with good subject matter." So he ignored everything critical in *Sink or Swim* and simply complimented himself for giving me good material from which to make a film! As much as I thought I knew him, that degree of egotism just floored me.

Typically, Friedrich's films arrive at a resolution, even though some endings are ambiguous or ironic. At the conclusion of *Sink or Swim*, Friedrich tells the story of how, instead of continuing her efforts to swim across the lake, as her father demanded, she decided turn back and rejoin her friends, an act of defiant self-assertion. Yet, as the song she sings at the end of the film suggests ("Now I know my A-B-Cs, tell me what you think of me"), Friedrich still yearns on some level for her father's love and approval. She explains, "I was angry at my father for many years, and it wasn't until I made *Sink or Swim* that I thought, 'It's not just about being angry, it's about admitting to yourself that you wanted to have a father who loved you.'"

Film and Religion: *Damned If You Don't* (1987)

A priest is by definition blameless and he's telling people "Look at your sin, look at your sin," and I'm saying, "I've sinned, I've sinned. And maybe you have too. And if you have, maybe it's not so bad."—Su Friedrich

The tension between repressive Catholicism and the expression of lesbian desire is an important subtext in much of Friedrich's work. With *Damned If You Don't*, Friedrich openly explores the conflict between the powerful vow of chastity and the irresistible lure of sexuality. At the beginning of *Damned If You Don't*, a woman falls asleep while watching a television broadcast of *Black Narcissus*, a melodramatic film about simmering sexuality in a secluded convent. Friedrich calls attention to the televised footage by leaving in the "roll bars" caused by filming television, and by casting the televised footage in black and white rather than in its original glowing color. In addition, Friedrich selects sequences of *Black Narcissus* that depict the tensions between the "good" nun, the "bad" nun, and Mr. Dean (the object of their desire), and this footage is accompanied by droll commentary in which a narrator underlines the sexual underpinning of the film. As *Damned If You Don't* proceeds, the woman shadows and finally confronts an attractive young nun. Friedrich introduces a reading from Judith C. Brown's 1986 *Immodest Acts: The Life of a Lesbian Nun in Renaissance Italy*, which includes sexually explicit testimony given by a nun regarding her seduction by another nun (the seducer was subsequently imprisoned for her transgressions), as well as recollections by a friend of Friedrich's about growing up Catholic. The film also includes candid footage of nuns on the streets, as well as images of whales, swans, and sea snakes undulating sensually. Friedrich ends *Damned If You Don't* with an extraordinarily erotic scene in which the woman slowly and ceremoniously removes one after another the many layers of the nun's habit until the nun stands nude before her. The eager lovemaking that follows is a consummation ideal for a film addressing the difficulties of achieving erotic release, although as critics have pointed out, it flies in the face of religious and feminist prohibitions against erotic depictions of women's bodies on film.[22]

Ela Troyano and
Peggy Healey in Su
Friedrich's *Damned
If You Don't*, 1987.
Courtesy of
Su Friedrich.

Noting the influence of Catholicism on her career, Friedrich draws
surprising parallels between filmmaking and sermonizing:

> When I make art I do feel that sometimes I'm exhorting people to deal
> with themselves or deal with a situation. "Are you afraid of your medical
> problems? Are you having trouble with having a gay identity? What's your
> relationship like with your parents? Whatever it might be, try to own up to
> that and do something about it and make your life better." I think that's
> kind of like sermonizing, but I didn't make the connection until a few
> years ago between my childhood experience of listening to the weekly
> Sunday sermons and this impulse I seem to have to exhort people to look
> seriously at their lives, consider the moral implications of their behavior
> and speak openly about the behavior of others.

The complexity of Friedrich's sound tracks is evident in *Damned If
You Don't*. In this film, she collages witty, spoken analysis of *Black Narcissus*, reading of Renaissance-era testimony, and present-day reminiscences. The film's concluding erotic scene is presented in breathless silence. For Friedrich, however, music is a more complicated issue. She
acknowledges that a growing challenge in her work has been whether and
when to use music as an element: "I'm no longer the purist that I was in
my first works, when I just wouldn't use music no matter how great the
temptation." She employs music for the first time in *Sink or Swim* (the
Schubert song and the "ABC" ditty), but withholds its extensive use until
First Comes Love (which she describes as having "wall-to-wall" music).
Music is also an important element in *Rules of the Road*, used by Friedrich to evoke the mood of the period.

Film and Cultural Iconography:
First Comes Love (1991) and *Rules of the Road* (1993)

In *First Comes Love*, Friedrich cuts together footage that traces conventional high points of four different weddings, using popular music as a counterpoint to the images. Friedrich's editing strategy has a disruptive effect, since no single wedding is viewed in a continuous way and no piece of music is heard in its entirety. Instead, Friedrich presents characteristic moments in a typical wedding: arrivals at the church, posing for photographs, and sweeping up rice. Focusing not on the whole, but on the telling details, her camera searches out bouquets, limousines, and gowns without individualizing particular couples or wedding parties. The film's transitions are purposefully abrupt, emphasizing the repetition and sameness of each "special event."

Friedrich's assertive technique, including rapid camera movements and jagged editing, as well as eclectic musical accompaniment, call attention to the fact that the events depicted are mediated by the filmmaker. The lyrics of the songs constitute Friedrich's observations on the action, from Al Green's "Let's Stay Together" to Willie Nelson's "You Were Always on My Mind." But the clearest evidence of Friedrich's presence occurs at the moment when the couples take their vows in church; she abruptly interrupts the wedding footage with a rolling title of the 120 countries where gay and lesbian couples cannot legally marry. The list is so long that the accompanying song—Gladys Knight's "That Should Have Been Me"—ends, and the names of countries continue to roll by in silence. Friedrich resumes the wedding footage, but as the film concludes, she inserts a final title stating that in 1990 Denmark became the first country to legalize same-sex marriage.

In 1991, Friedrich outraged some gay viewers by acknowledging the legitimacy of the desire for a legal marriage, and perhaps even the pomp and circumstance of a wedding ceremony. It seemed to some that Friedrich was expressing a yearning for heterosexual life.[23] Today, when homosexual marriage is passionately advocated by many gays and lesbians as a fundamental human right, *First Comes Love* seems prescient. However, as with all of her subjects, Friedrich's attitude toward weddings and marriage remains ambivalent. As the couples leave the church, the film becomes more contemplative, suggesting that, despite the excitement and appeal of the wedding rituals, the couples may not necessarily live happily ever after.[24]

Rules of the Road, one of Friedrich's strongest films, has a diaristic quality, chronicling the course of a relationship, while focusing on the automobile the couple shared (a 1983 beige Oldsmobile station wagon with fake wood paneling), which serves as an ongoing reminder of past love and present loss. Narrated by the filmmaker, who has lost touch with her former lover and their car, the film contains one image after another of nearly identical station wagons, interspersed with shots of hands playing games of solitaire with a Greyhound bus deck of cards. Images of cars still or in motion are accompanied by long silences or by Friedrich's deadpan recollections of how her lover's station wagon assumed a central place in their lives. Along with the spoken anecdotes, the sound track contains popular songs recorded to sound like music from a 1980s car radio. Most of the film is in color, but it also contains black-and-white views of a woman rowing on a lake, evoking Friedrich's longing for a prior time by "quoting" images from her early films *Hot Water* and *Gently Down the Stream*. These black-and-white images are accompanied by traffic noises, linking the otherwise unseen lover with the shared automobile.

The narrator's relationship with the car is both ironic and touching. She reports that, when her lover first drives up, it is something of a shock (she is taken aback by this "sensible family car"). Later the "homely" station wagon surprises her with its unexpected pickup. The car offers the freedom of travel outside the city but also traps the couple in a confined space during lengthy arguments to and from their destinations. For a brief period after their breakup, the narrator has limited access to the car when her ex-lover is away. Emotionally charged, these moments provide ghostlike evidence of her former lover in the radio station left on and in the smell of smoke permeating the seat covers. The narrator airs the car out in hopes of helping her ex-lover stop smoking. Poignant details like her admitting to scanning license plates to search for the car (while dreading to find it) give way to speculation about what might happen if it did appear. Like *First Comes Love*, *Rules of the Road* is about a cultural phenomenon, in this case, the place of cars in American life. A shared possession, it comes to stand for the relationship, simultaneously providing adventure and claustrophobia. Having a car is one way to participate in the larger society, but it also establishes solidarity between owners of similar cars: "By becoming the owner of one, she seemed to have been initiated into a special clan. And by sharing the car with her, I felt I had become an honorary member of that same family."

Film and Identity:
Hide and Seek (1996) and *The Odds of Recovery* (2002)

In *Hide and Seek*, Friedrich presents an ambitious narrative film about the sexual awakening of the film's twelve-year-old lesbian protagonist (Lou), intercut with interviews with adult lesbians recalling their own pubescence (about issues such as first sexual experiences, whether they ever wanted to be boys, or crushes on teachers). This interview material, often funny and touching, bolsters the narrative in which Lou and her girlfriends learn about their bodies and sex, enjoy intimate friendships with each other, dream about the future, dance, and play. Adolescent confusion about identity and "fitting in" is at the center of the film. Lou experiences jealousy over a friendship, escapes to a tree house, and entertains fantasies about travel to Africa.

Hide and Seek freely and poetically juxtaposes several different kinds of filmic material. These include narrative sequences tracing Lou's daily activities, stories from adult lesbians about their youth, sequences from 1950s sex education film, footage of animals in Africa (from the 1955 film *Simba*), dozens of photographs of lesbians as children (including two of Friedrich), and popular music from the period of Friedrich's adolescence. The film, which depicts typical girlhood situations from a lesbian perspective, explores an underreported subject yet avoids the rhetorical stance of conventional documentary. It is less journalistic than impressionistic, with most of its ideas and arguments bubbling up from a rich, intimate matrix of memories and associations.[25]

Friedrich was enthusiastic about the making of her most narrative film, *Hide and Seek*, on which she collaborated with her partner, painter Cathy Quinlan. Friedrich has said that she thoroughly enjoyed every aspect of the production, although she recognized that she would not continue making narrative films. Following the production of *Hide and Seek*, Friedrich endured a long, extremely painful period. *Hide and Seek* was well received but the distributor would not give it a limited theatrical release for financial reasons. However, the film was shown on public television because it had been funded by ITVS, and it ran for two years on the Sundance Channel. In addition, during this period Friedrich had her heart set on adapting a book called *Aquamarine* by Carol Anshaw, only to find that the book had already been optioned.

The Odds of Recovery, which takes Friedrich's history of illness as its subject, marks the completion of an important trajectory in Friedrich's

Su Friedrich with Ariel Mara and Chels Holland in *Hide and Seek*, 1996. Courtesy of Su Friedrich.

filmmaking—how best to interject herself into what are essentially auto-biographical works. Over a period of twenty-five years, Friedrich has gradually emerged from behind the camera into full view. In *Gently Down the Stream* and *But No One*, two early silent films inspired by her dream journal, and in *The Ties That Bind*, her first fully realized sound film, Friedrich scratches stories and questions directly onto the film stock. In *Damned If You Don't*, she sings the "I Won't Be a Nun" song offscreen. In *Sink or Swim*, she painstakingly scripts a series of emotionally charged autobiographical anecdotes told in the third person by a young girl, with-holding her own voice until she sings a children's song at the end of the film. *Sink or Swim* also offers glimpses of Friedrich drinking beer in a bathtub and smoking a cigarette on her bed. In *Rules of the Road*, Frie-drich enters the film to a much greater extent by delivering voiceover recollections about the car she and her lover once shared. In *Hide and Seek*, there are two photographs of Friedrich as a child, and she plays the teacher in the classroom. Still, as she points out, "unlike a lot of my other work, I wasn't in the film very directly, except of course Cathy and I wrote the script together, so it's very much our story, and so 'I'm there' in that sense." Finally, in *The Odds of Recovery*, Friedrich is fully the protagonist, narrating the film, making her medical history the topic of her storytell-ing, and turning the camera on herself in various states of dress and undress. As Friedrich sees it, "*The Odds of Recovery* was very much a way of owning up to who I am, both as a maker and as a person."

The Odds of Recovery is an extraordinarily intimate chronicle of Frie-drich's life as a series of illnesses. Taking herself as subject, Friedrich recounts the history of her encounters with the medical profession, in-cluding her undiagnosed hormonal imbalance and her many surgeries.

From Su Friedrich's
*The Odds of
Recovery*, 2002.
Courtesy of Su
Friedrich.

Friedrich calmly catalogs her medical procedures, nervously converses
with doctors in examining rooms, angrily addresses the camera when
struggling alone with an unruly hospital dressing gown, and anxiously
comments on the appearance of her bruised postbiopsy breast filmed in a
bathroom mirror. The film's postdubbed track is especially pure and
simple; it includes ambient sounds like dirt scraped into a planter and
songbirds that lend her backyard garden a cloistered calm. *The Odds of
Recovery* mixes footage of Friedrich's visits to hospitals with scenes involving her pursuit of alternative therapies: shopping for Chinese herbs, taking tai chi classes, and cooking health-inducing remedies. The film continually compares nature (the time it takes plants to grow) and the body
(the time it takes wounds to heal). This idea is best conveyed in images that
document Friedrich's gardening and her crewel work. Throughout the
film, her hands are glimpsed embroidering a vine that depicts in its twists
and turns the history of her surgeries. The vine's "flowers" are Friedrich's
affected organs. Camera movements up the vine lead the viewer to key
moments in her life; they also evoke the camera movements that pan
across her scars. At the end of the film, her story has been told, and the
embroidery, a map of her medical problems, is finished.[26]

One startling issue that the film raises is how Friedrich could continue
to make increasingly ambitious, painstakingly constructed films while
undergoing medical treatment. As the film lists the dates of her surgeries
and provides footage of her medical procedures, it also details Friedrich's
perseverance as an artist in the face of long and crippling illnesses. She
has written that it was only in hindsight that she realized that she had
been in denial. For example, while she was making *The Odds of Recovery*,
she had had a breast biopsy that developed complications but she still
took the video camera into the bathroom and filmed herself. Only after-

ward did she realize "that was not the thing to be doing at such a time." One factor that may have allowed her to continue working is that the making of *The Odds of Recovery* coincided with Friedrich's use of a computer to edit her work, simplifying and granting her more control over the process, although not streamlining it.[27]

Country and City Video Diaries: *The Head of a Pin* (2004) and *The All in the Small* (in progress)

With *The Head of a Pin* (which I don't think of as totally realized), I just went out and shot some footage based on the simple idea that "I'm out in the country and I don't know what the country is like, so I'll try to convey something of that feeling of ignorance and displacement."—Su Friedrich

A synch-sound videotape, *The Head of a Pin* is a relatively modest work in which Friedrich offers glimpses of herself and friends on a summer vacation in upstate New York. As with *The Odds of Recovery*, she was willing to let the film evolve, rather than preplanning it in a rigorous way. Repeated image clusters include views of a path in the woods and a rushing river. In fact, the piece turned out differently than she expected because Friedrich came across a determining image: a spider that had trapped a fly twice its size in its web. Their twitching, biting struggle to the death became the leitmotif of the film, returned to again and again, an emblem of nature's small but frightful dangers. While a less richly structured piece than her earlier films, *The Head of a Pin* is a first step in Friedrich's decision to make works in video.

Friedrich recently began making *The All in the Small*, a promising new project about the coffee pushcarts in New York City. Her long-range plan is to track the coffee from its harvesting to the time "it gets handed to you for 50 cents." Like many of her other films, it will trace a process from start to finish. To get a feel for the project, Friedrich has been looking at the pushcarts on the streets of Manhattan during the day and watching them driven back over the bridges to Brooklyn at night. She visited a garage where the coffee beans are stored, interviewed a Senegalese worker while he washed the pushcarts, visited a factory in Queens to see how the coffee is processed, and traveled to Charleston, South Carolina, to interview a coffee importer. She plans to go to Guatemala to videotape a coffee farm, to Miami to film the coffee arriving by ship, and to travel along the route of the shipment's transport up the East Coast. Friedrich also plans to interview the workers who make the ubiquitous "We Are Happy To Serve You" paper cups. Although the film will initially focus on the push-carts and the coffee they serve, Friedrich believes it could go in many different directions. Whatever form it takes, however, it is likely to be unconventional, and to tell us as much about Friedrich as about her ostensible "subject." In responding negatively to whether her new project would be a *regular* documentary, Friedrich said:

> I had to rack my brain to think why I constantly resist making a regular documentary. Or even a "regular" experimental film. If I think about ex-perimental film as a genre, there's always something about it that I think is different than my own work. Maybe *Gently Down the Stream* fits in, but once you get into *The Ties That Bind* or *Damned If You Don't*, and even *Rules of the Road*, they don't . . . I think there's something more purely visual in experimental films. They're not so driven by narrative. My work has *always* been driven by a kind of narrative, so I don't know. I just do what I do.

Coda: Friedrich on Her Career

Although Friedrich clearly uses recurring images, themes, and strategies in her work, she has never had a grand plan for her career. She continues to make both short and long works and to move freely between narrative, documentary, and experimental modes, determined to evolve as a film-maker. If Friedrich can be said to have any regrets, they are that her work, and the work of other experimental filmmakers, is not more widely seen beyond academic circles and various cable outlets. She is currently trying to remedy that by transferring her work to DVD, beginning with *Gently Down the Stream*, *Sink or Swim*, and *Hide and Seek*. In this, Friedrich has a mission to "contribute to raising the level of the culture" by making work that is serious about both form and subject matter more visible.[28]

At the same time, Friedrich has long harbored a dream of becoming a feature filmmaker. Admitting that this goal may not be meant for her, she says that she started out thinking that she would make films like Fass-binder.[29] At one point, just after *Sink or Swim*, she was asked by a pro-ducer whether she wanted to be the next Woody Allen. Although she declined, she has always been fascinated with the prospect.[30] Friedrich has a clear sense of the ways in which her films offer alternatives to mainstream commercial cinema. Compelled to make therapeutic, moral tales, Friedrich explores and exposes her own fears in her works, while urging others to take a fresh, critical view of themselves:

> My films will always attempt to face up to problems and invite others to do the same. They show my failings, or at least my sense that I haven't completely realized my desires. *Sink or Swim* shows the extent to which I really wanted to have a good Dad and I didn't. In *Rules of the Road*, I say a little bit about why I didn't do such a good job being in a relationship, and in *First Comes Love*, I admit that I have a soft spot for all of that [wedding-related] pomp and circumstance. So my films start from a feeling of some sort of weakness and then get past it. It's through my films that I can actually talk about it.

As Friedrich's work progresses, she will certainly continue to analyze troubling subjects, push the medium, and provide herself and her viewers with original, lucid ways of viewing film and understanding their lives.

Filmography

Hot Water, 1978 (12 min.): sd., b&w; Super 8
Cool Hands, Warm Heart, 1979 (16 min.): si., b&w; 16mm
Scar Tissue, 1979 (6 min.): si., b&w; 16mm
I Suggest Mine, 1980 (6 min.): si., b&w; 16mm
Gently Down the Stream, 1981 (14 min.): si., b&w; 16mm
But No One, 1982 (9 min.): si., b&w; 16mm
The Ties That Bind, 1984 (55 min.): sd., b&w; 16mm
Damned If You Don't, 1987 (42 min.): sd., b&w; 16mm
Sink or Swim, 1990 (48 min.): sd., b&w; 16mm
First Comes Love, 1991 (22 min.): sd., b&w; 16mm
Rules of the Road, 1993 (31 min.): sd., col.; 16mm
Lesbian Avengers Eat Fire, 1994 (60 min.): sd., col.; video
Hide and Seek, 1996 (65 min.): sd., b&w; 16mm
The Odds of Recovery, 2002 (65 min.): sd., col.; 16mm
The Head of a Pin, 2004 (21 min.): sd., col.; video
Seeing Red, 2005 (27 min.): sd., col.; video

Notes

I thank Su Friedrich for generously making her work available to me and for allowing me to interview her for this project. I am indebted to her and to Sam McElfresh and Paul Arthur for their contributions to this essay.

1   Holmlund, *Between the Sheets*, 134–35.

2   Holmlund, "Feminist Makeovers," 224.

3   Russell, *Experimental Ethnography*, 148, 276.

4   Renov, *The Subject of Documentary*, 22.

5   P. Adams Sitney categorizes avant-garde film genres in *Visionary Film*: the "psychodrama" is a quest for sexual identity; the "trance film" is a somnambulist's journey in which the central character's visionary experience, confronting the past and the self, leads to self-realization; the "structural film" is one in which structure and duration determine content, utilizing "fixed camera position, the flicker effect, loop printing, and rephotography off the screen" (18–22, 407–8). Jonas Mekas's comment that his own diary film "captures bits of life as a mode of reflection" ("The Diary Film," 191) is also useful here.

6   Jenkins, "Gently Down the Stream," 196–97.

7   Kotz, "An Unrequited Desire for the Sublime," 95.

8   MacDonald, *Avant-Garde Film*, 103.

9   As Jenkins points out, "Recent histories of American avant-garde cinema share a general acknowledgement that by the late 1970s and early 1980s experimental film had reached a critical impasse" ("Gently Down the Stream," 195). In an essay titled "End of the Avant-garde," Fred Camper names Su Friedrich as an exception, one of the few original artists "reshaping the medium toward their own concerns" (123). In a review in the *Village Voice*, Amy Taubin writes, "Just when it seemed as if half the avant-garde filmmakers born post-1948 were putting on the brakes . . . along comes Su Friedrich's sweetly passionate and genuinely innovative *Damned If You Don't* to make a case for not following the well-worn narrative path" ("Experimental Bent," 64).

10   Unless otherwise noted, Su Friedrich's quotes are from an unpublished interview with Janet Cutler, conducted on July 9, 2004, in Brooklyn, New York.

11   In his mid-1980s assessment of the avant-garde since 1966, Paul Arthur writes, "Admittedly the position of women in the American avant-garde, at least since the signal interventions of Maya Deren, Marie Menken, and Shirley Clarke, has been one of provisionality" ("The Last of the Last Machine?," 84). Rabinowitz identifies Maya Deren, Joyce Wieland, and Yvonne Rainer as filmmakers who were able to express a feminist perspective, although it was not always recognized, and who often faced challenges in their efforts to finance and distribute their work. She goes on to describe the work of those who came later as more aggressively challenging patriarchy, arguing for women's rights, and validating women's experience (*Points of Resistance*, 10, 190).

12   Friedrich currently teaches film and video at Princeton University.

13   Friedrich sometimes begins and abandons unrealized films; in the case of *I Suggest Mine* (1980), she completed the film (also titled *Someone Was Holding My Breath*) but was never completely satisfied with it. It is not in distribution.

14   Sitney, "Autobiography in Avant-Garde Film," 202.

15   Friedrich is one of the filmmakers who, in the 1980s, was responsible for the return of the written word after its virtual banishment from the avant-garde. In "Bodies, Language and the Impeachment of Vision," Arthur offers reasons why visual texts "fit into the avant-garde's reigning cultural politics," using various films and filmmakers, including Friedrich, to illustrate his points. He concludes: " . . . the introduction of language has had the paradoxical effect of reinvigorating the avant-garde's compass of permissible imagery by adding both another facet and a tool with which to interrogate, bend, or otherwise force new meanings onto diaristic or poetic schema" (*A Line of Sight*, 150).

16   *Gently Down the Stream* also exists as a small self-published booklet of text and images (1982).

17   MacDonald, *A Critical Cinema*, 290.

18   Friedrich has stated: "And particularly now, when we live in this completely lawless world (even though I obviously don't agree with a lot of the ideas of Catholicism, or any other organized religion, and I think that they got a lot of things wrong), I do think we all need some sort of moral compass. And to the extent that I got that and interacted with it sitting in the church (I might be disagreeing with what was being said, but I was processing it), I think there's something for me in that."

19   For a more detailed analysis of the film, see Fischer's *Cinematernity* and MacDonald's *Avant-Garde Film*.

20   Critics, including MacDonald, often note *Sink or Swim*'s parallels to Hollis Frampton's use of the alphabet in structuring *Zorns Lemma* (1970); also relevant are Stan Brakhage's excavations of childhood and parent-child relationships in *Scenes from Under Childhood* (1968–70) and other films. *Sink or Swim* has been analyzed extensively by Camper in *Chicago Reader*, MacDonald in the *Independent*, Renov in *The Subject of Documentary*, Zryd in *Senses of Cinema*, and by others.

21   "Just as there were things that happened in my childhood that make me behave as I do now, the same thing is true for him and his parents. So it was important for me to acknowledge that chain reaction, not necessarily to forgive him" (McElfresh, "An Interview with Filmmaker Su Friedrich").

22   As Scott MacDonald explains, "Some filmmakers and critics came to see traditional film pleasure as an implicit acceptance of the workings of patriarchy, and it seemed necessary to expunge female sexuality and nudity from serious cinema in the service of progressive feminism. . . . Friedrich's decision not only to include a representation of female sexuality but to use it as a triumphant conclusion of the film is crucial. Friedrich has cinematically appropriated the pleasure *of* women *for* women" (*A Critical Cinema*, 2:287). Kotz describes how "in a modern tale of girl gets girl [Friedrich succeeds in] creating pleasure in the discards of a repressive and highly constrained past, and of moving beyond feminist critique to selectively reinvest these images and memories with private and erotic meanings" ("An Unrequited Desire for the Sub-

lime," 98–99). Chris Holmlund ("Feminist Makeovers") and Chris Straayer (*Deviant Eyes, Deviant Bodies*) also address the issue of lesbian representation (and representations of lesbian desire) in *Damned If You Don't*.

23 While not agreeing with the sentiment, Alisa Lebow describes how in 1991 "screenings in queer festivals were marked by offended grumblings and huffy, premature walkouts" ("Lesbians Make Movies," 18). On a more positive note, Holmlund sees *First Comes Love* (and *Rules of the Road*) as "subtly expanding kinship to include lesbians as well as heterosexuals" (*Between the Sheets*, 134).

24 Because *First Comes Love* focuses on the codes and conventions of heterosexual wedding ceremonies, Holmlund believes it can be seen as a kind ethnographic exercise in which the filmmaker takes the position of the outsider looking in on the rites of the other (*Between the Sheets*, 134–35). In her program notes, Friedrich calls it the "rites and wrongs." Certainly, in contradiction to the film's title (the entire children's chant is recited at the opening of the film), "love" is not always followed by either "marriage" or a "baby carriage."

25 For a more detailed discussion of this film, see Russell's *Experimental Ethnography*.

26 In *The Odds of Recovery*, there is a great deal of attention to "women's spaces"—the kitchen and the garden—as well as to "women's art"—the crewel work. Interestingly, a needlepoint image of Christ's face is a cherished gift from the woman to the nun in *Damned If You Don't*.

27 Friedrich said, "One thing about working on the computer is that there's certainly a physical ease to editing images that just isn't there on a flatbed. However, I cut *Hide and Seek* on a flatbed and *The Odds of Recovery* on the computer, and even though I had more footage to use for *Hide and Seek* (I had about seventeen takes of each thing the girls did) and even though the computer is faster, each film took me about a year to cut. I think my way of processing information slows it down so I still end up taking a lot of time. . . . Working with the computer allows me complete control of the sound editing. When I was assembling *Hide and Seek* on film, there were a lot of layers so I did the basic layers and then had a sound editor come in and build up all the other stuff. But with *Odds of Recovery* I did all the sound editing myself, and I actually Foleyed the sound for all the sound effects. All the stuff in the garden where I'm digging and cutting and weeding, all the stuff in the kitchen—it's all artificial sound. I shot the film silent and put all the sound in later. So the more I'm able to work with sound in the computer, the more I can try out things that I'd never tried before."

28 Friedrich has long devoted her energies to improving the state of independent film distribution, including working on the Film-Makers' Cooperative rental and sales catalog, helping to launch and maintain the distribution efforts of Women Make Movies, and supporting other independent film distribution networks.

29   Friedrich cites the following filmmakers as influences on her work: "Rainer Werner Fassbinder, Akira Kurosawa, Billy Wilder, Maya Deren, Chantal Akerman, Leslie Thornton, Luis Buñuel, Pier Paolo Pasolini, Marlene Gorris, Ingmar Bergman, Leontine Sagan, Agnes Varda, Buster Keaton, Hollis Frampton, Anne Severson, Abbas Kiarostami, Valie Export, Preston Sturges, Vincent Grenier, Leighton Pierce, Frederick Wiseman, David Lee, Vilgot Sjoman, Jean Rouch, John Marshall, Satyajit Ray, Mike Leigh . . ."

30   Friedrich said, "I've also often fantasized about making classic ethnographic films in the style of John Marshall or Robert Gardner, whose work I love. I suppose as you get older you're forced to recognize that you have various dreams that can't be realized and you have to come to grips with the limits of your own talents, resources, funding, personality traits and uncontrollable urges. In my case, I'd say that I keep on wanting to do things against the grain even while I love a lot of the conventional ways of filmmaking."

KATHLEEN MCHUGH

The Experimental "Dunyementary"

A Cinematic Signature Effect

□

I am my own text.—Cheryl Dunye

Born in 1966, Cheryl Dunye grew up loving 1970s television, a taste that marks her as coming from a different generation than all but one of the filmmakers discussed in this volume. If she is a descendant of these earlier filmmakers, she assimilates their influence to the other, highly diverse traditions from which her filmmaking draws. These traditions include African American documentary, experimental film, the personal and autobiographical approaches of the classical avant-garde, European art cinema, homoerotic cinematic aesthetics, the Underground (and its love of popular culture),[1] and 1970s television. She also nurtured her talent in the academy, where her exposure to feminist theory led her to visual media as a creative outlet through which to explore issues that concerned her. Dunye's early student films, screened nationwide at lesbian and gay, women's, and community film and video festivals also attracted more mainstream media attention while she was still pursuing her MFA at Rutgers University. The rights to *Janine* (1990) and *She Don't Fade* (1991) were bought by WHYY, a Philadelphia PBS affiliate television station, and broadcast in 1991. From the outset, Dunye's work bridged popular and avant-garde sources, impulses, and outlets, and also creative and critical, or political, expression. Dunye articulated this bridge through reference to her own life story, community, and mediascape, each of which affirmed and was explored for its diversity and contradictions. In light of Dunye's intentional grounding in her particular life experience, I will begin with the referential field of Cheryl Dunye's biography, the material of her own text.

Vita

Cheryl Dunye was born in Liberia in 1966 to an African father and African American mother. She was raised in Philadelphia and received her BA from Temple University in 1990 and her MFA from Rutgers in 1992. After having her work shown in prestigious national and international screenings, she began accruing media awards from major foundations (Pew, Rockefeller, and MacArthur) and national arts institutions (the NEA) as well as prizes for her videos and films, all by 1993, the year after she received her MFA. By that time, she had made three student films at Rutgers, works that clearly established her as an up and coming video artist: *Janine, She Don't Fade,* and *Vanilla Sex* (1992). She called these films "Dunyementaries," a genre that combined autobiography, documentary, fiction, and humor with an experimental style. She followed this work with *Untitled Portrait* (1993), *The Potluck and the Passion* (1993), and *Greetings from Africa* (1994) before moving to feature filmmaking.

During this time, Dunye wrote, directed, edited, and acted within an artisanal mode of production, her crew and her videos including friends and lovers working and playing themselves on both sides of the camera.[2] In her article "Building Subjects," Dunye cites Michelle Parkerson and Marlon Riggs as models, since their work showed her that aspects of her life "as part of a black gay and lesbian community [were] valid subjects" for her art. Dunye's work incorporates an autoethnographic focus, "building a visual language for black lesbian life that focuses on our creativity, our culture, and our concerns about a world where we are forgotten."[3] Dunye's use of the term *forgotten* rather than the often-used *invisible* shifts the focus of her endeavor from a theoretical quality ascribed to women overall ("invisible") to altering a situation that black lesbians have been put in by the active agency of others ("forgotten"). The existence and visibility of this community, however forgotten, is never in question.

Dunye then wrote, directed, and starred (as herself) in her first feature, *The Watermelon Woman* (1996), which was produced by Barry Swimar

Cheryl Dunye
in *Greetings from
Africa*. Courtesy
of Women Make
Movies, www
.wmm.com.

and Alexandra Juhasz and distributed in the United States by First Run Features. In keeping with the inter-/extratextual approach that had characterized the earlier Dunyementaries, Juhasz, her companion at the time, was also the film's producer and an actor in its narrative. Today, in addition to its theatrical release, the film plays regularly on the BET channel (Black Entertainment Television), was shown at the Whitney Biennial and in film festivals, women's cinema festivals, and gay and lesbian festivals in Hong Kong, Amsterdam, Tokyo, Taorino, London, New York, Taipei, San Francisco, and many other cities. It won the Teddy Award in Berlin and audience award prizes at several of these festivals. After *The Watermelon Woman*, which Dunye said in interviews was both "full-blown Cheryl" and "the death of Cheryl in such a straightforward way," Dunye ceased working in an autobiographical mode and made the acclaimed *Stranger Inside* (2000) for HBO.[4] She most recently has completed her first studio film, *My Baby's Daddy*.[5]

By her own account, Dunye grew up loving popular culture and television. She cites *The Addams Family* and *The Brady Bunch*, as well as contemporaneous feminist experimental films (which she saw as an undergraduate in the 1980s), as signal, if very different, influences on her work. The sitcoms and the feminist experimental work share an emphasis on domestic space. Yet the work of filmmakers Barbara Hammer, Carolee Schneemann, and Chantal Akerman, whom Dunye has referred to as models, explores what the sitcoms could only allude to in a surreal and cartoonish way. While Hammer and Schneemann generally eschew narrative and explore explicit female and lesbian sexuality through formal erotics, Akerman emphasizes her heroines' relationships to sex, women,

men, and domestic space in narratives that frequently employ real time to underscore the duration involved in women's enduring conventional domestic, sexual, and familial arrangements. Dunye also found inspiration in Charles Burnett's *Killer of Sheep* (1977), Jean-Luc Godard's *Masculin-Feminin* (1966), Jim McBride's *David Holzman's Diary* (1967), and Michelle Citron's *Daughter Rite* (1979).[6] These films all combine elements of documentary and fictional aesthetics to effect critical, politically inflected commentary through narrative.

In her university classrooms, Dunye read theory, especially feminist theory, and this experience, although important to her, led her to visual media as an alternative form of expression. As she remarks, "When I was exploring feminism, it was a bunch of *books* that made you a feminist. I like work that is not just talking about issues but is doing something with the form to push the issues. That's why I make media, to push it one step further."[7] Dunye's "one step further" positions media as a form that not only talks but does, and is therefore *activist* in some sense. Like the filmmakers of the Underground, Dunye is enamored of and appropriates elements from popular culture, rather than constituting her work in opposition to it. Her work takes from the 1970s family sitcom its comedy, droll parodic sensibility, family-oriented content, and mass cultural reach. Dunye locates her exploration of alternative sexualities and African American subcultures within videos and films that blend the rhetoric and reach of the television sitcom with experimental and documentary film techniques. For her, the activism of which media are capable involves access, not only to mass outlets like television, but also in relation to content. In other words, she experiments with accessible form.

In this sense, Dunye's work inclines to narrative. When asked by T. Haslett about the tendency of white feminist avant-garde filmmakers such as Barbara Hammer "to do away with conventional narrative structure altogether," Dunye responded: "My challenge is to say that that stuff is important [what her work documents] and more people need to see it. How do more people get to see something? You know, put a little narrative in there and people do and use humor. So my trick is to actually try to figure out that balance."[8]

Dunye's theoretically informed use of narrative draws from a tradition of African American engagement with theory articulated by Barbara Christian in her seminal 1987 essay, "The Race for Theory." Christian noted that this tradition mobilized theory in an active sense, as a verb ("theorizing") rather than a noun, and frequently articulated it within narrative forms "since dynamic rather than fixed ideas seem more to our liking." Adapting Christian's ideas to an analysis of black women filmmakers, Judylyn Ryan observes these filmmakers' tendency to theorize within experimental cinematic narrative.[9] Dunye, therefore, in pushing theory "one step further" to accessible form, works within an African American synthetic tradition that blends storytelling and theorizing in a range of different media, from prose to poetry to cinema.

Further, Dunye sees her relationship to theory as autobiographical, that is, as a material consequence of the historical moment and her specific position within it: "I am from the academy. Most of us have received some sort of academic training and know what are hot issues in popular culture: identity politics, multiculturalism, issues dealing with race, sex, class. My life story as an individual . . . is all about that. I am my own text. So I talk about myself, and that becomes interesting. If I'm being honest, I'm being theoretical."[10] Dunye's relationship to her work about herself and her life is mediated by academic training, by theoretical frameworks concerning identity that make her a "hot" topic. Her adjective evokes "hot" in the McLuhan sense "of being well filled with data," as well as that of being timely, of the moment, and also concerned with sexuality.[11] Cheryl is a text wherein Dunye reads, or better sees, or better makes theory in the form of autobiographical film. Juhasz observes: "Thus [Dunye] and her generation add to the familiar feminist adage the following twist: the personal is the political is the theoretical."[12]

To do something with form to push the issues, as Dunye might put it, she trains the camera on herself, her community, her everyday activities, her work, and her emotional and sexual relationships, foci that variously mark not only the work of Hammer and Schneemann, but that also go back to Maya Deren and Stan Brakhage. Yet unlike Brakhage and Deren's oppositional explorations of their own idiosyncratic visions (in the mode of the romantic artist) and Schneemann and Hammer's nonnarrative explorations of women's and lesbian sexuality, Dunye conceives of her project as making her life and her community accessible and familiar in what could be seen as an ongoing experimental sitcom of black lesbian life. The activist theoretical project of the Dunyementary began with a phone call to an old high school friend.

Projecting the "I" of the Other: *Janine*

In *Janine*, for example, I tell the tale of my relationship with a white girl in high school—"she seemed so perfect and I just seemed so imperfect." Rather than continuing to internalize Janine's effects, I put her in my video.—Cheryl Dunye

The first Dunyementary came into being by way of what Dunye called "a big light bulb" moment late one night as she was attempting to make a documentary to address the question, "Why are there so few African American woman artists?" Viewing the pictures of such artists that she had taped to the wall for inspiration, what came to her mind instead was a recent conversation she had had with Janine, a white girl she had had a crush on in her Catholic high school. Dunye then decided "to sit down and rip the pictures off the wall and sit in front of the camera and tell the story that was burning inside of me. I wanted to get out all these issues . . . not just the crush, but that she was a white woman and came from a different class background. . . . It was two takes. It started coming out like sweat."[13] To make her film, Dunye took her own pictures and family photos and put them on the wall in place of those of the artists who preceded her.

The resulting ten-minute film, *Janine*, begins with a tight close-up of two candles and of Cheryl, who is nude but whose body is obscured by the framing and lights. The film returns to these candles several times, as Cheryl blows one out, then the other, and in the end blows both out as if they were birthday candles. But the pith of the film consists of Cheryl's monologue, her confession, her testimony about her relationship with Janine, illustrated by shots of Dunye sitting directly addressing the camera or in voice-off as we see footage of her family and school photos and explanatory or emphatic intertitles.[14] Cheryl met Janine when they played basketball together on the school team. Janine was from the "right" side of town (as the film says), and, as we see from a photo of her, was blonde, blue-eyed—"the epitome of whiteness." Cheryl wanted to get into her circle, "into her game," and wanted to be more like her. Reflecting on the relationship, Cheryl states: "I wanted to be more white." A simple but telling anecdote—Janine chastising Cheryl for not using shampoo correctly—captures Janine's role in the relationship, a role which Cheryl accepted at the time, but then realized was a misrecognition in which she herself participated, and which she documented in the video.

Cheryl recounts how her identification *with* Janine became a desire *for* her as she came to understand that she was lesbian. The narration of her coming out in the video is framed specifically as her coming out to Janine.

Janine initially feigns approval, then admits to Cheryl that she was "terrified and upset" by this news. She has her mother call Cheryl and offer her money so that she can go to a doctor to talk about her problems. An intertitle reads: "about MY PROBLEMS!!!!" Needless to say, that event marks the end of their relationship.

Ten years later, in the conversation that prompted the film, Cheryl calls Janine, who can talk only about the past and how much fun they had in high school. Cheryl's memories of the past are quite different—high school was not fun for her—and Janine's banality and conservatism prompt her to find "a quick way out of the conversation." The film ends with Cheryl saying, "That's about it" over a picture of her in her high school cap and gown. The photo superimposes two moments represented in the film, Cheryl's high school graduation and her graduation from the difficult issues raised by her relationship with Janine, issues she resolves in making the video, *Janine*. But the photo also functions in another way. Its implicit superimposition of the two graduations referenced in the video mimics the extratextual superimposition that generated the film itself: Dunye's placing of her own photos over those of earlier women artists. Dunye's cathartic narration, both in her video and in interviews recounting how the video came to be, links her resolution of her relationship to Janine with her assuming a place on the wall of artistic achievement—the two acts are one and the same. Together they represent her graduation, her "moment of artistic vocation."[15]

In one of the first articles written on cinematic autobiography, "Autobiography in Avant-Garde Film," P. Adams Sitney argued for the fundamental reflexivity of this genre, one that customarily aligns the filmmaking process (shooting, editing) with the filmmaker's life process. He observed that, as with literary autobiography, avant-garde autobiographical film frequently privileges the moment that the autobiographer decides to become a filmmaker, "the moment of artistic vocation." Several things are notable about *Janine's* representation of this moment. First, although the video records—indeed enacts—this moment, it does not register it as such. The reflexivity of the moment does not arise within the text itself but from the context from which it derives, one in which the psychic, aesthetic, and historical effects of racism are registered, and in print media interviews Dunye has given. Thus the meaning of the Dunyementary does not end with Cheryl's life or the text itself, but exists within an extensive referential field generated in part by Dunye's name or signature throughout various media. These interviews supplement the text, provide a backstory in the form of a historical question—why are there so few African American women artists? Thus Dunye's textual and extra-textual references to superimpositions or a palimpsestic structure pointedly inverts the latter's conventional psychoanalytic use. Here it is the materiality of historical absence rather than the family romance that serves as Cheryl's and the video's generative "screen memory."

Second, Dunye's description of her moment of inspiration and her implementation of it in the making of the video actively confounds the usual separation maintained between inspiration (the light bulb, candles) and perspiration, evoking images of the body, labor, and sweat. Her monologue was "two takes. It started coming out like sweat." In equating aesthetic inspiration with sweat, Dunye affiliates artistic production with the body and with acts that induce sweat—sex and labor—the customarily repressed affiliations that run all through the Dunyementaries.

In addition, the referential field of Dunye's imagination far exceeds the textual reflexivity described by Sitney or the historical context she alludes to in her anecdote concerning the video's production. Dunye's pinning the images of African American women artists on the wall implicitly references a cultural field that not only includes white women's searches for artistic forbears (that typically did not include women of color), but also Sal's Wall of Fame in Spike Lee's 1989 film, *Do the Right Thing*.[16] Sal only has Italian American celebrities (actors, writers, and politicians) on his wall, although his customers are almost exclusively African American. His refusal to integrate the wall leads to the riot that destroys his pizzeria, at the culmination of which a character pins the image of Malcolm X and Martin Luther King to the wall. The wall that gives rise to Dunye's video reminds us of a fundamental absence that has structured white feminists' and African American men's cultural engagements with inequality; they have both tended to "forget" women of color. Dunye superimposes herself, positions herself within this historical, representational absence, finding herself within it.

Finally, her inspiration comes not only from an aesthetic tradition she has put up on her wall, but also from a contingent, seemingly trivial event, a chance phone call with a high school classmate whom she once identified with and desired. Where she once looked up to Janine, the video records her discovery years later about how misguided she was, and how her admiration was shaped by her own projections. Fittingly, she names her first video projection for its reconfigured object, a white privileged teenage friend who first made Cheryl feel her difference and in so doing, later helped her to realize it (in all senses of the word).

Self as Genre: The Dunyementary

After having made *Janine*, Dunye labeled each of her films a "Dunyementary." In fashioning a pun from her name, one that blurred the subject and object of her autobiographical films, she designated the genre in which she was working and labeled her aesthetic process and product. The Dunyementary animates and textualizes several convergences or crossovers: between the singularity of the proper name and the textual community of genre, and between autobiography and documentary, life and art, biology and biography. The Dunyementaries thereby activate and popularize a strategy that Jacques Derrida has called "the signature effect." In his view, the writer's proper name discursively aligns, transects two bodies—"the corpus and the body," "the work and the life"—forming a borderline both internal and external to the text.[17] Derrida sees the signature effect as operating throughout these two bodies according to a rhetorical figure wherein one substitutes a proper name for a common noun or vice-versa. He listens for the common nouns that can be heard in an author's name (the "sponge" in "Ponge," for example) and uses them to read that author's work for its distinctive poetics. That is, the proper name of the author "moves from designating a particular individual to become the key to a . . . theory of rhetorical invention."[18]

While Derrida sees the signature as an effect of language, a phenomenon that sounds through and out of literary or philosophical writings regardless of an author's intention or control, Dunye redoubles this effect, actively *naming* her own key. In signing, she theorizes her process of cinematic invention (using form to push the issues) and makes her proper name not only common but generic. In interviews, she has signaled her auteurism precisely in relation to genre and her signature, saying, "I like to experiment with genre . . . to do remakes of genres that have a relationship to my own media history . . . to put my twist on it, *sign my name on it.*"[19] One such generic twist is that the individual Dunyementaries are at once singular and exemplary of a larger category, just as their focus on Dunye's life or bios is also a focus on community or an ethnos.[20] This connection between the self-referential and the auto-ethnographic becomes more and more pronounced and explicit as the Dunyementaries progress. They move from the developmental and racialized misrecognition in *Janine* to a consideration of aesthetic, self, and couple production within the community in *She Don't Fade* to the auto-ethnography of *The Potluck and the Passion.*

Inspiration and Perspiration: *She Don't Fade*

In *Janine*, Dunye employed the intimate first-person address and structure of the diary film, naming it not for herself, but for the high school friend who first enabled her own self-misrecognition. She thereby documents the interpersonal dynamic of internalized racism, discovering and then excising the Janine inside herself. She converts a psychic projection to a literal and an aesthetic one. Her second tape, *She Don't Fade*, maintains an intimate tone but turns to social groups formed around the crucial issues of love and sexuality and profession and labor. The video's title simultaneously evokes a film technique ("fade") and a woman who does not vanish or disappear. Using a "film within a film" structure, *She Don't Fade* alternates between a fictional narrative and ongoing commentary and narration by the crew making that narrative. Drawing from the techniques of the French New Wave, particularly Godardian uses of direct address, multiple diegesis, and multiple narrators, Dunye's ensemble cast is drawn from the production crew involved in making the tape. These techniques of baring the devices conventionally used to foreground the mechanics of representation and to underscore the interpermeability of truth and fiction both refer to and extend its applications by the French New Wave. *She Don't Fade* juxtaposes what is "real" and what is "represented" at the same time that it invites spectators to look behind the scenes of the video's production and at the lesbian community that it depicts, thereby documenting two things usually kept off screen—labor and lesbian sexuality.[21] Rather than using these techniques to distance the audience and defamiliarize the narrative, Dunye employs them to make the lesbian community accessible and familiar, to erase or attenuate the distinction between insider spectators (members of that community) and outsiders (nonlesbian viewers). She thereby cultivates our identity with the production endeavor and the community rather than with any narrative arc or individual character.

This approach is signaled from the outset. "Zoie" walks on screen, takes a seat in front of a white backdrop, looks directly at the camera, and introduces herself as a "dyke yenta"; she proceeds to give us the "lowdown" on what will happen "before it does." To guide us through the "wild world of lesbianism" depicted in the video, she lays out all the crucial elements of the plot that follows: we will be watching the exploits of a woman who is "confused," who takes up with one woman and then meets another, a "somewhat familiar story" that will get "down and dirty." She then gets up and walks off camera, as we hear her interact with someone else in voice off, saying, "Great. I'm satisfied." From the first, then, the importance of the plot of *She Don't Fade* is dispensed with in favor of its narration. Since we already know what will happen, what remains is to see how it will be recounted. The fact that our first narrator identifies herself as a dyke yenta locates the narration in the mode of gossip, in other words, as insider information that is being directly shared with a consequently insider audience. The studio framing and direct address of this opening shot are repeated throughout the tape with its two other narrators, Cheryl and Paula, who appear singly or together. These narrational segments alternate with narrative action.

The subsequent title sequence initiates this alternation, depicting, in brief shots, a woman (Dunye) setting up a vending table on the street, interacting with customers, and folding up shop, in between which we see shots of the video's title and director. We then cut to Cheryl, sitting in the chair Zoie occupied, who tells us: "I'm Cheryl and in this video, I play Shae Clarke. Shae is twenty-nine years old, she broke up with her lover of three years about a year ago and she just started a vending business." Then, in the space of a sentence, Cheryl shifts from introducing her character to becoming her, slipping from third person to first as she tells us that her business "got me into myself." She finishes by blurring the issues of love and work; she tells us that going out with women has been "my livelihood" and she is now going to approach dating differently. An intertitle appears, reading: "Shae's new approach."

Shae's new approach, which we see in the next sequence, consists of filming women as they are walking down the street and following them. As the camera captures one such woman, we hear Cheryl/Shae's voice calling out to her: "Hi. I'm working on this video about women and stuff [close-up of the woman]. You seem like you might have the look for this video and I was wondering if I could interview you." Obviously annoyed and uncomfortable, the woman says, "No, I'm sorry." This sequence blurs the identities of Dunye, the filmmaker, and Shae Clarke, the street vendor, as well as the pursuits of filmmaking/interviewing and dating.

We then cut back to Cheryl/Shae in the studio, facing the camera; she tells us about her friend Paula who has been her good friend since she came out and "who's here." She calls out to Paula to come on camera and we hear Paula refusing, saying, "No, I don't want to say anything." Immediately afterward, we cut to Paula who is in the chair and quips, "I'm Paula and in this film I play, guess who . . . Paula." She tells us that, "I'm not an actress" and that she "works on the camera, lighting, and sound," which is much "easier" than being in front of the camera. Solicited to straddle crew and cast, she plays Shae's confidant, even as her production tasks are also highlighted throughout the tape.

Together, these different narrator/characters register the multiple diegesis that the video mobilizes: the metanarrative story space invoked by Zoie's gossip; the production story space concerning the making of the film and its crew; and the story space of the narrative itself, the latter including both exterior action and interior fantasy sequences. Thus Dunye mobilizes distinct story spaces of narration, creative labor, and romantic narrative to align the endeavors of making love, making community, and making a film. What ties all these spaces and endeavors together is Dunye, in her interrelated roles as director, actor, and black lesbian artist, who wittily renders her life, loves, and work as part of a "forgotten" community. At the same time, she interweaves fictional and purportedly documentary footage ("Hi, I'm Cheryl and in this video, I play Shae Clarke"), such that as she represents a "forgotten" community, she foregrounds the fiction at work (and the work of fiction). Dunye "casts [her] own history as an allegory for a community or culture that cannot be essentialized," even as she inscribes this allegory in her self-portrait of the artist she is becoming.[22]

We can see this dynamic, and the humor Dunye evokes from it, in *She Don't Fade*'s first sex scene. It begins with Shae and Margo, sitting on a bed, looking at a book together. They begin to kiss; they get naked; they continue to kiss and caress each other, in the middle of which, Shae/Cheryl says, "You all don't have to get so quiet." The crew, offscreen, laughs and starts to instruct "Cheryl" and "Wanda" on how to effectively act out Shae and Margo's sex act. The moment rendered is incredibly awkward, certainly funny rather than erotic. In this explicit staging of sex for the camera, Cheryl, letting us watch her play Shae, also establishes her self-reflexive persona. Her identity as actor and filmmaker appear, or surface, in the body of and in the place of her character and subject—the life, loves, and professional labors of a black lesbian. This is not quite autobiography, not quite documentary, not quite fiction, but some approximation of all three. These approximations allow the audience to come close, to get near a sense of the community, the identity of which is represented without either being defined or reified.

Throughout the video, Dunye cultivates this effect by layering, doubling, and confusing the roles she is playing (Cheryl/Shae), the work she is doing (street-vending/filmmaking), and the desires she is pursuing (women/work). Thus Shae's central narrative conflict of being "torn between two lovers" is multiply reiterated in *Fade*'s dual diegetic structure (direct address sequences alternating with narrative action sequences) and in the intertwined communities (and narratives) of the production staff and the cast. At one point, Dunye faces the camera and actually sings two full verses of the song "Torn between Two Lovers." Gay or straight, we are all familiar with this song—and we all know it is an awful song. Building on this familiarity, Dunye structures the moment as a particularly funny and inclusive in-joke, embellishing it by singing the song badly and off-key.

In these moments and in the overall structure of the video, Dunye humorously maps the problem of defining what is truth and what is fiction onto a related question that underpins her rendering of a lifestyle and community predicated on alternative erotic choices. In the act of representing her life and community, she asks: what is work and what is desire? Fittingly, everything comes together in the party scene that ends the film, which is introduced by the intertitle: "Guess who Shae meets." Nikki, a woman Shae saw briefly on a bridge and has not been able to get out of her mind, shows up at a party attended by Zoie, Paula, and Shae, among others. Paula knows who she is (as crew she would; as character, her knowledge is inexplicable) and winks at us as she goes to find Shae. She urges Shae to go talk to Nikki, but to "be cool." The two talk briefly and then decide to go "someplace quiet" as Zoie picks up a mike lying on a chair, walks up to the camera, and says, "So, seriously, sisters, the rest is history . . . or, sorry, herstory."

Genre: Herstory, Mystory, Dunyementary

The Dunyementaries raise the question: what does it mean to turn oneself into a genre by means of one's signature? In order to answer that question, I first consider Dunye's self-classification in relation to two other historiographic moments, one of which *She Don't Fade* explicitly references, wherein the creation or invention of a specialized genre intervenes in conventions of the historical: *herstory* and *mystory*. Puns and neologisms, the very sounding of which opened up new areas and methods of research, generated both of these moments. "Herstory" articulated a feminist critique of history predicated on what had been left out or excluded from *his*tory. The alternative it proposed was based on this exclusion and so operated as a kind of supplement. In the famous phrase "the personal is political," the herstoriographical intervention opened up an entire realm—that of women's space, of the private, the domestic, the reproductive and the sexual—to historical consideration, a realm much in evidence, in *She Don't Fade*.

Citing this feminist intervention, as well as the dissolution of grand metanarratives and the rise of situated knowledges, Greg Ulmer proposed *mystoriography*, a generic invention marked by the convergence of "history, politics, language, thought and technology."[23] Mystory insists on knowledge conditioned by creativity, an analysis predicated on pattern and pun exemplified by the neologism itself. In its allusion to the *my* that is definitive of autobiography and the *mys* of mystery, *mystory* starts with the individual but adds a social project, an inquiry into the autobiographer "as narrated by the social body."[24] Mystory invents a genre or mode of academic writing that is not fully invested in referential analytics as the basis for knowledge. It is a practice of using anecdotes, conjecture, plots, and hermeneutics to imagine and to image the complexity of what is intelligible, theoretical, and conventionally articulated in essay, argument, and word. It is the "one step further" of which Dunye speaks, the move from "talking about the issues to doing something with the form to push the issues." In her articulation of the Dunyementary—both the films themselves and her naming of them—Dunye demonstrates some of the insights of herstory and mystory as she fashions herself both as text and genre and as experiment in moving pictures. In fact, she sees her work in mystorical terms, observing that it "fits in with certain academic discourse. My work is like a sample tape for it."[25] Yet, while herstory and mystory intervene in generic conventions of academic research, the Dunyementary rearticulates the genre of nonfiction film. Writing her signature, her patronym over the *doc* in *documentary*, Dunye mobilizes pun and neologism to body, to name the example and proof that the word *documentary* etymologically expresses (Latin *documentum*—example or proof, from *docere*, to teach). In the echo of *documentary* heard in *Dunyementary*, the problematic objectivity of nonfiction films (a source of much theorization and debate) is sounded and rewritten as a signature effect. In her signing, Dunye mobilizes a subjective authority in her films at the same time that she takes herself and her community up as a phenomenon to be (fictitiously) objectified, generalized, and observed. In *The Potluck and the Passion*, she makes an autoethnographic film that "takes on" the theoretical pretensions and assertions of ethnography to explore lesbian interracial romance and the elusive contours of any community.

The Potluck and the Passion:
Realizing, not Idealizing, Community

The Dunyementaries feature recurring characters, in the mode of a sit-com, and Dunye is the one who runs through them all, although her characters have different names (for example, Shae in *She Don't Fade*). Yet in addition to manifesting elements of plot progression, her "character arc" also articulates nonnarrative meditations on genre, on Dunye's own development as an artist, and on issues concerning community and representation that greatly exceed plot concerns. In the final Dunyementary I will discuss, *The Potluck and the Passion*, the plot takes up a year or so after *She Don't Fade* left off, opening with a shot of Nikki and Cheryl, whose coupling resolved the earlier video. Cheryl now plays a character called Linda, and she and Nikki are hosting a potluck dinner to celebrate their first year anniversary together. The potluck will bring together their different sets of friends to "meet and eat." The motif of the communally produced dinner aligns community making with lesbian lovemaking, here around Dunye's naughty double entendre and the two kinds of eating to which it refers.

Dunye's use of wordplay runs all through the tape, notably in the intertitles that mark the progression of the narrative: "6:20 p.m. Homo-place"; "7:15 p.m. Failing the chitlin test"; "8:07 p.m. A Pot can't call a Kettle Black." She sounds the "homo" in *home* and the "black" in an everyday aphorism, also referencing the test that determines who is really black. In aligning lesbian erotics with questions of race, she frames the tape's concern with the difficulty of discerning the difference between interracial lesbian desire and racialized fetishism. This concern, which will also animate *The Watermelon Woman*, signals Dunye's engagement with an issue much in evidence in films by African American men around this time, from Marlon Riggs's 1989 *Tongues Untied* to Spike Lee's 1991 *Jungle Fever*.[26]

The first part of the video, dealing with the party preparation, focuses on the couple's gay friend Robert advising Nikki on her clothing choices and housecleaning. Once the party begins, very little screen time is devoted to Linda and Nikki, but rather the story revolves around several people whose direct address to the camera punctuates footage of the dinner and of one couple (Lisa and Kendra) trying to make it to the dinner. The actors playing Tracy, an African American graduate student studying the nineteenth-century Irish novel, and Megan, a white woman who considers herself an expert on the third world, Ethiopia, and all things African American as well, introduce themselves and their characters. Although Tracy and Megan have come to the party together, we quickly understand from their testimonies to the camera that they each have a very different understanding of what their relationship means. Megan is controlling and possessive, while Tracy, increasingly annoyed at Megan and her attitude, finds that she is very interested in another guest, Evelyn, who is also African American. The couple that came to the party together is not the couple that leaves together.

Dunye makes use of the multiple passions (intellectual, culinary, sexual) of the various characters to bring them together and split them apart, while the dynamics of food sharing hilariously belie any fantasy of lesbians as a homogeneous community. At the potluck, vegans (no meat, no dairy) sit elbow to elbow with enthusiastic carnivores. Someone has brought ambrosia, a retro-style salad featuring marshmallows, and it sits on the table next to southern fried chicken and a tofu dish. Everyone's food aversions are raised by some item on this table. Evelyn and Tracy bond over the spicy chicken dish that Evelyn brought, which she confesses she has "toned down" for the party. Tracy tells Evelyn that she would like her to make the chicken dish for her and the two exchange phone numbers. The film ends with Megan exiting the party in a huff after Tracy refuses to leave with her. She literally runs into Kendra and Lisa, knocking over the dish they brought as they arrive, very, very late to the potluck.

Underlying this entire video is the coy double entendre of this particular group getting together to meet and eat. Yet, as the title of the piece, *The Potluck and the Passion*, suggests, Dunye mobilizes this sexual innuendo to particular purpose. Each installation of the Dunyementaries also mimics and alters a "host" genre. While *Janine* emulates the diary film, and *She Don't Fade* the self-reflexivity of the French New Wave, *The Potluck and the Passion* parodies the conventions of participant-observer ethnography in its use of the autoethnographic mode that Dunye developed throughout the Dunyementaries. The title of the video signals this intention, as it playfully invokes and blends together a classic text of structural anthropology (Claude Lévi-Strauss's 1964 *The Raw and the Cooked*) and concept (potlatch) derived from the field.

In *The Raw and the Cooked*, Lévi-Strauss asserted that just as the linguist can derive from a limited number of sentences, the grammar of a language, so "the anthropologist should be able to produce an account of" a culture from a limited set of its practices.[27] As the title of this work indicates, Lévi-Strauss explored the dependency of prevalent cultural structures and myths on fundamental binary oppositions (for example, raw/cooked, male/female). If feminism has fully explored the operation of the binary male/female, the stark oppositions of gender cannot fully apprehend same-sex desire and the cultures articulated around that desire.

While Dunye's title uses alliteration (*potluck* and *passion*) to parody the structure of a binary opposition, it also wittily sounds the homophonic relation between *potluck* and the anthropological concept of *potlatch*, the latter, referring to ceremonies used to display wealth and status, much studied and written about in contemporaneous academic scholarship. In the echo of *potlatch* we hear *potluck*, as Dunye's wordplay names an everyday familiar dinner practice and puts it in the place of an arcane academic concept. While her video depicts women who share sexual preference and practices, she cannily throws food culture into the mix, taboos on what can and cannot be eaten wreaking havoc with the contours of any stable grouping based on sexuality.

Through these Dunyementaries, Dunye has not yet expressed directly her vocation as a filmmaker. After playing Linda in *The Potluck and the Passion*, she appears as Cheryl in both *Greetings from Africa* and *The Watermelon Woman*. Each film features direct address and narration, either by Dunye and other characters (*She Don't Fade* and *Potluck*) or by Dunye alone (*Greetings* and *The Watermelon Woman*). Intertitles, voiceover, stills with or without voiceover, and direct address punctuate the dramatic action, filmed in a docu-narrative style wherein characters in the narrative resolve a dramatic scene by turning and speaking directly to the audience. These videos and films narrate the Cheryl characters' desire for work, for self-expression, but most often for sexual connection. Significantly however, sexuality and sexual desire are never depicted as distinct or separate from work and aesthetic self-expression. The Dunyementaries investigate their filmmaker documenting herself as constructed— and, further, constructed as becoming a member of a profession and becoming an identity that does not yet exist. What she becomes is revealed in the last of the series, *The Watermelon Woman*, a film already becoming something other than a Dunyementary as its maker moves into industry feature production. Early in this film, Dunye faces the camera and says she's *working on* becoming a filmmaker. She has found a subject for her film project, an obscure African American actress credited only as "the watermelon woman" in old Hollywood films, and the subsequent film recounts her search for this woman even as it covers, in the manner of the earlier Dunyementaries, Dunye's friendships and her love life. In

The Watermelon Woman, Dunye makes the film she set out to make in 1990 about African American women artists, a film that both invents an artistic predecessor with whom she can identify and also "finds" Cheryl herself as the artist that she seeks. As Dunye identifies herself as a black lesbian filmmaker, this last Dunyementary comes to an end and its maker moves on, crossing over to HBO and studio production.

In this very trajectory, the Dunyementary's affinity with and clever manipulation of the popular (for example, 1970s sitcoms) generates a certain cultural mobility. Writing the academic script of such experiments, Ulmer notes that they "appropriate the stereotypes and conventions of available genres as well as the materials of particular works as part of a didactic invention. What remains to be developed is a genre capable of sampling at once the archives of the family, the school, and popular culture. This genre, in other words, is designed to facilitate the postmodernist process of 'crossover,' joining areas of culture that until now have been held apart as if autonomous."[28]

The genre Dunyementary, 1990–96, answers this call to generic invention. Through these films, Dunye's signature genre performs a proleptic auteurism as a mode of invention and intervention. First the genre anticipates its maker's identity. Second, the Dunyementaries effectively join "areas of culture that had been held apart as if autonomous" as the destination of Dunye's signature.

Signature and Auteur

The problem of the author is a problem of the inside and outside of the text, how it will be framed and interpreted in relation to its maker, writer, and creator. Traditionally, the frameworks thereby mobilized, such as biography, psychology, and the unconscious, limit the work according to a humanist logic incommensurate with the operations of textuality and have been repeatedly critiqued on that basis. Yet again and again, the author who has died but who will not go away persists in the necessary signing of texts, in the author's proper name that lives on after its possessor's decease, and in the scholarship that can neither resolve nor relinquish the critically suspect category of the author.

Among other instantiations, *The Watermelon Woman*, the ultimate Dunyementary, activated Cheryl Dunye's signature in places that extended beyond its semantics—most notably in the U.S. Congress and national newspapers in the furor over the film's NEA funding. In 1995,

Dunye received a $31,500 NEA grant through Women Make Movies, the largest distributor of films made by women in the United States. In the summer of 1996, Michigan Republican Peter Hoeskra, chairman of a subcommittee overseeing the NEA, requested a copy of *The Watermelon Woman*, having been alerted to a film review that mentioned that it contained "the hottest dyke sex scene on celluloid." After viewing the tape, the Congressman "went ballistic" and demanded an amendment to the NEA's 1997 budget that would deduct the amount of Dunye's grant from it. Although he later dropped this request (his Republican colleagues assured him they could get rid of the NEA altogether), he resumed his attack in January of the following year based on his investigation of the Women Make Movies catalogue and fourteen films whose descriptions caught his eye. The descriptions alone led him to accuse the NEA of funding child pornography in addition to obscene material (Su Friedrich's *Hide and Seek*, a coming-of-age narrative about adolescent girls, is an example of the films included on the list).

In the media frenzy that followed, Dunye's film, her name, and Women Make Movies were cited in almost every article. Most people would not have seen the film, but Cheryl Dunye was now widely known, from Congress to CNN and beyond, as a black lesbian filmmaker. This is the signature effect that exceeds the text itself. Although her supporters and detractors repeatedly invoked her in this way, it is important to note that she had said it, had signed it first. Thus I will end this essay with her words. At the end of *The Watermelon Woman*, she faces the camera for the last time and says: "What I understand is that *I'm going to be the one* who says I am a black lesbian filmmaker who's just beginning, but I am going to say a lot more and have a lot more work to do."

Filmography

Janine, 1990 (10 min.): sd., col.; video
She Don't Fade, 1991 (24 min.): sd., b&w; video
Vanilla Sex, 1992 (4 min.): sd., b&w; video
The Potluck and the Passion, 1993 (30 min.): sd., col.; video
An Untitled Portrait, 1993 (3 min.): sd., b&w, col.; video
Greetings from Africa, 1994 (8 min.): sd., col.; 16mm
The Watermelon Woman, 1996 (90 min.): sd., col.; 16mm
Stranger Inside, 2000 (94 min.): sd., col.; 35mm
My Baby's Daddy, 2004 (86 min.): sd., col.; 35mm

Notes

I thank my wonderful writing group—Wendy Belcher, Mary Bush, Ellen Kraut Hasegawa, Harryette Mullen, and Alice Wexler—and, always, Chon Noriega, for reading this essay and offering me helpful suggestions on revising it.

1   The Underground, a very public moment in the history of American avant-garde film that Parker Tyler notes began in 1959 and ended in the late 1960s, was characterized by, among other things, its ambivalent fascination with American pop culture and its frequent appropriation of recognizable images from industry cinema, advertising, and other entertainment media. See Tyler, *Underground Film*, v, and Suárez, *Bike Boys, Drag Queens, and Superstars*, 54.

2   Cook, "The Point of Self-Expression in Avant-Garde Film," 272–74.

3   Dunye, "Building Subjects," 4.

4   Washington, "Takes on Hollywood's Invisible Color Lines," 1, and Haslett, "Interview with Cheryl Dunye," 9.

5   See Cheryl Dunye's vita at *CherylDunye.com*.

6   Dunye identifies these influences in an excellent interview she did with Juhasz in her invaluable collection *Women of Vision*, 299–300.

7   Ibid., 300.

8   Haslett, "Interview with Cheryl Dunye," 7.

9   Ryan, "Outing the Black Feminist Filmmaker in Julie Dash's *Illusions*," 1323.

10   Juhasz, *Women of Vision*, 298.

11   McLuhan, *Understanding Media*, 22.

12   Juhasz, *Women of Vision*, 292.

13   Ibid., 298.

14   Julia Lesage cites *Janine* as an example of one specific type of feminist experimental autobiographical video in which the verbal narration is primary and the images serve to illustrate that narration ("Women's Fragmented Consciousness in Feminist Experimental Autobiographical Video," 312, 335).

15   Sitney, "Autobiography in Avant-Garde Film," 232.

16   Thanks to Harryette Mullen for mentioning the reference to Spike Lee's Wall of Fame.

17   Derrida, *The Ear of the Other*, 5–6.

18   Ulmer, "Mystory," 257.

19   Juhasz, *Women of Vision*, 294, emphasis mine.

20   See Lionnet, "Autoethnography," and Russell's "Autoethnography." Russell observes: "Autobiography becomes ethnographic at the point where the film- or videomaker understands his or her personal history to be implicated in larger social formations and historical processes. Identity is no longer a transcendental or essential self that is revealed, but a 'staging of subjectivity'" (276).

21 In my book *American Domesticity*, I consider the multiple purposes that the suppression of images of labor serves.

22 Russell, "Autoethnography," 278.

23 Ulmer, *Teletheory*, 83.

24 Ibid., 89.

25 Juhasz, *Women of Vision*, 298.

26 Thanks to Carole-Anne Tyler for mentioning Marlon Riggs's exploration of his own racialized fetishism in *Tongues Untied*.

27 Culler, *Structuralist Poetics*, 41.

28 Ulmer, *Teletheory*, 14.

SCOTT MACDONALD

Conclusion:

Women's Experimental Cinema

Some Pedagogical Challenges

□

The Nitty-Gritty of Film Exhibition

For those of us who have taught what is variously called "avant-garde film," "alternative cinema," "underground film," and "experimental film" (the proliferation of monikers is a function of the size and diversity of this field), the arrival of a new collection of scholarly discussions of women's contributions to this history is fraught with paradox. Because academics, including academics who teach and write about film, have been irresponsible about insuring the longevity of the full spectrum of film history, an increased awareness of contributions by women filmmakers could be achieved just as much of the field itself vanishes! The reason? Across North America, college and university audiovisual offices and faculties have convinced themselves and each other that the arrival of new video and digital technologies has rendered film itself—and in particular, 16mm film, which has been the standard academic gauge for half a century—obsolete. Had the evolution of film studies taken a different route, we might not need to begin by discussing technical matters, but given the realities of our current moment, there is no sensible option—assuming, of course, that the reader is interested in the contributions of women to a living art form. The problem is that if you want to experience the major contributions to alternative cinema by women (and men), 16mm exhibition remains not just the best, but in most cases, the only option and familiarity with it is essential. (My apologies in advance to those for whom the following information is already second nature.)

Of course, working with film in an academic context has always posed challenges of one kind or another, and fortunately, the challenges of the moment, while grave, are hardly insurmountable. Indeed, were more academics willing to confront these challenges, by committing to the remarkable achievements and the inimitable pedagogical value of alternative cinema, there is every reason to think that this field could continue to invigorate college classrooms, scholarly writing, and thinking about cinema for generations to come. The first challenge for a teacher interested in availing herself of the opportunity offered by alternative film (including the particular films I discuss later in this chapter) is to be sure that she has adequate physical facilities for presenting 16mm films well. The second challenge, at least the final one I will deal with here, is deciding on the particular films to use and learning how to use these films effectively in the classroom. The second part of this essay discusses some films that I have found especially successful in invigorating my classes over the years and in some instances describes ways of helping students come to grips with them.

Insofar as facilities are concerned, there are basically two issues: 16mm projectors and the projection space. Fortunately, most educational institutions still have adequate 16mm projectors, and audiovisual specialists who can run them, or better, who can teach you to run them—though my guess is that your request for 16mm equipment and for assistance may be met with some surprise. Of course, some projectors are better than others. In my experience, the easiest good projectors to work with have been the portable Eikis, which are in relatively wide circulation—though there are other excellent projectors. The quality of the better projectors is a function of the luminous image they provide and their gentleness with film prints. Projector gates must be regularly cleaned with cotton swabs and alcohol or with forced air to be sure the gate is dust-free and will not damage the print or be distracting during the screening.

Ideally, films should be presented in a room especially designed for screenings: that is, a room that can be completely darkened and that has a projection booth. A good many alternative films (including several I discuss later) rely on visual subtleties that can easily get lost if the films are presented with a projector that has inadequate light or in a room with too much ambient light. Part of the pleasure of working with these films is that, like serious writers or painters, their makers are often deeply committed to the particularities of the experiences their work creates. Further, my experience suggests that students take films seriously when it is clear that their instructor does. Indeed, when students sense that their instructor has made special arrangements so that they can see films, and see them well, they are more likely to be open to the unusual, challenging, and often transformative experiences these films can provide. Screening conditions are of particular importance since in most instances, students will see a film—no matter how complex or subtle it is—only once.

The challenge of developing a budget for renting 16mm prints of films can seem formidable, especially because many academic institutions are struggling financially and most popular films are available inexpensively in VHS or on DVD. In other fields—literature or music, for example—the classics are often comparable in price, and even less expensive, than popular favorites. But renting independent films in 16mm remains substantially more expensive than renting or even buying videos or DVDs of more popular, and longer, works (renting *prints* of pop films *is* very expensive, but these days, few teachers rent prints of feature films). Unfortunately, there is no real option here: most alternative films are available only in 16mm; and even in those instances where VHS or DVD versions are available, these versions are often markedly inferior.

How much of a budget is necessary? The leading distributors of alternative film usually charge, roughly, $2 per minute for prints: that is, a ten-minute film might cost $20 or $25, plus shipping; a twenty-minute film, $40 or $50, plus shipping; an hour film, $100 or $125, and so on. A good course on women independents should have a rental budget of at least $2,000. While this can sound like a lot, especially for faculty who are not experienced in raising money within an academic institution, it is easy to overestimate the difficulties. For many years, I taught at Utica College of Syracuse University, a small, private college with no endowment to speak of and many financial problems, and I had a generous budget for film rentals, year after year. Indeed, like most allocations, the money for film rentals for my courses—once it was originally included in the budget— did not need to be rejustified every year but became a regular operating expense in much the same way the (much greater) costs of running laboratories are regular operating expenses in science courses.

There are ways of supplementing classroom rental budgets and simultaneously invigorating film courses and campus life in general. The most obvious is to host accomplished visiting filmmakers. Indeed, for many independent makers campus visits are a financial lifeline (as, of course, are classroom rentals of their films). Generally, there is broad interest in filmmakers of all kinds, and as a result, financial support for campus visits is not all that difficult to find, either in offices that fund student activities, or in offices dedicated to encouraging diversity on campus and to providing opportunities for women. Often, student organizations are happy to support campus visits of filmmakers. Hosting visiting filmmakers does require that the teacher not only raise adequate funding for a visit but work to insure a decent audience for these events. This can be done either through publicity, or, better, by means of advance planning with colleagues so that such events are part of the curriculum of specific courses. The work of many filmmakers is relevant for a variety of classes and fields of study; in addition, bringing several groups together for a public or campuswide film event often creates a healthy academic energy.

What one pays a visiting filmmaker depends not only on the maker's level of accomplishment, but also on the particular circumstances. During the 1990s, I tended to pay any filmmaker who traveled a distance to present work at a campuswide or public event $1,000, plus travel and accommodations (I usually assumed the rentals for the films presented came out of the honorarium—in most cases, filmmakers brought the films with them). For many makers a $1,000 fee seems quite generous, and there are, of course, accomplished film artists who will present work for less. However, since many filmmakers do not have full-time jobs and most struggle to make ends meet, I have always felt embarrassed to ask makers to present films for an amount of money that can hardly make a difference in their lives or in their filmmaking. Of course, some filmmakers require more than $1,000. One noteworthy instance is Trinh T. Minh-ha, who recognized, early on, that her work was relevant to a very wide range of academic disciplines (film studies, anthropology, ethnic studies, women's studies, cultural studies, art history); Trinh has tended to demand a fee that requires a variety of campus groups to collaborate. Of course, such collaboration is often a worthy end in itself, and, I suspect, is a process that Trinh has always meant to instigate.

Finally, should a professor be willing to initiate, develop, and host an ongoing exhibition program, with regular visits by makers, funding may be available from community or state arts councils. In my experience, a first-rate exhibition program is always considered a valuable addition to campus life, and at times, I was not only able to garner campus, community, and state support from New York for presenting films and filmmakers, but also was able to get a reduction in load for the (considerable) labors involved in planning, promoting, and hosting these events. I recognize that my situation may have been unusual, but it is one of the embarrassments of academic film studies that so few institutions have committed to regular, seriously curated exhibition programs in the way that they commit to regular art shows in campus galleries or to regular concert programs. Too often, film programming on campus is left to students, who nearly always follow in the steps of commercial theater chains. An inventive exhibition program is an intellectual nexus for any campus and should be recognized as a form of scholarly activity on the part of the programmer, who must do considerable research in deciding which films might be most valuable to show and must make sure these events are presented in a manner that can maximize their educational value.

The issue of film exhibition is a crucial one, especially given current pressures on the field resulting from the arrival of new media technologies. For all the obvious popularity and ubiquity of the commercial cinema, the serious study of film differs from the study of other art forms in fundamental ways. Those dedicated to serious literature know that even if students do not take college courses in poetry or fiction, a very broad range of literature is available through any bookstore, conveniently and inexpensively. But this is not true of cinema, where only commercial works are easily accessible. If students are to understand the accomplishments and potential of cinema—and, in particular, of the remarkable women who have contributed in major ways to film history—college and university faculty must make a more serious effort to include the full range of filmmaking within campus life, while such inclusion remains possible.

Films/Filmmakers That Can Invigorate Teaching

The following recommendations are based on thirty years of teaching this work, and of talking with others who have worked with the films. The films were selected on the assumption that one of the most valuable things a teacher can do for students is to interrupt and counter their experiences of the commercial media. Each of the particular films I will discuss confronts standard viewing habits and expectations in one or more ways; therefore, teachers must be prepared to deal with the sometimes passionate reactions of students who are generally protective of their training as television watchers and commercial moviegoers. At the same time, each film I have chosen offers a positive alternative to the mass media, and especially to the still-pervasive marketing of women's bodies and marginalization of women's concerns and needs. It is a rare conventional entertainment film that can compete with the films on the following list in generating serious, long-term thinking by students (and their teachers). I have included only films (and several filmmakers) not discussed in the earlier chapters of this book.

No. 4 (Bottoms) (1966) by Yoko Ono

Perhaps the most fundamental training we receive from the mass media involves the rate at which we learn to consume imagery. The fast pace of nearly all editing in commercial cinema and on television models a form of hyperactivity that works in the interests of advertisers: the more we consume and the faster we consume it, the better—for them. By the 1960s, a full-fledged response to the accelerating pace of mass media was under way. Filmmakers were finding ways of slowing down the rate of consumption and creating new cinematic experiences that demanded both careful attention and patience. Two of the major instigators of the tendency toward deceleration were Andy Warhol, whose long, super-slow films of the mid-1960s became legendary, and Yoko Ono, whose conceptual cinema was an aggressive confrontation of conventional mass-media spectatorship.

Ono's considerable accomplishments as an artist continue to be eclipsed by her fame as John Lennon's partner and as a pop musician. However, the recent "Yes: Yoko Ono" show, curated by Alexandra Munroe (with Jon Hendricks), has gone a long way in reminding us how inventive and prolific Ono has been since her arrival in New York as a young composer and performance artist at the end of the 1950s. Ono's achievements as an artist are wide-ranging, but one of her most remarkable accomplishments is the series of films she produced, first as part of the Fluxus movement, and subsequently in collaboration with Lennon. During the five years between 1966 and 1971, Ono was involved in fifteen films, including several features. The earliest of the features, *No. 4 (Bottoms)*, remains a film of considerable power, partly because its original confrontation of moviegoers was so unusual, and also because the film provides one measure of how our assumptions about the body have changed during the past half-century.

During the eighty minutes of *No. 4 (Bottoms)*, viewers see nothing but naked human buttocks, in close-up, framed so that each buttocks fills the

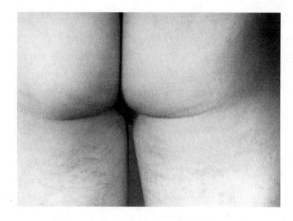

From Yoko Ono's
No. 4. (Bottoms),
1966. Courtesy of
Yoko Ono.

frame and is in continual motion: the buttocks of dozens of volunteers were filmed, one by one, as each performer walked on a treadmill. Each buttocks is onscreen for a single, continuous shot roughly fifteen seconds long: that is, we see approximately four naked, walking butts per minute, for eighty minutes. The sound track provides some variety by documenting various aspects of the production of the film: there are interviews with many who volunteered to appear in the film, and many who decided not to, and instances of media coverage of the production of the film (including comments by Ono). In general, speakers on the sound track voice many of the objections to the project that were voiced in 1966 and that are voiced when the film is shown now.

Few films provide a more aggressive confrontation of the mass media, and the audience it has produced, than *No. 4 (Bottoms)*. The film's relentlessly serial pace causes its eighty minutes to seem much longer, and it takes a courageous teacher to let the film run its full length. Of course, Ono was well aware of how confrontational the film was; in 1988, she explained, "*Film No. 4* mainly supplied a lot of laughs for people all over the world, most of whom never actually saw the film. Just the idea of it gave them a giggle. I found out much later that they were even giggling behind the Iron Curtain. No wonder my artistic friends dropped me. It was a total antithesis to Art per se. But actually *I* was the ultimate snob. I was going 'Up yours!' to the whole world including the avant-garde. It was a great high but also a lonely one."[1]

For contemporary viewers now, and especially for American college students, *No. 4 (Bottoms)* is often infuriating, not merely because of its length and its formal relentlessness, but because the bottoms Ono films are *real* bottoms—hair, pimples, droopiness, and all—*exactly* the kinds of bottoms that so much of contemporary advertising presents as defective. These are buttocks that our training tells us have no right to be represented. Every time I have shown *No. 4 (Bottoms)*, the first hairy male butt creates a virtual detonation in the audience. Whatever humor an earlier generation found in the experience is far rarer now. Students vent their disgust, their aggravation, and begin storing up their wrath toward Ono as the perpetrator of this outrage. I never expect that students will stay for the whole film (though I also do not suggest that they should leave if they get bored). I do ask them to consider both the film and the virulence of their own reactions to it.

No. 4 (Bottoms) raises a wide range of issues, about bodies, about film form, about the effects of advertising and the evolution of history, even about the nature of the art scene of the mid-1960s in London, where *No. 4* was filmed, when few people of color were in evidence. It provides an opportunity—as so many alternative films do—for a retraining of perception. Even during the eighty minutes of Ono's film, some viewers get over their fear of bottoms that have not been "colonized" by advertisers; by the end of the film those hairy and droopy bottoms are no longer shocking: they are just butts, like our own—the humble seat of all film pleasure.

Near the Big Chakra (1972) by Ann Severson (Alice Anne Parker)

While *Near the Big Chakra* has much in common with Ono's *No. 4 (Bottoms)*, both in Severson's choice of subject matter and in her presentation of it, the experience of the film is quite different, largely because of its obviously feminist politic. Severson's seventeen-minute film presents a series of extreme close-ups of the vulvas of thirty-seven females ranging in age from three months to sixty-three years. Each vulva is presented in a single, continuous shot, though the shots vary in length (also, from time-to-time Severson adjusts her zoom lens during the shot). *Near the Big Chakra* is silent, and as a result, seems far longer than seventeen minutes. During the film, the tradition of transforming female bodies into lifeless, conventionally "erotic" icons is continually subverted: tampon strings are visible in some shots, some of the women contract their muscles, and occasionally there is mucous.

Few films create as intense a screening experience as *Near the Big Chakra*; indeed, few films so clearly confront the general avoidance of the body still typical of the classroom. And few films demonstrate the widespread investment—even on the part of students who consider themselves progressive—in the conventional imaging of women. In fact, the film provides a measure of the degree to which our experiences with commercial film, television, and magazines have caused us to romanticize women's bodies. The degree of an individual's shock or disgust with the film—and these are standard reactions, even now—is a gauge of that viewer's acceptance of the idea of women as beautiful (inorganic) objects. Of course, the enlargement of these vulvas by the process of filming and projection is the cause of the often powerful responses the film creates, but after all, the "perfect" bodies marketed by the mass media are also enlarged by projection (in several senses). Severson's goal is to provide a kind of cinematic shock treatment that will, in the long run, work to create a more sensible, healthy relationship between women and men, and women's bodies.

Near the Big Chakra was the product of a certain moment in the history of sexual liberation and feminism in the Bay Area. It began when Severson found herself staring at her teenage daughter's vulva when she was sunbathing, and was reprimanded by her embarrassed daughter: "Later it seemed odd to me that, first, I had not looked at that part of her body since she was very small, and second, that my curiosity had made me uncomfortable, as though there was something wrong with my interest. I realized that I had never seen any woman's vagina except in crotch-shots in pornographic films and magazines or close-ups in birth films."[2] Severson worked with the Glide Methodist Church in San Francisco, at that time a center for research into human sexuality, to produce the film and to find volunteers to be filmed. *Chakra* refers to the traditional centers of consciousness in much eastern thought: "The second [chakra] is where all psychological energy is erotic or creative. I was jokingly calling it 'the big chakra' because in the early seventies we all seemed stuck at this level of development," Severson said.

As may be obvious, one of the challenges in dealing with *Near the Big Chakra* is overcoming student (and teacher) embarrassment about discussing the film. Our culture's failure to develop nonembarrassing terminology for genitalia is nowhere more obvious (when she traveled with *Near the Big Chakra*, Severson often referred to it as "the cunt film"—in an attempt to detoxify *cunt*). But as with any aspect of our lives where cultural fear and prejudice constrict healthy discourse, discussing the experience of Severson's film, and our discomfort with it, can be therapeutic and liberating. And the teacher can be sure that whatever conversation about *Near the Big Chakra* begins in the classroom, students will be talking about the film outside of class for weeks, even months.

Take Off (1972) by Gunvor Nelson

Made the same year as *Near the Big Chakra*, and within the same artistic milieu (filmmaker Robert Nelson, Gunvor Nelson's husband until 1972, was the first person to support Severson's idea to make *Near the Big Chakra*), *Take Off* uses a similar shock tactic to confront conventional representations of women, although its particular method creates a very different experience from the Severson film. Also, like *Near the Big Chakra*, *Take Off* was made as a collaboration of several women: Magda, who had the original concept for the film; an aging Bay Area stripper named Ellion Ness (a stage name based on Elliot Ness); and Nelson herself. The goal of the project was to deconstruct the entertainment ritual of the striptease by reducing it to absurdity.

Take Off opens with an evocation of striptease music and the appearance of Ellion Ness, dressed in a conventionally feminine dress. During the ten minutes of the film, Ness dances seductively for her audience (she consistently looks directly at the camera—at us), while removing article after article of her clothing. When she is entirely nude, however, the strip tease does not stop: Ness continues dancing and, usually to the audible shock and amusement of the film audience, removes first her wig, revealing a bald head; then her arms, her legs, her breasts, her ears, and nose, her head, leaving only a torso that "takes off" and is seen, at the very end of the film, spinning among asteroids in outer space.

The classroom experience of *Take Off* generally has several phases. Early on, students can hardly help but wonder not only why their instructor is showing a film of a striptease, but also—especially if the instructor is male—how he can get away with showing the film: most contemporary students are clear that feminists abhor the implications of this sort of performance. If the instructor is a woman, students are likely to assume that an attack on the film will be forthcoming once the screening is complete. At the moment when Ellion Ness removes her wig, however, the experience of the film is transformed, and students are either mystified by what happens next, or recognize the effectiveness of Nelson's revelation of the psychic damage to women of those societal practices that involve women performing with their bodies for the pleasure of men. Stripping, Nelson and her collaborators suggest, is not merely a slow, sexy disrobing, it is an implicit attack that reduces a woman to body *parts*, and by doing so, does damage to women's selfhood. The old stripping cliché, "Take it off; take it *all* off!" (heard more often in the era when

Take Off was made) receives in Nelson's film a response that undercuts the traditional assumption that men determine when women's eroticism begins and ends.

Of course, the brilliance of *Take Off* is that while it reveals the essential misogyny of the striptease, it provides not only a deconstruction of the performance, but a complex counter to it. The moment Ellion Ness removes her wig, the audience must confront the fact that they have underestimated Ness, Nelson, and the film. What looked like a typical stripper's ingratiating smile at her male audience is now revealed as Ness's smile of complicity with her collaborators at the naive assumption of her audience and of her pleasure in defying what is expected of her. After all, as her hair and body parts disappear, Ness's (and Nelson's) intelligence and spirit are increasingly evident.

As Lucy Fischer has demonstrated, Nelson's film rethinks the long tradition of magic in which male magicians perform tricks on women for the pleasure of audiences—a tradition quickly incorporated into cinema by George Méliès and other early makers of "trick films."[3] Here, a woman film magician uses precisely the tricks developed during the early decades of film history as a way not merely of recognizing the problematic elements of this tradition, but of transforming its implications once and for all: my guess (my hope) is that anyone who has experienced *Take Off* will never be able to see a conventional striptease—and even those many other filmic moments that are essentially striptease—without remembering the Nelson film and its implications.

Riddles of the Sphinx (1977) by Laura Mulvey and Peter Wollen

During the 1970s, many feminist filmmakers made films that demonstrated a rebellion not only against Hollywood, but also against forms of avant-garde cinema that—despite their own rebellion against the psychological/philosophical/aesthetic simplicities of the commercial cinema—seemed either unconscious of or unconcerned about the social inequities with which women were dealing. For some women struggling to express their frustrations, the sense of formal rigor, and in some cases beauty, that characterized many of the landmark films of the late 1960s and early 1970s—for instance, Michael Snow's *Wavelength* (1967), Hollis Frampton's *Zorns Lemma* (1970), J. J. Murphy's *Print Generation* (1974), or even Yoko Ono's *No. 4 (Bottoms)* and *Film No. 5 (Smile)* (1968)—seemed pointlessly self-indulgent extravagances that had no place in a seriously political cinema. But for other women, the major "structural films" of the

From Laura
Mulvey and Peter
Wollen's *Riddles
of the Sphinx*, 1977.
Courtesy of the
British Film
Institute.

1960s and 1970s offered new opportunities for exploring gender inequities and attempting to deal with them. One of the most remarkable films to take advantage of these opportunities was a collaboration by two noted film theorists (and one-time marriage partners), Laura Mulvey and Peter Wollen: *Riddles of the Sphinx*.

I know of no feature narrative film that (still, nearly thirty years later) creates a more powerful challenge for most college students. The focus of *Riddles* (motherhood and domestic labor) and its formal strategy (the main body of the film is a series of long, continuous, 360-degree pans of the mundane, middle-class spaces where the central character, Louise, lives and works) seem—as they were meant to seem—the very antitheses of cinematic pleasure, even to otherwise sophisticated students. Mulvey and Wollen built upon the structure of Frampton's *Zorns Lemma* in order to provide a critique of the conventional cinema that evoked both the challenges to narrative politics posed by experimental narrative directors like Jean-Luc Godard, Luis Buñuel, Jean-Marie Straub and Danièle Huillet, and others and the wide range of formal challenges to commercial media that were characteristic of avant-garde filmmaking during the 1960s and early 1970s. *Riddles* is formally organized so that the story of Louise dealing with her new life is presented in a series of complex tableaux, sandwiched between three opening and three closing sections that are considerably more abstract. "Louise's Story" evokes European challenges to feature-length melodrama, and each of the more abstract sections evokes a form of avant-garde cinema that emerged during the 1960s and early 1970s.

In my experience, *Riddles* creates such consternation that, after some years, I decided to institute a ritual to assist students in dealing with their anger with the film before beginning to discuss it. As soon as the screening is over, I ask students to write the name of the film and the names of the directors on a piece of paper, and to crumple the paper into a tight ball: "The more annoyed with the film you are, the tighter the ball should be." Then I ask them to stand and "stone" me with the balls of paper. They seem to enjoy this ritual stoning immensely.

Then we can begin to explore why students find *Riddles* so boring. What generally becomes clear is that, in addition to the film's refusal of conventional melodramatic pleasure, Mulvey and Wollen's decision to see parenthood and domestic work as important—however problematic the gender politics of particular divisions of parental and domestic labor may be—is a bit frightening. For a good many American college students, male and female, college is an escape from parenthood and domestic labor. Of course, many male students assume that domestic work, including the raising of young children, will not be required of them; and many young women fear motherhood and domestic labor as if it means—as historically it often has meant—the termination of their professional ambitions and their creativity. *Riddles of the Sphinx* makes quite clear the "bad news" that even intelligent, creative, politically astute men and women must deal with the realities of domesticity and, often, child rearing, and, further, that they feel a responsibility to their children to deal with these realities well. We do not know why Louise and her partner have split up; we know only that they have decided they can no longer live together, despite the difficulties that splitting up will bring. Louise must go back to work at a low-paying job and see to day care for their daughter, Anna, and the couple's home will be sold, even though, as the husband suggests, "It's not a good time to sell." ("It's a good time for *me* to sell," Louise responds.)

The power of *Riddles of the Sphinx* is a function of the intricacy of its mirror-like structure and of the mise-en-scène of the thirteen shots of Louise's story. A detailed discussion of the opening shot of "Louise's Story"—Louise is in the kitchen cooking an egg for Anna—makes obvious how much thought has gone into this and subsequent shots. The 360-degree pan around the kitchen reveals myriad suggestions of circularity and roundness that provide a counter to the phallic directionality inherent in the relentless forward thrust of most conventional narrative and in the Renaissance-perspectival conventions of the photographic image. Indeed, *Riddles of the Sphinx* is so dense with formal "riddles" and with suggestive detail that one of the deepest messages of a first experience of the film is how blind our cinematic prejudices can make us, and how little of life the conventional cinema enables us to see. *Riddles* allows students to rethink the ways in which the commercial cinema (and the educational process) constrict our awareness of the demands and opportunities of domestic life.

Privilege (1991) by Yvonne Rainer

It would be hard to think of a topic less likely to excite conventional film-goers, including students who consider themselves reasonably sophisticated about women's issues, than menopause. Indeed, in most modern cultural discourse, menopause seems the antipathy to pleasure, the conclusion of youth and energy, the beginning of the end. The irony is that Yvonne Rainer's film about menopause—the onset of her own, and menopause in general—is remarkably engaging for women and men alike. Rainer approaches this "grim" topic with humor and high spirits.

Rainer's mixture of personal interview and dramatic reenactment, of image and text, provides a telling challenge to conventional film pleasure by confronting its most fundamental assumptions in a manner that is both revealing and enjoyable. During *Privilege* we follow the story of Jenny, a menopausal woman talking with her therapist about her experiences in New York City beginning with her early years as a dancer. Rainer's formal method is to tell a coherent, evolving story within a mise-en-scène that is continually shifting and revealing its own construction. From one shot to the next, the characters' dress, or the decor of the space, or the mood of the scene is continually shifting. Challenging at first, but increasingly understandable as the film evolves, these gaps in continuity force viewers to understand that we are constructing the story, reminding us that our lives, including our filmgoing experiences, are in fact constructions in which we can directly participate, and that the smooth continuities of conventional cinema are, in part, *about* avoiding the inevitable interruption within the life cycle created by aging and the physical changes it brings.

Privilege was made at that moment in the 1990s when feminism was confronting a tendency evident in earlier decades to focus primarily on the struggles of middle-class white women. Rainer weaves the themes of race and ethnicity into *Privilege* by recognizing how the American cultural focus on young heterosexual romance (within society in general and certainly within cinema) disenfranchises not only older women—and the older they are, the more cinematically disenfranchised they become—but also all those who do not fit the Hollywood paradigm of the lovely young (white) actress and the men who pursue her. *Privilege* provides a cross-section of contemporary America in which women and men of various heritages struggle together to live full, rich lives, whatever age they are.

Chronicles of a Lying Spirit (by Kelly Gabron) (1992) by Cauleen Smith

Within that area of American independent cinema usually called "avant-garde" or "experimental" film, the paucity of African American and Hispanic contributors has generally been considered something of an embarrassment. The interest in countering Hollywood paradigms often brings with it at least an intellectual commitment to the idea of cultural diversity, and the fact that so few women of color seem to have seen avant-garde/experimental film as an arena worth exploring has tended to render the field so white as to seem politically retrograde.[4] As a result, when a woman of color has made a noteworthy contribution, it has been a cause for celebration. When, for example, Cauleen Smith's short film *Chronicles of a Lying Spirit (by Kelly Gabron)* was shown at the Robert Flaherty Film Seminar in 1992, seminarians demanded it be shown a second time and it *was*, a rarity at the Flaherty.

Chronicles has much in common, in both subject matter and form, with *Privilege*, although it is both shorter and denser. The film pretends to review the life of a woman named Kelly Gabron (the name is a modification of Khalil Gibron), who is clearly a version of Smith herself. Gabron's story is narrated by two voices: a white male voice that attempts to see her as "typical" of African American women's struggles and Smith's own (very sensual and engaging) voice, which frequently counters the assertions of the male voice. The two voices are heard simultaneously through the film, but the female voice slowly, subtly gains ascendancy and, at the conclusion of the film, when the male voice says, "Sound out," Smith provides a final counter by allowing the sound to continue. Visually, the film collages a variety of images recycled from popular culture and bits of visual text—originally collected as a scrapbook when Smith was a student of Lynn Hershman at San Francisco State University—into a dense, fluidly edited montage. The greater part of the film is repeated a second time, because "when I was showing it to people in the fine cut on the flatbed, the first thing . . . [people] would do before commenting on the film, was to rewind and watch it again."[5]

What emerges during a viewing of the film is the complexity of the idea of African American identity and Smith's struggle, as a middle-class, suburban black to both respect and honor the African American past while living a life outside the difficulties of financial deprivation, or at least far enough outside deprivation to have access to the possibility of making a film, even if there seem to be few opportunities to have the film seen by a large audience: "I know now that the only way I'm gonna get on TV is to make my *own* goddamn tapes and play them for *myself.*" Smith has gone on to make the narrative feature *Drylongso* (1998).

Kristallnacht (1979) by Chick Stand

Chick Strand has made important contributions to American independent film in at least two ways. She was a member of a small group of men and women (others include filmmaker Bruce Baillie, and editor/author Chick Callenbach) who originated Canyon Cinema, a screening and workshop collective that evolved into the San Francisco Cinematheque, still one of the bellwether exhibitors of alternative cinema in the United States, and Canyon Cinema, this nation's most dependable distributor of avant-garde cinema. She has been making her own films since 1966. Strand has worked in a variety of ways. She has made experimental documentaries in Mexico and complex, poetic evocations of states of feelings, of which *Kristallnacht* is among the most remarkable.

Kristallnacht is a deceptively simple film, focusing on reflections of light on water, seemingly at night. The seven-minute film divides into two distinct passages: during the first we see crystalline ripples of water accompanied by nighttime sounds of crickets and frogs, and of young women apparently enjoying the water; then, after the sound of a distant train and of a gong, the rippling effect is more regular and pronounced and is accompanied by haunting, rhythmic music (the voices are no longer heard). Visually, *Kristallnacht* is exquisite, a paean to the innocent pleasure of enjoying a nighttime swim during warm weather. But because of the film's title, and Strand's framing the water imagery with two texts—at the beginning, a haiku: "White chrysanthemum / before that perfect flower / scissors hesitate," and at the end, "For Anne Frank"—this innocence is recontextualized by its opposite. *Kristallnacht*, of course, refers to the "night of broken glass," November 9–10, 1938, when the Nazis expanded their persecution of European Jewry by destroying synagogues, looting stores, and arresting thousands of Jews. Within this context the haiku suggests the sacrifice of Anne Frank and the train we hear on the sound track comes to suggest the transportation of millions of Jews to their death during Hitler's "Final Solution."

For Strand, who was part of the postwar generation for whom the Holocaust was a fundamental political reality, the challenge was how to use film as a means of functioning positively in a world capable of the ultimate horror. Her answer is to demand a space for innocence, even in (*especially* in) a world where innocence has come to seem problematic. After all, if the beauty of the moment captured by the sounds and sights of *Kristallnacht*—and the innocence and freedom such a moment represents—is no longer possible, if we refuse the experience of innocent ecstatic pleasure, then the forces of destruction and oppression have won. While one must never forget how precarious and fragile such moments are, while we must remember the horrors our brothers and sisters throughout the world have experienced and continue to experience, we must never surrender the idea of innocence and its expression within our lives and within cinema. Without its opposite, after all, horror becomes the norm, and the world is doomed to choose only between circles of hell.

The particular value of using *Kristallnacht* in the college classroom is that it models a way of dealing with political realities without giving in to self-righteous anger or cynicism. It suggests that students, all of us, can *live* in ways that offer a counterpart to the negative, destructive forces that seem so pervasive in the news. Strand demonstrates, in contradistinction to the action-adventure blockbusters that pervade local movie theaters here and abroad, that cinema can also be a place for beauty and for (politically aware) mindfulness.

The Sky on Location (1983) by Babette Mangolte

Babette Mangolte's *The Sky on Location* remains one of the most accomplished and least recognized films to be made by a woman during that productive decade and a half that begins with Yvonne Rainer's features and ends with the emergence of Su Friedrich, Leslie Thornton, and Peggy Ahwesh. On one hand, the lack of recognition accorded Mangolte's fourth feature-length film is surprising, given the fact that Mangolte's accomplished cinematography played an important role in a number of the remarkable feminist films of those years—including Rainer's *Film about a Woman Who . . .* and *Lives of Performers* (1972), Sally Potter's *The Gold Diggers* (1983), Chantal Akerman's *Jeanne Dielman . . .* (1975) and *News from Home* (1977), and Anthony McCall's, Claire Pajaczkowska's, Andrew Tyndall's, and Jane Weinstock's *Sigmund Freud's Dora* (1979)—and given that her own *The Cold Eye (My Darling, Be Careful)* (1980) is an important and still underappreciated early contribution to the debate about "the male gaze." The reason that *The Sky on Location* is not well known has to do with subject matter and timing:

Mangolte's subject is the landscape of the American West, and in 1983 few topics seemed less relevant to feminists.

By 1983 Mangolte could no longer resist the urge to explore the American West, which had been such a crucial location for John Ford, one of the popular filmmakers (Jean Renoir is the other) whose films reveal what Mangolte calls a "clarity and trust," a realism "that feeds me."[6] Mangolte drove close to 20,000 miles during 1980 and 1981, criss-crossing the West from Montana to Arizona, and from Colorado to California, recording landscape imagery with the kind of solemn respect evident in the paintings of the Rocky Mountain school of American landscape painting (Thomas Moran, Albert Bierstadt) and in the photography of William Henry Jackson, Carleton Watkins, and Ansel Adams. Indeed, Mangolte credits art historian Barbara Novak as a major influence on *The Sky on Location*.[7]

Mangolte's imagery is nearly devoid of human presence; Mangolte wanted to provide a sense of what the original explorers might have felt upon first seeing these spaces. The exception is the sound track, where three voices—Mangolte herself, plus one other woman (Honora Ferguson) and one man (Bruce Boston)—discuss the cultural history of these landscapes and their implications for modern life. The comments of these discussants are sometimes abrasive and generally work against the grain of the visual experience of Mangolte's consistently stunning imagery, and this discord is at the heart of the film. The sound track reflects the divided consciousness we all have when faced with the magnificent vistas of the west and with our awareness of what was involved in appropriating them for the American nation and what is happening to them now. While Mangolte's landscapes are nearly empty of people, we know that the exploitation of these landscapes was, and is, relentless and ongoing.

For most moviegoers, landscape is, at most, the background for melodramatic narrative, and to bring that background into the foreground can raise a range of cinematic and sociological issues. Most college students see college life as virtually placeless, an escape from the geographic and historical aspects of place and its implicit demands. For a woman filmmaker to lead the way toward an engagement with place (defying all those stereotypes about the inability of women to read maps!) may have been a subtle form of feminist intervention in 1983. Yet Mangolte's expedition and the undeniable quality of her cinematography remain a valuable model for young women thinking about cinema.

Glimpse of the Garden (1957) by Marie Menken

The fact that Menken is so little known is one of the more poignant realities in the history of women's filmmaking. Even those few who recognize her achievements and her considerable influence have often been less than energetic in their support of her work. P. Adams Sitney has often said that his "biggest regret" as a chronicler of American avant-garde filmmaking in the post–World War II era is that he did not include Menken in his ground-breaking *Visionary Film*. Until very recently, only filmmaker Stan Brakhage has written at any length about Menken, in *Film at Wit's End*.[8] That Brakhage should be Menken's champion is not surprising, since he is one of a number of major avant-garde filmmakers to profit from her influence (Jonas Mekas is another).

Originally a painter, Menken became interested in filmmaking in the 1940s, although she had already been involved in the classic film *Geography of the Body* (1943), made by her partner, Willard Maas. From the late 1940s though the 1960s, Maas and Menken were fixtures in the New York City cultural scene, hosting many of those who would become movers and shakers (Andy Warhol, Sitney, Marilyn Monroe, Norman McLaren, Kenneth Anger, Edward Albee) in their ramshackle "penthouse" in Brooklyn Heights.

Unlike so many of the filmmakers working during those years, including Maas, Menken remained unusually informal about her filmmaking, attempting to be serious without being pretentious. She was a hard-working, politically aware woman (for much of her married life, her work at Time-Life supported both her and Maas), without being anti-intellectual or disdainful of aesthetics. *Glimpse of the Garden* is a perfect embodiment of Menken's aesthetic, and a perfect reflection of Menken and Maas's unusual marriage. Maas was a homosexual, at the time an unusually flamboyant homosexual, and Dwight Ripley, whose garden is the subject of Menken's film, had been one of Maas's many lovers. Ripley and Menken became good friends and, as was true of so many of Menken's little films, *Glimpse* was homage to friendship and a way of honoring a friend's aesthetic passion. *Glimpse of the Garden* is a five-minute evocation of Ripley's garden, filmed with the handheld, gestural camera characteristic of Menken's work. Menken may have been the first filmmaker to make gestural camerawork a hallmark of style. In her era, her wildly improvisational visual explorations of art and place (beginning with her evocation of an Isamu Noguchi sculpture in *Visual Variations on Noguchi* of 1945) were seen as closely related to abstract-expressionist

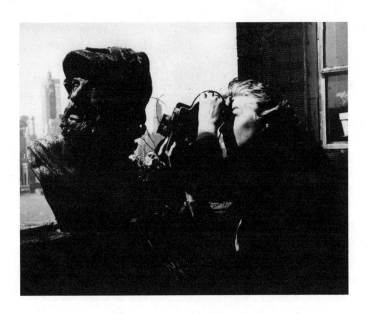

Marie Menken at work. Courtesy of Anthology Film Archives.

gestural painting and certainly were a major influence on Brakhage and Mekas. In *Glimpse of the Garden*, her camera flits from flower to flower, from space to space, like a bird, glimpsing Ripley's elaborate garden (the film's sound track is made up of bird sounds).

In contrast to the free-form camerawork, and even to the informality of Menken's failure to clean her camera (at one point dirt in the camera gate is visible), Menken's sixty-odd shots are densely, carefully edited: clusters of glimpses of one sector of the garden are followed by more stable and extended shots of other sectors. While there are a number of lovely shots, especially near the end of the film—almost as if to say, "I *can* make conventionally beautiful shots"—*Glimpse of the Garden* does not pretend to be a beautiful film; it remains an informal engagement with Ripley and his creative enterprise, an evocation of their friendship. This very informality, this horror of pretentiousness, this commitment to allow films to evolve out of personal life distinguishes Menken's work— and causes students difficulty. The slick surfaces of commercial movies, of commercial products in general (and of digital imagery especially), are ubiquitous and seductive. The slicker we become, the more sloppy and unimpressive Menken's films can look. But it is precisely her defiance of commerce that allows Menken's films to provide a powerful intervention—an intervention that has been regularly echoed in the years since Menken died (in December 1970) in the work of women film-makers—from Carolee Schneemann to Peggy Ahwesh—who have been determined to allow their films to emerge out of the nitty-gritty of day-to-day experience.

Teatro Amazonas (1999) by Sharon Lockhart

Like several of the women discussed in this anthology, Sharon Lockhart did not start out as an independent filmmaker but came to filmmaking as an accomplished artist from another field, in this case, like Babette Mangolte, from photography. Like Laura Mulvey, she came to filmmaking already deeply influenced by the formal rigor of structural cinema, especially the films of Hollis Frampton, Michael Snow, James Benning, Morgan Fisher, and Chantal Akerman. But she *also* was fascinated with how cinema represents people of other cultures and how it might negotiate the distinctions between different cultures. For *Goshogaoka* (1997), Lockhart worked with Japanese schoolgirls, specifically, a girls' basketball team, to create a set of rigorously framed performances that lie somewhere in between calisthenics and postmodern dance, and between American and Japanese. At first, the film seems to be a documentary, and in a sense it is, but our sense of what exactly is being documented evolves during the film.

The interface between different cultures dramatized in *Goshogaoka* was subsequently literalized in the film that followed, the forty-minute, 35mm *Teatro Amazonas*, which is constructed of a single, continuous, thirty-minute shot of an audience in an opera house in Manaus, Brazil, followed by a credit sequence that reveals the names of the three hundred and eight men and women in the audience, plus the individuals who make up the crew and the sixty-person choir that provides the sound. While the audience in the theater looks at the audience in the opera house looking at the camera, both groups listen to what at first seems to be a wall of sound, a musical composition performed by a choir (located in the orchestra pit so that it is invisible to both audiences). As the film proceeds, the singers drop out, one by one, until at the end of the shot the only remaining sounds are those made by the audiences themselves and by the traffic and other environmental sounds audible outside the two theaters. It is as if both audiences are, for a magical moment, in the same space—and in a conceptual sense they are.

As may be obvious from this description, *Teatro Amazonas* offers two kinds of challenges—and two kinds of opportunities. First, anyone wanting to show the film must find a theater that can show 35mm—a rarity especially on most small campuses (in fact, the film requires a special 35mm platter system, since it must be shown without a break). That is, for many, showing or seeing *Teatro Amazonas* would require a journey beyond campus boundaries. Of course, Lockhart knew that her decision to make this film would place it in a kind of no-woman's-land: as a film, it exists between two very different cinema cultures. This "problem," however, is also a pedagogical opportunity to demonstrate to students what earlier generations of cineastes knew so well: that film developed as an experience that required movement out of the home and into public life, and that not long after its invention, cinema had become in many cities a ritual meeting place where various cultures and classes shared experiences.

The other challenge, of course, is a function of the length of the film and its minimalism—the same challenge posed by the Ono film with which I began. In fact, the challenge of the film's length works two ways: a thirty-minute shot is a considerable test of audience patience, regardless of the subject matter, but at the same time, forty minutes is much too short for a film shown in conventional 35mm theaters these days. Each of the film's limitations is a conceptual confrontation of the way film has come to function in the world at large and in the lives of our students. The relentless visual/auditory overload of most theatrical cinema and television and the paucity of opportunities for sharing media experiences with people of different cultures are evidence of the ongoing cooption of the real potentials of cinema by big governments and big money. The value of *Teatro Amazonas*—and of experimental film in general, including the particular films discussed in this essay and book—is precisely its demonstration that there are cultural and cinematic alternatives that deserve and will reward ever greater exposure.

Film Sources

Yoko Ono's films are available from the Museum of Modern Art Circulating Film Program (MoMA); *Near the Big Chakra* and *Take Off*, from Canyon Cinema; *Riddles of the Sphinx*, from MoMA; Yvonne Rainer's *Privilege*, from Zeitgeist in New York City; *Chronicles of a Lying Spirit (by Kelly Gabron)* and *Kristallnacht*, from Canyon; *The Sky on Location* and *Glimpse of the Garden*, from the Film-Makers' Cooperative in New York; and Sharon Lockhart's films, from Blum and Poe Gallery, 2042 Broadway, Santa Monica, Calif. 90404.

To learn the full range of what films are available and how they might be useful in the classroom, use the catalogues published by the leading distributors of alternative film. These include Canyon Cinema; the Film-Makers' Cooperative, and Women Make Movies in the United States and the Canadian Filmmakers Distribution Centre in Toronto. All these organizations have extensive catalogues of the films they offer for rent, both online and as books. These catalogues are a pleasure to explore and can lead readers to possibilities they would otherwise not consider. The staff at these organizations can provide useful suggestions.

Notes

1   Ono, "Addendum '88," 22.

2   Ann Severson quoted in MacDonald, *A Critical Cinema*, 2: 326.

3   Fischer, *Shot/Counter Shot*, 3–31.

4   Because videotaping has for some time been far less expensive than shooting film, a good many young African American women have turned to video and made films that have much in common with the films that are the subject of this volume.

5   Cauleen Smith quoted in MacDonald, *A Critical Cinema*, 3: 305.

6   Babette Mangolte quoted in MacDonald, *A Critical Cinema*, 1: 292.

7   See Novak, *American Painting in the Nineteenth Century* and *Nature and Culture*.

8   See Sitney, *Visionary Film*, and Brakhage, *Film at Wit's End*. Sitney is currently completing a book that discusses Menken's work at length.

Film Distribution

□

Most of the films discussed in this anthology are available from one or more of the following distributors.

Canadian Filmmakers Distribution Centre
37 Hanna Ave., Suite 220
Toronto, Ontario, Canada M6K 1W9
416-588-0725
barbara@cfmdc.org
www.cfmdc.org

Canyon Cinema
145 Ninth St., Suite 260
San Francisco, Calif. 94103
415-626-2255
film@canyoncinema.com
www.canyoncinema.com

Facets Multi-Media
1517 W. Fullerton Ave.
Chicago, Ill. 06014
800-331-6917

sales@facets.org
www.facets.org

LUX Video
18 Shacklewell Lane
London E8 2EZ
United Kingdom

Museum of Modern Art Circulating Film Library
11 West 53rd Street
New York, N.Y. 10019
212–708–9530
library@moma.org

New American Cinema Group
c/o the Clocktower Gallery
108 Leonard St, 13th Floor
New York, N.Y. 10013
film6000@aol.com
www.film-makerscoop.com

Women Make Movies
462 Broadway, Suite 505L
New York, N.Y. 10013
212-925-0606
orders@wmm.com
www.wmm.com

Bibliography

□

Ahwesh, Peggy. "Lara Croft: Tomb Raider." *Film Comment* 37 (2001): 77.

———. "Film, Baby." In *Big as Life: An American History of 8mm Film*, edited by Albert Kilchesty, 79–82. San Francisco: Foundation for Art in Film, 1998.

———. "Nocturne." In *Lux: A Decade of Artists' Film and Video*, edited by Steve Reinke and Tom Taylor, 312–15. Toronto: XYZ Books and Pleasure Dome, 2000.

Andersson, Fred. "Technology and Poetry." In *Gunvor Nelson: Still Moving i ljud och bild*, edited by John Sundholm, 91–98. Karlstad, Sweden: Centre for the Creative Arts, Karlstad University, 2002.

Angell, Callie. *The Films of Andy Warhol: Part II*. New York: Whitney Museum of Art, 1994.

Anker, Steve. "The Films of Gunvor Nelson." In *Gunvor Nelson: Still Moving i ljud och bild*, edited by John Sundholm, 7–30. Karlstad, Sweden: Centre for the Creative Arts, Karlstad University, 2002.

———. "Gunvor Nelson and the American Avant-Garde Film." In *Gunvor Nelson and the Avant-Garde*, edited by John Sundholm, 109–24. Frankfurt am Main: Peter Lang, 2003.

Armatage, Kay. "The Feminine Body: Joyce Wieland's *Water Sark*." In *The Films of Joyce Wieland*, edited by Kathryn Elder, 135–46. Toronto: Toronto International Film Festival Group, 1999.

———. "Kay Armatage Interviews Joyce Wieland." In *The Films of Joyce Wie-*

land, edited by Kathryn Elder, 153–61. Toronto: Toronto International Film Festival Group, 1999.

Artaud, Antonin. "The Theater and Its Double." In *Antonin Artaud: Selected Writings,* edited by Susan Sontag, 215–16. Berkeley: University of California Press, 1988.

Arthur, Paul. "The Last of the Last Machine? Avant-Garde Film since 1966." *Millennium Film Journal,* no. 16–18 (1986–87): 69–93.

——. "Letter to Marjorie Keller." *Millennium Film Journal,* no. 28 (1995): 64–67.

——. *A Line of Sight: American Avant-Garde Film since 1965.* Minneapolis: University of Minnesota Press, 2005.

——. "*Quixote* and Its Contexts." *Film Culture* 67–69 (1979): 32–55.

Ball, Gordon. *66 Frames.* Minneapolis: Coffee House Press, 1999.

Banes, Sally. "Dance, Emotion, Film: The Case of Yvonne Rainer." A talk at the Symposium on the Work of Yvonne Rainer sponsored by the Humanities Institute of New York University, April 1999.

——. *Dancing Women: Female Bodies on Stage.* London: Routledge, 1998.

——. *Greenwich Village 1963: Avant-Garde Performance and the Effervescent Body.* Durham, N.C.: Duke University Press, 1993.

——. *Terpsichore in Sneakers.* 2nd ed. Middletown, Conn.: Wesleyan University Press, 1987.

Banning, Kass. "The Mummification of Mommy: Joyce Wieland as the AGO's First Living Other." In *The Films of Joyce Wieland,* edited by Kathryn Elder, 29–44. Toronto: Toronto International Film Festival Group, 1999.

Barthes, Roland. *Camera Lucida: Reflections on Photography.* Translated by Richard Howard. New York: Hill and Wang, 1981.

——. "The Death of the Author." *Image, Music, Text.* Edited and translated by Stephen Heath, 142–48. New York: Hill and Wang, 1977.

——. *Empire of Signs.* Translated by Richard Howard. New York: Hill and Wang, 1982.

Bazin, André. "Death Every Afternoon." Translated by Mark A. Cohen. In *Rites of Realism: Essays on Corporeal Cinema,* edited by Ivone Margulies, 27–31. Durham, N.C.: Duke University Press, 2003.

——. "The Ontology of the Photographic Image." In *What Is Cinema?* Vol. 1. Translated by Hugh Gray, 9–16. Berkeley: University of California Press, 1967.

Belasco, Daniel. "A Note from the Underground." *Westchester: The Jewish Week.* September 22, 2000.

Bell, Lynn and Michael Zryd. "Su Friedrich." *Senses of Cinema* (2002). < sensesofcinema.com/contents/directors/02/friedrich.html>

Benedikt, Michael, ed. *Theatre Experiment.* Garden City, N.Y.: Doubleday, 1967.

Benjamin, Walter. "Unpacking My Library: A Talk About Book Collecting." In *Illuminations,* edited by Hannah Arendt, 59–67. New York: Schocken Books, 1969.

Beroes, Stephanie. "Interview: Leslie Thornton." *Cinematograph* 2 (1986): 65–68.

Blaetz, Robin. "In Search of the Mother Tongue: Childbirth and the Cinema." *The Velvet Light Trap* 29 (Spring 1992): 15–20.

Boccino, Joan. "A Talk with Barbara Hammer: Part One, Personal Reflections." *The Empty Chair* (November 1993): 10–11.

———. "A Talk with Barbara Hammer: Part Two, Reflections on Work." *The Empty Chair* (December 1993/January 1994): 10–12.

Bockris, Victor. *The Life and Death of Andy Warhol.* New York: Bantam, 1989.

Borger, Irene. "An Interview with Leslie Thornton." *Senses of Cinema.* www.sensesofcinema.com/contents/02/22/thornton_interview.html. Accessed June 1998.

———, ed. "Leslie Thornton." *The Force of Curiosity: CalArts/Alpert Award in the Arts 1994–1998.* Los Angeles: CalArts/Alpert Foundation, 1999.

Braderman, Joan. "First Festival of Women's Films." *Artforum,* September 1972, 87.

Brakhage, Stan. *Film at Wit's End.* Kingston, N.Y.: Documentext/McPherson, 1989.

———. "Marie Menken." In *Film at Wit's End.* 33–48.

———. "On Marie Menken." In *Brakhage Scrapbook: Collected Writings,* edited by Robert Haller, 91–93. New York: McPherson, 1982.

———. "Metaphors on Vision." *Film Culture* 30 (1963).

Brownworth, Victoria. "Out in the World: An Interview with Barbara Hammer." *Metroline* 18, 1 (January 1995): 18–19, 21.

———. "Reel Women: The Iconoclastic Art of Barbara Hammer." *Deneuve* 5, 5 (October 1995): 44–47.

Bruno, Giuliana. "Women in Avant-Garde Film: An Interview with Annette Michelson." *Millennium Film Journal,* no. 16–18 (1986–87): 141–48.

Buchloh, Benjamin H. D. "Andy Warhol's One-Dimensional Art, 1956–1966" (1989) and "Robert Watts: Animate Objects, Inanimate Subjects" (2000). 531–53. In *Neo-Avantgarde and Culture Industry: Essays on European and American Art from 1955 to 1975.* Cambridge, Mass.: MIT Press, 2000.

Butler, Alison. *Women's Cinema: The Contested Screen.* London: Wallflower, 2002.

Callenbach, E. "*Mosori Monika.*" *Film Quarterly* 25, no. 2 (1971–72): 57.

Camper, Fred. "End of the Avant-Garde." *Millennium Film Journal,* no. 16–18 (1986–87): 99–124.

Canyon Cinema Cooperative. *Film Video Catalogue 7.* San Francisco: Canyon Cinema, 1992.

———. *Canyon Cinema Film/Video Catalogue 2000.* San Francisco: Canyon Cinema, 2000.

Carroll, Noël. "Avant-Garde Art and the Problem of Theory." *Journal of Aesthetic Education* 29, no. 3 (1995): 1–13.

———. "Avant-Garde Film and Film Theory." In *Theorizing the Moving Image*, edited by Noël Carroll, 162–68. New York: Cambridge University Press, 1996.

———. *The Philosophy of Horror*. New York: Routledge, 1990.

Cherchi Usai, Paolo. *The Death of Cinema: History, Cultural Memory and the Digital Dark Age*. London: British Film Institute, 2001.

Child, Abigail. *Mob*. Oakland, CA: O Press, 1994.

———. *A Motive for Mayhem*. Hartford, CT: Potes and Poets Press, 1989.

———. *Scatter Matrix*. New York: Roof Books, 1996.

———. *This Is Called Moving: A Critical Poetics of Film*. Tuscaloosa: University of Alabama Press, 2005.

———. "Truth Serum." *Cinematograph*, 4 (1991): 43–52.

Chua, Laurence. "Usually Moving Pictures." *Artforum* (May 1993): 17.

Citron, Michelle. *Home Movies and Necessary Fictions*. Minneapolis: University of Minnesota Press, 1999.

Clark, Vévé, Millicent Hodson, and Catrina Neiman. *The Legend of Maya Deren: A Documentary Biography and Collected Works, Parts I and II*. New York: Anthology Film Archives, 1984–1988.

Cook, Pam. "The Point of Self-Expression in Avant-Garde Film." In *Theories of Authorship*, edited by John Caughie, 271–81. New York: Routledge, 1988.

Cooper, Harry and Ron Spronk. *Mondrian: The Transatlantic Paintings*. New Haven, Conn.: Yale University Press, 2001.

Culler, Jonathan. *Structuralist Poetics: Structuralism, Linguistics, and the Study of Literature*. New York: Cornell University Press, 1975.

Curtis, David. *Experimental Cinema*. New York: Delta Publishing Co., Inc., 1971.

Dargis, Manohla. "Beyond Brakhage: Avant-Garde Film and Feminism." In *A Passage Illuminated: The American Avant-Garde Film, 1980–1990*, edited by Nelly Voorhuis and Paul Arthur, 55–68. Amsterdam: Foundation Mecano, 1991.

De Lauretis, Teresa. *Technologies of Gender: Essays on Theory, Film, and Fiction*. Bloomington: Indiana University Press, 1987.

Deleuze, Gilles. *Cinema 1: The Movement-Image* and *Cinema 2: The Time-Image*. Translated by Hugh Tomlinson and Barbara Habberjam. Minneapolis: University of Minnesota Press, 1989.

———. *Difference and Repetition*. 1968. Translated by Paul Patton. New York: Columbia University Press, 1994.

Deren, Maya. "An Anagram of Ideas on Art, Form and Film." In *Maya Deren and the American Avant-Garde*, edited by Bill Nichols, 267–322. Berkeley: University of California Press, 2001.

———. "Program Notes on Three Early Films." *Film Culture* 39 (1965): 1.

Derrida, Jacques. *The Ear of the Other: Otobiography, Transference, Transla-*

tion. English edition edited by Christie McDonald and translated by Peggy Kamuf. Lincoln: University of Nebraska Press, 1985.

Desmond, Jane. "Ethnography, Orientalism and the Avant-Garde." *Visual Anthropology* 4 (1991).

DiBattista, Maria. "Marjorie Keller: A Remembrance." *Film Culture* 78 (Summer 1994): 15–17.

DiMatteo, Robert. "Gunvor Nelson: Capturing the Nether Regions of Femininity on Film." *San Francisco Bay Guardian*, October 15, 1976.

Dixon, Wheeler Winston. *The Exploding Eye: A Re-Visionary History of 1960s American Experimental Cinema*. Albany: State University of New York Press, 1997.

——, and Gwendolyn Audrey Foster. *Experimental Cinema: The Film Reader*. New York: Routledge, 2002.

Doane, Mary Anne. *Femmes Fatales: Feminism, Film Theory, and Psychoanalysis*. New York: Routledge, 1991.

Doty, Alexander. *Flaming Classics: Queering the Film Canon*. New York: Routledge, 2000.

Dunning, Jennifer. "Free-Spirited Progeny of the Long Romance Between Dance and Film." *New York Times*, December 7, 1996.

Dunye, Cheryl. "Building Subjects." *Movement Research, the Performance Arts Journal* 4 (1992): 18.

——, and Shu Lea Cheang. "Vanilla Sex." In *The Wild Good: Lesbian Photographs and Writings on Love*, 39. New York: Anchor Books, 1996.

Dyer, Richard. *Now You See It*. New York: Routledge, 1990.

Eder, Richard. "The Screen: Cultural Intrusion." *New York Times*, December 10, 1976.

Eisenstein, Sergei. "Methods of Montage." In *Film Form*. Translated by Jay Leyda, 72–83. New York: Harcourt Brace, 1949.

Elder, Kathryn. *The Films of Joyce Wieland*. Toronto: Cinema Ontario, 1999.

Elder, R. Bruce. *The Films of Stan Brakhage in the American Tradition of Ezra Pound, Gertrude Stein, and Charles Olson*. Waterloo, Ontario: Wilfrid Laurier University Press, 1998.

Film-Makers' Cooperative Catalogue, no. 7. New York: The New American Cinema Group, 1989.

Filmverkstan. *Skeppsholmen, 1973–1993*. Catalogue. Stockholm: Tryckgruppen, 1993.

Fischer, Lucy. *Cinematernity*. Princeton, N.J.: Princeton University Press, 1996.

——. *Shot/Counter Shot: Film Tradition and Women's Cinema*. Princeton, N.J.: Princeton University Press, 1989.

Foster, Gwendolyn Audrey. "Barbara Hammer, an Interview: Re/Constructing Lesbian Auto/biographies in *Tender Fictions* and *Nitrate Kisses*." *Post Script, Essays in Film and Humanities* 16, no. 3 (1997): 3–16.

Foucault, Michel. "Nietzsche, Genealogy, History." In *The Foucault Reader*, edited by Paul Rabinow, 76–100. New York: Pantheon Books, 1984.

Frampton, Hollis. *Circles of Confusion: Film, Photography, Video Texts, 1968–1980*. Rochester, N.Y.: Visual Studies Workshop, 1983.

Frampton, Hollis, and Joyce Wieland. "I Don't Even Know about the Second Stanza." In *The Films of Joyce Wieland*, edited by Kathryn Elder, 161–82. Toronto: Toronto International Film Festival Group, 1999.

Freud, Sigmund. *Three Essays on the Theory of Sexuality*. Translated by James Strachey. New York: Basic Books, 2000.

Friedberg, Ann. "*Misconception* = The 'Division of Labor' in the Childbirth Film." *Millennium Film Journal*, no. 3 (1979): 64–70.

Friedrich, Su. "Radical Form: Radical Content?" *Millennium Film Journal*, no. 22 (1989–90): 117–23.

——. "*Jennifer, Where Are You?*: A Film By Leslie Thornton." *Downtown Review* 3, no. 1–2 (1981–82).

Gaffrey, Jake. "Off the Beaten Tracks with Chick Strand." *Village Voice*, December 27, 1976.

Gangitano, Lia. "Warhol's Grave." In *Lux: A Decade of Artists' Film and Video*, edited by Steve Reinke and Tom Taylor, 306–11. Toronto: XYZ Books and Pleasure Dome, 2000.

Ganguly, Suranjan. "Stan Brakhage: The Sixtieth Birthday Interview." In *Experimental Cinema: The Film Reader*, edited by Wheeler Winston Dixon and Gwendolyn Audrey Foster, 139–62. London: Routledge, 2002.

Gill, June M. "The Films of Gunvor Nelson." *Film Quarterly* 30, no. 3 (1977): 28–36.

Gorbman, Claudia. "Body Displaced, Body Discovered." *Jump Cut* 32 (1986): 12–14.

Greenfield, Amy. "Dance as Film." *Filmmakers Newsletter*, January 1969, 1–2, 27.

——. "The Kinesthetics of Avant-Garde Dance Film: Deren and Harris." In *Envisioning Dance on Film and Video*, ed. Judy Mitoma, 21–26. New York: Routledge, 2002.

Gunning, Tom. "The Cinema of Attractions: Early Film, Its Spectator and the Avant-Garde." In *Early Cinema: Space, Frame, Narrative*, edited by Thomas Elsaesser and Adam Barker, 56–67. London: British Film Institute, 1989.

——. "Toward a Minor Cinema: Fonoroff, Herwitz, Ahwesh, Klahr and Solomon." *Motion Picture* 3, no. 1–2 (1989–90): 2–3.

Gurwitsch, Aron. *Compossibility and Incompossibility in Leibniz*. The Hague: Martinus Nijhoff, 1975.

Haller, Robert. "Amy Greenfield." *Millennium Film Journal* 6 (1980): 103–6.

Halter, Ed. "Festivals: Tomb Raiding Filmmakers Dig Up Pixels at NY Video Fest." www.indiewire.com/film/festivals/fes_01NYVideoFest_010716.html. Accessed August 16, 2001.

Hansen, Christian, Catherine Needham, and Bill Nichols. "Pornography, Eth-
nography and the Discourse of Power." In *Representing Reality: Issues and
Concepts in Documentary*, edited by Bill Nichols, 201–28. Bloomington:
Indiana University Press, 1991.

Haskell, Barbara. "Yoko Ono: Objects." In *Yoko Ono: Objects/Films*. New York:
Whitney Museum of American Art, 1989.

Haslett, T., and N. Abiaka. "Interview with Cheryl Dunye." *Black Cultural
Studies Website Collective*. April 12, 1997. www.cheryldunye.com/pages/
interview.html.

Haug, Kate. "An Interview with Chick Strand." *Wide Angle* 20, no. 1 (1998):
106–37.

——. "Interview with Kate Haug." In *Imaging Her Erotics*, edited by Carolee
Schneemann, 20–45. Cambridge, Mass.: MIT Press, 2002.

Helmersson, Stina. "Filma är som att måla." *Aftonbladet*, January 10, 1985.

"Hilary Harris: Interviews, Documents." Memorial Program Folder. New York:
Anthology Film Archives, 2000.

Hoberman, J. "Personal Best." *Village Voice*, May 3, 1983. Reprinted as "Teen
Angel," in *Vulgar Modernism: Writings on Movies and other Media*, edited by
J. Hoberman, 141–42. Philadelphia: Temple University Press, 1991.

——. Obituary for Marjorie Keller. *Village Voice*, March 8, 1994.

Holmlund, Chris. "Feminist Makeovers: The Celluloid Surgery of Valie Export
and Su Friedrich." In *Play It Again, Sam: Retakes on Remakes*, edited by
Andrew Horton and Stuart Y. McDougal, 217–37. Berkeley: University of
California Press, 1998.

——. "From Rupture to Rapture Through Experimental Bio-pics: Leslie Thornton's *There Was An Unseen Cloud Moving*." In *Feminism and Documentary*,
eds. Janet Walker and Diane Waldman, 287–308. Minneapolis: University of
Minnesota Press, 1998.

——. "Gunvor Nelson." Biography, filmography, critical description. In *Women
Filmmakers and Their Films*, edited by Amy L. Unterburger, 130–31. Detroit:
St. James Press, 1998.

——, and Cynthia Fuchs, eds. *Between the Sheets, in the Streets: Queer, Lesbian,
Gay Documentary*. Minneapolis: University of Minnesota Press, 1997.

Iles, Chrissie, "Erotic Conceptualism: The Films of Yoko Ono." In *Yes Yoko
Ono*, edited by Alexandra Munroe and Jon Hendricks, 201–7. New York:
Japan Society and Harry N. Abrams, Inc., 2000.

Irigaray, Luce. *This Sex Which Is Not One*. Translated by Catherine Porter with
Carolyn Burke. Ithaca, N.Y.: Cornell University Press, 1985.

Jackson, Renata. "The Modernist Poetics of Maya Deren." In *Maya Deren and
the American Avant-Garde*, edited by Bill Nichols, 47–76. Berkeley: University of California Press, 2001.

James, David. *Allegories of Cinema: American Films in the Sixties*. Princeton, N.J.: Princeton University Press, 1989.

——. "Film Diary/Diary Film: Practice and Product in *Walden*." In *To Free the Cinema: Jonas Mekas and the New York Underground*, edited by David James, 145–77. Princeton, N.J.: Princeton University Press, 1992.

——. "An Interview with Pat O'Neill." *Millennium Film Journal*, no. 30–31 (1997): 192–32.

——. "Notes from Los Angeles Film Forum Retrospective." 2000. www.light housecinema.org/winter_spring2001.php. Accessed August 26, 2004.

Jenkins, Bruce. "Gently Down the Stream." *Millennium Film Journal*, no. 16–18 (1986–87): 195–98.

Jones, Kristin M. "Ahwesh at the Whitney." *Artforum* 36 (November 1997): 118–19.

Jones, Kristin. "*Ming Green:* The Color of Memory." *Millennium Film Journal* 32/33 (Fall 1998): 99–102.

Juhasz, Alexandra. *Women of Vision: Histories of Feminist Film and Video*. Minneapolis: Minnesota University Press, 2001.

Kaplan, Dora. "Part 3: Selected Short Subjects/First International Women's Film Festival." *Women and Film* 1, no. 2 (1972): 37–39.

Kaplan, E. Ann. "Travel, Traveling Identities and the Look." In *Looking for the Other: Feminism, Film and the Imperial Gaze*, 3–26. New York: Routledge, 1997.

——. *Women and Film: Both Sides of the Camera*. New York: Routledge, 1983.

Kaufman, Anthony. "War! What Is It Good For? Errol Morris Finds Out with *Fog of War*." www.indiewire.com/people/people_031229morris.html.

Keller, Marjorie. "Is This What You Were Born For?" *Xdream* 1, 1 (Autumn 1986): 1–5.

——. "Montage of Voices." *Millennium Film Journal* 16–18 (Fall/Winter 1986–87): 250.

——. *The Moon on the Porch*. A Chicago Book, 1986.

——. "Report from Knokke-Exprmentl 5." *Women and Film* 2, no. 7 (1975): 28–33.

——. "Review of E. Ann Kaplan's *Women and Film*." *Millennium Film Journal*, no. 14–15 (1984–85): 43–47.

——. *The Untutored Eye: Childhood in the Films of Cocteau, Cornell, and Brakhage*. New Brunswick, N.J.: Fairleigh-Dickinson, 1986.

Klein, Melanie. "Early Stages of the Oedipus Conflict and of Super-Ego Formation." In *The Psycho-Analysis of Children*. Translated by Alix Strachey, 123–48. New York: Delacorte, 1975.

Kinder, Marsha. "Soft Fiction." *Film Quarterly* 33, no. 3 (1980): 50–57.

Kotz, Liz. "Complicity: Women Artists Investigating Masculinity." In *Dirty Looks: Women, Pornography and Power*, edited by Pamela Church Gibson and Roma Gibson, 101–23. London: British Film Institute, 1993.

———. "An Unrequited Desire for the Sublime: Looking at Lesbian Representation across the Works of Abigail Child, Cecilia Dougherty, and Su Friedrich." In *Queer Looks: Perspectives on Lesbian and Gay Film and Video*, edited by Martha Gever, John Greyson, and Pratibha Parmar, 86–102. New York: Routledge, 1993.

Lavin, Maud. *Cut with a Kitchen Knife: The Weimar Photomontages of Hannah Hoch*. New Haven, Conn.: Yale University Press, 1993.

Lebow, Alisa. "Lesbians Make Movies." *Cineaste* 24, no. 1 (December 1993).

Leimbacher, Irina. "Chick Strand." *Wide Angle* 20, no. 1 (1998): 138–43.

Lellis, George. "*La Raison avant la passion*." In *The Films of Joyce Wieland*, edited by Kathryn Elder, 57–64. Toronto: Toronto International Film Festival Group, 1999.

Lesage, Julia. "Feminist Film Criticism: Theory and Practice." *Women and Film* 1, no. 5–6 (1974): 12–19.

———. "Women's Fragmented Consciousness in Feminist Experimental Autobiographical Video." In *Feminism and Documentary*, edited by Diane Waldman and Janet Walker, 309–37. Minneapolis: University of Minnesota Press, 1999.

Levi Strauss, David. "Love Rides Aristotle through the Audience: Body, Image and Idea in the Work of Carolee Schneemann." In *Imaging Her Erotics*, edited by Carolee Schneemann, 316–25. Cambridge, Mass.: MIT Press, 2002.

Lind, Jane. *Joyce Wieland: Artist on Fire*. Toronto: James Lorimer and Co., 2001.

Lionnet, Françoise. "Autoethnography: The An-Archic Style of Dust Tracks on a Road." In *Autobiographical Voices: Race, Gender, Self-Portraiture*, 97–129. Ithaca, N.Y.: Cornell University Press, 1989.

Lyotard, Jean-François. *The Libidinal Economy*. Bloomington: Indiana University Press, 1993.

MacDonald, Christine. "Sharing Tender Fictions: New Work by Lesbian Filmmaker Barbara Hammer." *Sojourner* 22, 6 (February 1997): 10–11.

MacDonald, Scott. *Avant-Garde Film: Motion Studies*. New York: Cambridge University Press, 1993.

———. "Carolee Schneemann's Autobiographical Trilogy." *Film Quarterly* 34, no. 1 (1980): 27–32.

———. *A Critical Cinema: Interviews with Independent Filmmakers*. 5 vols. Berkeley: University of California Press, 1988–2005.

———. *The Garden in the Machine: A Field Guide to Independent Films about Place*. Berkeley: University of California Press, 2001.

———. "Gunvor Nelson." In *A Critical Cinema*, 3: 181–95. Berkeley: University of California Press, 1998.

———. "An Interview with Carolee Schneemann." *AfterImage* 10–11 (1980): 10–11.

———. "Peggy Ahwesh" (interview). *Millennium Film Journal*, no. 39–40 (2003): 1–30.

Magidson, Deborah, and Judy Wright. "True Patriot Love." In *The Films of Joyce Wieland*, edited by Kathryn Elder, 81–86. Toronto: Toronto International Film Festival Group, 1999.

Margulies, Ivone. "After the Fall: Peggy Ahwesh's Vérité." *Motion Picture* 3, no. 1–2 (1989–90): 31–33.

Markopoulos, Gregory J. "The Intuition of Space." *Millennium Film Journal*, no. 32–33 (1998): 71–75.

Marks, Laura. *The Skin of the Film*. Durham, N.C.: Duke University Press, 2000.

——. *Touch: Sensuous Theory and Multisensory Media*. Minneapolis: University of Minnesota Press, 2002.

Martineau, Barbara. "Women's Film Daily." *Women and Film* 1, no. 5–6 (1974): 36.

Mayne, Judith. "Theory Speak(s)." In *A Woman Who . . . Essays, Interviews, Scripts*, edited by Yvonne Rainer, 18–26. Baltimore: Johns Hopkins University Press, 1999.

——. *Woman at the Keyhole: Feminism and Women's Cinema*. Bloomington: Indiana University Press, 1990.

McElfresh, Sam. "An Interview with Filmmaker Su Friedrich." *American Federation of the Arts Newsletter*. Autumn 1991: 4–5.

McHugh, Kathleen. *American Domesticity: From How-to Manual to Hollywood Melodrama*. New York: Oxford University Press, 1999.

McLuhan, Marshall. *Understanding Media: The Extensions of Man*. Cambridge, Mass.: MIT Press, 1997.

McPherson, Bruce. "Wieland: An Epiphany of North." In *The Films of Joyce Wieland*, edited by Kathryn Elder, 11–20. Toronto: International Film Festival Group, 1999.

Mekas, Jonas. "The Diary Film." In *The Avant-Garde Film: A Reader of Theory and Criticism*, edited by P. Adams Sitney, 190–98. New York: New York University Press, 1978.

——. *"Flaming Creatures* at Knokke-Le-Zoute." In *Movie Journal: The Rise of a New American Cinema, 1959–1971*, 111–15. New York: Macmillan, 1972.

——. "More on the New Sensibilities in Cinema." 1967. In *Movie Journal: The Rise of a New American Cinema, 1959–1971*, 275–77. New York: Macmillan, 1972.

——. "Interview with Barbara Rubin." *Village Voice*, March 2, 1972.

——. "Notes on Some New Movies and Happiness." In *Film Culture Reader*, edited by P. Adams Sitney, 317–25. New York: Praeger, 1970.

——. "On the Tactile Interactions in Cinema, or Creation with Your Total Body." 1966. In *Movie Journal: The Rise of a New American Cinema, 1959–1971*. New York: Macmillan, 1972.

——. "Praise to Marie Menken, the Film Poet." In *Movie Journal: The Rise of a New American Cinema, 1959–1971*, 46–48. New York: Macmillan, 1972.

Mellencamp, Patricia. *Indiscretions: Avant-Garde Film, Video, and Feminism.* Bloomington: Indiana University Press, 1990.

Michelson, Annette. *New Forms in Film.* Montreux, Switzerland: Imprimerie Corbaz, 1974.

——. "Yvonne Rainer, Part I: The Dancer and the Dance." *Artforum* 12, no. 5 (1974): 57–63.

——, and P. Adams Sitney. "A Conversation on Knokke and the Independent Filmmaker." *Artforum* 13, no. 9 (1975): 63–66.

Milutis, Joe. "All the Girls Without the Cameras in Their Heads: An Interview with Leslie Thornton." *Afterimage* 27, no. 4 (February 2000).

Morris, Gary. "Raging and Flaming: Jack Smith in Retrospect." *Bright Lights Film Journal* 29 (2000). www.brightlights.com/29/jacksmith.html.

Mulvey, Laura. "Feminism, Film, and the Avant-Garde." *Framework* 10 (Spring 1979): 6.

——. "Visual Pleasure and Narrative Cinema." *Screen* 16, no. 3 (1975): 6–18.

Munroe, Alexandra, and Jon Hendricks. *Yes Yoko Ono.* New York: Japan Society: Harry N. Abrams, 2000.

Nelson, D. "Imagery of the Archetypal Feminine in the Works of Six Women Filmmakers." *Quarterly Review of Film Studies* 3 (1978): 495–506.

Nichols, Bill, ed. *Maya Deren and the American Avant-Garde.* Berkeley: University of California Press, 2001.

Novak, Barbara. *American Painting in the Nineteenth Century.* New York: Praeger, 1969.

——. *Nature and Culture: American Landscape Painting, 1825–1875.* New York: Oxford University Press, 1984.

Nowell, Iris. *Joyce Wieland: A Life in Art.* Toronto: ECW Press, 2001.

Ono, Yoko. "Addendum '88." *Film Quarterly* 43, no.1 (1989): 21–23.

O'Pray, Michael. *Avant-Garde Film: Forms, Themes, and Passions.* New York: Wallflower, 2003.

Peckham, Linda. "The Aftermath of Intelligence: *Peggy and Fred in Hell.*" *Unsound* 2 (1983).

——. "Not Speaking With Language/Speaking With No Language: Leslie Thornton's *Adynata.*" In *Psychoanalysis and Cinema,* edited by E. Ann Kaplan, 181–87. New York: Routledge, 1990.

——. "The Overflow of Ecstasy into Speech: Leslie Thornton's *There Was An Unseen Cloud Moving.*" *Cinematograph* no. 4 (1991): 91–95.

Peirce, Charles Sanders. *Peirce on Signs: Writings on Semiotic by Charles Sanders Peirce.* Edited by James Hoopes. Chapel Hill: University of North Carolina Press, 1991.

Peterson, James. *Dreams of Chaos, Visions of Order.* Detroit: Wayne State University Press, 1994.

Peterson, Vicki. "Two Films by Chick Strand." *Millennium Film Journal* (Spring/Summer 1978): 110–13.

Petrolle, Jean, and Virginia Wright Wexman, eds. *Women and Experimental Filmmaking*. Urbana: University of Illinois Press, 2005.

Pettersson, Anders. "Interview." In *Gunvor Nelson: Still Moving i ljud och bild*, edited by John Sundholm, 31–47. Karlstad, Sweden: Centre for the Creative Arts, Karlstad University, 2002.

——. *Gunvor Nelson: Om avantgardefilm i allmänhet och 'personal film' i synnerhet*. Karlstad, Sweden: Karlstad University Studies, 2002.

——. "Interview with Gunvor Nelson." In *Gunvor Nelson and the Avant-Garde*, edited by John Sundholm, 137–62. Frankfurt am Main: Peter Lang, 2003.

Phelan, Peggy. "Yvonne Rainer: From Dance to Film." In *A Woman Who . . . Essays, Interviews, Scripts*, edited by Yvonne Rainer, 3–17. Baltimore: Johns Hopkins University Press, 1999.

Pipolo, Tony. "Making *Antigone/Rites of Passion:* An Interview with Amy Greenfield." *Millennium Film Journal* 26 (Fall 1992): 34–55.

Pramaggiore, Maria T. *Seeing Double(s): Performance and Self Representation in the Films of Maya Deren, Barbara Hammer, and Yvonne Rainer*. Emory University, doctoral thesis, 1993.

Pruitt, John. "Review of *The Untutored Eye: Childhood in the Films of Cocteau, Cornell, and Brakhage*." *Millennium Film Journal*, no. 28 (1995): 78–85.

Rabinowitz, Lauren. "The Development of Feminist Strategies in the Experimental Films of Joyce Wieland." In *The Films of Joyce Wieland*, edited by Kathryn Elder, 107–18. Toronto: Toronto International Film Festival Group, 1999.

——. "*The Far Shore:* Feminist Family Melodrama." In *The Films of Joyce Wieland*, edited by Kathryn Elder, 119–26. Toronto: Toronto International Film Festival Group, 1999.

——. *Points of Resistance: Women, Power, and Politics in the New York Avant-Garde Cinema, 1943–1971*. Chicago: University of Illinois Press, 1991.

Rainer, Yvonne. *Lives of Performers*. In *The Films of Yvonne Rainer*, edited by Yvonne Rainer, 59–76. Bloomington: Indiana University Press, 1989.

——, ed. *A Woman Who . . . Essays, Interviews, Scripts*. Baltimore: Johns Hopkins University Press, 1999.

——. *Work, 1961–1973*. Halifax: Press of the Nova Scotia College of Art and Design, 1974.

Rajchman, John. "Foucault's Art of Seeing." In *Critical Essays on Michel Foucault*, edited by Karlis Racevskis, 141. New York: G. K. Hull and Co., 1999.

Raymond, Monica. "The Pastoral in Abigail Child's *Covert Action* and *Mayhem*." *Cinematograph* 3 (1988): 61–64.

Reed, Christopher. "International Conference Ponders Homosexuality." *Gay Community News*, April 10–16, 1988, 6–7.

Rees, A. L. *A History of Experimental Film and Video*. London: British Film Institute, 1999.

Reich, William. *The Mass Psychology of Fascism*. New York: Farrar, Straus & Giroux, 1970.

Reisman, Linda. "Personal Film/Feminist Film." *Camera Obscura*, no. 11 (1983): 60–85.

Renov, Michael. *The Subject of Documentary*. Minneapolis: University of Minnesota Press, 2004.

Rich, B. Ruby. *Chick Flicks: Theories and Memories of the Feminist Film Movement*. Durham, N.C.: Duke University Press, 1998.

——. "Yvonne Rainer: An Introduction." In *The Films of Yvonne Rainer*, edited by Yvonne Rainer, 1–23. Bloomington: Indiana University Press, 1989.

Richardson, Brenda. "An Interview with Gunvor Nelson and Dorothy Wiley." *Film Quarterly* 25, no. 1 (1971): 34–39.

Rimbaud, Arthur. "Morning." In *A Season in Hell/The Illuminations*. Translated by Enid Rhodes Peschal, 101. New York: Oxford University Press, 1973.

Rodowick, D. N. *Gilles Deleuze's Time Machine*. Durham, N.C.: Duke University Press, 1997.

Rosenbaum, Jonathan. "Leslie Thornton." *Film: The Front Line 1983*. Denver: Arden Press, 1983.

——. "*Peggy and Fred in Hell:* The Complete Cycle." *Chicago Reader*, October 18, 1996.

Russell, Catherine. *Experimental Ethnography: The Work of Film in the Age of Video*. Durham, N.C.: Duke University Press, 1999.

——. "Culture as Fiction: The Ethnographic Impulse in the Films of Peggy Ahwesh, Su Friedrich and Leslie Thornton." In *The New American Cinema*, edited by Jon Lewis, 353–78. Durham, N.C.: Duke University Press, 1998.

Ryan, Judylyn S. "Outing the Black Feminist Filmmaker in Julie Dash's *Illusions*." *Signs* 30 (2004): 1319–44.

Schivelbusch, Wolfgang. *The Railway Journey: The Industrialization of Time and Space in the Nineteenth Century*. Berkeley: University of California Press, 1986.

Schjeldahl, Peter. "Art as Life: The Matisse We Never Knew." *New Yorker*, August 29, 2005, 78–83.

Schneemann, Carolee. "Disruptive Consciousness." Lecture at The Kitchen, New York, N.Y., Summer Institute Media Arts–Public Talks. June 19, 2003.

——. *Imaging Her Erotics: Essays, Interviews, Projects*. Cambridge, Mass.: MIT Press, 2002.

——. *More Than Meat Joy*. New Paltz, N.Y.: Documentext, 1979.

Schneider, Rebecca. *The Explicit Body in Performance*. London: Routledge, 1997.

Scott, Jay. "Full Circle—True Patriot Womanhood: The Thirty-Year Passage of Joyce Wieland." In *The Films of Joyce Wieland*, edited by Kathryn Elder, 21–28. Toronto: Toronto International Film Festival Group, 1999.

Silverman, Kaja. *The Acoustic Mirror: The Female Voice in Psychoanalysis and Cinema.* Bloomington: Indiana University Press, 1988.

Simonds, Cylena. "Spontaneous Combustion: An Interview with Barbara Hammer." *Afterimage* (December 1993): 5–7.

Sitney, P. Adams. "Autobiography in Avant-Garde Film." In *The Avant-Garde Film: A Reader of Theory and Criticism,* edited by P. Adams Sitney, 199–246. New York: New York University Press, 1978.

——. *The Essential Cinema.* New York: Anthology Film Archives, 1975.

——. *Film Culture Reader.* New York: Cooper Square Press, 2003.

——. *Visionary Film: The American Avant-Garde, 1943–2000.* New York: Oxford University Press, 2002.

Smith, Gavin. "The Way of All Flesh." *Film Comment* 31, no. 4 (1995): 18.

Squire, Susan. "Why Did the Palette Cross the Road?" *Los Angeles Magazine,* September 1980. www.members.aol.com/tedalvy/neon4.htm. Accessed August 28, 2004.

Staiger, Janet. "Authorship Approaches." In *Authorship and Film,* edited by David A. Gerstner and Janet Staiger, 27–57. London: Routledge, 2003.

Starr, Cecile. "Hilla Rebay and the Guggenheim Nexus." In *Articulated Light: Abstract Film in America.* Boston: Harvard Film/Anthology Film Archives, 1995.

——. "Maya: The Mother of the Avant Garde Film." *New York Times,* May 1, 1976.

Stiles, Kristine. "The Painter as an Instrument of Real Time." In *Imaging Her Erotics,* edited by Carolee Schneemann, 3–16. Cambridge, Mass.: MIT Press, 2002.

——. "Unbosoming Lennon: The Politics of Yoko Ono's Experience." *Art Criticism* 7, no. 2 (1992): 21–52.

Straayer, Chris. *Deviant Eyes, Deviant Bodies.* New York: Columbia University Press, 1996.

Strand, Chick. "Chick Strand at the Cinematheque." *Cinema News* 80, no. 3–5 (1980): 10–17.

——. "Conversation with Chick Strand," *Cinema News* 80, no. 3/4/5 (1980): 18–22.

——. "Notes on Ethnographic Film by a Film Artist." *Wide Angle* 2, no. 3 (1978): 44–51.

Suárez, Juan A. *Bike Boys, Drag Queens and Superstars: Avant-Garde, Mass Culture, and Gay Identities in the 1960s Underground Cinema.* Bloomington: Indiana University Press, 1996.

Suarez-Araùz, Nicomedes. *Amnesis Art: The Art of the Lost Object.* New York: Lascaux Publishers, 1988.

Sullivan, James. "Punk Master of the Absurd Winston Smith Shows His Art." *San Francisco Chronicle,* December 6–12, 1998. www.winstonsmith.com/winfo/press/sfchron.98.12.06.html.

Sundholm, John. "Biography." In *Gunvor Nelson: Still Moving i ljud och bild,* edited by John Sundholm, 110–11. Karlstad, Sweden: Centre for the Creative Arts, Karlstad University, 2002.

——. "Gunvor Nelson and the Aesthetics of Sensual Materiality." *Vers*, May 28, 2004. www.avantofestival.com.

——, ed. *Gunvor Nelson and the Avant-Garde*. Frankfurt am Main: Peter Lang, 2003.

Taubin, Amy. "*Daughters of Chaos:* Feminist and Avant-Garde Filmmakers." *Village Voice* (November 30, 1982): 80–1, 87.

——. "Experimental Bent." *Village Voice*, September 15, 1987.

——. "Interview with Marjorie Keller." *Idiolects* 6 (1978).

——. "Review of *Daughters of Chaos.*" *Artforum* (Summer 1981): 91–92.

——. "Women Were Out Front, Too." *New York Times*, June 25, 2000.

Testa, Bart. *Spirit in the Landscape*. Toronto: Art Gallery of Ontario, 1989.

Thompson, Kristin, and David Bordwell. *Film History: An Introduction*. 2nd edition. New York: McGraw-Hill, 2003.

Thornton, Leslie. "Culture As Fiction." *Unsound* 2 (1983).

——. "Dear Su . . . from a list of things to tell you . . . /Letters." *Idiolects* 13 (1982).

——. "Interview: Leslie Thornton." *Art Papers* (1989).

——. "*Peggy and Fred in Hell,*" [first version]. *Subjects/Objects* 3 (1985).

——. "We Ground Things Now On A Moving Earth." *Motion Picture* 3, no. 1–2 (1989–90).

——. "Women in Film: Interview with Laura Theilen." *Cinezine* (October 1984).

Tinkcom, Matthew. *Working Like a Homosexual: Camp, Capital, Cinema*. Durham, N.C.: Duke University Press, 2002.

Trinh T. Minh-ha. "Which Way To Political Cinema?/Trinh Minh-ha, Leslie Thornton, Laleen Jayamane." In *Framer Framed*, 243–68. New York: Routledge, 1992.

Turim, Maureen. "Art/Music/Video.com." In *Medium Cool: Music Videos from Soundies to Cellphones*, edited by Roger Beebe and Jason Middleton, 83–110. Durham, N.C.: Duke University Press, 2007.

——. "Childhood Memories and Household Events in the Feminist Avant Garde." *Journal of Film and Video*, 38 (1986): 86–92.

——. "The Ethics of Form: Structure and Gender in Maya Deren's Challenge to the Cinema." In *Maya Deren and the American Avant-Garde*, edited by Bill Nichols, 77–102. Berkeley: University of California Press, 2001.

——. "A Look at the Violence of Female Desire in Avant-Garde Films." In *Women and Experimental Filmmaking*, edited by Jean Petrolle and Virginia Wright Wexman, 71–90. Urbana: University of Illinois Press, 2005.

——. "Reminiscences, Subjectivities, and Truths." In *To Free the Cinema: Jonas Mekas and the New York Underground*, edited by David James, 193–212. Princeton, N.J.: Princeton University Press, 1992.

Tyler, Parker. *Underground Film: A Critical History*. 1969. New York: Da Capo Press, 1995.

Ulmer, Greg. "Mystory." *Teletheory: Grammatology in the Age of Video.* New York: Routledge, 1989.

Walker, Janet, and Diane Waldman, eds. *Feminism and Documentary.* Minneapolis: University of Minnesota Press, 1999.

Washington, Laurence. "Takes on Hollywood's Invisible Color Lines." Blackflix .com.www.blackflix.com/articles/watermelon.html. Accessed June 1, 2004.

Watson, Steven. *Factory Made: Warhol and the Sixties.* New York: Pantheon, 2003.

Wees, William C. "Carrying On: Leslie Thornton, Su Friedrich, Abigail Child and American Avant-Garde Film in the Eighties." *Canadian Journal of Film Studies* 10, no. 1 (2002): 70–95.

——. "'Let's Set the Record Straight': The International Experimental Film Congress, Toronto 1989." *Canadian Journal of Film Studies* 9 (2000): 101–111.

——. *Light Moving in Time.* Berkeley: University of California Press, 1992.

——. *Recycled Images: The Art and Politics of Found Footage Films.* New York: Anthology Film Archives, 1993.

Weiss, Andrea. *Vampires and Violets.* New York: Routledge, 1992.

——. "*Women I Love* and *Double Strength:* Lesbian Cinema and Romantic Love." *Jump Cut* 24–25 (March 1991): 30.

Wheeler, Dennis, ed. *Form and Structure in Recent Films.* Vancouver: Vancouver Art Gallery/Talonbooks, 1972.

Widding, Astrid Söderbergh. "Ett kabinett för vardagens visuella under." *Svenska Dagbladet,* August 28, 2002.

——. "The Material World Transformed: Gunvor Nelson's Videoworks." In *Gunvor Nelson and the Avant-Garde,* edited by John Sundholm, 125–34. Frankfurt am Main: Peter Lang, 2003.

Wilkin, Karen, *Tibor de Nagy Gallery: The First Fifty Years.* 2005. www.tibor denagy.com/history.html.

Williams, Linda. *Hard Core: Power, Pleasure and the Frenzy of the Visible.* Berkeley: University of California Press, 1999.

Willis, Holly. "Uncommon History: An Interview with Barbara Hammer." *Film Quarterly* (Summer 1994): 7–13.

Zita, Jacquelyn. "Films of Barbara Hammer, Counter-Currencies of a Lesbian Iconography." *Jump Cut* 24–25 (March 1991): 26–30.

Zryd, Michael. "A Report on Canadian Experimental Film Institutions, 1980–2000." In *North of Everything: English-Canadian Cinema since 1980,* edited by William Beard and Jerry White, 392–401. Edmonton: Arberle, 2002.

——. "'There Are Many Joyces': The Critical Reception of the Films of Joyce Wieland." In *The Films of Joyce Wieland,* edited by Kathryn Elder, 195–212. Toronto: Cinema Ontario, 1999.

Zummer, Thomas. "Leslie Thornton." *Senses of Cinema.* www.sensesofcinema .com/contents/directors/02/thornton.html. Accessed November 2002.

Contributors

◻

PAUL ARTHUR is a professor of film and literature at Montclair State University. He is a regular contributor to *Film Comment* and *Cineaste* magazines and coedits *Millennium Film Journal*. His collection of essays, *A Line of Sight: American Avant-Garde Film, 1965 to the Present*, was published in 2005.

ROBIN BLAETZ is an associate professor and chair of the film studies program at Mount Holyoke College. She is the author of *Visions of the Maid: Joan of Arc in American Film and Culture* and is working on a book titled *Home Movies*.

NOËL CARROLL is the Andrew W. Mellon Term Professor in the Humanities in the department of philosophy at Temple University. He is the author of fifteen books and over one hundred essays in aesthetics and film criticism. He is currently working on a project about jokes and humor.

JANET CUTLER is a professor of English and director of the film studies program at Montclair State University. She is coeditor of and contributor to *Struggles for Representation: African-American Documentary Film and Video*.

MARY ANN DOANE is the George Hazard Crooker Professor of Modern Culture and Media and English at Brown University. She is the author of *The Desire to Desire: The Woman's Film of the 1940s* and *Femmes Fatales: Feminism, Film Theory, Psychoanalysis*. She is completing a book on technologies of representation and temporality in the early twentieth century.

ROBERT A. HALLER is the director of collections and special projects at Anthology Film Archives in New York. He has published edited books about Stan Brakhage and Jim Davis, a monograph on Kenneth Anger, and catalogs on Fritz Lang, Ed Emshwiller, and Omer Kavur. With Scott MacDonald, he is an editor of a collection of documents titled *Art in Cinema: Documents Toward a History of the Film Society*.

CHRIS HOLMLUND is the Lindsay Young Professor of Cinema Studies, Women's Studies, and French at the University of Tennessee. She is the author of *Impossible Bodies*, coeditor of *Contemporary American Independent Film: From the Margins to the Mainstream* and *Between the Sheets, In the Streets: Queer, Lesbian, Gay Documentary*. Current projects include *American Cinema of the 1990s: Themes and Variations* and a book on stars in action films.

CHUCK KLEINHANS is the coeditor of *JUMP CUT* (ejumpcut.org) and teaches in the radio/television/film department at Northwestern University. Recent articles include Hong Kong cinema's relation to Hollywood, virtual child pornography, Court TV, porn and documentary, and the early 1990s making and marketing of blockbuster and indy films.

SCOTT MACDONALD is a visiting professor of art history at Hamilton College. The fifth volume of his series, *A Critical Cinema: Interviews with Independent Filmmakers*, was published in 2006. His *The Garden in the Machine: A Field Guide to Independent Films about Place* appeared in 2002; *Cinema 16: Documents Toward a History of the Film Society* in 2002.

KATHLEEN MCHUGH is the director of the UCLA Center for the Study of Women and teaches in the English department and the FTV critical studies program. She is the author of *American Domesticity: From How-To Manual to Hollywood Melodrama* and coeditor of *South Korean Golden Age Melodrama: Gender, Genre and National Cinema*. Her book on Jane Campion is forthcoming from the University of Illinois Press.

ARA OSTERWEIL is an assistant professor of film studies at Muhlenberg College. She completed a dissertation, titled "Flesh Cinema: The Corporeal Avant-Garde, 1962–1972."

MARIA PRAMAGGIORE is an associate professor of English and the director of film studies at North Carolina State University. She coedited *Representing Bisexualities: Subjects and Cultures of Fluid Desire* and writes film and theater criticism for the *Independent Weekly* in Raleigh.

MELISSA RAGONA is a visiting assistant professor of art at Carnegie Mellon University, where she teaches critical theory and media and sound studies. She is completing a book on the uses of sound in experimental film work (1970 to the present) as well as a project on the recordings of Andy Warhol.

KATHRYN RAMEY is a filmmaker and doctoral candidate at Temple University, completing her dissertation, "Between Art, Industry and Academia: The Fragile Balancing Act of the Film Avant-Garde." She is currently a Pennsylvania Council on the Arts Fellow and assistant professor in the department of Visual and Media Arts at Emerson College.

M. M. SERRA is an adjunct professor in media studies in the communications department at the New School for Social Research. Her work as an experimental film and video artist and a scholar focuses on women and erotica. As the Executive Director of the New American Cinema Group/the Film-Makers' Cooperative, she has curated and presented numerous programs and touring exhibitions of experimental film worldwide.

MAUREEN TURIM is a professor of film studies at the University of Florida. She is the author of *Abstraction in Avant-Garde Films, Flashbacks in Film: Memory and History*, and *The Films of Oshima: Images of a Japanese Iconoclast*. Her current book project is titled *Desire and Its Ends: The Driving Forces of Recent Cinema, Literature, and Art.*

WILLIAM C. WEES is an emeritus professor at McGill University and the editor of the *Canadian Journal of Film Studies*. He is the author of *Vorticism and the English Avant-Garde, Light Moving in Time: Studies in the Visual Aesthetics of Avant-Garde Film*, and *Recycled Images: The Art and Politics of Found Footage Films*.

Index

□

Eberhardt, Isabelle, 252–257, 260

Edinburgh International Film Festival, 3–4

8mm film, 17

Eight million (Child), 278, 283–284

Eisenstein, Sergei, 264, 276, 279

Elasticity (Strand), 194

Element (Greenfield), 159, 162, 164

Emotion, 15; in work of Yvonne Rainer, 95–98

Empire (Warhol), 36

Empire of Signs (Barthes), 249

Emunah (Rubin), 128

Encounter (Greenfield), 153, 157, 162

Endangered (Hammer), 172

Enthusiasm (Vertov), 281

Erdman, John, 93–94

Ethnographic film, 189–190, 192; of Strand, 193–208; of Thornton, 257–258

Experimental Ethnography (Russell), 195

Eye Body: 36 Transformative Actions for Camera (Schneemann), 104–105

Fake Fruit (Strand), 194

Fallen World, The (Keller), 219–220

Family Album, The (Berliner), 264

Far Shore (Wieland), 49, 51

Female body, 11–12, 155, 170–171; "active nude" and, 155, 159; bilabilism and, 140; in work of Child, 12, 267, 270, 272, 274–278, 283–285; in work of Friedrich, 316–319, 325–326; in work of Greenfield, 155, 159, 163–165; in work of Hammer, 171–172; in work of Ono, 139–140; in work of Rubin, 134–136, 138–141; in work of Schneemann, 104–108, 111–113, 123–124, 139–140, 155; in work of Wieland, 61

Female Man, The (Russ), 306

Feminism, 172, 228–232; Child and, 263, 267; Dunye and, 342; feminist film, 227; Friedrich and, 317–319, 321; Greenfield and, 162–163; Hammer and, 171; Nelson and, 10, 67–68, 80; power of the gaze and, 189; and rejection of feminist film theory by Keller, 211–213, 227–228, 235; Rubin and, 130, 141; *Still Point* and, 170; *Thriller* as ideal women filmmakers' non-identification with, 10, 80, 130

Festival of Free Expression, 106

Field Study #2 (Nelson), 68, 81

"Film Body: An Implantation of Perversions," 136

Film Culture, 141–142

"Film diary," 8; and diary film, 24; and Menken as film diarist, 23–25

Film festivals, 2–4; change in ethos of, 173–174; critics of, 3–4

Film journals, 3

Film Library Quarterly (journal), 3

Film-Makers' Cooperative, 10, 132, 215, 382

Film series, 266. See also *Is This What You Were Born For?* (Child)

Film studies: evolution of, 360–361

Filmmakers Newsletter, 154, 156–157

Filmverkstan, 71–72

First Comes Love (Friedrich), 312–313, 326–327

First International Festival of Women's Films, 3–4

Fischer, Lucy, 6

Flaming Creatures (Smith), 130, 138, 141–142, 273

Flavin, Dan, 27

Fog Pumas (Nelson), 77

Foreign Parts (Keller), 221–223, 225

Foreman, Richard, 132

Foucault, Michel, 217–218, 227

Found footage, 14–15, 264–265; Conner and, 264; of pornography in *The Color of Love*, 301; silent cinema and, 14; in work of Child, 264, 267, 270, 272, 276–278; in work of Strand,

Library of Congress Cataloging-in-Publication Data

Women's experimental cinema : critical frameworks /
Robin Blaetz, editor.

p. cm.

Includes bibliographical references and index.

ISBN-13: 978-0-8223-4023-2 (cloth : alk. paper)

ISBN-13: 978-0-8223-4044-7 (pbk. : alk. paper)

1. Experimental films—United States—History and
criticism. 2. Women motion picture producers and
directors—United States. I. Blaetz, Robin, 1955-

PN1995.9.E96W68 2007

791.4302.33082—dc22   2007009344